RE-FIGURING HAYDEN WHITE

Cultural Memory
in
the
Present

Mieke Bal and Hent de Vries, Editors

Hayden White
Photograph by Richard Todd

RE-FIGURING HAYDEN WHITE

EDITED BY
Frank Ankersmit,
Ewa Domańska,
AND *Hans Kellner*

STANFORD UNIVERSITY PRESS

STANFORD, CALIFORNIA

Stanford University Press
Stanford, California

Printed in the United States of America on acid-free, archival-quality paper

Library of Congress Cataloging-in-Publication Data
Re-figuring Hayden White / edited by Frank Ankersmit, Ewa Domańska, and Hans Kellner.
    p.   cm.—(Cultural memory in the present)
    Includes bibliographical references and index.
    ISBN 978-0-8047-6003-4 (cloth : alk. paper)—ISBN 978-0-8047-6275-5 (pbk. : alk. paper)
    1. White, Hayden V., 1928—Influence.   2. Historiography.
3. History—Philosophy.   4. Literature and history.   I. Ankersmit, F. R.
II. Domańska, Ewa.   III. Kellner, Hans, 1945–
    D15.W46R42 2009
    907.2'02—dc22

                               2008046635

Typeset by Motto Publishing Services in 11/13.5 Adobe Garamond

Contents

RE-FIGURING HAYDEN WHITE

A Distinctively Human Life

Hans Kellner

This volume celebrates the eightieth birthday of Hayden White. The contributors are White's students, colleagues, friends; all of us have been instructed by his work. We continue to be inspired by his presence. Ewa Domańska and Frank Ankersmit conceived this project, and they did most of the work of organizing it. I am pleased to be the third editor, although by participating in this project, I am breaking a promise. A number of years ago, at an event in honor of a senior scholar, Hayden White looked at me and muttered, "Don't you ever do anything like this for me," and I agreed. Perhaps this order followed logically from the wisdom found in another piece of advice he once gave me: "Never expect gratitude." White has always seemed to live above the economy of tributes. There are, however, some things that cannot *not* be done. This volume of tribute and interrogation is one of those things.

In September 1966 I walked into White's office in Rush Rhees Library of the University of Rochester, a room large enough to hold a seminar table and a large blackboard as well as his desk and chair. This graduate seminar in European intellectual history was on the decade of the 1830s. The professor, not yet 40, was elegantly dressed; he had recently stepped down as chair of the department, but was still a dominant (and, even then, controversial) figure. The academia of forty years ago was rather different from that of today. The History Department at Rochester, for example, had no women on the faculty. Intellectual history was at the cutting edge; its young faculty expositors seemed radically critical of their profession. The political turmoil we now associate with the sixties was just about to occur. Our seminar room, White's office, was filled with smoke, from student cigarettes snuffed in Styrofoam coffee cups and from the professor's pipe. White was then, as now, the embodiment of the credo of the Sophist Gorgias, answering his opponent's seriousness with humor, his humor with seriousness. This drove some of his older colleagues crazy, and they worked hard to instill the graduate students with the notion that working with the faculty around White—scholars like Sidney Monas, Michael Cherniavsky, Harry Harootunian, R. J. Kaufmann, Loren Baritz—would lead to dead ends. White's group, apparently, did not take the right things seriously.

White loved blackboards. He would often jump up and draw a scheme on the board that none of us could seem to grasp or explain to each other after class, but which apparently satisfied his desire for spatial representation. He often taught by aiming a student, like a glance more than an arrow, in a direction that might lead any number of places. At the end of the first semester, I turned in to him a particularly dreary essay on François Guizot's politics, which he returned to me with appropriately lukewarm comments. In a private conference, he looked at the essay, then pushed an (apparently) random book across the table to me, saying something like, "Here, see if this helps." The book was Roland Barthes' *Mythologies*, the pages of the library's copy were uncut, and, after a very puzzled weekend of revision, driven by those scattered pieces on contemporary French popular culture, sketches which struck me as having nothing to do with the subject of my paper, I must confess, it *did* help—a lot. His advice was typically—"go off and read"—thus he advised me a few years later, when I despaired of writing anything. And, the writing began. Unexpected connections appeared.

The Hayden White I first encountered had not yet written *Metahistory*, or the essays that make up the three books that followed it. There is one exception. In 1966 *History and Theory* published "The Burden of History," an essay (discussed in this volume by David Harlan) that cast a gauntlet before the historical profession by noting that the pathbreaking historical work of the twentieth century was typically the work of such nonhistorians as Ernst Gombrich, Michel Foucault, or White's friend Norman O. Brown. The twentieth-century historian, the essay implied, was wedded to nineteenth-century science and nineteenth-century art. Deriding professional history as an obsolete art and an obsolete science—"art *and* science" being the formula that allowed the historical profession to have it both ways, while avoiding any real accountability to the strictures of either one—White called for a renewal from outside, the discovery of new modes of conceptualizing the past and creating new forms of discourse. What struck this hidebound graduate student about "The Burden of History" was its lack of documentation. Where, I wanted to know, were the footnotes? Since his door seemed always to be open, I timidly entered White's office, and ventured to ask him about this. He replied, ironically: "Oh, I used to do all that." I later learned, and Dick Vann's essay here reminds us, that he had indeed done all that. He knows the protocols of every genre, and will deploy them as required.

In the late sixties, White seemed to be looking for something, but it wasn't clear what it was. He was reading the texts that would inform *Metahistory*, and was teaching the classic nineteenth-century histories, to which he had turned after his medievalist entry into the scholarly career, but things hadn't yet come together. Certainly, I heard no talk of tropes or of figuralism in his seminars, although both Giambattista Vico and Erich Auerbach were then parts of White's intellectual arsenal. At that moment, they served other purposes. And yet, in one remarkable, brief gesture, an obscure talk that he never chose to place in a published volume of his own, White made a point that heralded his later work and his break from the commonsense logic of things. Toward the end of 1967, White spoke in Denver at a conference devoted to the relation of biology and history. In that talk, delivered to an odd assortment of scientists, philosophers, and humanists, White maintained that the difference between a historical system and a biological system is that the biological past is given, and so determines what follows from it, while the historical past is constituted backwards, so that, in effect, we decide who our ancestors were.

In speaking of the course of biological systems, we do not speak of "choice, purpose, or intent" on the part of the organisms themselves, and it would be a mistake to do so. Cultures, however, are often spoken of as having a "life" of their own, as if they were endowed with a genetic identity that governed their existence. Thus, we can speak of the "death" of a culture and the "birth" of a new social formation.[1] And this, White insisted, was mistaken. "Socio-cultural systems do not have lives of their own; they exist solely as a function of the choices of individuals to live their lives this way and not another, regardless of what the environment would seem to require for survival. And when individuals cease to choose a given way of life, this way of life ceases to exist."[2] Thus, although changes may take place at a pace that spans generations, making genetic explanations appealing, the business of history is accomplished by individuals, for whom education and indoctrination are merely signs of the unnatural state of culture. After all, if culture were natural, these institutions of *Bildung* would not be necessary. The extended metaphor that describes medieval Christendom as conceived and maturing in the womb of pagan Rome is misleading insofar as it implies that processes that may be perceived in a long-range perspective can be felt at all in the micro-experience of individuals. To be sure, such processes are the stuff of our historical understanding, but the meaning it offers us is won at a great price: we lose our awareness of the fact that socio-cultural systems are precariously built upon "fictions" that may be rejected quite unexpectedly, and at any time. When this rejection occurs, it presents us not only with a historical crisis, but also with the crisis of many separate lives.[3]

In what I have just recounted, White holds true to the existentialist ideas that formed his intellectual *Gestalt*, and which have long been noted.[4] It is what comes next in this talk that is of interest to me here. White again refers to the end of Roman civilization.

What happened between the third and eighth centuries was that men ceased to regard themselves as descendents of their Roman forebears and began to treat themselves as descendents of their Judeo-Christian predecessors. And it was the constitution of this fictional cultural ancestry which signaled the abandonment of the Roman socio-cultural system.[5]

To act *as if* one could choose one's ancestors, cultural ancestors, the ones that matter, is to create a different fictional past and to make it real by living it in the present. The historical past provides a sort of expanse over which we may, if we must, range in search of models. If a generation fails to find any figures adequate to their legitimate needs and desires in the models that the existing culture offers it, they will turn away from their historical culture and create another by choosing a different past. This is cultural revolution. When it happens, this newly chosen past becomes *the* past for that group, in defiance of evidence and even utility. This "process of retrospective ancestral constitution" is what historical consciousness is all about. "Eliminate it and historical systems would not exist at all."[6]

Ancestry is created retrospectively by the sons and daughters. Under certain circumstances, no sort of determinism, no idea that the past leads to the present in a necessary way, is possible, unless it is freely chosen or else inculcated by a set of cultural fictions that may be cast aside with surprising speed, as when the Germanic peoples of northern Europe cast aside their Teutonic and Roman identities in order to find, however tenuously, ancestral models in long-dead Palestinian Jews. And those who turn to new ancestors will be certain that these were their *true* ancestors, that what they have chosen was a necessary course of events; history will make this into an orderly process.[7] That created past will then justify the present.

This creates, White remarks, a delicate balance. "By constructing our past, we assert our freedom; by seeking retroactive justification for it in our past, we silently strip ourselves of the freedom that has allowed us to become what we are."[8]

Lasting freedom, White implied here, would seem to require that we remain ungrounded in any past, either real (whatever that might be taken to mean) or chosen. We would be suspended in a permanent, "free," anti-foundational anti-essentialism, rejecting the binaries that allow us to distinguish things, and apologizing eternally for speaking from any given subject position. This lasting attitude, in my view, we do not want, and cannot have. It is no more desirable than its opposite, the cultural cryogenics that freezes a culture permanently in place. Keith Jenkins, in his essay describing a radical history, see things rather differently; and Frank Ankersmit admits that White's political commitment has "a quite peculiar nature." I see White's commitment in yet another way. As White's sentence above implies, we use the freedom to choose, to redefine ourselves, in times of sensed crisis, only to put that freedom aside subsequently in exchange for the illusion that the things we have chosen had to be as they are. This solution to the problem of creating a place for human will in a lovably stable world—leading "a distinctively human life," to borrow White's phrase—involves oscillation between the "serious" and the "rhetorical" view of life. The serious approach sees the past as the force that determines who we are, what we can and cannot accomplish, and what the scope of our world may be. This, at its worst, is the vision of human culture as a second-rate imitation of biological systems, determined by inner forces, growing, maturing, aging, dying. It is to be found in any strict socio-biological or ecological view of things. There is no place here for a distinctively human life. The rhetorical view—I borrow this serious/rhetorical binary from Richard Lanham—sees us as playing self-chosen roles, adjusting to various situations as they occur, and creating them as we perform in them.[9] It is performative, playful, streetwise, and suspicious.

The power of the serious view is enormous, particularly in history, where the authoritative view of a subject is generally, and conveniently, the most recently acknowledged one. We now know best, we are told, against all logic and evidence; old history, like old science, is necessarily bad. The *practice* of history, however, is quite another thing. Revisionism—celebrating the power to see things differently—wins the prizes and the big careers. The textual model of this oscillation was laid down for history by Thucydides, who creates a narrative speech–narrative pattern that alternates the serious and the rhetorical, narrator and actor; it is carried on into modern Western letters as the novelistic alternation of points of view coming from nowhere (the serious narrator) and from somewhere (the rhetorical character). White's recognition of the importance of the European novel may reflect this sense that it embodies a more complete representation of humanity than either drama or historical report can; Herman Paul is astute in framing his discussion in this volume with citations from Hermann Hesse.

White's chosen intellectual forebears are not difficult to list, but none is more powerfully present throughout his career than Erich Auerbach, both as form and as content. Auerbach provided another way of articulating the existentialist intuition that we create ourselves by choosing our ancestral past. In the figure/fulfillment relationship chosen by the Christian Church Fathers to keep and transfigure their Hebrew forebears, White would find a literary language that could supplement the Nietzschean term *genealogy*; Auerbach also provided the notion of an "aesthetic historism," and showed how to unfold levels of meaning from a small piece of text. *Metahistory* shows its debt to *Mimesis* in many ways, as a fulfillment of Auerbach's *figura*.

The essays in this *Festschrift* are meant to be fulfillments of figures in Hayden White's work. He is their cause in a historical, which is to say, an aesthetic, sense. Whether they follow his path, or reject it, or wander off altogether, they show themselves as unquestionably part of a genealogy. But they proceed in many directions. As Andrew Baird suggests in his essay here, the final destination is never clear. To push whatever book is on your table toward a student may seem random, but that apparent randomness brings home to us forcefully that the association of ideas is created unpredictably, to be determined by the future, not the past. As White wrote in his essay on Auerbach:

The fulfillment of a figure over the course of a given period of time or narrative diachrony is not predictable on the basis of whatever might be known about the figure itself apart from its fulfilled form. No more could one predict that a promise will necessarily be fulfilled on the basis of whatever might be known about the person who made the promise.[10]

In other words, Hayden White bears no responsibility for the essays we present to him. Because they choose him, he has no obligation to respond, or to affiliate with them. And yet, since fulfillments of a figure are "the kinds of actions of which morally responsible persons are thought to be capable, actions such as fulfilling a promise, cleaving to the terms of an oath, carrying out assumed duties, remaining faithful to a friend, and the like,"[11] he plays an ambiguous role. Each of these descriptions of Auerbach's notion of *Erfüllung* seems appropriate to our tributes to Hayden, but they place the emphasis too much on us, on those who attempt to fulfill, and in doing so, can only produce further figures. Our duties and our faithfulness, although quite different for each one of us, are random variations on a larger theme, which is the influence of Hayden White on our vision of cultural possibility, our personal obligations, the things we cannot *not* do. These expressions are quite inadequate to that influence, but they do suggest how promises can be both broken and kept by the same action, how fulfillments become figures.

The participants in this volume were asked to address, not simply the work of Hayden White, but also the questions he has addressed, the areas he has influenced, the concepts he has developed. The four sections of this Festschrift move from the theoretical to the practical via discourse and narrative. Part 1, Philosophy, is devoted to broad issues in the philosophy of history, particularly the figures of Kant and Hegel. Part 2, Discourse, deals with what has come to be called historical theory, where White's contributions have made the greatest impact. Part 3, Narrative, explores White's recurrent theme, the representation of our "distinctively human" effort to make sense of living with change. Finally, Part 4, Practice, presents the applications of White's ideas and suggests his personal influence as a teacher and scholar. The essays range widely, from philosophy to pedagogy, from the rhetorical to the sublime, but all, we hope, are informed with the spirit of Hayden White—generous, inquiring, and always full of youth, with an eye on the future.

Notes

1. Hayden White, "What Is a Historical System?" in *Biology, History and Natural Philosophy*, ed. Allen D. Breck and Wolfgang Yourgrau (New York: Plenum Press, 1972), 235–6.

2. Ibid., 236.

3. Ibid., 238.

4. See Hans Kellner, *Language and Historical Representation: Getting the Story Crooked* (Madison: University of Wisconsin Press, 1989), 193–227, and Hayden White, "The Ironic Poetics of Late Modernity," interview by Angelica Koufou and Margarita Miliori, http://www.historein.gr/vol2_interview.htm (accessed January 14, 2008).

5. White, "The Ironic Poets," 239.

6. Ibid., 241.

7. Ibid., 242.

8. Ibid.

9. Richard Lanham, *Motives of Eloquence: Literary Rhetoric in the Renaissance* (New Haven: Yale University Press, 1983).

10. Hayden White, *Figural Realism: Studies in the Mimesis Effect* (Baltimore: Johns Hopkins University Press, 1999), 89.

11. Ibid., 88.

PART ONE

PHILOSOPHY

Philosophy, an Introduction

Ewa Domańska

Part 1 of the collection considers various philosophical aspects of White's writings, which are rarely addressed by readers interested primarily in the discursive and tropological elements of White's theory. David Carr observes that whereas scholars often stress the importance of White's theory of the historical work formulated in his *Metahistory* on the basis of discussions of Leopold von Ranke, Jules Michelet, Alexis de Tocqueville, and Jacob Burckhardt, they tend to forget that *Metahistory* also contains substantial discussions of several nineteenth-century philosophers of history, including Georg Wilhelm Friedrich Hegel, Karl Marx, Friedrich Nietzsche, and Benedetto Croce. According to Carr, White should be regarded not only as a theorist who has significantly changed our approach to the epistemology of history, but also as a scholar whose work, like that of Karl Popper and others, is a reaction to nineteenth-century philosophy of history. In this way, White can be subsumed within the project Carr refers to as a "metaphilosophy of history." Carr suggests a re-examination of the classical or speculative philosophy of history, stressing its continued vitality. (*Speculative* is for Carr a negative term he wants to eliminate.) He argues that the classical philosophy of history must be understood less as a theoretical enterprise and more as a practical one, displaying historical events along a temporal axis geared to a projected future, not to be speculated on but to be realized. The practical aspect of these narratives is located in their redescriptive rather than prescriptive character. They organize the past in order to make a case for a particular future.

In his essay "White's 'New Neo-Kantianism': Aesthetics, Ethics, and Politics," Frank Ankersmit also emphasizes the philosophical aspect of White's works and proposes a reading of *Metahistory* from a philosophical perspective. He points to a fundamental lack of interest in philosophy on the part of philosophers of history, and a corresponding lack of interest in philosophy of history on the part of philosophers. Comparing Kant's categories of the understanding and White's tropology, Ankersmit observes that while Kant's categories of the understanding do not function as alternatives to each other, White's tropes and modes of emplotment are optional. In order to reconcile Kant and White, Ankersmit attempts to find in White's system a deeper level where the options no longer exist and also seeks in the Kantian system a counterpart to White's optionality. He finds the deeper level in White's theory of the "prefiguration" of the historical field, which forms the transcendental condition of the possibility of historical knowing, and optionality in Kant's conception of the imagination and his analytics of the beautiful. Further, Ankersmit addresses the relation between ethics and politics in White's writings, indicating that although White had a strong political commitment, he refrains from explicitly stating whether it follows from his own philosophy of history, and if it does, how. Furthermore, Ankersmit contends that White privileges ethics over politics in his written works and then suggests that future generations of philosophers of history should explore the consequences of White's and his followers' emphasis on ethics at the expense of politics.

Herman Paul's essay discusses White's writings in the context of the "crisis of historicism." He suggests that there is a difference between a pre-*Metahistory* "liberal humanist" phase, when White seemed to be concerned about the possible threat of historicism and advocated historical variety in narratives of humanist advancement, and his writings from the 1970s and 1980s, when a Sartrean emphasis on individual moral choices led White to deny that people should hope for moral wisdom beyond the limits of their historical situation. Paul maintains that White's early work is driven by a specific "humanist historicism" that emphasizes the human will as the primary agent in human history. Paul claims that White's later works, especially *Metahistory*, address "the crisis of historicism," but that this crisis pertains specifically to moral concerns about the ironic condition of historical studies and is characterized as a "condition of Irony." The problem is the inability to relate historical studies to irrational (mythic, religious) modes of thought. Because, according to White, all moral aspirations and political visions require some "irrational" element, irony could play an important role as a mediator between history and myth. It failed to do so, however. This is why, Paul argues, White shows in his studies of Tocqueville, Marx, and Nietzsche that it is possible to reject irony and to focus on other ways of unifying history, reason, and myth.

1

On the Metaphilosophy of History

David Carr

Hayden White's Agenda for the Metaphilosophy of History

As everyone knows, Hayden White's *Metahistory* changed the philosophy of history for good. Anyone who has wanted to do serious work in the philosophy of history since its appearance in 1973 has had to come to terms with this now-classic work.

White's thesis and his approach are stated in the first two pages of his book. By considering "the historical work" as "a verbal structure in the form of a narrative prose discourse," he wants to affirm that "the historical consciousness on which Western man has prided himself since the beginning of the nineteenth century may be little more than a theoretical basis for [an] ideological position."[1] He then lays out his elaborate "theory of the historical work,"[2] and proceeds to apply it to the writings of a large collection of celebrated nineteenth-century authors.

I want to call attention to an interesting feature of White's work that has, I believe, gone largely unappreciated. He addresses himself, in the passages quoted above, to "the historical work," and the book received considerable attention for his analyses of the works of historians Leopold von Ranke, Jules Michelet, Alexis de Tocqueville, and Jacob Burckhardt. And much of White's subsequent work has been devoted to extending certain features of his "theory of the historical work" to historians in general, beyond the confines of the nineteenth century. Thus what mattered, for both White and his readers, was the impact of his analyses on our understanding and evaluation of works of history.

A large part of *Metahistory* is devoted to examining texts that are usually considered not "works of history" at all, but works of philosophy. He deals with as many philosophers of history (Georg Wilhelm Friedrich Hegel, Karl Marx, Friedrich Nietzsche, Benedetto Croce) as historians. The common rubric, of course, is "the historical consciousness of the nineteenth century," to which the philosophers, no less than the historians, give expression. Neither they nor their readers, however, would think of them as historians: the difference between history and philosophy, and indeed between history and the philosophy of history, was by the nineteenth century generally accepted. White, of course, finds the elements of his "theory of the historical work" in the writings of the philosophers as well as the historians, namely explanation by formal argument, emplotment, and ideological implication. These elements are discerned in philosophical theories about history, not historical narratives proper. Thus, it is important that Hayden White be recognized for his analysis and evaluation of the philosophy of history in the nineteenth century, and not only for what he says about historians.

This allows us to view Hayden White's work in a significantly different context from the usual one, and to put him into a somewhat different company of thinkers. He is usually viewed, quite correctly, as contributing to the epistemology of history (sometimes called the analytical or critical philosophy of history), which, as a field, is concerned with evaluating historians' claims to knowledge about the past. But he also belongs to the ranks of those twentieth-century philosophers who evaluated the "substantive" claims about the historical process, claims made primarily by nineteenth-century philosophers like Hegel and Marx. To be sure, these two groups of philosophers overlapped to some degree, since some analytic philosophers felt the need to dispose of the substantive philosophy of history before turning to their own epistemological analysis.[3] But other thinkers, not associated with the analytic philosophy of history (Karl Popper and Karl Löwith are good examples), joined in this evaluation, and we can think of this project, the critique of the substantive or "classical" philosophy of history, as constituting a significant chapter in twentieth-century thought, especially in the post–World War II period.

Hayden White belongs to this group too, then, and can be seen as part of the mid- to late-twentieth-century reaction to the nineteenth-century philosophy of history.

This project, it seems to me, deserves to be called something other than "metahistory," which many people now use as a generic term for the analysis of works of history; I suggest metaphilosophy of history, or the philosophy of the philosophy of history.

There are good reasons why Hayden White's contribution to this project has not attracted as much notice as other aspects of his work. By 1973 the evaluation of the classical philosophy of history had been under-way for some time, and the consensus seemed unanimously negative: the classical philosophy of history was dead. Though they advanced different reasons, most philosophers concluded that its project, usually described as finding the "meaning" in the whole of history, could not be realized. Hayden White seemed to agree, and there was nothing remarkable about that. What was remarkable was what he said about history itself. Most critics of the classical philosophy of history had contrasted it unfavorably with history itself, which seemed to them capable of attaining genuine and possibly even objective knowledge. But in his analysis, White appeared to attack this view as well, and *that*, of course, is what attracted attention.

I think there are good reasons for returning to the examination of the classical philosophy of history and for taking Hayden White's contribution to that examination seriously. Many philosophers who dismissed the classical philosophy of history thought they had disposed of it for good and that we need no longer deal with it. But there are important issues and questions about it that remain vital, as I shall argue. Many people who read White on history itself thought he was simply dismissing history as a serious enterprise and consigning it to the scrap heap; that was never his intent, however. Indeed, because of the new light he shed on historical writing, it deserved to be examined all the more intently. The same thing is true of the classical philosophy of history: in part because of White's treatment of it, but also for other reasons, it merits a new look and a reexamination.

In this essay, I will not be writing about Hayden White's views on the philosophy of history; instead, I will reexplore the classical philosophy of history which takes account of his critique. That is, I want to undertake a post–Hayden White metaphilosophy of history. I will not limit myself to an examination written in his style or even with his basic concepts; in fact, I will be employing some strategies that are considerably at variance with his approach.

The Survival of the Classical Philosophy of History

I begin by recalling an interesting phenomenon of the last years of the twentieth century. Many philosophers and historians did a double take in 1992 when they learned of a much-discussed book by Francis Fukuyama called *The End of History and the Last Man*. Their puzzlement could be explained by the fact that this author seemed to be advancing anew the most notorious claim associated with Hegel's philosophy of history, namely that Freedom would triumph in the course of History. But as we've seen, Hegel's project had long since been pronounced dead. Had nobody informed Fukuyama of this?

When Fukuyama's book hit the *New York Times* bestseller list— and was widely discussed in the popular press—the professionals could smile condescendingly and recognize a familiar phenomenon. Arnold J. Toynbee had published his twelve-volume *A Study of History*, which William Dray calls "the twentieth century's best known speculative account of history as a whole," in mid-century, and Dray, one of the major figures of the analytic philosophy of history, remarks that "it was *Time* and *Life* magazines, not scholarly journals, which received that account with highest acclaim."[4] Fukuyama's book could be safely dismissed as unserious, then, and the serious among us could spare themselves the trouble of reading it.

I mention Fukuyama's book in order to introduce my proposed new look at the classical philosophy of history. Many of the criticisms directed at some of its best-known practitioners, including Hegel, and at the whole project of such a philosophy of history, are fully justified, provided we understand this project in a certain way, namely as a theoretical enterprise advancing cognitive claims about the whole of history. And this is largely how it has been understood, not only by its critics but also by some of its advocates.

There is another way of understanding it, one which makes it both more interesting and possibly more understandable as an enterprise, perhaps less deserving of being dismissed. Dray, continuing in the passage I just quoted, hints at this: "Perhaps because an understanding of the past matters so much to most of us, and because the belief that it ought to be meaningful is so strong, interest in the speculative philosophy of history has not entirely disappeared." By this he means that its classical texts continue to be studied, though often not in the spirit intended by their authors.

I want to say something even stronger. The interest in as well as the practice of speculative philosophy continues, as the appearance of Fukuyama's book shows. I think it is also practiced in other forms, not so explicitly labeled as Fukuyama's effort. While Dray is right about why it continues, it is appropriate to inquire further into why the understanding of the past matters so much to us and why the belief is so strong that it ought to be "meaningful." Such an inquiry will convince us, I think, that not only has such philosophy not disappeared, but it is unlikely to disappear any time soon.

This is the much stronger claim that I want to advance. It requires a renewed understanding of this form of philosophy of history, one which I will pursue by returning to some of its classical texts to seek out the motivations behind the questions asked and the solutions proposed. In particular, I want to claim that the classical philosophy of history must be understood more as a practical enterprise than a theoretical one, which displays historical events along a temporal axis geared to a projected future, a future not be speculated on but to be realized. This is one reason why I want to eliminate the pejorative term "speculative" in the course of my argument. The terms "meaning" and "meaningful," used by Dray and many others in discussing this philosophy of history, must be understood in practical terms; the critics and practioners of this philosophy of history have construed "meaning" as a theoretical concept rather than as action or practice. The place to look for an understanding of the classical philosophy of history is the sense of meaning that relates to action and practice—social action and social practice, more precisely, in the temporal world. If we come to understand how our view of history is deeply rooted in the temporal structures inherent in action in the social sphere, then it will come as no surprise to us that the philosophy of history has a way of turning up again and again, long after its very possibility has been convincingly called into question.

History and the Philosophy of History

We have undertaken this re-examination of the classical philosophy of history under the assumption that it really differs from history proper. But is this assumption justified? Before the late eighteenth century, probably not. The task of telling the story of the past and that of seeking its ultimate meaning, especially in theological terms, were so closely intertwined that the distinction would be an artificial imposition. It is only after history begins to establish itself as an autonomous enterprise and to acquire the status of an academic discipline that the two tasks can be separated. As Hayden White notes, university chairs of history were first established in Berlin in 1810 and Paris in 1812,[5] and it is only a few years after this that Hegel starts giving his lectures on the philosophy of history. Ranke famously renounces the task that had traditionally been associated with history, that of finding edification and moral lessons in past events, and encourages the development of a discipline which is nonpartisan, objective, and based strictly on documentary evidence. Hegel, in the opening pages of his lectures, endorses the division of labor between history proper and the philosophy of history, and later feels he has to defend himself against the charge that he is encroaching on "a science that regards itself as empirical."[6]

Thus historically, at least, the establishment of history as a serious academic discipline and the establishment of the philosophy of history as a separate undertaking go hand in hand. Perhaps the new discipline of history, by restricting itself to certain very limited tasks, was leaving untouched some questions about the past and the course of history that needed to be asked and answered. The consensus among critics of the philosophy of history—and it had its detractors right from the start—was that while its questions may differ from those of history proper, the answers it comes up with are meant to be continuous with the theoretical claims made by historians. That is, like history, it wants to tell us the truth about the historical process; it wants to tell us about history as a whole rather than just some part of it; and it wants to tell us something about its ultimate meaning, not just the facts of what happens.

This view of the classical philosophy of history was shared by some of its most important twentieth-century critics. Karl Löwith famously characterized the whole project of seeking meaning in history, up through

Hegel and Marx, as a secularized version of the Christian story of salvation, "secularized" meaning, among other things, that its religious foundation was disguised as science.[7] Karl Popper likewise denounced what he called "historicism" as pseudo–social science.[8] Arthur Danto, in his analysis of what he calls the substantive philosophy of history, makes the claim that philosophers, like historians, examine past events in terms of their causal relation to later events, and that this feature of past events is what we call their "meaning"; but historians do this legitimately because the later events they refer to are events that have already happened or are happening. Philosophers of history, by contrast, postulate latest or ultimate events (the "end of history" idea), which they cannot justify, and derive from these their sense of meaning for the whole of history. Thus their claims extend the legitimate inquiry of history beyond the realm in which such claims can be justified.[9]

The Importance of Hegel's Lectures

Danto speaks of the substantive philosophy of history as a generic project or set of questions not identified with any particular philosopher. But his critique seems tailored to Hegel's lectures on the philosophy of history—and logically so, for in many ways Hegel created and continues to define the field. It is true that the expression "philosophy of history" had been used by Voltaire and Herder before him, but in neither case was the impact so great. Delivered in the 1820s and published shortly after his death, the lectures represent Hegel at the height of his influence, and their relatively brief (less than 100 pages) introduction is as clear and straightforward as it is comprehensive. Soon translated into other languages (for example, English in 1857), it has become probably the most widely read of Hegel's works. So great was Hegel's impact, that his approach to history became paradigmatic not only for many who followed his lead, but also for those who later attacked the very project of the philosophy of history. What is more, philosophers who reflected on history before Hegel are often thought, anachronistically, to have been engaged in the same kind of inquiry he was.

Any attempt, then, to understand the classical philosophy of history must first of all come to terms with Hegel's text. Let us recall the main outlines of his famous introduction to the lectures. As we have pointed out, he begins *philosophische Weltgeschichte* from history proper. Philosophy, he says, has "thoughts of its own," a priori thoughts, to bring to the study of history.[10] The "only" thought, however, that philosophy brings to the study of history is that of reason—"that reason rules the world"—and thus world history, like everything else, can be seen as a rational or reasonable (*vernuenftig*) affair.[11] Reason not only sets the goal for history but also governs the realization of that goal. Hegel did not invent this idea, he reminds us; the idea that reason rules the world is that of Anaxagoras, and it has also been expressed in the idea of divine providence. This too suggests a rational plan, God's plan, but providence is usually portrayed as being hidden from us. Unwilling to settle for pious ignorance, Hegel believes that the rationality of providence can be known and explained. If we take seriously the idea of providence, the demonstration of its rationality would amount to a theodicy or "justification of God."[12]

The embodiment of reason is Spirit (*Geist*), both in individuals and in peoples, whose nature is to be conscious and self-conscious, and whose actualization is to be autonomous and self-sufficient, that is, to be free. This actualization is a temporal process, and that process is history. Spirit actualizes itself and achieves freedom through history, drawing its energy from human passions and intentions; the result of this process is often at odds with the actual intentions of the individuals and peoples involved. Hegel speaks famously of the "cunning of reason,"[13] since reason achieves ends of its own by using the ends of others. In history, it is only when individuals and peoples organize themselves into states that freedom can finally be truly realized. The "positive reality and satisfaction of freedom"[14] are to be found in law, the ethical life of the community and political order, not in the mere absence of constraint.

The actual course of history can be seen as the human "drive [of] perfectibility"[15] in the gradual realization of freedom. This pathway is not a smooth one, however, but consists in the spirit's "hard and endless struggle against itself." Spirit hides its own nature from itself and is even "proud and full of enjoyment in this self-estrangement."[16] Individuals and peoples struggle against each other, and many morally good and virtuous people suffer unjustly. But history moves on a different plane, and the acts of individuals, especially those of the great figures of history, are not to be judged by moral standards. The spirit of a people, not individuals, is the agent of history, "progressing in a necessary series of stages," but only as "phases of the one universal Spirit" through which the "World-Spirit elevates and completes itself in history, into a self-comprehending *totality*."[17] The self-comprehension of World-Spirit is philosophy itself.

In several places in the lectures, Hegel presents in the broadest outlines the necessary stages through which the World-Spirit has passed on its path toward the realization of freedom. In the ancient Oriental world only one—the emperor or tyrant—is free. In the Greek and Roman worlds only *some* persons are free. It was first the "Germanic peoples, through Christianity, who came to the awareness that every human is free by virtue of being human."[18] The realization of freedom is the goal that gives meaning to what happens in history, and the place of this realization is within history itself, not beyond it. Moreover, it has occurred or is occurring in "our world," "our time," "the last stage of history."[19]

Hegel's sweeping treatment of world history beautifully exemplifies Danto's formal analysis—no accident, because Danto's account of "substantive philosophy of history" was in my view tailored primarily to fit Hegel. The realization of freedom is taken as the end point and goal of the historical process; and it is from the perspective of this end point that the broad outlines of history can be understood. "Meaning" is attributed to the large-scale events of world history insofar as they contribute to this end. Indeed, we could go so far as to say that what counts as an event—at least a historical event—is determined by the relation to this goal. For Danto, Hegel's procedure is formally equivalent to that of a historian of the Second World War. Knowing the end, in this case the Allied victory, the historian decides what events are worthy of inclusion, and thus of having "meaning," by the degree to which these events relate to the war's outcome. The difference between the historian and the philosopher is obvious, however: we know that the Allies won the war; the claim that freedom is finally and fully realized "in our time"—that is, in Hegel's time—is very questionable, to say the least. It seems to be speculative, in the pejorative sense of that term.

Hayden White's formal analysis of Hegel's philosophy of history has similar features to Danto's reading of Hegel. Hegel first emplots the course of history in terms of irony and tragedy, stressing the struggle of points of view, the "panorama of sin and suffering," that is, the suffering of the good and the triumph of the wicked, the failure of human passions to attain their ends. But then this tale of tragedy is enveloped and taken up into the Christian "divine comedy" in which Creator and Creation are fully reconciled.[20] Again the goal of freedom for all gives retrospective meaning to the tragic events of history, elevating them to a different plane and providing them with a sense they could not have had for those involved.

Narrative and Practice

Danto and White stress the narrative form displayed in the classical philosophy of history; both belong to the "narrativist" revolution which sought to understand historiography by comparing it to literature, indeed fictional literature, rather than science. In White's case, this led to a very skeptical view of history: narrative form was claiming cognitive or "scientific" status for something that has its proper application in the realm of fiction. This assessment was unremarkable when applied to the classical philosophy of history: it just provided reinforcement for the low esteem in which this philosophy was generally held.

The narrative form can be seen to have much broader application, beyond its uses in literature and history alone. Danto acknowledged this in *Narration and Knowledge*. There he called narrative the "metaphysics of everyday life."[21] What he meant, I think, is that the idea of structuring events retrospectively in relation to an end is simply the teleological form, one which is found in many aspects of ordinary experience, especially action. Like the events in stories, and like historical events, our actions are made up of events spread across time, and we don't just live through or observe them, we perform them. In action, we envisage the future and consult the past, and arrange the present as the passage between the two. What we encounter in the present has significance as obstacle or instrument to our objectives. In fact, we can see a close kinship between the beginning-middle-end structure of narrative and the means-end structure of action. In both cases "end" is not merely temporal but also teleological, and the same can be said for the related concepts of middle and means. The beginning of an action is the situation perceived by the agent, a divergence between what is the case and what is to be done. This divergence constitutes a problem or predicament, which is overcome or resolved by the achievement of the end. The role of the agent is thus both prospective and retrospective, or perhaps quasi-retrospective, since the agent views the past and present *as if* looking back from a point in the future not yet realized. This lends to the agent a role not unlike that of the narrator of a story, organizing the present by actively selecting, from a range of possibilities, the means to employ in the realization of an end. Sometimes, in fact, we call this "plotting," and we can see the connection between this and the narrativist concept of "emplotment" used by Hayden White.

Suppose we were now to look at the classical philosophy of history not as a cognitive or theoretical embodiment of the teleological structure, but as a *practical* embodiment of it. What would this mean?

First, the application we propose would involve a reinterpretation of the mode or register in which these theories are put forth. We would have to try to understand them not as metaphysical claims about the reality of the historical process, but as a kind of discourse more appropriately compared with the political-rhetorical kind of storytelling we encounter in political discourse. To the extent that their theories involve reference to an end point or conclusion of the historical process, philosophers, through their own activity as philosophers, work to bring it about.

This is not to say, however, that their discourse is *prescriptive* rather than *descriptive* in character. This would be a misleading oversimplification of the practical aspect of their narratives. What they give us, after all, is a story that includes the past and the present as well as the future. The past, of course, cannot be prescribed, nor can the present; so a large part of the narrative is still descriptive in character. But the description is tailored to fit the larger story, and this may require that present and past be described in a new way. Thus we can say that they are being *redescribed*, and indeed that *redescription* is a large part of what goes on here.

Another general point concerns the scale or scope of the philosophy of history in its classical forms. Whatever else it is, this philosophy has always presented itself as an account not limited to any particular stretch of history or to any particular state, region, or people; it claims to be an account of "history as a whole," "universal history," or "world history." Action and practice, even considered at the social and political levels, are still describable as particular actions, no matter how sweeping their scope. Fighting wars, undertaking revolutions, and other such collective actions are still particular events. What is more, such actions are performed by particular social agents, even if these are collective agents like communities or other "we" subjects. Any reinterpretation of the philosophers' historical narratives in practical terms will have to consider whether the narrative structures we have considered so far are really applicable at such a scale. In other words, if such an application is to work, our account must find in these classical theories something that corresponds to the types of action and the sorts of agents that we found in our earlier examples.

Kant and Marx

Is it possible to read the classical philosophers of history in this way? In fact, this was the approach of important philosophers of history both before and after Hegel. Kant is usually not associated with the philosophy of history, and he does not use the term, but he did write on the subject. His essay "Idea for a Universal History from a Cosmopolitan Point of View" (1784), his best-known work on history, argues only for the very limited thesis that the course of past history "permits us to hope" for "a steady and progressive though slow evolution" toward a better state for mankind. Kant wants to share the Enlightenment belief in progress, but his critical reason forces him to limit its pretensions. Progress in history, should it be found, would be toward "the achievement of a universal civic society which administers laws among men," which is "the most difficult and the last [problem] to be solved by mankind."[22]

By the time he reaches this point, the status of Kant's discourse on history should be clear to the reader. He is not making claims about the actual course of history; rather, he is outlining the ideal conditions under which alone, he thinks, history could exhibit any progress. Because these conditions are, in his day, far from having been realized, Kant's claims are clearly practical or moral in character. Thus, he can assure practicing historians that he is making no attempt to displace their work, since he is propounding an Idea of world history based upon an a priori principle,[23] an "Idea of how the course of the world must be if it is to lead to certain rational ends."[24] By using the term *Idea*, Kant indicates a rational concept whose empirical reality is not, and, according to the *Critique*, *cannot* be exhibited in experience. Like human freedom itself, neither can its possibility be empirically denied. The course of history does not provide evidence that the "civic union of the human race" will ever be achieved, but it does not prove that it never will be, either. Its realization must at least be regarded as possible, and the Idea that we have of it may help bring it to pass.[25] Kant is telling us not where history is going but where it *ought* to be going. Only in this very minimal sense can philosophy help "make sense" of history, namely by articulating the "cosmopolitan stand-point" from which alone it can be freed from its apparent moral chaos. In *Idea for a Universal History*, the concepts of a universal civic society, or league of nations, and of history as progressing toward it, legitimize certain political choices. Those concepts are Ideas capable of guiding our action in the social sphere. Kant anticipates the project of expanding his ethical principles, with such notions as a kingdom of ends, into a political theory. Ethics and politics alike belong to Kant's practical philosophy, not his theoretical philosophy. Their central concern is what we ought to do. And the same is true of his philosophy of history.

It was primarily the "Western Marxists," who emerged in Europe before and after the Second World War, who found ways of taking Marx seriously without accepting the standard determinist reading of his philosophy of history. In their view, Marx's account of past history, and the present situation as he described it, were ways of setting the stage for political organization and action. Rather than a theoretical account of how history unfolds and where it is inevitably heading, Marx's account is a blueprint of the social forces that must be understood if concrete steps are to be taken toward the realization of a desired outcome. This interpretation, inspired by attention to Marx's early writings, can also be applied to later works like the *Communist Manifesto*.

From this view, Marx's account of history could be said to stem from an analysis of what is wrong with the present state of affairs and what needs to be done to correct it. His originality lies in shifting the focus of political critique away from the discourse of democratic participation in social decisions and toward underlying material conditions. The idea of class results from viewing political realities as based on the economic substructure of the ownership of the means of production rather than on "abstract" notions of freedom. The class concept allows Marx to look beyond the constitutional arrangements of the existing nation-states of Europe and to discern the conditions shared by the working class across national boundaries. Understanding the situation of European countries in the nineteenth century in terms of class struggle calls forth an account of how the class struggle came to its present state. The familiar historical background of the overthrow of feudalism, the attack on the monarchies, and the rise of modern constitutional states, is now seen in a completely new light. The French Revolution is not the triumph of human freedom but the triumph of a particular class, the bourgeoisie; this coincides with and contributes to the beginnings of capitalism and the Industrial Revolution. In turn, these developments generate the new working class of the modern industrial states. The *Communist Manifesto* is devoted primarily to telling this story.

It is easy enough to read Marx's philosophy of history in this way because he thought of himself more as a reformer and activist than as a philosopher. Indeed, he famously contrasted his role with that of the philosophers, who had only "interpreted" the world in various ways. The point is to change it, he said. That is the point of the *Communist Manifesto*, which ends with a stirring call to arms: "working men of all countries, unite!"[26] But changing the world, for him and for Engels, required telling a story that would make sense of the change. This story takes the form of a narrative that is neither cognitive nor aesthetic, but practical.

Considered as a narrative in the practical sense, with a predicament or problem to be addressed by action, Marx's account of history has a beginning, a middle, and an end. It also has a central subject or protagonist, the proletariat. In spite of Marx's rejection of the "idealist" background and his pretension to a strictly "scientific" theory, he portrays the proletariat as both suffering and eventually collectively acting. This class is portrayed as the culmination of a history of class struggle, a class whose emancipation will "forever" release "the whole of society from exploitation, oppression, and class struggles."[27] Thus, the proletariat is not so much a particular group or community as a universal subject who represents the aspirations of mankind as such. The proletariat stands in for all of us. So, implicitly and indirectly, "we" are all part of this struggle. All the features of practical storytelling are preserved even though Marx's story encompasses all people and all history.

Hegel's World-Historical Rhetoric

Let us now return to Hegel's philosophy of history with the structures of practical narrative in mind. It may seem difficult initially to discern these structures in Hegel's text, especially if we begin where we just concluded our discussion of Marx, with the idea of the central subject or protagonist. One of the most striking and, to some, troubling features of Hegel's account is the role accorded to Spirit, or more precisely World-Spirit, in the course of history. There is no doubt that Hegel's account of history has a central subject or protagonist, and this is it: the World-Spirit. Moreover, the term *"Geist"* suggests subjectivity and agency—certainly more so than the notion of "class" in Marx—and Hegel indeed attributes to Spirit activity, intentions, thought, and, of course, reason.

But one of the reasons this notion is found troubling—as well as unconvincing—is that this protagonist seems to operate completely on its own, marching through history according to its own plan, oblivious to and seemingly contemptuous of the thoughts, needs, desires, and interests of individuals in history. Even those giants Hegel calls world-historical individuals —Caesar, Alexander, Napoleon—are in the end nothing but unwitting tools, used by the World-Spirit in pursuit of its own ends. If a story is being told here, it seems to be about something or someone that is remote from and even alien to the lives of ordinary individuals. By contrast, part of the notion of practical narrative is the communal "we" subject with which one can identify, denoting a group to which one belongs and in whose action one participates. This may seem plausible in the case of Marx's proletariat, but does it work with Hegel's World-Spirit?

In order to answer this question, it is necessary to look more closely at the important notion of Spirit (*Geist*) and its function in Hegel's thought. The World-Spirit (*Weltgeist*) is important, but it is not the only spirit among the dramatis personae of the lectures on the philosophy of history. According to one passage, the world or universal spirit is the result of the activities of *Volksgeister*—national spirits or spirits of a people, which are moments or phases that make it up. These in turn result in each case from the development of a people. "A people," Hegel writes, "goes through a series of stages [*Bildungsstufen*] until it reaches the one which is the universal stage of its spirit."[28] The key to the understanding of the World-Spirit lies in the understanding of these stages and what it means to go through them.

At this point in the lectures Hegel's description is very sketchy. He says that a particular form of spirit "does not merely pass away naturally in time, but is negated (*aufgehoben*) in the self-activating, self-reflecting activity of self-consciousness." This process is both a "preservation and a transfiguration [*Erhalten und Verklären*]."[29] Spirit is the "result of its own activity: its activity is the transcending of what is immediately there, by negating it and returning into itself."[30] These passages recall Hegel's description of history as the Spirit's "hard and endless struggle against itself," its "self-estrangement," which is not the "harmless and peaceful progress" that we find "in the realm of organic life."[31] "Spirit, within its own self, stands in opposition to itself. It must overcome itself as its own truly hostile hindrance."[32] These brief references to the well-known "dialectical" movement of history (Hegel does not use the term himself, at least not here) remain tantalizing because Hegel does not relate them concretely to what he describes as the broad movements of the World-Spirit in history.

We should note that in the lectures the term *Geist* is first introduced on its own: not, that is, as part of the complex forms *Volksgeist* and *Weltgeist*. Hegel begins with the broad distinction between Spirit and nature, or Spirit and matter, and says that he wants to put forward some "abstract" features of spirit before going on to its "most concrete" embodiments in history. These descriptions are abstract, then, in the sense that they apply to all instances of spirit, whether at the level of peoples, states, etc. Here Hegel mentions self-consciousness, self-knowledge, and self-sufficiency, each having its center (*sein Mittelpunkt*) in itself, being by itself (*bei-sich selbst-sein*). These are summed up in the notion of freedom, which is the "essence," the "only truth," of spirit.[33] But again these general descriptions are not related to the dialectical movement of self-opposition and self-negation described elsewhere.

This produces in the text of the lectures a kind of disconnect that has driven many commentators to look elsewhere in Hegel's work in order to fill in the gaps. The favorite choice has been the *Phenomenology of Spirit* (1807), a difficult work that can, at least in part, be itself read as a philosophy of history. A passage in the lectures, following those quoted above in which the "abstract" concept of spirit is introduced, points us toward the *Phenomenology*: "According to this abstract definition, we can say of world history that it is the exhibition [*Darstellung*] of the spirit, the working out of the explicit knowledge of what it potentially is. Just as the germ of the plant carries within itself the entire nature of the tree . . . so the first traces of spirit virtually contain all history."[34] It is this reference to the "first traces of spirit" that sends us to the *Phenomenology*, since there the spirit is shown to arise for the first time out of more basic elements.

In the text of the *Phenomenology* itself, Hegel uses the term *Geist*—the true subject, after all, of the *Phänomenologie des Geistes*—for the first time in a passage which introduces a section titled "Independence and Dependence of Self-Consciousness; Lordship and Bondage [*Herrschaft und Knechtschaft*]." This section is probably the most famous and most quoted and commented-upon section in the *Phenomenology*. It can be and has been read in many ways: as a description of psychological or interpersonal relations, social and political dynamics, or historical developments, or even merely as a description of the internal relation of individual consciousness with itself. Perhaps it is all these at once. A couple of its features make it especially useful for understanding Hegel's philosophy of history, and for our interpretation in particular. First, it is clearly the description of a threefold process, development, or progression, and Hegel *seems* to be saying that *Geist* is generated or constitutes itself out of this process. It culminates in mutual recognition and reconciliation. Thus we are likely to find here an exemplary account of what Hegel means by *Geist*, a term that has a prominent role in his philosophy of history. Second, when he introduces the term *Geist*, Hegel describes it in language that is familiar to us, namely as "an I that is We, a We that is I."[35] Hegel's concept of *Geist*, then, seems to reflect or incorporate the very notion of the first-person plural that is central to our account of *practical* narrative.

If we look at Hegel's narrative in this way, we can see it not as describing the history of mankind, but as urging that it move in a certain direction. He is organizing the past in order to make a case for a particular future, that of the realization of human freedom. In the 1820s, when the reaction of European countries to the French Revolution and the Napoleonic conquests was still being formed, it was significant to argue in favor of human freedom, rather than simply order and restoration, as the direction of history. Hegel is addressing his European contemporaries and saying: *we* constitute a community in virtue of what we have been through together. Because of our common experience, history can now be seen to have a significance that could not be seen by those who lived through it. He is urging that the contentious history of modern Europe be transformed dialectically from bloody conflict and the seesaw of domination to the emergence of a new community.

It is true that Hegel's narrative is not limited to Europe but is projected onto humanity as a whole. We know retrospectively that part of Hegel's problem is that he identified the future of humanity with that of Europe; his work has been criticized for its false predictions or implausible claims about the end of history. But the major problem of Hegel's philosophy of history is not merely that it is Eurocentric. If it is in fact a failure, its failure is not theoretical but practical. When it is understood as a kind of world-historical rhetoric rather than a putative science, its problem becomes this: it is not able to constitute a community of humanity by telling a persuasive story about it. In this sense, its failure may be even more predictable or inevitable than in its theoretical interpretation, and perhaps even more tragic.

But Hegel's philosophy of history need not be viewed simply as a failure. Seen as a practical narrative, rather than as a speculative science, it exemplifies certain features of the way we view history in light of narrative and time. First, we look at ourselves as parts of larger-scale communities, and at the limit, these communities can expand to encompass humanity as a whole. Though the idea of the "human community" has repeatedly proved to be wildly impractical as a motivating force for collective action, it still offers a possible background for human endeavor. Second, we see the problems of the present as the culmination of a process that points us in a certain direction. Part of human historicity is that we see ourselves and our present situation as the dramatic turning point between past and future, and we arrange the past in such a way as to make a certain future meaningful if not inevitable. In this sense narrative is not only the metaphysics of everyday life, as Danto said, but also the metaphysics of social and historical life as well. In this sense, because of what Kant might have called a transcendental and unavoidable illusion, we are always at the end, or at least very near the end, of history.

Notes

1. Hayden White, *Metahistory* (Baltimore: Johns Hopkins University Press, 1973), 2.

2. Ibid., 5.

3. See W. H. Walsh, *The Philosophy of History* (New York: Harper & Row,

1960), chs. 1, 6, 7; Arthur Danto, *Narration and Knowledge* (New York: Columbia University Press, 1985), ch. 1.

4. William Dray, *Philosophy of History*, 2nd ed. (Englewood Cliffs, NJ: Prentice Hall, 1993) 2.

5. White, *Metahistory*, 136.

6. G. W. F. Hegel, *Introduction to the Philosophy of History*, trans. Leo Rauch (Indianapolis: Hackett, 1988), 68; G. W. F. Hegel, *Vorlesungen über die Philosophie der Geschichte* (Frankfurt: Suhrkamp Verlag, 1976), 87. Hereafter, page numbers of the German edition will follow the English page references in parentheses.

7. Karl Löwith, *Meaning in History* (Chicago: University of Chicago Press, 1949), 1 and passim.

8. Karl Popper, *The Poverty of Historicism* (London: Routledge, 1957).

9. Danto, *Narration and Knowledge*, ch. 1.

10. Hegel, *Introduction*, 10 (20).

11. Ibid., 12 (20).

12. Ibid., 18 (28).

13. Ibid., 35 (49).

14. Ibid., 41 (56).

15. Ibid., 57 (74).

16. Ibid., 59 (76).

17. Ibid., 82 (105).

18. Ibid., 21 (31).

19. Hegel, *Vorlesungen*, 524.

20. White, *Metahistory*, 126–27.

21. Danto, *Narration and Knowledge*, xiv.

22. Immanuel Kant, *On History*, ed. L.W. Beck (New York: Macmillan, 1963), 16ff.

23. Ibid., 25.

24. Ibid., 24.

25. Ibid.

26. Karl Marx and Friedrich Engels, *The Communist Manifesto*, ed. D. McLellan (Oxford: Oxford University Press, 1992), 39.

27. Ibid., 44.

28. Hegel, *Introduction*, 81 (104).

29. Ibid., 81 (103).

30. Ibid., 82 (104).

31. Ibid., 59 (76).

32. Ibid., 58ff. (76).

33. Ibid., 19ff. (29ff.).

34. Ibid., 21 (31).

2

White's "New Neo-Kantianism"

AESTHETICS, ETHICS, AND POLITICS

Frank Ankersmit

Hayden White has dominated debate in philosophy of history in the last three decades. Contemporary philosophy of history is mainly what White has made it. So the question of the future of philosophy of history is, essentially, a question about how to extrapolate from White to the future, although this is not an attempt to predict the (near) future of philosophy of history. Popper has cured us forever of the hope of being able to do so. Maybe some young scholar is presently writing a book in some out-of-the-way corner of the intellectual world that will have an impact similar to that of *Metahistory* and that will pitilessly condemn all we are presently doing to oblivion and obsolescence. Not very likely, though, but one can never tell.

Hence, I shall focus on what one might paradoxically call the "foreseeable future." With that scope, I have in mind the big questions raised by White's oeuvre and that still await satisfactory treatment. One of these big questions surely is how to read that oeuvre from a philosophical perspective. Obviously, this is a somewhat surprising observation about an oeuvre that will ordinarily be said to belong to the philosophy of history. Is a philosopher of history not primarily a philosopher? And will his writings not primarily be read as expressing philosophical claims about our relationship to and our knowledge of the past?

But, as we all know, this is not how things are: since the 1960s, philosophers have never shown any interest in what philosophers of history have been discussing. Or, to be more precise, the traffic between mainstream philosophy (of language and of science) and philosophy of history has been since then exclusively one-way. Philosophers of history with a scientist cast of mind have tried, with more or less success, to import to philosophy of history what had been achieved in philosophy of language and of science. But nobody traveled in the opposite direction.

White's oeuvre may give us part of the explanation. When looking for theoretical inspiration, White preferably turned to literary theorists like Northrop Frye, Roland Barthes, Fredric Jameson, Émile Benveniste, or Erich Auerbach, to historians such as Michel Foucault or E. P. Thompson, and to older philosophers such as Giambattista Vico, Georg Wilhelm Friedrich Hegel, Karl Marx, or Benedetto Croce, none of whom score particularly high on the hit lists of contemporary philosophers (of language and of science). White does not once cite such names as Willard Van Orman Quine, Sir Peter Frederick Strawson, Donald Davidson, Peter Geach, John Searle, Wilfred Sellars, Thomas Nagel, Hilary Putnam, John McDowell, or even Richard Rorty.

One might infer that White (and the philosophers of history inspired by him) and philosophers of language and of science apparently have nothing to say to each other. It would seem like a *dialogue des sourds*; they would appear to inhabit completely different intellectual worlds. I would not be surprised if this is actually how White and his colleagues in the philosophy department look at each other. However, it might also be that both sides have taken insufficient notice of each other and that they truly have to tell each other a few things that are of considerable interest to both of them and that both parties should heed.

This will be the intrigue of my story here: I shall take my point of departure in White's philosophy of history and hope to show, next, in what way it may, or ought, to have its impact on contemporary philosophy of language. Finally, most of my essay will be devoted to the old Machiavellian—and still unresolved—issue of the relationship between ethics and politics. For this is where White's philosophy of history is especially enlightening.

White's Transcendentalism

Let's start with the well-known Whitean quasi-structuralist grid of the four tropes metaphor, metonymy, synecdoche, and irony, which are listed with their modes of emplotment, argument, and ideological implication. The grid is introduced in the introduction of *Metahistory*, then applied to eight historians and philosophers of history in the substance of the book and theoretically refined in *Tropics of Discourse*.[1] The truly amazing claim made here is that the grid is optional: one may just as well choose one trope plus emplotment, argument, and ideological implication as another. As far as I know, a similar claim has never been made by any philosopher (of history). The trajectory between the world, as an object of knowledge, and what is said about it, is always presented as a route without alternatives. "Optionalism" never had any popularity in philosophy.

For a proper assessment of White's claim, it must be emphasized that he does not have in mind anything so trivial as that we are free to say about the world what we want. We may say about a chair that is made of wood, that it has four legs, etc.; and, indeed, the set of alternatives is truly infinite. So it is with history: when writing on the French Revolution, one may focus on its political history, or, instead, on its military or economic aspects. But with regard to the chair, we can be sure that it has four legs, if it has four legs. We have no alternatives anymore. If a history of the French Revolution states that King Louis XVI was guillotined on January 21, 1793, the relationship between the event itself and the statement in question does not leave room for alternatives. Truth is a jealous god, suffering no rivals.

So White's amazing optionalism will have to be interpreted differently, if we wish to get an adequate grasp of its philosophical implications. We may get closer to the truth if we focus on some similarities with the Kantian system. Hans Kellner already argued that one could hardly fail to recognize the similarities between White's four tropes and the four sets of Kant's categories of the understanding.[2] Indeed, it makes sense to say that the Kantian categories of the understanding make knowledge possible and that White's tropology, in its turn, explains how historical knowledge is possible. Furthermore, as we all know, Kant was awakened from his dogmatic slumbers by David Hume's treatment of causality. Hume had shown that cause and effect do not belong to the inventory of the world and are part of what the mind brings to the world.[3]

In his first *Critique*, Kant radicalized Hume's strategy by arguing that space and time and our cognitive grasp of the world do also have their (transcendental) conditions in the human mind. This deep "transcendental" insight enabled him to demarcate the correct uses of reason from its misuses (as in metaphysics) and to overcome the dogmatic rationalism of both Cartesian rationalism and of the Lockean and Humean empiricism of his time. A similar story can be told for White's tropology. Tropology also is something that "the mind brings" to (past) reality and that is not part of the past itself. But whereas Kant's contemporaries were surprisingly quick to grasp the revolutionary and proto-idealistic implications of Kant's transcendentalism, White's contemporaries either stubbornly stuck to their dogmatic empiricism or accepted tropology without recognizing in what way tropology might succeed in reconciling the claims of empiricism with those of transcendental historical reason. It should be added, however, that the latter category of White's readers should be forgiven much of their disappointing grasp of his argument, because White has not always been the best advocate of his own case. For example, when eagerly emphasizing the "fictional" component of tropology, he deliberately exploits the ambiguity of the word *fiction*, insofar as that word may refer both to what is "made" by the mind, and to what is fiction in the sense that the novel is fiction. In this way, White himself provided his enemies with the ammunition that they often used against him so effectively.

Prefiguration as a Transcendental Strategy

Nevertheless, there is a striking difference between Kant's categories of the understanding and White's tropology: in his "transcendental analytics," Kant insisted that *all* of the categories of the understanding are conditional of our knowledge of the world. They do not function as potential alternatives for each other. No "optionalism" here. But this is clearly quite different in White's tropology: the tropes, and the modes of emplotment, argument, and ideological implication "consonant" with them are all optional. One may freely choose among them or even combine all of them (as was the case, according to White, with Marx). Self-evidently, introducing this kind of optionalism into the Kantian system would reduce it to utter nonsense. It would result in a Babylonian confusion of coexisting "knowledges," and in the epistemologist's intellectual suicide. Truth is not optional, as Aristotle already made abundantly clear.

There seem to be two strategies for reconciling Kant and White. In the first place, it can be argued that there is a still deeper level in White's system where the optional aspect no longer exists. Secondly, one might try to find a counterpart to the optional aspect elsewhere in the Kantian system.

Let's begin with the first strategy. The search for the "deeper" level will bring us to White's notion of *prefiguration*, which he describes as follows:

> Before the historian can bring to bear upon the data of the historical field the conceptual apparatus he will have to represent and to explain it, he must first prefigure the field—that is to say, constitute it as an object of mental perception. This poetic act is indistinguishable from the linguistic act in which the field is made ready for interpretation as a domain of a particular kind. That is to say, before a given domain can be interpreted, it must first be construed as a ground inhabited by discernible figures. The figures, in turn, must be conceived to be classifiable as distinctive orders, classes, genera, and species of phenomena.[4]

Needless to say, this is, once again, a very Kantian statement: just as Kant exchanged the dogmatic rationalism of empiricism and Cartesian rationalism for a critical analysis of Reason, so does White exchange naive confidence in historical Reason for an investigation of the limits of historical Reason. And the Whitean counterpart to Kant's transcendental aesthetics and transcendental analytics is to be found in his theory of the "prefiguration" of the historical field, preceding all that the historian might wish to say about the past. Hence, *prefiguration no longer is optional*: it can truly be said to be the transcendental condition of the possibility of historical knowing. At the (deeper) level of prefiguration, we have no options: there simply is no alternative for prefiguration. Alternatives and options enter the scene only when the subsidiary question arises of what specific kind of prefiguration shall be adopted. So on this (deeper) level of prefiguration, the parallelism with the Kantian system seems to be happily restored.

In this context, we should also observe that in his later work, White more frequently relies on prefiguration (and cognate concepts) than on the tropes.[5] The title of his last collection of essays was *Figural Realism*, suggesting that the notion of *figura* may help us understand how we conceive of historical reality and in what way figura is conditional of our understanding of it. Though figura is clearly related to prefiguration, White did not hit on the notion through further analysis of the latter, but in his confrontation with Erich Auerbach's use of it in *Mimesis*. I shall not here enter into the very complicated intellectual history of figura;[6] I restrict myself to the observation that figura is meant to tie together two historical phenomena (separated from each other by sometimes thousands of years) on the basis of a certain structural similarity. For example, one might say that there is such a structural or semantic similarity between the journey of the Israelite people through the Red Sea as recounted in Exodus and the baptism of Christ by St. John, or, more plausibly, between the Revolution of 1789 and that of 1848. And then one might infer that the first event is conditional for an understanding of the second, or even, as White in his later work likes to emphasize, that the second event can be seen as the *fulfillment* of the first.[7] White insists, moreover, on the moral or political use that can be and has been made of figura by presenting a desired present or future as the "fulfillment" of some antecedent event in the past. It could be argued that White seems to be more interested in this moral or political application of figura rather than in what the historian may do with it.

Needless to say, this way of dealing with historical events and our understanding of them is riddled with nasty problems. First, what is to *count* as a pair of structurally similar events? The structural similarities between the Jews crossing the Red Sea and the baptism of Christ by St. John will be far from obvious to many people, to say the least. Second, the figuralist approach reduces the scope of the historian to only those events that happen to have a believable twin somewhere in the past. But the approach is even at odds with what one should expect from historical writing, insofar as the historian's professional interest is in where one period differs from another. Worse still, the approach seems to give the ill-famed covering law model a new lease on life—though in a peculiarly counterintuitive and antediluvian guise. Third, a discussion of the plausibility of claims about structural similarities necessarily presupposes the kind of historical knowledge that the figuralist approach is precisely expected to justify. The approach then appears to beg the question dramatically. And, last, the approach focuses on two events in the past itself, bypassing the dimension of language and historical meaning. It is therefore sui generis, incapable of addressing transcendental questions, let alone of dealing with them adequately.

But let's skip such objections, serious though they are. Of interest in the present context is something else: namely, that figura and prefiguration tend to get fixed to *individual* historical events or phenomena. Recall that we moved a moment ago from tropology to prefiguration because this seemed to enable us to avoid the optionality of tropology. But if figura ties one individual historical event or phenomenon to just one other event or phenomenon, we shall inevitably be back to optionality again. One specific argument in favor of the claim that a structural similarity exists between the two events or phenomena in question can then no longer be preferred to any other. Any argument singling out a number of similarities between the two events or phenomena will then do, and any preference that one might have here will be wholly arbitrary and will not permit of rational justification.

White's Tropology and Kant's Analytics of the Beautiful

Nevertheless, there is a way in which the preceding account of figura can be fitted within the Kantian transcendental system. This fitting will bring us to a second strategy for upholding the symmetry of the Kantian system and White's tropology. In order to see this, we shall now focus on Kant's notion of the imagination (*Einbildungskraft*). The imagination is, roughly, the faculty enabling us to reduce the manifold of our perception of the world to the appropriate concept. Suppose we are looking at an apple. We shall then perceive something that is round and red, but this is not yet the perception of an *apple*. The imagination will then add to and subtract from these perceptions in a very complex mental process; it will, for example, add the side of the apple that we do not see, it will add its white flesh and it juiciness, it also will eliminate irrelevant contingencies peculiar to this apple only—and only then will we recognize the perceived object *as* an apple. This, then, is what the imagination does. Put in one sentence, one may say that the imagination mediates, or negotiates, between perception and conceptualization.

In the first *Critique*, Kant lengthily dwells on the distinction between what he refers to as "schematization" and "conceptualization." Schematization is "phenomenal" in the sense of dealing with the object of perception *as it is given to us* when seeing it from a certain perspective and as presented to us in a certain relationship to ourselves. Conceptualization abstracts from this and gives us the pure *concept* of the apple *as such*. This is done by what Kant refers to as the "productive imagination." Kant's argument is quite complicated and often far from clear. It has thus provoked avalanches of theoretical speculation by two centuries of commentators on the relevant passages of the first *Critique*.

The philosopher of history studying Kant and his commentators cannot fail to be struck by the profound relevance of the Kantian notion of the imagination for how the historian conceptualizes the past. For whereas Kant's analysis of the imagination may sometimes seem needlessly complex and elaborate for the perception of objects as apples or dogs, all the technicalities of his exposition acquire unexpected value and meaning if applied to the issue of how the historian may come to conceptualize such events or phenomena of the past as, say, a "war" or a "revolution." What is almost inextricably entangled in visual perception is dissolved into a number of clearly distinct and separately identifiable mental steps in the historian's (attempts at a) conceptualization of the past. Because neo-Kantian philosophers of history ordinarily took their point of departure in the second *Critique* and in the question of how the notions of freedom and norms and values may (co-)determine our knowledge of the past (think of Rickert), the question of how we may apply Kant's conception of the imagination to the issue of historical understanding still awaits its proper and full treatment. In the present volume, the main question is what promises White's philosophy of history may have for future research in the philosophy of history. From that perspective, White's "new neo-Kantianism" is certainly suggestive of new avenues of thought that still await exploration. So much is to be expected from a return to Kant!

In the third *Critique*, Kant returns again to the notion of the imagination in his analytics of the beautiful. The emphasis is different here from that in the first *Critique*. In the case of the perception of the beautiful object, the imagination is no longer guided by a concept (such as that of an apple or a dog) in its effort to achieve a synthesis of the manifold of sensible intuitions. The function of the imagination here could be described as the search of a concept while, in fact, no concept is actually available for a satisfactory subsumption of what is presented to the senses. As a consequence, the understanding has nothing to go on here—except itself. It is, so to say, left *free* to move in the logical space defined by itself. And this is where Kant situates the source of aesthetic pleasure:

If pleasure is connected with the mere apprehension . . . of the form of an object of intuition, apart from any reference it may have to a concept, for the purpose of a definite cognition, this does not make the representation referable to the Object, but solely to the Subject. In such a case, the pleasure can express nothing but the conformity of the Object to the cognitive faculties brought into play in the reflective judgment.[8]

That is to say, in such a case the object provokes "a free play" of the faculties of the mind, free in the sense that these faculties are now no longer guided or bound by any concept. The object refers these faculties to themselves and by doing so, is even more suggestive of meaning than objects lending themselves to conceptualization; at the same time, a final meaning can never be given. There is no "closure," as contemporary literary theorists would put it. What we have, instead, is a continuous shuttling back and forth between perception, and these always failing attempts at conceptualization, and the free play of our cognitive faculties in the process invites them to reveal all their strength and cognitive resources. Hence, the feeling of pleasure produced by our perception of the object.[9]

Much the same pattern can be discerned in White's tropology, though a lack of theoretical precision in White's tropology makes it a bit speculative and hazardous to graft the tropology onto Kant's analysis of the beautiful. Nevertheless, it seems fairly uncontroversial to see White's prefiguration as analogous to what is achieved by Kant's categories of the understanding. *Prefiguration* is, roughly, a specific combination of the sixteen components of the tropological grid in terms of which the historian determines the nature of the historical field and, hence, what kind of events make up the past and what is the nature of the relationship between them. Put differently, prefiguration transforms the chaos—"the manifold," as Kant would put it—of the past into a reality that can be mapped, investigated, and discussed. The writing of history is only possible after prefiguration has taken place. However, prefiguration does not determine what the historian will actually *say* about the past, just as the Kantian categories of the understanding still allow for the possibility of competing scientific theories and for a discussion of their respective merits. Historical writing within White's tropological analysis will be a continuous moving back and forth between the tropological constitution of historical reality and what is explicitly said about the past in the historian's text. In both the "surface" of the historical text and its prefigurative "depth," the nature of historical reality is at stake. In what is one of the most perceptive analyses of White's philosophy of history ever written, Hans Kellner puts it as follows:

White views discourse as a dynamic force that mediates between the preliminary [that is, prefigurational] and the final stages of linguistic process [that is, the historical text or historical debate]. Once a field of data has been described, the process of discourse engages, acting like a "shuttle" in order to commute between the phenomena and the argument or narrative that the phenomena have been chosen to serve. Thus conceived, discourse is what brings together in textual practice the description of things, and the meaning presented by its encoding in a text. . . . The important thing to note about White's "diatactical" definition of discourse is its dynamic function; discourse is always moving back and forth in its shuttle diplomacy.[10]

The similarity to Kant's analysis of the beautiful will be obvious. In both cases we have to do with the process of a continuous "shuttling back and forth," to use Kellner's terminology, between what is given to us and our effort to make sense of it. And in both cases the always-elusive aim is final, successful conceptualization. In the case of Kant's analysis of the beautiful, this aim will never realized, because in the Kantian reflective judgment there is no pre-given concept in terms of which the realization of the aim could be established. Facts do not determine theories, as Quine might have phrased it. And in history the aim is never achieved because all of history moves in the logical space prior to successful conceptualization. If universally acceptable conceptualization were to be achieved in historical writing, we would automatically have left the domain of historical writing and moved into the domain of how we relate to the world in daily life—with its apples, dogs, etc.—and where things possess a fixity that they typically lack as long as we are doing history.[11]

Finally, the parallelism that I have attempted to demonstrate here between the Kantian analysis of the beautiful and White's tropology is self-evidently in agreement with White's own openly professed aestheticism. It should be added, however, that this is an aestheticism in which all the strongly cognitivist propensities of Kant's aesthetic have been carefully preserved. The historian convinced of the rationality of his discipline and of historical discussion has little to fear from *this* variant of aestheticism. This variant of aestheticism is not an invasion of the irrational into historical thought; instead, it will amount to an extension of the claims of Reason to domains that we hitherto believed to be beyond the reach of Reason. In sum, White's tropology is not the attack on historical rationality so often perceived in it: on the contrary, it is a vindication of the rationality of historical writing.

The Transcendentalization of Narrative

As one might expect from such a pronouncedly Kantian philosopher, White repeats in his own philosophy of history what is undoubtedly one of the main features of Kantian epistemology, that is, the distinction between the phenomenal and the noumenal world. This feature announces itself in White's work in a most appropriate way. White begins with the following observation in what has been said to be the most often cited of his essays:

Far from being a problem, then, narrative might well be considered a solution to a problem of general human concern, namely, the problem of how to translate knowing into telling, the problem of fashioning human experience into a form assimilable to structures of meaning that are generally human rather than culture specific.[12]

Note this "structures of meaning that are generally human rather than culture specific," and it will be clear that we are dealing here with an argument aiming at transcendentalist claims. Nevertheless, it may surprise that White attempts to substantiate his claim with an argument relying on what is "culture specific" rather than on what seems to be a "general" property of human knowing. White proceeds with opposing what I shall provisionally call here "the early medieval historical consciousness" to that of later times. When doing so, White focuses on chronicles and annals. He points out that the early medieval chronicle, such as the *Annals of Saint Gall*, will typically give a mere list mentioning for each year what interesting events occurred in that year (or just a blank if there were no interesting events at all), while no effort is being made to fit them into some kind of story. He then goes on to say that we should not interpret this as a sign of medieval backwardness but rather as a most appropriate expression of how people in the early Middle Ages must have experienced their world. So, from their "culture specific" perspective, this is how one should write history.[13]

When Western man took the fate of the world out of the hands of God and discovered the work of his own hands in the past, the early medieval historical consciousness made no sense anymore. Western man now needed the story, narratives recounting and explaining his dealings with the human, historical world.

As I suggested a moment ago, it will be clear that this kind of argument would entail that narrative is "culture specific" rather than a "general" (or transcendental) feature of the human mind. Anyway, White could counter this argument by declaring that historical consciousness only came into being with the Renaissance's discovery that man is the maker of his own fate and that, thus, there simply is no such thing as an "early medieval historical consciousness." Assuming this to be the most sensible and fruitful way of dealing with the issue, it follows that we have only history if we have narratives about the past and that, to put it in the terminology used in this essay, narrative truly is the "transcendental condition of the possibility of historical knowledge."[14] Of interest in this strategy is that it radically disconnects what one might call "life" from "history." For no one will doubt that the life of people in the early Middle Ages was subject to much the same variables—love, hate, fear, compassion, joy, despair, pain and pleasure, etc.—as is our own, however much the color of these variables may differ in time, as has so cogently been argued in the history of mentalities.

But there was *one* big difference: they had no historical consciousness, as we have it in the West, at least since the end of the eighteenth century. And this is, surely, something that one can do without. For there is little, if anything, about how we live our daily lives that makes having historical consciousness absolutely imperative, just as many people can do without art or music—however strange this must seem to most of us. But this indubitable fact does *not* rule out the transcendentalism of history. Similarly, epistemological claims about science and scientific truth are not refuted by the mere fact that there have been people, or perhaps even whole civilizations, having no interest in science.

Obviously, we have been rehearsing here, though in a somewhat deviant (Kantian) terminology, the old discussion of whether there is a continuity between life and narrative or history. That there is no such continuity was famously claimed by Louis O. Mink with the argument that narratives are to be found in books (or in stories that we tell each other), but not in life itself. He summed up his view in the powerful slogan that "stories are not lived but told."[15] Against Mink, David Carr pointed out that all human thought and action presupposes narrativization. We not only tell stories or listen to them, we also organize our lives narratively; narrative is the ineluctable pattern organizing all our actions and thinking. Carr therefore concluded: "Louis Mink was thus operating with a totally false distinction when he said that stories are not lived but told. They are told in being lived and lived in being told."[16] The weakness of Carr's argument is, however, that he may well be right about narrative being part of how we organize our life, but this fact by no means proves his case. For Mink might now riposte that even at the level of life itself we must distinguish between life and action, on the one hand, and how we may narrativize our thought and action on the other. In a way, we are indeed necessarily the historians of ourselves. But *not* at the moment we act. Our past, present, and future thought and actions may well be the subject of narratives that we tell ourselves and these may even be indispensable for all meaningful social behavior, but these thoughts and actions *themselves* are not narratives: they are only referred to in these narratives, or quoted, or recounted within quotation marks, so to say. Narratives should not be confused with what they are about.

But if we agree with Mink's argument against Carr—as White is likely to do[17]—we are in trouble. For a moment ago we had argued that for White history and historical consciousness only made their entry into the West's history somewhere between the early Middle Ages and the Renaissance (let's keep the margins comfortably broad). And this clearly is at odds with the claim that everyone may be the historian of his or her own life (even though this does not entail a fusion of (his-)story and life, as we saw a moment ago). So White's monks writing their weird chronicle of the monastery of St. Gall can be expected to have been the (more or less) reliable historians of their own lives. And then we must conclude that history existed already at that time.

The Politics of Transcendentalist Narrativism: White and Hegel

The solution to the puzzle is to be found in another big discovery of the Renaissance. Think of what Isaiah Berlin wrote on Machiavelli:

What he [Machiavelli] institutes is something that cuts deeper still—a differentiation between two incompatible ideals of life, and therefore two moralities. One is the morality of the pagan world: its values of courage, vigor, fortitude in adversity, public achievement, order, discipline, happiness, strength, justice, above all assertion of one's proper claims and the knowledge and power needed to secure their satisfaction. . . . Against this moral universe . . . stands in the first and foremost place Christian morality. The ideals of Christianity are charity, mercy, sacrifice, love of God, forgiveness of enemies, contempt for the goods of this world, faith in the life hereafter, belief in the salvation of the individual soul as being of incomparable value—higher than, indeed wholly incommensurable with any social, or political or terrestrial goals, any economic or military or aesthetic consideration.[18]

I shall not say that I can agree with all the details of Berlin's argument; but what is of interest in the present context is the opposition he construes between a public and a private morality. There is, on the one hand, private morality, Christian morality, focusing on the individual and his salvation, and on what God requires us to do and to avoid. Surely we can build a moral universe on these foundations; and one might say that this is what the Middle Ages attempted to do.

The "originality of Machiavelli" (to use Berlin's terminology) has been to demonstrate the insuperable limitations of this morality. One might be the perfect Christian, fulfill all the high requirements of Christian morality—and yet be a curse and unmitigated disaster to one's fellow human beings. Not because anything is wrong with Christian morality and a better, more perfect morality should replace it. No, in a certain sense, Christian morality is beyond perfection. The crux is rather—and this is the essence of Machiavelli's tragic message—that Christian morality is a *private* morality and that it, therefore, has no application in the *public* domain. That is a different moral world. For in the public domain not Christian, but pagan morality (as summarized above in Berlin's quote) is our best and only guide. These two moralities are truly incommensurable; even when they would require us to do the same thing under certain circumstances (and we shall self-evidently be always in search of such happy agreements!), this will never be more than mere coincidence. For the private and the public domain truly constitute two different moral universes. It follows from Machiavelli's (and Berlin's) impeccable argument that the same incommensurability separating the two moralities also separates the domain of the private and the public. So we could rephrase Machiavelli's discovery as the (re-)discovery of the wisdom of Livy, Cicero, Tacitus that what private morality demands that we do will not work for the public domain—and vice versa.

When discussing what was at stake in the transition from the historical consciousness of the early Middle Ages (or, rather its absence at that time) to its modern Western successor, White turns to Hegel. He then refers us to the following passage from *Die Vernunft in der Geschichte*:

> Only the State provides us with a content that is not only appropriate for the prose of history but that also codetermines it. A public consciousness gradually crystallizing out, and taking on a more or less fixed form in the State, requires not only subjective acts of government that are merely fit for the moment, but above all commandments, laws, and universally valid determinations; and in this way the State stimulates both the production of and an interest in events that rationally confirm themselves in their results and effects, and to which Mnemosyne is compelled to add lasting memory for the benefit of the self-perpetuating purposes of the State's presently existing nature and form. (my translation)

> (Aber der Staat erst führt einen Inhalt herbei, der für die Prosa der Geschichte nicht nur geeignet ist, sondern sie selbst mit erzeugt. Statt nur subjektiver, für das Bedürfnis des Augenblicks genügender Befehle des Regierens erfordert ein festwerdendes, zum Staate sich erhebendes Gemeinwesen Gebote, Gesetze, allgemeine und allgemein gültige Bestimmungen und erzeugt damit sowohl einen Vortrag als ein Interesse von verständigen, in sich bestimmten und für sich selbst in ihren Resultaten dauernden Taten und Begebenheiten, welchen die Mnemosyne zum Behuf des selbst perennierenden Zwecks dieser noch gegenwärtigen Gestaltung und Beschaffenheit des Staates, die Dauer des Andenkens hinzuzufügen getrieben ist.)[19]

So, according to Hegel, it is only the state that may lift us out of an ahistorical blindness to why history matters. And this for a double reason: in the first place, because the state is, whether we like it or not, the paradigmatic historical actor (here we have to do with the level of the res gestae themselves), and, secondly, because the state is the entity we need for our being able to tell the *story* of the past (this is the level of the *historia rerum gestarum*). Every (hi-)story needs a subject whose (hi-)story is being narrated—and in the case of history, the state is the most obvious candidate.

In *Metahistory*, White had already discussed that the state is the main protagonist on the scene of world history:

Every actual state . . . fails to attain this harmonious reconciliation of individual interests, desires, and needs with the common good. This failure of any given state to incarnate the ideal, however, is to be experienced as a cause for jubilation rather than despair, for it is precisely this *imbalance of private with public (or public with private)* interests which provides the space for the exercise of a specifically human freedom [italics in original].[20]

This passage (and its wordings) are of interest for several reasons. First, this never-ending, but never completely successful effort to reconcile the private and the public interest and the "jubilation" it should provoke in us, cannot fail to remind us of Kant's analytics of the beautiful. All the more so, since the freedom mediating between private and public interests seems to have its anticipation in the "free play" of the imagination between perception and conceptualization in Kant's aesthetics. This seems to suggest an aestheticist conception of the state.[21] Next, observe that White defines the activities of the state in terms of this mediation between public and private interests. This has the advantage of exchanging Hegel's own emphasis on the state for one on politics as such, insofar as the relationship between the public and the private can be said to be at stake in *all* politics. Lastly, and most importantly, crucial to both Hegel's and White's arguments is the ultimate irreconcilability of the public and the private. This is, of course, a rephrasing of Machiavelli's insight into the irreconcilability of (Christian) ethics and politics. A result that need not surprise us from such a profoundly Machiavellian philosopher as Hegel!

And now all the elements of my exposition will fall into their proper place. In the first place, we shall now see that not Carr but Mink was right: there *is* no continuity between life and history, and stories are not lived but told. This has a very deep explanation: the distinction between life and (hi-)story has its basis in the distinction between ethics and politics. In its turn, this distinction is as necessary and inevitable as the distinction between the public and the private domain. This may also help explain why historical consciousness came into being during the Renaissance. Recall that in this time, the modern Western state came into being and—what is of no less importance—that feudalism was the legal system reducing all public law to private law.[22] But the most far-reaching implication of my argument is, of course, the irreducibility of politics to ethics. Ethics has its proper place in the sphere of the private; politics and history must remain restricted to the public domain. Surely both politicians and

historians may become interested what is to be situated in the private domain. But they should never forget that this is unnatural to them.

Conclusion

No reader of White's oeuvre can fail to be struck by its profound
awareness of the political dimension of all historical writing. In his tropology, White leaves ample room for the modes of ideological implication, and *Metahistory* comments lengthily on the political orientation of
the historians and philosophers of history discussed in it. Further, White
himself is a man of strong political conviction, as everyone who has had
the pleasure of talking to him will be able to testify.

It is, then, all the more to be regretted that there is so little real political commitment in all of White's body of work. And I deliberately use
here the term *commitment*, for one need only recall *Metahistory*'s "modes
of ideological implication" to recognize that White was well aware of the
political dimension of all historical writing. Yet this never led him to reflect on how the historian—*as* historian—should respond to the political challenges of his own time. This is surprising, if only because he did
not hesitate to castigate Burckhardt, Nietzsche, and Croce for their alleged reluctance to translate their historical insights into politics.[23] Undoubtedly, part of the explanation is that American intellectuals (with the
one unfortunate exception of the neocons of the recent past) rarely feel
tempted to pronounce on political issues; and, if they do so, they ordinarily restrict themselves to lofty but vague and unpractical declarations
on how to achieve a better and more just world. One need only think
here of academic American political philosophy— "*enivré d'abstractions*,"
as Daniel Mornet once described French political philosophy on the eve
of the Revolution. Meanwhile, the oldest democracy is going down the
drain under their very noses.

But even this leaves something to be explained. In his excellent
book on White, Herman Paul has wrestled with the problem of White's
dislike of political commitment.[24] He focuses on irony and emphasizes
how important this trope is for White. Irony comes closest to defining
how White himself thinks about history and historical writing. We might
then be tempted to explain White's political abstention as an expression
of (political) irony. This would be wholly wrong, Paul convincingly ar-

gues. For, as he goes on to say, White's political commitment is truly total, but it is a commitment of a quite peculiar nature. It has its source in existentialist thought and in the idea of the Sartrean *mauvaise foi*, that is to say, in the existentialist thesis that the claims of freedom and of ethical obligation are boundless and may never be curtailed by an appeal to how we—or others—are determined by the past. Surely, a kind of moralism that one would hardly expect from a historian or philosopher of history!

But of even more importance is this: Sartrean ethics is, perhaps, the most total and uncompromising kind of ethics that has ever been conceived. In this way, it could be said to be the purest variant of ethics in the history of that discipline. In this essay, however, we have seen that there is an unbridgeable gap between ethics and politics and, further, that White privileged ethics over politics in his written work (as these notions have been defined here). The question arises of what must or should happen when White's commitment to ethics is shifted from ethics to politics. This is a major question, and one that White's unsurpassed contribution to historical thought invites us—and future generations of philosophers of history and politics—to investigate.

Notes

I would like to thank Herman Paul for his most valuable comments on a previous version of this essay.

1. See Hayden White, *Metahistory: The Historical Imagination in Nineteenth-Century Europe* (Baltimore: Johns Hopkins UP, 1973); 29ff.; the most succinct and convincing of White's theoretical claims in question is to be found in Hayden White, "The Historical Text as a Literary Artifact," in *Tropics of Discourse* (Baltimore: Johns Hopkins UP, 1978); 81–101.

2. H. Kellner, "Hayden White and the Kantian Discourse: Tropology, Narrative, and Freedom," in *The Philosophy of Discourse. The Rhetorical Turn in Twentieth-Century Thought*, ed. Charles Sills (Portsmouth, NH: Boynton/Cook Publishers, 1992). The present essay can well be seen as an elaboration of Kellner's.

3. Discussing "necessary connexion," Hume wrote: "this connexion, which we feel in the mind, this customary transition of the imagination from one object to its usual attendant, is the sentiment or impression from which we form the idea of power or necessary connexion. Nothing farther is the case." See David Hume, *An Enquiry Concerning Human Understanding and Concerning the Principles of Morals* (1777, repr., Oxford: Oxford UP, 1972); 75. Note, furthermore, Hume's emphasis of the mere "contiguity" of cause and effect (Hume, *An*

Enquiry; 74) and recall that contiguity is how metonymy, as defined by White, relates things to things. Philosophers outraged by White's tropology then should be well aware that consistency would require them to be similarly outraged by Hume's argument about causality. Indeed, when reading White's opponents, one often feels tempted to exclaim that they seem to have completely forgotten what they (should) have learned from Hume and Kant.

4. White, *Metahistory*; 30.

5. In the 1990s, he often said that he would go deeper into tropology, but until now he has not taken it up again.

6. For a competent exposition of this intellectual history and for how it may help us to understand White's use of figura, see the erudite and exhaustive master's thesis by Herman Paul titled "Figura. *De semantische ontwikkeling van een patristisch begrip bij Erich Auerbach en Hayden White*" (Groningen University, 2001).

7. Hayden White, "Auerbach's Literary History: Figural Causation and Modernist Historicism," in *Figural Realism* (Baltimore: Johns Hopkins UP, 2000); 87–101.

8. Immanuel Kant, *Critique of Judgement*, trans. J. C. Meredith (Indianapolis: Hackett, 1987); 30.

9. Paul Crowther, *The Kantian Sublime: From Morality to Art* (Oxford: Oxford UP, 1991); 51ff.

10. Kellner, "Kantian Discourse"; 249.

11. Frank Ankersmit, *Narrative Logic* (The Hague: Martinus Nijhoff, 1983); chapter 5.

12. Hayden White, "The Value of Narrativity in the Representation of Reality," in *The Content of the Form* (Baltimore: Johns Hopkins UP, 1987); 1.

13. White, "Value of Narrativity," 6ff. For a closely similar argument, see John Pocock, *The Machiavellian Moment in the Atlantic Tradition* (Princeton: Princeton UP, 1975); Pocock relies on St. Augustine and on Boethius's *De Consolatione Philosophiae* in order to substantiate his claim.

14. This is where we may discern a surprising agreement between White's argument and that of his fellow student from Wayne State University, Arthur Danto—both of them being great admirers of their teacher William Bossenbrook. See for this Frank Ankersmit, "Arthur Danto's Philosophy of History in Retrospect," in *Narration and Knowledge*, ed. A. C. Danto (New York: Columbia UP, 2007), and where I use Hans Michael Baumgartner's work to expound Danto's transcendentalism. See also chapter 9 by Allan Megill in this volume.

15. Louis Mink, *Historical Understanding* (Ithaca: Cornell UP, 1987); 60.

16. D. Carr, "Narrative and the Real World," *History and Theory* 25 (1986); 125, 126. The same argument inspires most of Ricoeur's impressive three-volume *Time and Narrative* (Chicago: University of Chicago Press, 1983).

17. "No one and nothing lives a story." See White, *Tropics*; 111. Recall, fur-

thermore, that White and Mink were close colleagues at Wesleyan University, who mutually respected and inspired each other, so that by its very phrasing this quote can be taken to be an implicit reference (and an endorsement) of Mink's slogan discussed above. And elsewhere, White writes: "Does the world really present itself to perception in the form of well-made stories, with central subjects, proper beginnings, middles, and ends, and a 'coherence' that permits us to see 'the end' in every beginning? Or does it present itself more in the forms that the annals and chronicles suggest, either as a mere sequence without beginning or end or as sequences of beginnings that only terminate and never conclude? And does the world, even the social world, ever really come to us as already narrativized, already 'speaking itself' from beyond the horizon of our capacity to make scientific sense of it?" See White, "Value of Narrativity"; 24, 25.

18. Isaiah Berlin, "The Originality of Machiavelli," in *The Proper Study of Mankind: An Anthology of Essays*, ed. Henry Hardy and Roger Hausheer (London: Chatto & Windus, 1997); 289.

19. Georg Wilhelm Friedrich Hegel, *Vorlesungen über die Philosophie der Weltgeschichte. Band I. Die Vernunft in der Geschichte* (Hamburg: Felix Meiner Verlag, 1970); 164.

20. White, *Metahistory*; 108, 109.

21. I had advocated this myself (though for different reasons) in Frank Ankersmit, *The Aesthetic State: Political Philosophy Beyond Fact and Value* (Stanford: Stanford UP, 1997).

22. Of course, this is only part of the whole story. For a lengthier discussion of this issue, see Frank Ankersmit, *Sublime Historical Experience* (Stanford: Stanford UP, 2005); chapter 8.

23. One may wonder whether the criticism was well founded. Burckhardt was clear enough about his conservative politics and, further, he was convinced that the teaching of history is, at least partly, a political mission in the Renaissance tradition of civic humanism. See Lionel Gossman, *Basel in the Age of Burckhardt* (Chicago: University of Chicago Press, 2000). Croce was a prominent member of the liberal party of the Italy of his time; he was a firm opponent of Mussolini and even minister of education for several years. So not quite an apolitical man, Croce!

24. What follows is a short summary of the relevant parts of Herman Paul, *Masks of Meaning: Existentialist Humanism in Hayden White's Philosophy of History* (Groningen: eigen beheer, 2006).

3

Hayden White and
the Crisis of Historicism

Herman Paul

> To study history means submitting to chaos and nevertheless retaining faith
> in order and meaning. It is a very serious task, young man, and possibly a
> tragic one.
> —Hermann Hesse, *The Glass Bead Game*, 1943

When Joseph Knecht, the strong-minded hero in Hermann Hesse's celebrated novel, starts some good conversations with Father Jacobus, the Benedictine scholar-in-residence at the monastery of Mariafels, he learns a few things about historical scholarship that would strike no historian as surprising or remarkable: always historicize, never allow any anachronisms, avoid reading your own opinions into the views of others, be attentive to both changes and continuities in human history. As for the subject of their first conversation—the speculations of an eighteenth-century theologian—Joseph has few objections against this historicist program. Things get more complicated, though, when these historicist hermeneutics are applied to the ideals governing the institution that has delegated Knecht to Mariafels. This is the Castalian Order: an intellectual community proud of its skills in "ordering" the world of thought by juxtaposing, contrasting, and combining ideas from different historical and geographical contexts in thought experiments known as the Glass Bead Game. "I have no quarrel with the student of history who brings to his work a touchingly childish, innocent faith in the power of our minds and our methods to order reality," Father Jacobus declares, "but first and foremost he must respect the incomprehensible truth, reality, and uniqueness of events."[1]

This is far from innocent advice, as Joseph is quick to find out. By drawing attention to the particularity and context-dependency of historical events, it poses a dilemma to all those who, like the Glass Bead Game players, treat historical events as bearers of transhistorical, supratemporal meanings. Either they have to reject the historicist approach of a Father Jacobus (as the Castalian Order does), or they have to abandon the game and affirm that there is no other reality than the infinitely varied, complicated history of human stirrings and failures (as Joseph, near the end of the novel, does). Or perhaps a more subtle effect can be attributed to the historicist lessons of that white-haired historian at Mariafels. His instruction makes Joseph sensitive to historical change in such a tacit and gradual manner that after a while, it "ripened within him in the course of his historical studies"; historicism naturally seems to emerge as more plausible than the timeless truths of the game players.[2] Once the novel's primary character has learned to see the world in historical terms, there is no way back. Exposure to historicism has irreversible effects. This is why the study of history, as Father Jacobus tells his visitor, is not only "very serious," but potentially "tragic" as well. By "submitting to chaos," historians run a risk of losing "faith in order and meaning," at least as long as these are understood in nonhistorical terms. Eventually, in Hesse's version, an act of will, a strong personal determination of the kind that Joseph displays when he resigns from his Castalian office and escapes into the "real" world, assures that "history" and "meaning" do not exclude each other—that meaning can be found (or made) *within* the particularities of the historical contexts in which human persons, outside the Castalian province, shape their lives.

Is there a sense in which Hayden White's long-term contributions to the field of historical theory share the concerns that led Joseph out of Castalia? Is there a sense in which White invites his readers to "submit to chaos and nevertheless retain faith in order and meaning"? To what extent do White's epistemological skepticism, his readiness to challenge historical orthodoxies, and his "nominalist" understanding of historical narrative presuppose the existence of a human subject that lives by will alone in a world "full of change, history, struggles, and eternally new beginnings"?[3] Of course, White's work is usually read in narrativist terms. It is honored and criticized for breaking down traditional boundaries between historical and literary writing, for analyzing linguistic aspects and constraints of historical knowledge and for challenging historians to acknowledge that moral and aesthetic preferences are the only grounds for favoring one type of narrative representation over another. Judged by the inspiration it has provided for historians and literary theorists in the past few decades, this narrativist reading has not been unproductive. Moreover, as an interpretative proposal, it finds support in a good many of White's essays from the 1970s and 1980s (as well as in the introduction and conclusion to *Metahistory*, which are presumably the most-cited pages White has ever written). But for two reasons, it falls short in explaining what is at stake in White's historical theory. First, it generally neglects large parts of White's oeuvre, in particular the more than fifty titles (books, essays, introductions, reviews) published before *Metahistory*. Secondly, this "standard interpretation" does not usually explain *why* White is fascinated by historical narratives, for what *reasons* he insists on the legitimacy of different modes of representation, and what *motivates* him to provoke controversies over matters of meaning, freedom, and responsibility. These deficiencies are, perhaps, related, in so far as the clearest indications of the questions and concerns that inspire White's philosophy of history can be found in his earliest writings.

Following the helpful suggestion that, in some specific sense, White advocates a "return of the moral imagination" in historical thought,[4] this chapter proposes to read White against the background of what is known as the "crisis of historicism." Because of a Babylonian confusion about the word *historicism*, a twofold clarification is needed. First, the "crisis of historicism" denotes a number of distinct crises. These include, but are not limited to, (a) the intuition, articulated by such philosophers as Wilhelm Dilthey and Martin Heidegger, that the linear narratives of nineteenth-century historical thought were inadequate because of their indebtedness to a transcendental, Cartesian subject-position, (b) the fear that "historical criticism" would undermine traditional religious authorities such as the Bible, the "historical Jesus," and the lives of the saints, and, most importantly, (c) the uncertainty, famously expressed by Ernst Troeltsch, but also by some characters in Hesse's novel, whether any moral absolutes would survive the challenge of historical contextualization.[5] In what follows, "the crisis of historicism" initially refers to this third type of crisis: to the disquieting thought that there are, perhaps, no moral standards that transcend the limits of our historical condition. It will, however, soon become clear that, in White's oeuvre, the "crisis of historicism" has its own particular meaning.

Secondly, albeit reaching a climax in the interwar years, the crisis of historicism in Troeltsch's sense was (and is) experienced at various times and places. There is an element of nonsimultaneity (*Ungleichzeitigkeit*) in the crisis of historicism. Presupposing some kind of clash between a growing historical consciousness and a desire to reach beyond the individual and the particular to the absolute or universal, the crisis only occurs if both conditions are met. Simply abandon the search for universals or deny that historical change has any significant effect on human values, and the crisis will be eliminated. The "crisis of historicism" may therefore well be called a traveling problem, or a challenge that faces different groups at different times and places, depending on whether and when they fulfill the conditions that may cause them to feel torn between historicism and its rivals.[6] Because of this, no anachronism is involved in suggesting that White's scholarly agenda, half a century after Troeltsch (and a full century after Jacob Burckhardt, the historian who reportedly served as a model for Hesse's Father Jacobus), was shaped by concerns stemming from the crisis of historicism.

Now, it may not be insignificant that, throughout his oeuvre, White addresses the relation between historical studies and moral inquiry, but hardly ever spends more than a few words on Troeltsch's worry that an excessive historical consciousness may threaten moral values. Likewise, one cannot fail to notice that, in his early work in particular, White finds lots of inspiration in sociologists like Max Weber, but never reads these thinkers as responding to the crisis of historicism that arguably served as the context in which their thought took shape.[7] Does this "absence" of Troeltsch's crisis of historicism in White's writings indicate that the desire to reach beyond historical situatedness makes no appearance in his thought? Does White envision a historicism without crises, without disturbing implications in the sphere of moral thought, without the risk of tragic loss envisaged by Father Jacobus? In what follows, I will argue that, after a "liberal humanist" phase in which the author averts the possible threat of historicism by embedding historical variety in narratives of humanist progress, White in the 1970s and 1980s indeed appears to have few problems with the moral "relativism" that Troeltsch feared. This is because an strongly voluntarist understanding of morality leads White to emphasize the individuality and singularity of each moral situation to such an extent as to deny that people should long or hope for moral wisdom transcending the limits of their historical situation. Yet, as few have pointed out, in the early 1970s, White encounters another "crisis" caused by historicist thought, or a profound concern resulting from the kind of conclusions that Troeltsch *cum suis* hesitated to draw. If indeed all moral inquiry is context-bound, then does this imply that the study of the past is morally irrelevant? Why should one want to study the past, if there is no moral education to be gained from it? According to my reading of *Metahistory*, White suggests a monumental mode of dealing with the past exemplified, in the last chapter of *The Glass Bead Game*, by Joseph Knecht's heroic self-affirmation in the face of history's absurdity.

Humanist Historicism

Among White's largely forgotten pre-*Metahistory* writings are three textbooks, conceived in the now almost equally forgotten tradition of the Western Civilization course.[8] Coauthored with Willson H. Coates, *The Emergence of Liberal Humanism* (1966) and *The Ordeal of Liberal Humanism* (1970) tell a glorious story of expanding liberty. They relate how, from the Italian Renaissance onward, new ideas about nature, the self, religion, politics, freedom, and the common good transformed "the European mind" to the extent that modern liberal humanism could have qualified as "the most nearly triumphant philosophy" in the entire Western world if "the irrational propensities of Western European man" had not stopped its advancement in the early twentieth century. A third book, published (in White's own Major Traditions of World Civilization series) as *The Greco-Roman Tradition* (1973), covered "the rise and fall of the classical humanistic ideal" in Greece and Rome.[9] As the authors themselves admit, these books proceed from the assumption that "freedom of conscience and liberty in all its aspects constitute the most important tradition in Western civilization." Deeply indebted to a 1960s version of the secularization thesis, the two earliest volumes in particular read like a

Whig history of modern, secular humanism. Typically, story elements that run counter to this liberal narrative—Pius IX's *Syllabus of Errors* or Hitler's rise to power—are presented as "challenges" and "dilemmas" that liberal-minded Europeans had to face. Thus emplotting modern European history as a battle between forces of light and darkness, the authors do not conceal their critical attitude toward "practices of magic, myth, and superstitious beliefs of the most archaic kind" or "the unsurpassed agonies of the witch trials." Likewise, they frankly speak of "failure" and "irrelevance" if such phenomena as Romanticism in an industrializing society and "ethics of ambiguity" in times of political decision appear to them as anachronistic.[10] Indeed, by Father Jacobus's criteria, these volumes cannot be called historicist, exactly.

This should not come as a surprise: nowhere in his early historical writings does White display a particular affinity with a hermeneutics of "otherness" and "difference." To be sure, in his praise for Croce, most eloquently expressed in "The Abiding Relevance of Croce's Idea of History" (1963), White fully endorses the Italian thinker's resistance against sociological typologies and "general laws" in the name of history's individuality, particularity, and unpredictability. His translation of Carlo Antoni's *Dallo storicismo alla sociologia* (1959)—an outright condemnation of Dilthey's, Troeltsch's, and Weber's classificatory methods—also indicates a genuine interest in what Russell Jacoby calls "the specificity of history."[11] But in White's own historical writings, typologies, ideal types, and schemes borrowed from Weber, Arnold J. Toynbee, and (in the late 1960s) Giambattista Vico always serve as means for ordering history and exploring that "foreign country" called the past. In offering a threefold typology of historicisms, White's introduction to Antoni's book even employs the very same classificatory methods that the Italian author so passionately warns against.[12] The large amounts of criticism that White's work in medieval church history received during the late 1950s and early 1960s also can be summed up as too rigidly imposing Weberian ideal types, insufficiently respecting the "otherness" of twelfth-century Roman Christianity, and, in general, not being historicist enough in the hermeneutical sense of the word.[13]

Yet, if not historicist in their hermeneutics, White's textbooks on "liberal humanism," like his Croce essay, are certainly historicist in their *Weltanschauung* or presuppositions about the nature of historical reality. Indebted to what Michel Foucault, in *The Order of Things*, criticizes as "humanist historicism," these volumes insist on the endless variety, multiplicity, and unpredictability of human history, without fearing, as Troeltsch did, that moral values suffer from such a consequent historical contextualization. The books do so, first, by insisting on the primacy of human agents as actors in history's drama. Humanism, so they tell their readers, is "an attitude of mind which takes man as the effective qualitative center of the universe and as sole responsible agent for the creation of order in the world of human affairs." Downplaying social contexts, cultural conventions, collective actions, and unintended consequences of intentional conduct, this "humanism" treats the human individual and, more specifically, the human will as the primary actor in human history. Whereas this definition already implies a rejection of any and all religion, White adds, significantly, that he considers "liberation from all transcendentalist aspiration" an important aim of modern humanism. Take your life into your own hands, without ever projecting moral authority or moral responsibility into whatever transcendental realm, is the humanist message White's textbooks convey. Secondly, a blanket condemnation of any supposedly timeless truth "as both fundamentally unhistorical and philosophically naïve" indicates how much this humanism intends to respect historical variety. All this is, thirdly, embedded in a narrative of progress, which portrays humankind as a collective personality, growing in time and showing a remarkable ability for adaptation and transformation. If, within this narrative, varieties in human moral discourse can be seen as corresponding to distinct phases in a process of human self-realization, and if "all attempts at knowledge are essentially efforts at human self-understanding," as *The Emergence of Liberal Humanism* puts it, then the possible threat of historicism is effectively averted. Then, indeed, White can be as openly historicist as Herder was, because the "sacred canopy" of his belief in progress provides an overall meaning to the historical process in the same way that (as *Metahistory* explains at length) Herder's belief in a "unified organic force" in which all human life participates enabled him to rejoice in whatever historical varieties he encountered.[14]

Nineteenth-century German historicism felt the first pangs of a crisis as soon as it left this Herderian organicism behind.[15] This suggests the question whether White faces a crisis of historicism, too, when (shortly after Foucault's *The Order of Things*) the language of progressive development disappears from his writings. Does White's humanist historicism, increasingly weaned from its belief in progress, persist in emphasizing the desirability of human self-determination in the face of historical change, difference, and dissimilarity? Or does the author agree that, without belief in progress, "submitting to chaos" may threaten "faith in order and meaning"? In my reading, *Metahistory* indeed engages in a vigorous struggle with "the crisis of historicism," but in a distinct sense of the word. Not Castalian fears or Troeltschean worries, but moral concerns about the ironic condition of historical studies lead White to pit himself against "the crisis of historicism."

A Crisis of Historicism

In its hermeneutics, *Metahistory* is even less historicist than the textbooks mentioned above. Hypostatizing historical "ages" and attributing "integral consistency" to how people understood reality within such long-time epochs as "the Medieval period," the book deals in broad generalizations, looks for patterns rather than for particularities, and focuses on "family characteristics" between "types" of human thought. Moreover, just as White's 1955 Ph.D. dissertation explains the rise and fall of twelfth-century papal leadership ideals with the help of a large-scale model of how social institutions ideal-typically evolve, so *Metahistory* identifies Enlightenment historiography and the subsequent forms that Western historical consciousness took between the days of Herder and Burckhardt with four phases of a cyclical model, which White still in the late 1980s believes to have the nature of an "iron law."[16]

However, as the cycle indicates, the spread of these historical modes of thought in Western Europe is *not* identified with a progressive realization of human rationality. *Metahistory* differs from White's humanism textbooks in acknowledging that "rationality" and "irrationality," or wisdom and foolishness, cannot simply be contrasted in terms of binary oppositions, as is assumed in classic "Western civilization" narratives about the triumph of reason over myth and superstition. After Max Horkheimer's, Theodor Adorno's, and Michel Foucault's critical diagnoses of Enlightenment rationality, White discerns a need for theory that takes "unreason," "myth," "dreams," and "religious speculation" as modes of human inquiry as seriously as it does "reason," "history," "science," and "liberalism." An "adequate psychological theory" or "theory of human consciousness" would not set reason over "against imagination as the basis of truth against the basis of error," but recognize "the *continuity* between reason and fantasy." "[T]he mode of their relationship as parts of a more general process of human inquiry into a world incompletely known might be sought, and the process in which fantasy or imagination contributed as much to the discovery of truth as did reason itself might be perceived."[17] Hence White's enthusiasm, expressed in the first two chapters of the book, for such philosophers as Gottfried Wilhelm Leibniz, Giambattista Vico, Johann Gottfried von Herder, Georg Wilhelm Friedrich Hegel or Friedrich Nietzsche, all of whom attempted not to contrast history and myth, or reason and imagination, but to conceptualize these modes of inquiry as "parts" of a "whole." (It is perhaps no coincidence that a fragment of *Metahistory*'s first draft, published in 1966, focuses on Hegel.)[18] What White hopes to derive from these thinkers is not an alternative narrative of progress or an overarching philosophy of history providing "ultimate" meanings to the contingencies of history—after his humanism textbooks, White no longer trusts such *grand récits*—but a "metahistorical" mode of thought that can foster a creative interaction between rational and imaginative dimensions in human thought.

Following White's exposition of his "tropology" in the book's introduction, many readers have identified the four phases in White's model with "linguistic" paradigms and their "closed-cycle development" with a gradual elaboration of "the possibilities of tropological prefiguration . . . contained in poetic language in general."[19] However, given the striking dissimilarities between the introduction and the subsequent chapters of *Metahistory*, it may be preferable to examine how White actually *uses* these tropes throughout his book, rather than to repeat his own definitions.[20] This operation yields complex results: since the tropes (literally: "turns") are relational terms, they can be, and are in fact, used for mapping diverse types of relationships (texts to contexts, past to present, thought to action, etc.). In the first two chapters of the book, however, White's "master tropes" primarily denote response patterns to the question asked a moment ago: how to relate history and myth, reason and imagination, fact and fiction, reality and vision.

Starting with eighteenth-century French historians such as Voltaire and Hume, White asserts that, "under the auspices of a Metonymical paradigm—that is, in the mode of severance or extrinsic opposition"— Enlightenment historiography destroyed an "original" (metaphorical) unity of the truthful and the fabulous, thereby raising the Vichian question how the former can possibly emerge from the latter. "The Enlighteners, because they viewed the relationship of reason to fantasy in terms of an opposition rather than as a part-whole relationship, were unable to formulate this question in a historiographically profitable way."[21] Kant, too, is said to have conceptualized "the historical field metonymically, . . . as merely a conflict, an *unresolvable* conflict, between *eternally opposed* principles of human nature: rational on the one hand, irrational on the other."[22] This metonymical mode works well as long as its adherents are so convinced of the power and promise of their rationalism as to be able to reject its opposites: unreason, superstition, and myth. "Put as a rule," however, this metonymical "modality of comprehension" meets a sufficient number of challenges—the observation that large parts of humankind fail to live up to its rational standards, or critical analyses of the Enlightenment's own "dialectics"—as to "degenerate" into irony, that is, into a helpless awareness of its own one-sidedness, its limitations as a means for understanding the fullness of human reality.[23]

Unlike their metonymic forerunners, ironic thinkers like Burckhardt and Croce (White's examples) realized that the world cannot be ruled by reason alone, that "demythologization" will not solve societal problems. But they failed to relate history to myth, or reason to imagination, and consequently isolated "rational inquiry" from what Hesse's novel describes as the blatant irrationalities of political life.[24] In White's version, such a "dead end" can be avoided by "neutralizing" metonymical tensions in some kind of "higher unity," as Herder did, when he tried to integrate the rational and the fabulous into a synecdochic harmony, arguing that both history and myth articulate some truth about the universe. By rational standards, however, this attempt at a reunion of history and myth was itself entirely mythical in nature, as Kant pointed out to Herder, and was therefore more likely to be defeated by metonymic and ironic forces than to overcome them.[25] Hence White's somewhat indefinite hope that a more radical overthrow of conceptual barriers, associated with Nietzsche's "metaphorical" effacement of the distinctions between history and myth, might provide a means for returning to a mode of thought in which the two creatively interact.[26] In short, in White's schematic understanding, "metaphor" denotes a unity of reason and imagination, or history and myth; "metonymy," a binary opposition between the two; "synecdoche," a higher unity of both; and "irony," that which is left after the unity has broken down: an inability to meaningfully relate the rational and the fabulous.

Now, when *Metahistory* addresses the "crisis of historicism," this crisis is characterized as a "condition of Irony," as an "Ironic condition of mind" and as "the descent into Irony which was to characterize the historical consciousness" of the late nineteenth and twentieth centuries.[27] In spite of White's inconsistent use of "irony"—Eugene O. Golob has counted no less than twenty possible meanings of this term in *Metahistory* alone[28]—the author leaves no doubt as to his conviction that "the true content of the 'crisis of historicism'" was an awareness of limitations in the sense just explained: an inability, if not unwillingness, to relate historical studies to mythic, religious, and other "irrational" modes of thought. Burckhardt, for example, is associated with disdain for "political and religious impulses" and with an "explosion of all formulas, all myths, in the interest of pure 'contemplation' and resignation to the world of 'things as they are.'" Croce is blamed for having moved historical studies out of "the fullness of the noonday sun" to "the partial light of the new moon"—that is, from participation in an effort to integrate human knowledge to the monastic sphere of merely historical contemplation.[29] More specifically, both thinkers are criticized for having separated "rational" historical inquiry from the "irrational" domains of moral and political commitment. This is as unsatisfying as it is dangerous, as White believes that all commitment or involvement requires some kind of myth, dream, or "irrational" vision of what life should look like. According to *Metahistory*, all moral aspirations, all efforts to make a difference in life, require a "fictional construction of the world." All political visions ("Activism," "Communism," "Transcendentalism," "Chauvinism," and so forth) require some form of "irrationalism."[30] These irrationalities, argues White, need to be constructively engaged, rather than opposed or ignored, lest they go their own way, just as the Romanticists once opposed the Enlightenment, and "ultimately plunge[d] European civilization into the abyss of totalitarian error." Thus, the ironic failure to mediate between history and myth may not be without consequences: it may eventually "bring about the end of civilization itself."[31]

All this seems to indicate that White's crisis of historicism is an entirely different problem than the one faced by Hesse's Castalian characters and early-twentieth-century theology. Nowhere does *Metahistory* associate the crisis of historicism with Troeltsch's attempt to escape "moral relativism" (Troeltsch's name does not even appear in the index). Nowhere does the author show himself concerned about "crises" that an increasing awareness of historical variety and multiplicity may cause in the domain of moral certitude. Rather, for White, the "crisis of historicism" denotes the unfortunate circumstance that, in the 1970s as much as in the late nineteenth century, "academic historiography remains locked within the Ironic perspective" and fails to engage in productive interaction with imagination, dream and myth.[32] Yet, my contention is that these two elements in White—the absence of a Troeltschean crisis and his anti-ironic attitude—are closely related. White's aim to rescue historical studies from their ironic cage is motivated by the belief that human beings need to be inspired to take the step that Troeltsch hesitated, and finally refused, to take: to accept full responsibility for the meaning of their lives and the moral values they want to promote.[33]

Monumental Historiography

Many readers of *Metahistory* have noticed that White is particularly fascinated by the theme of human freedom.[34] Whereas freedom in *The Emergence* and *The Ordeal of Liberal Humanism* is predominantly defined in negative terms—liberal humanism has produced freedom *from* religion, myth, tradition, superstition, and ignorance—the notion of freedom receives a more positive definition in *Metahistory*. Not only does White consider human beings free to think, believe, and act in whatever ways they find appropriate; they are also granted a right "to conceptualize history, to perceive its contents, and to construct narrative accounts of its processes in whatever modality of consciousness is most consistent with their own moral and aesthetic aspirations."[35] (Note that this is not the same as declaring that people are free to say whatever they please about the past: in this passage, at least, White merely claims that human beings have a freedom to decide whether to relate history and myth in metaphoric, metonymical, synecdochic, or ironic "modalities of consciousness.") These types of freedom are related in so far as historical representations reflect the author's moral and political positions and, vice versa, in so far as ideals, dreams, and utopian visions presuppose a certain attitude toward the past.[36] Importantly, White takes these to be *individual* freedoms. Not the state, the church, or the historical discipline tells individuals how to interpret their past, present, and future: according to humanist reason, they are individually responsible for how they interpret their lives.

White, unlike Father Jacobus, does not see this meaning become "serious" or even "tragic" if confronted with historicist versions of the past because White does not believe such meaning to transcend the limits of the individual's situation. He conceives of moral meaning in thoroughly historicist terms. This is not to say that White insists on a radical "otherness of the past." In fact, consistent with his hermeneutics, the theme of otherness ("they do things differently there") is largely absent in White's book. But since the author regards moral meaning as created solely by individual acts of will, and since he attributes to individuals a freedom to apprehend the "spectacle of history-in-general in terms of felt needs and aspirations that are ultimately personal," he is at pains to point out that these individual perceptions of reality cannot be limited, restricted, or disciplined by what others in their situations saw as the meaning, purpose, or "proper" mode of understanding reality. White's Marx chapter can therefore state that "one can either adopt Marx's philosophy as providing the perspective from which one *wills* to view one's own place in the stream of historical becoming or one can reject it on similarly voluntaristic grounds."[37] Likewise, in spite of White's praise for Tocqueville, it is the individual reader who has to decide whether or not to accept this Frenchman's tragic conception of reality. In fact, for White, Tocqueville's greatness lies precisely in forcing "the reader to decide for himself 'what actually happened' in terms of what he desires to happen in his own future, asking him to choose between a comfortable drifting on history's stream and a struggle against its currents."[38] Thus, the primacy of the individual will—characterized by Hans Kellner as the only "foundationalism" that *Metahistory* is prepared to endorse[39]—leads White to preclude or deny the possibility of supra-individual standards for interpreting reality or judging good and evil. Accordingly, the Castalian world of timeless truths and moral universals is utterly foreign to White's book. White does not fear a crisis of historicism as Troeltsch or

Father Jacobus did, because his voluntarism prevents him from assuming that there is any worth in the "moral absolutes" threatened by historicist thought.

However, if moral decision-making is a here-and-now activity, as White presumes, then why should human beings wish to study the past? If there is no wisdom to be gained in the contemplation of human successes and failures in the past, what, then, is the moral significance of historical studies? Besides, it is one thing to say that reason and imagination need to build upon each other, but another to claim that historical studies should facilitate this interaction. Why cannot literature, philosophy, or the social sciences help people deal with this challenge? In short, if White opts for "situational" or even "presentist" ethics, then why does he not abandon history and further contribute to the marginalization of historical studies described in "The Burden of History"?

Kellner has made the pertinent point that White's book should probably not be titled *Metahistory*, but *Metahistories*. The book has multiple dimensions, each with its own agenda, horizon, and intended audience.[40] Having said this, one might nevertheless argue that the moral significance of historical studies is one of the dominant themes in White's study. "The question for the historian today is not *how* history ought to be studied, but *if* it ought to be studied at all," wrote White in 1965.[41] His *opus magnum* is an attempt to answer this question, notwithstanding the fact that other purposes are pursued along the way. This is also to say, *pace* some critics of White's book,[42] that *Metahistory* does not primarily aim to analyze professional historiography or ask academic historians to increase their "moral commitment." Instead of taking present-day historical writing as his frame of reference, White wonders if there is any sense at all in which "the general intellectual and artistic life of our time" may need historical reflection.[43]

Metahistory provides a threefold answer. First, following Kant, White argues that all moral positions, including those articulated within "the general intellectual and artistic life of our time," presuppose a vision of the past. The way I live my life depends not only on my moral ideals, but also on how I locate these ideals vis-à-vis the historical process:

If I conceive the historical process as a spectacle of degeneration . . . I will live history in such a way as to bring about a degenerate end to the process. And similarly, if I conceive that spectacle as "one damn thing after another," I shall act in such a way as to turn the age in which I live into a static age, one in which no progress will be possible.[44]

Thus, for instance, a metonymical opposition between reason and imagination constructed by French Enlighteners in the service of a rational ideal of society led Voltaire to regard the past as a time of unreason, the present as a struggle, and the future as a period in which a greater rationality would be realized. In Voltaire's philosophy of history, the past served as a dark contrast to (what was destined to become) a splendid future. Leibniz's synecdochic understanding of reason and imagination, by contrast, did not require such an opposition. "When Leibniz surveyed the remote past he saw there precisely the same powers at play which he saw all around him in the present, and in the same proportions."[45] Consequently, unlike Voltaire, Leibniz did not need a break from the past. To White, these examples indicate that a vision of the past helps explain how a moral vision can be realized.

Secondly, however, all moral visions, whether progressive, conservative, or reactionary in nature, require dreams and myths. As outlined in the previous section, White believes that a "fictional construction of the world" ("I have a dream") is part of every moral aspiration, including the Enlightenment quest for greater rationality. If such aspirations are to be prevented from stumbling into irony, White argues, then they must be articulated within a synecdochic or metaphoric comprehension of reality. They need, to put it differently, a configuration of "reason" and "unreason" that will not tolerate the erroneous idea that human beings will finally become more rational or indulge in the naive thought that today's irrationalities are worse than yesterday's. In a synecdochic or metaphoric mode, history can teach individuals that reason and unreason have always coexisted—and that human beings have to live their moral life *within* this situation. "What Voltaire might have concluded from his consideration of Charles's career," adds White, referring to Voltaire's *Histoire de Charles XII*, "was that unreason is a part of the world and of man, as ineluctable and as irreducible as reason itself, and a power which is not to be eliminated in time so much as it is to be tamed, sublimated, and directed into creative and humanly useful channels."[46]

This brings us to the third answer, which is anticipated in White's 1963 Croce essay. Speaking about what lessons, if any, can be learned from the past, White states that "history alone (and here it surpasses both philosophy and art in its powers of moral suasion) provides us with *living* models of human beings willing to act within the limits (. . .) given and teaches us that, potentially at least, we too possess a similar courage."[47] History not only reminds individuals that they live in a world where reason and unreason coexist, but also tells them that, *within* this far from perfect reality, a courageous moral life is possible. This is why White's *opus magnum* tends to favor a "monumental" historiography, in Nietzsche's sense of the word.[48] It tends to favor a mode of history that "pertains to the active and powerful, to the person who is involved in a great struggle and who needs exemplars, teachers, and comforters, but is unable to find them among his contemporaries and in the present age."[49] Obviously, White does not expect such "teachers" to exemplify how others should live—for that would violate his individual voluntarism. Neither does *Metahistory* support a monumental history that gives "late-comers" on the stage of history the uncomfortable feeling that everything worthwhile has already been accomplished ("Look, great art already exists!"). Rather, White favors historical studies that, in Nietzsche's words, make their readers believe "that the greatness that once existed was at least *possible* at one time, and that it therefore will probably be possible once again."[50] Precisely this is the reason why *Metahistory* reminds its readers of the "golden age" of history, of figures like Tocqueville, Marx, and Nietzsche, of visionary thinkers who believed that history, reason, myth, and imagination have to join forces in the realization of moral ideals. Their examples aim to show White's readers that it is possible for them to break away from irony—"we have only to reject this Ironic perspective and to *will* to view history from another, anti-Ironic perspective"—and to instill in them a courage to take their lives into their own hands, to learn again to dream, and to develop a historical vision that sustains rather than destroys their imaginative faculty.[51]

So, White's final answer to the question posed by what he calls "the crisis of historicism"—is there anything morally significant to be expected from the study of the past?—is that historical studies, in a monumental sense, may inspire the reader to become as courageous a moral actor as is Joseph, in the final chapter of *The Glass Bead Game*: a man who knows better than most how transitory our historical conditions are, how human beings are blinded by instincts, impulses, and sinful desires—a man who, nonetheless, affirms this mixture of "reason" and "unreason," trusts in the soundness of his judgment and in the strength of his will, breaks with the Castalian Order, and begins a new life, rejoicing in his freedom and looking forward to whatever comes next.[52]

Notes

Parts of this essay are based on my doctoral dissertation, "Masks of Meaning: Existentialist Humanism in Hayden White's Philosophy of History" (University of Groningen, 2006). I gratefully mention Professor White's generosity in making time to respond to my thoughts and intuitions about his work, first during a weeklong visit to Stanford University and later at conferences in Turku, Budapest, and Groningen. Pretending not to understand why anybody would write a doctoral thesis on Hayden White, he helped me discover "the politics of style" by refusing to answer my questions in any straightforward manner, offering more challenging, more thought-provoking reflections on history, philosophy of history, and the state of the Western world instead. I consider Professor White's support a particular privilege and gladly express at this occasion my thanks for his interest in my readings of his oeuvre. Two published interviews resulted from our conversations: "Zonder god rest ons niets dan geschiedenis," *De Groene Amsterdammer* 129, no. 43 (2005): 22–25; "Een beslissend moment van geschiedenis: Hayden White en de erfenis van het existentialisme," *Groniek* 38 (2005): 581–91.

1. Hermann Hesse, *The Glass Bead Game* (*Magister Ludi*), trans. Richard and Clara Winston (New York: Holt, Rinehart and Winston, 1969), 168–69.

2. Ibid., 265.

3. Ibid., 400.

4. David Harlan, "The Return of the Moral Imagination," in *The Degradation of American History* (Chicago: University of Chicago Press, 1997), 105–126; Hans Kellner, "A Bedrock of Order: Hayden White's Linguistic Humanism," in *Language and Historical Representation: Getting the Story Crooked* (Madison: University of Wisconsin Press, 1989), 193–227. More recently, A. Dirk Moses also emphasized this moral aspect in his "Hayden White, Traumatic Nationalism, and the Public Role of History," *History and Theory* 44 (2005): 311–32.

5. A variety of crises associated with nineteenth-century historicism are explored in *Krise des Historismus, Krise der Wirklichkeit: Wissenschaft, Kunst und Literatur, 1880–1932*, ed. Otto Gerhard Oexle (Göttingen: Vandenhoeck & Ruprecht, 2007). That nineteenth-century historical thought ("classical historicism," as distinguished from "crisis historicism") suffered, rather than caused, a crisis is the argument of my essay, "A Collapse of Trust: Reconceptualizing the Crisis of Historicism," *Journal of the Philosophy of History* 2, no. 1 (2008): 63–82. The *locus classicus* remains, of course, Ernst Troeltsch, *Der Historismus*

und seine Probleme: Das Logische Problem der Geschichtsphilosophie (Tübingen: J. C. B. Mohr, 1922).

6. The allusion is to Mieke Bal, *Travelling Concepts in the Humanities: A Rough Guide* (Toronto: University of Toronto Press, 2002).

7. See Patrick Dassen, *De onttovering van de wereld: Max Weber en het probleem van de moderniteit in Duitsland, 1890–1920* (Amsterdam: G. A. van Oorschot, 1999). Weber's influence on the "young" White is the subject of my essay, "A Weberian Medievalist: Hayden White in the 1950s," *Rethinking History* 12, no. 1 (2008): 75–102.

8. Gilbert Allardyce, "The Rise and Fall of the Western Civilization Course," *The American Historical Review* 87 (1982): 695–725.

9. Willson H. Coates and Hayden V. White, *The Ordeal of Liberal Humanism: An Intellectual History of Western Europe*, vol. 2, *Since the French Revolution* (New York: McGraw-Hill, 1970), 3, 448; Hayden V. White, *The Greco-Roman Tradition* (New York: Harper & Row, 1973), ix.

10. Willson H. Coates, Hayden V. White, and J. Salwyn Schapiro, eds., *The Emergence of Liberal Humanism: An Intellectual History of Western Europe*, vol. 1, *From the Italian Renaissance to the French Revolution* (New York: McGraw-Hill, 1966), v, 69; Coates and White, *Ordeal of Liberal Humanism*, 37, 79, 290, 452; White, *Greco-Roman Tradition*, 6.

11. Russell Jacoby, "A New Intellectual History?" *The American Historical Review* 97 (1992): 407.

12. Hayden V. White, "Translator's Introduction: On History and Historicisms," in *From History to Sociology: The Transition in German Historical Thinking*, Carlo Antoni, trans. Hayden V. White (Detroit: Wayne State University Press, 1959), xix–xxv.

13. See Paul, "Weberian Medievalist," 80.

14. Coates, White, and Shapiro, *Emergence of Liberal Humanism*, 194, 195; Hayden White, *Metahistory: The Historical Imagination in Nineteenth-Century Europe* (Baltimore; London: Johns Hopkins University Press, 1973), 77.

15. Paul, "Collapse of Trust," 65.

16. White, *Metahistory*, 2, 46, 47; Hayden V. White, "The Conflict of Papal Leadership Ideals from Gregory VII to St. Bernard of Clairvaux with Special Reference to the Schism of 1130" (Ph.D. diss., University of Michigan, 1955). White uses the iron law metaphor in an interview with Willem Otterspeer and Michaël Zeeman: "De valse verhalen van de geschiedenis," *NRC Handelsblad*, cultural supplement "Beeldspraak" (June 9, 1989), 4.

17. White, *Metahistory*, 51. A few pages later, White makes a similar statement: "The modality of *opposition*, by which things in history are related in thought, has not given place to the modality of *continuity and interchange*, which alone could generate an adequate appreciation of the concreteness, individuality, and vividness of historical events" (57–58).

18. Hayden V. White, "Hegel: Historicism as Tragic Realism," *Colloquium* 5, no. 2 (1966): 10–19.

19. White, *Metahistory*, ix, xii, 38.

20. See F. R. Ankersmit, "Hayden White's Appeal to the Historians," in *Historical Representation* (Stanford: Stanford University Press, 2001), 253; as well as my "bottom up" reconstruction of White's tropology in "Metahistorical Prefigurations: Towards a Reinterpretation of Tropology in Hayden White," *Journal of Interdisciplinary Studies in History and Archaeology* 1, no. 2 (2004): 1–19.

21. White, *Metahistory*, 69.

22. Ibid., 52, 58, 62.

23. Ibid., 67, 92, 108.

24. Ibid., 234–37, 401; Hesse, *Glass Bead Game*, 277.

25. White, *Metahistory*, 69, 71, 77, 80.

26. Ibid., chapter 9.

27. Ibid., xii, 40, 41.

28. See Golob's review in *History and Theory* 14 (1975): 81.

29. White, *Metahistory*, 41, 230, 233, 385.

30. Ibid., 397, 400, 423. See chapter 8 of *The Ordeal of Liberal Humanism*, on "The Place of the Irrational in Culture and Society."

31. White, *Metahistory*, 85, 108, 236.

32. Ibid., 433. See the book's epigraph: "One can study only what one has first dreamed about." Clear evidence of White's desire to reunite "dream" and "reason" in historical studies can also be found in his review article on George Armstrong Kelly's *Idealism, Politics and History: Sources of Hegelian Thought*, in *History and Theory* 9 (1970): 343–63.

33. I leave aside the problem that *Metahistory*, in White's own words, "is itself cast in an Ironic mode" (xii). How White's "turning of the Ironic consciousness against Irony itself" (xii) can be understood is the subject of my article, "An Ironic Battle Against Irony: Epistemological and Ideological Irony in Hayden White's Philosophy of History, 1955–1973," in *Tropes for the Past: Hayden White and the History/Literature Debate*, ed. Kuisma Korhonen (Amsterdam; New York: Rodopi, 2006), 35–44. An extended version of this essay appeared in Dutch as "Tegen zure regen: Hayden White, anti-ironisme en existentialistisch humanisme," *Tijdschrift voor Geschiedenis* 120 (2007): 74–84.

34. Peter Novick even refers to White's "existentialist quasi obsession with the historian's liberty of choice. It is not too much to call him historiography's philosopher of freedom." *That Noble Dream: The "Objectivity Question" and the American Historical Profession* (Cambridge: Cambridge University Press, 1988), 601. Hans Kellner and Ewa Domańska, among others, have also drawn attention to the significance of "freedom" in White.

35. White, *Metahistory*, 434.

36. "In choosing our past, we choose a present; and vice versa. We use the

one to *justify* the other." Hayden V. White, "What Is a Historical System?" in *Biology, History, and Natural Philosophy*, ed. Allen D. Breck and Wolfgang Yourgrau (New York: Plenum Press, 1972), 242.

37. White, *Metahistory*, 283.

38. Ibid., 227.

39. Hans Kellner, "Twenty Years After: A Note on *Metahistories* and Their Horizons," *Storia della Storiografia* 24 (1993): 115.

40. Ibid., 109.

41. *History* by John Higham (in collaboration with Leonard Krieger and Felix Gilbert), reviewed in *AHA Newsletter* 3, no. 5 (1965): 6.

42. E.g., Jörn Stückrath, "Typologie statt Theorie? Zur Rekonstruktion und Kritik von Hayden Whites Begrifflichkeit in 'Metahistory,'" in *Metageschichte: Hayden White und Paul Ricoeur: Dargestellte Wirklichkeit in der europäischen Kultur im Kontext von Husserl, Weber, Auerbach und Gombrich*, ed. Jörn Stückradt and Jürg Zbinden (Baden-Baden: Nomos, 1997), 86–103; Siegfried Kohlhammer, "Die Welt im Viererpack: Zu Hayden White," *Merkur* 52 (1998): 898–907.

43. This expression, taken from "Burden of History," 48, frequently occurs in White's writings from the 1960s and early 1970s.

44. White, *Metahistory*, 57.

45. Ibid., 62.

46. Ibid., 64.

47. Hayden V. White, "The Abiding Relevance of Croce's Idea of History," *The Journal of Modern History* 35 (1963): 118.

48. White occasionally recommends Nietzsche's critical mode of history, as Moses, "Hayden White," 313, observes, but only to create space for monumental historiography.

49. Friedrich Nietzsche, "On the Utility and Liability of History for Life," in *Unfashionable Observations*, trans. Richard T. Gray (Stanford: Stanford University Press, 1995), 96. White lists Nietzsche's reservations about this type of historiography in *Metahistory*, 349–50.

50. Nietzsche, "Utility and Liability," 98, 101. "[H]e goes his way with more courage," continues Nietzsche, referring to the (male) reader of such monumental historiography, "for the doubt that befalls him in his weaker moments—Is he not, in fact, striving for the impossible?—is now banished."

51. White, *Metahistory*, 434 (emphasis added).

52. Hesse, *Glass Bead Game*, 266–67, 406–9.

PART TWO

NARRATIVE

Narrative, an Introduction

Frank Ankersmit

White is best known for his introduction of the so-called linguistic turn into historical theory. Hence, the claim that all knowledge requires language for its expression and that an adequate grasp of the nature of knowledge will minimally require an account of the conditions of meaningful language use. In philosophy the notion of the "linguistic turn" is ordinarily related to the work of Quine, and especially to his seminal essay on the "two dogmas of empiricism" of half a century ago.

White's embrace of the "linguistic turn" had, however, a different origin. He observed that the historical theory of the 1950s and 1960s focused exclusively on the *components* of the historical text (that is, the individual descriptions and explanations of historical events that we may find in the historical text), while being both unwilling and unable to deal with the historical text *as a narrative whole*. He then looked for help to authors who might help him to address this issue of the narrative whole of the historian's text. He found this help in the writings of literary theorists saying how we should read, analyze, interpret, and understand literary texts and, above all, the novel. This may explain how and why literary theory could become such a very prominent element in the discourse of historical theory since White and why his historical theory has often been characterized as "narrativist."

In practice, this resulted in a reading of historical texts (as a whole) with the technical instruments provided by literary theory. This gave us a wholly new kind of "historiography" (that is, history of historical writing). Before White, historiography was restricted to an enumeration of the great historians from the past and the present, to a summary of how the past was represented in their writings, to the moral and political bias that could be discerned in these writings, and to what influence the "Zeitgeist" and previous historians must have had on them. But the historical text was never analyzed as a linguistic "machinery" for the production of historical meaning. Though it should be added, in all fairness, that White did have his precursors here (such as Roland Barthes or Lionel Gossman). Nevertheless, the literary *déniaisement* of historiography is something that we owe, above all, to White. This has, arguably, been his most important contribution to historical theory and will undoubtedly prove to be his lasting legacy to that discipline. It is simply inconceivable that future historical theorists and historiographers will ever be prepared to abandon again what White has made them see. It has been the discovery of a wholly new intellectual universe.

In her essay, Nancy Partner adds still another dimension to the foregoing. She insists that the linguistic turn had always comprised not just narrative, but also semiotics, (post-)structuralism, deconstructivism, psychological and psychoanalytical approaches, etc. Her main argument is that all these other exemplifications of the linguistic turn are on their way out now, whereas narrativism clearly is here to stay. Each fashion in "theory" has, apart from what afterwards will be recognized to have been its lunatic fringe, its hard core as well, containing a message for later generations. And in the case of the "linguistic turn" this happens to be narrativism.

Keith Jenkins emphasizes that narrativism requires us to recognize that we must contribute to narrative a certain autonomy with regard to the past itself. It is a quasi-Kantian category not having its exact counterpart in the world itself. Or, rather, narrativism is a category we project on the non-narrative past in order to make sense of it. He elaborates this argument by questioning the referentiality of historical narrative: all the (narrative) trends, developments, evolutions, ruptures, etc., so assiduously investigated and discussed by historians, do not have a referent in the past itself, in the way that phrases such as "Nelson's flagship *Victoria*" undoubtedly do possess such a referent. Narrative may yield what Jenkins nicely captures as "inferred reference," but this is not reference in the proper sense of the word. "Radical" historians and historical theorists openly recognize, and even rejoice in, this nonreferentiality of history. Jenkins concludes his essay by saying that the White of *Metahistory* has been the "radical" historian *par excellence.*

Andrew Baird capitalizes on the fact that having beginnings, middles, and endings is the most basic feature of all (historical) narrative. In his essay he takes his point of departure in the notion of "anabasis," and then reminds us—with Alain Badiou in the latter's *Le Siècle* (2005)— that the Greek word may mean both "to embark" and "to return." The Greek word thus questions our commonsense notion about beginnings (to embark) and endings (to return home), and Baird agrees with Badiou that this is how we should read Xenophon's account of the uncertain march of the "ten-thousand" through Persia. Put differently, our notion of the relationship between beginnings and endings is consistently "ironized" by the word *anabasis.* Baird relates anabasis to Schlegel's "romantic irony," which had been best defined as "dialectics without the happy closure" (that is, there is no moment of synthesis, as in Hegel and Marx). Instead, the moment of synthesis is exchanged for a permanent impasse in which the mind comes to stand in a relationship to itself.[1] As Schlegel formulated it himself, "irony is a permanent *parekbasis.*" Now, if we replace "mind" by the more fashionable term "language," we shall find, as Baird insists, how we should take White's notion of "irony," and why, for White, the historian's language is a permanent comment on itself without ever encountering clear beginnings and endings.

These insights must bring us to the notion of myth. For if all historical explanation is necessarily provisional and radically uncertain because of this radical uncertainty about all beginnings and endings—hence, an uncertainty involving the main frame of all historical writing—what does then still protect the discipline against the accusation of producing mere "myths"? And this accusation should not be reduced to a philistine criticism that historical writing lacks proper "foundations" (as we may find these in the sciences). The idea is, rather, that any choice with regard to these beginnings and endings of narrative is always made thanks to an appeal to something outside, or beyond, the narrative in question *itself.* So the cogency of narrative depends on something not explicitly stated in it. This makes all historical writing essentially "enthymemic," in the sense that its claim to present us with the Truth about the past is always based on one or more tacit assumptions the reader is asked to add to the text himself. Now, these tacit assumptions—that both the historian and his readers are unaware of—can well be described as myth, insofar as these are *ex hypothesi* necessarily outside what is explicitly said in the historical text itself (as soon as this was *not* the case, we no longer would have to do with "unstated assumptions"). Myth has to be situated outside, previous to, or beyond all "historical time" as recounted in the discourse of disciplinary historical writing. This is how Roland Barthes had defined myth in his *Mythologies* of 1957, a definition inviting us to see in myth the perennial blind spot of all historical writing, accompanying it wherever it goes. In his essay, Stephen Bann lucidly demonstrates that White's reading of Vico brought him quite close to Barthes's "enthymemic" conception of myth.

Note

1. Obviously, this is why one may well see Schlegel as the Derrida of Romanticism.

4

Narrative Persistence

THE POST-POSTMODERN LIFE
OF NARRATIVE THEORY

Nancy Partner

Post-Postmodernism:
What Exactly Has Been Left Behind?

The discipline of history, at least in its theory-saturated precincts, seems to be shifting its temporal/theoretical self-definition from postmodern to post-postmodern. I cannot state with any certainty exactly when this began, but this cultural passage (for lack of a better word) surely took place sometime just before I became aware of it. And in that disconcerting way, just out of my perceptual range, which, I have to admit, is the way all these things seem to happen in the current intellectual atmosphere. It is hard to say with any specificity what this post-postmodern state includes and what is being left behind (as modernism so adamantly was by postmodernism), except that we are not returning to quasi-scientific positivism, naive empiricism, or any of the pre-postmodern assumptions that informed the writing of history. As theory-informed historians, we seem to be taking stock: pausing and evaluating the aftermath of postmodernist achievement, including its excesses, asking what changes seem permanent, what conceptual instruments became indispensable, and what now looks like ephemeral fashion. This ongoing process of stocktaking involves revisiting postmodernism, worrying over the apparently unsolvable problem of fiction undermining history, seeing what the implications of acknowledging the "constructedness" of knowledge in every humanist area actually involves.[1]

All attempts to define postmodernism and assess its implications revolve around language, around the true role of language in all the areas of intellectual life that have no existence independent of language—thus the directional phrase "the linguistic turn," turning around and around in circles, is the one we conflate with postmodernism. Consider what the linguistic turn meant for history: the destabilizing of the traditional impersonal voice of authority; deconstruction of the simple evidentiary value of documents; application of literary critical techniques and discourse analysis to historical writing. Through a scrutiny of language so insistent and systemic that now it feels like an ordinary routine of academic life, the linguistic turn posed its fundamental challenge to the truth-value of any writing claiming to represent the past. If post-postmodernism involves a turn away from the linguistic turn, it is exceptionally difficult to map out that direction.

In a review article in the current issue of *History and Theory*, the cutting-edge venue for these topics, Michael Roth (an exceptionally sophisticated cultural historian) opens: "For the last decade or so, recognition has been spreading that the linguistic turn that had motivated much advanced work in the humanities is over . . . the massive tide of language . . . has receded; we are now able to look across the sand to see what might be worth salvaging before the next waves of theory and research begin to pound the shore."[2] Among the tentative candidates vying for critical attention, Roth names ethics, intensity, postcolonialism, empire, the sacred, cosmopolitanism, trauma, animals. I would add memory (a well-established contender accelerating through the disciplines), experience, agency (making a strong return after the Foucault-style "death of the author"), and religion, along with the subject of the book Roth reviews—the sublime (Frank Ankersmit's *Sublime Historical Experience*). All of these topics or focal points for investigation share a common desire to escape language, restore a pure and immediate connection with the past or at least some central aspect of experience, and generally deny the power of language to contaminate "history" with its own uncontrollable meanings. Admittedly, a long-developing and generalized revolt against the prisonhouse of language makes intuitive sense; very few people ever really accepted the more extreme logic of endlessly deferred meaning, or conceded that language established no connection at all with an external and objective reality, even the problematic reality of the past. But research and teaching combine to convince me that the linguistic turn, and the dense web of concepts and interpretive assumptions we collect under the term, made an impact on historians and historical practice that cannot and will not be erased. The very fact that we are being offered trauma, memory, experience, and the sublime as post-postmodern interests should tell us clearly enough that we are not turning back to any place that looks empirical in the old confident sense. The new anti-language approach working its way through academic history departments seems to use postmodernism as a locus to gather together a number of strands that have yet to be adequately untangled and sorted out.

Here is my abbreviated history of postmodernism from a historian's purview. Sometime around 1990 or maybe a little after, the linguistic turn had succeeded in turning everything into a text. Artifacts that hitherto had been variously called books, articles, documents, evidence, histories, novels, and scripture, all collapsed into one categorical descriptor: text. Textuality exerted an irresistible and hegemonic dominance over linguistic artifacts, indeed, but events, ritual, law, social institutions, memories, identities, bodies, and sex acts fell under this "text" rubric as well, by virtue of their susceptibility to interpretation. Once everything made of language, associated with language, or "discourse" as we took to calling it, was definitively and conveniently collected in this way, these textual artifacts could be subjected to a variety of interpretive procedures suitable to their "textuality" (their intertextuality, their metatextuality)—procedures themselves collected under linguistic rubrics like critical theory and discourse analysis. Historical documents no longer promised to be transparent windows on the past, and historical scholarship built on these documents no longer claimed an unproblematic or unmediated relation to past lives and processes. All artifacts, however businesslike and pragmatic in their production, were the products of culture; even a shopping list or account book embodied a cultural poetics and could be read for more than its literal content. Everything was a text, and everyone in his or her more radical moments was willing to claim that there was nothing outside the text (at least in French, where the somewhat more ambiguous "il n'y a pas de hors-texte" carried a mysterioso plausibility missing in blunter English). One of the markers of post-postmodernism is that we don't say that anymore. The exhilaration of the idea has drained out of it. The combined weight of recent reality and the immemorial authority of Western Realism (our collective superego) have forced us to return to a much more earnest, indeed grimmer, epistemological place—mimesis, however we repress it, is our lot.

It is not hard to be satirical in retrospect about linguistic turn excesses, but in its essentials this was no fad. From my point of view as a historian (I am a medieval historian by traditional training), the late modernist breakthrough in history's self-analysis was the forced clarity of an unblinking attention on the semantic, syntactic, tropological, poly-referential, and formal powers of literary language to control meaning beyond the superficial reach of the historian's conscious intention. In a fundamental sense, the textuality of the historical document, and the textuality of the kind of professional history written over an armature of documentary research are now permanent aspects of the modern discipline. This much is not reversible. But excited debates over the death of the author, or the evisceration of facts, the Big Ideas about language offered by postmodernism, were both too radical and too vague to change the entire discipline. In research, historical understanding, or writing, the real influence of linguistic turn concepts and techniques has been extremely uneven. In a 2005 review of a book on patronage and the visual arts in Renaissance Florence, the historian Lauro Martines (whose scholarly reputation is long established in Renaissance studies) frankly complains about the "narrowly positivist approach to documents" in "the art-historical profession itself," the lingering tendency to read documents in "an innocently empirical key," taking fraught terms like "love" and "friendship" at face value, forgetting about rhetoric and that "texts might not be what they seemed."[3] Elizabeth Clark's important book, *History, Theory, Text: Historians and the Linguistic Turn*, which surveys the major debates about history and epistemological theory from Rankean empiricism to the near-present moment, and argues the importance of linguistic turn theory for her field of early Christianity in Roman Antiquity was published only in 2004. Clark brings the full earned weight of her reputation as a major scholar of early Christianity to "convince historians that partisans of theory need not be branded as disciplinary insurrectionaries. . . . More particularly, I wish to persuade scholars of Western premodernity (and especially those of ancient Christianity) that the texts they study are highly amenable to the types of literary/philosophical/theoretical critique that have excited—and indeed, have now transformed—other humanities disciplines under the rubric of post-structuralism."[4] The

Israeli historian Boaz Shoshan applies literary critical modes of discourse analysis to medieval Islamic historiography in his groundbreaking work *Poetics of Islamic Historiography*, also published in 2004. Shoshan notes, "Like most students of history I have been trained to regard historiography—be it an ancient "source" or a modern "reconstruction"—as essentially a body of fact." His expanded and revitalized change of orientation he credits to the work of Hayden White primarily and others who analyze historical writing with literary theory instruments.[5] These historical fields, early Christianity, medieval Islamic historiography, Renaissance art history, are hardly minor or marginal by any standard and still have not been adequately exposed to the postmodernist tide Roth accurately sees as receding from the shores of fields based in modernity.

As Martines, Clark, and Shoshan clearly understand, to have any real effect, the implications of seeing truth-claim discourse (alias: history) as a form of writing (whatever else it might claim for itself), seeing the source document as text, have to be demonstrated in detail using an array of techniques and conceptual instruments addressed to complex language in its cultural surround, and mostly borrowed from literary criticism and classical rhetoric. Semantic analysis, large-scale structural analysis, rhetoric, and tropes (elements that had been deliberately disconnected from history since the nineteenth century) are the main lines of approach, and are still being learned and experimentally applied in fields long committed to traditional pre-postmodern approaches. My examples of scholars of ancient, medieval, and Renaissance history are few but, I think, characteristic in showing which aspects of the linguistic turn now seem unalarmingly valuable to very traditionalist scholarly fields. Acceptance of linguistic turn insights and techniques in long-resistant areas offers clear proof of how mainstream yesterday's radicalism can look, once the critical instruments are freed from the debunking rhetoric of the culture wars.

As I understand the post-postmodern moment among those who embraced postmodernism when it came into being, the task is to evaluate what is still with us, what has to be packed every time we set out to unpack a text, what really has been discarded, and the fate of postmodern theory that has escaped from academic custody. What my personal ongoing stocktaking reveals is that a lot of stock from the linguistic-turn armory reached its shelf date surprisingly soon, and some is in ever-greater demand for purposes we never foresaw.

I will begin with a quick rundown of the "ubi sunt" of linguistic turn theory (for non-medievalists, "ubi sunt"—Latin for "where are they now?"—a medieval subgenre of moral literature, teaching "contemptus mundi"). Semiotics: I find that it does not feel necessary to think or teach anything in terms of the signifier, its relation to the signified, their triangulated and futile reach for the referent, or codified systems of meaning. The distinctions among the *langue*, the *langage*, and the *parole* left the room with them. The discipline called semiotics still exists; there are specialized journals, conferences, the institutional organs of academic life— but that's not the point for the wider diffusion of semiotics throughout the humanities. With semiotics, we are talking now about an important stage in the history of linguistics, with significant implications for the epistemology of word/world reference incorporating the work of Ferdinand de Saussure. But for actual work of the sort historians do, using concepts to think with and read with, none of it feels useful or necessary or does anything that other literary critical concepts don't do better. I rarely come across the term in current academic writing, and never outside it.

A real surprise has been the pathetic and instructive fate of deconstruction—*there* is a term I see or hear almost every day. Deracinated, domesticated, defanged—used confidently in print and in conversation with an intended meaning quite different from its initial swaggering entrée onto the cultural scene. Deconstruction was the bad child of Saussurean linguistics: mad, bad, and dangerous to everything it came near. The original deconstructive technique of parsing out the hidden supporting and silently negated concepts underlying every "natural" or self-apparent positive descriptor was, so it was repeatedly claimed, the death ray of naive positivist illusions about race, sex, power, nature, and the state. Deconstruction unburied the hidden "femme" in every masculine, the silenced minority voices within the collective "citizen"; the variant practices, which the sexually "natural" made "unnatural." Deconstruction exposed every suppressed "other" under the lexical foot of self-justifying authority. If anything in linguistic turn theory could be predicted to hold its edge, resist assimilationist blunting, surely it would be deconstruction—the heavy artillery of the culture wars. But the technique of deconstructing a text is unusually difficult—demonstrating the semantic instability of major categorical terms and working out the implications for entire complex arguments is hard to do, and requires a sensitive educated ear for metaphor and careful appreciation for buried structures of reasoning. Its philosophic underpinnings are demanding. In Robert Stein's summary, "In the strict sense, deconstruction applies properly only to the philosophical work of Jacques Derrida, and particularly to his effort to understand the logic of Husserlian and Heideggerian metaphysics, a philosophical task that led him to an extensive and thorough meditation on the properties of writing."[6] In application, its reading techniques bear a close resemblance to the fastidious close readings of the old New Criticism (of the 1950s) and demand just that kind of literate concentration. While the word *deconstruction* itself, alas, seems to announce something else—merely something closer to "reverse engineering" or just taking something apart to see how it's made—sometimes with a slight debunking intention. That is how it has been adopted and popularly used, and it is too late to do anything about it. In his lucid essay introducing historians to the central techniques of text analysis, Stein does not invoke deconstruction in the "strict sense"; he explains the procedures of "reading that we can loosely call deconstructive." "In the weaker sense that I am using here, deconstruction refers in the first instance to a particular kind of critical reading devoted to understanding the operations that construct a text as a meaningful object."[7] In this "weaker sense," deconstruction proves to have extraordinary pedagogical usefulness, for teaching students how to do the critical reading that exposes the operations that constitute a text. But as artillery in the po-mo culture wars, the supposed death ray for vaporizing all traditional values, the stability of received knowledge, the authority of authority, deconstruction has lost its heat charge—it's a culturally neutral word now.

The Persistence of Narrative: At Home Everywhere

Who knew that the real linguistic-turn contender with the strongest reach into post-postmodernism would be narrative? Gentle narrative, so apparently soft-edged and only lightly theoretical, with its childlike alternative term of *story*, is out there acquiring a cultural weight we are barely keeping track of in our seminar rooms. Narrative seems like the least controversial weapon of the linguistic turn theory armory, or the least aggressive in its applications. I am aware of course of the quite fierce attacks that Hayden White has encountered in the course of demonstrating the structural analogues grounding the cultural repertoire of fictional and historical plots. His mapping of the basic tropes of thought onto historical explanation, and his descriptions of the traditional large-scale plot structures common to fiction and history, have offended people who considered that he was moving fiction, and fictional amorality, too close to the historical reality of the Holocaust. Books like Richard Evans's *In Defense of History* (1997, very influential in the U.K.) have popularized the bizarre idea that the analysis of historical plot structures as cultural constructions leads to moral slippage and radical relativism (alias: Holocaust denial).[8] I don't think the charge is fair or warranted; in fact, I think it doesn't deserve discussion, but at least there is a certain seriousness in it.

But that particular controversy has not soured narrative for the rest of the world, where ideas about narrative, its peculiar efficacy, its persuasive powers, and its slippery ability to morph have, for some time, been attracting attention. In 2004 William Safire, in his column On Language in the *New York Times*, noted that "narrative" was being used to explain almost everything political, a phenomenon he described as political science raiding the terminology of literary criticism.[9] "A narrative is the key to everything," he quoted John Kerry's pollster; and the Republicans "had a narrative." James Carville, famous political consultant, agreed about the "Republican narrative." Peter Brooks, an academic who knows a thing or two about narrative, credited the impact of the Starr Report on the Clinton/Lewinsky scandal with its deployment of Narrative for presenting its findings. Nearly everyone Safire approached had something cogent to say about the coherence or efficacy, the centrality, of campaign narrative in the political process. These political observations were from 2004. More recently, the campaign manager for Barack Obama is seen, and sees himself, as the creator of Obama's narrative. A pollster working on behalf of a gay rights organization notes on the topic of gays in the military: "Iraq and the war on terror have created a whole new narrative around the issue of gays serving in the military."[10] Reframing contentious issues (here, military service in the post–September 11 era) apparently rewrites an entire political and social narrative. In a review of books written by presidential candidates, Michiko Kakutani observes that "these candidates' books remind us that the ability to construct a powerful narrative is an essential skill for a politician, for it confers the ability to articulate a coherent vision of the world, to make sense of history and to define the author—before he or she is defined by opponents and the news media."[11]

Unsurprisingly from this exceptionally acute literary critic, the core concepts are singled out for attention: construction, coherence, history, intelligibility, and self-definition.

Now, after the most theory-receptive of the academic humanities are prematurely treating narrative (as embedded in postmodernism) as thoroughly assimilated, drained of problematic excitement, the world outside academe seems to be recognizing ideas that White first and best laid out for inspection. "The Value of Narrativity in the Representation of Reality" rewards rereading in its fresh "right on" impact: "To raise the question of the nature of narrative is to invite reflection on the very nature of culture and, possibly, even on the nature of humanity itself."[12] The idea of narrative strangely combines the universal and inevitable—so deeply is it embedded in human linguistic and cognitive structures—with the ability to be manipulated to validate or substantiate personal and public claims that are partisan and aggressive. Narrative form is so readily understandable, so apparently natural, that talking about it is like trying to step out of the river of time. Or, from Hayden White quoting Roland Barthes: narrative "is simply there like life itself . . . international, transhistorical, transcultural."[13] It is both self-evident and real, understood by everyone, and the weapon of choice for asserting controverted claims of political collectivities—while at the same time, narrative develops and maintains the individual self in its relation to the world.

Talking about narrative as "less a form of representation than as a manner of speaking about events" would seem too abstruse for any forum outside the university seminar.[14] But not so. After keeping a slightly haphazard but open-ended file of narrative-related comment from outside of academe that seems to float in with the media tide, I can say with some confidence that there is nothing that cannot be narrativized, and is not. Reporting on the March 2004 fashion shows in Paris, a fashion journalist explained the meaning of one designer's vision: "[The designer] evokes a notion of femininity that embraces neither girlish modesty nor matronly ascent. His gift lies in creating narratives in suspension: put on the clothes and finish the story yourself." I'm not sure I really understand that, but I think the writer did.[15] At a step up the aesthetic hierarchy, the reopening of the Museum of Modern Art in New York was presented several times over in terms of its narrative, or the art historical story implied by the placement and sequence of art objects within the newly designed exhibition space. Michael Kimmelman notes of the fifth floor: "Here is the familiar, early story of modernism that the Modern virtually invented . . . The story is now retold in an installation."[16] Another art critic noted that MOMA was reopening "at a time when even its own curators no longer believe that art progresses like science. Narratives overlap and intertwine; instead of one big story, there are many competing stories"—sounding much like a historian from a decade or so ago. But, he concedes, "A story must begin somewhere." He proceeds to discuss the traditional rationale for placing Cézanne's painting *The Bather* at the beginning of the story of modern art.[17]

At the other end of the spectrum of scale, narrative is increasingly regarded as an essential cohering function of individual human identity, and at the core of belief, opinion, decision making, and judgment. Howard Gardner, psychologist at the Harvard School of Education, has written a book called *Changing Minds: The Art and Science of Changing Our Own and Other People's Minds*, which turns on narrative as the key to forming and changing belief and action, private, political, and commercial.[18] Formulating narratives, reformulating facts and events into new narratives, embodying or acting in accord with one's preferred narrative (recommended for politicians or business leaders), are regarded as the entrée to exerting measurable influence over people in large numbers. Narrative is also a central motif in the work of the influential sociologist Anthony Giddens on the construction and protection of modern identities in a fragmenting post-traditional world.[19]

The concept of "psychological narrativity" is taken most seriously by its singular opponent, the British philosopher Galen Strawson, who has described his collective adversary as: "a vast chorus of assent [rising] from the humanities—from literary studies, psychology, anthropology, sociology, philosophy, political theory, religious studies, echoed back by psychotherapy, medicine, law, marketing, design . . . : human beings typically experience their lives as a narrative or story of some sort. . . ."[20] Strawson himself is defiantly against-the-grain, and against the expanding mainstream on the narrative self, and I am quoting him here from a long article in the *Times Literary Supplement* (excerpted from a much longer scholarly article) in which he opposes the Diachronic to the Episodic self in a complex and counterintuitive argument. But his bold list of acknowledged pro-narrative adversaries, starting with Plato and Augustine and including Dostoyevsky and Joseph Conrad, elevate this debate to a high level of philosophic and literary seriousness. His argument is lucid and careful, but he isn't going to make many converts—his alternative, the "episodic" self, is a bit too postmodern for current tastes.

My scatter of examples can be traced into a follow-the-dots map of the places where narrative has made major inroads, from the arenas of active political life through every level of articulated culture to the interiority of the individual self. The examples offered here might be sparse, but they are significant and hardly isolated; a cultural map more systematically surveyed would cover nearly all areas of private and public life that have produced self-conscious explication. Before historical theorists move on from postmodernism, from the linguistic turn, as if all its important work has been accomplished, we would do well to pay attention to this deepening traction of self-conscious narrative construction throughout our intellectual and political world.

The aspect of narrative theory that postmodern historians most thoroughly deconstructed (in the debunking sense) was the grand narrative—the teleological, unifying story line connecting (by aggressively selecting) historical events over long periods of time into an intelligible arc of progress towards some large telos which itself "explained" and justified the latent principle of selection. The Rise of the West, From Magic to Science, From Feudalism to Capitalism, The Emergence of the Individual—these great linear themes that organized the chaos and miscellany of history into self-explanatory narrative form all now sound clumsily archaic, so evidently artificial that their "constructedness" announces itself. The joints and forced articulations of such metanarrative constructions are so "unnaturally" visible these days that undergraduates (in my experience) easily deconstruct William Stubbs's *Constitutional History of England*, a work of empiricist scientific rigor by the Rankean standards of the 1880s, which assembles the shambling multitudinous evidence for medieval England into an ineluctable narrative (and nationalist) march toward parliament and constitutional monarchy. Most of these historical plots linger on as empty containers of convenience. Their social and political contents had been shattered and drained of intellectual authority long before postmodernism addressed them specifically *as* narrative constructions. Linguistic turn weapons merely finished them off.

But grand narratives, metanarratives in their most ambitious traditional forms, represent only a very small portion of narrative construction in historical work. The narratives that act as a force field of vivid energy in so many areas of daily life are of a different and more tractable scale, large enough to become available for public inspection and small enough to be grounded in very specific events and experiences. Individuals and small groups can connect their own personal stories to these narratives and the collective story draws emotional energy from its deep anchorage in collective memory. These are the newer national narratives: persistent, elastic, resonant to large numbers of people.

Narrative Along National Fissures: Ex-Yugoslavia, Israel/Palestine, and Others

The newest investment in the power of narrative is being made by the partisans from every part of the globe whose nationalist aspirations were invigorated by the end of the Cold War. Every piece of disputed territory marked by political conflict is also mapped with overlapping and conflicting narratives, with different collective protagonists embarked on their different quests of heroic fulfillment or sanctified (and endlessly repeated) victimhood. The ethnic cleansing warfare between Albanians and Serbs in the Kosovo province of ex-Yugoslavia during the 1990s gave me my personal illumination on the central role of narrative in resurgent nationalism. In the course of reading, and forgetting, and just not "getting" the earnest explanations from our more respectable media for readers not conversant with the history of Eastern European ethnic conflict, I finally read something I understood: that two separate, parallel historical narratives "explained" the enduring grievances and current injustices of this place, from antiquity onward, each story turning around a fourteenth-century battle over "the field of blackbirds," which issued in Ottoman Turkish dominance over the region. The Kosovar Albanian narrative had its own beginning, narrative arc, litany of injustices and triumphs, and looked to a certain sort of culmination. The Serbian protagonist narrative covered ostensibly the same ground but with a different chronology, causality, and moral arc. Each version was self-evidently correct in its own terms, and could not be disproved (or substantiated) by the other because the narratives didn't connect, except over the one battle whose historical meaning was determined by narrative embedding. No one suggests that the violence, ethnic cleansing, and ongoing instability of Kosovo have been effectively *caused* by narrative conflict, but every schoolchild in Kosovo and Serbia knows "the story" about the battle of the field of blackbirds—either the Albanian or Serbian version; each one grounds ethnic and political ideology in historical reality.

Narrative does not cause political conflict, but narrative form encapsulates emotion and memory in the service of political causes, and does its work effectively in preventing political compromise. The Scholars' Initiative recognizes the gravity of entrenched, unchallenged histories. This international project is designed to bring the rigorous research techniques and the dispassionate, nonpartisan approach of the modern (as in pre-postmodern) historical discipline to bear on the lingering unresolved problems of ex-Yugoslavia. The project began about 2000, created by historian Charles Ingrao of Purdue University, and has now reached its final stage.[21] The plan was to create research teams combining reputable scholars from Balkan countries with specialists from the United States, Canada, and Western Europe. Each team would work together on a sensitive flashpoint topic of regional history, arrive at a consensus, and write a report. Amazingly, Charles Ingrao found the institutional support and has made this happen: about 260 historians were organized into eleven research teams charged with impossibly hard topics. Team 1 undertook "Kosovo Under Autonomy in 1974–1990" to examine how the Serbs in Kosovo were treated by the Albanian majority. Team 4 handled "Ethnic Cleansing and War Crimes Between 1991 and 1995"—and was charged with reporting on violence between Croats, Serbs, and Bosnian Muslims and faced with the question whether there is a distinction between ethnic cleansing and genocide. Team 5 investigated the role of the United States and the European community in the dissolution of Yugoslavia; Team 7 wrote on the war in Croatia, the treatment of the Serb minority there, and the responsibility of the Croatian government for war crimes. Armed with the critical rationality and anti-ideological impartiality of the post-Enlightenment empiricist historian, the project teams had to charge head-on into the impossible places, do battle with "competing national myths," and emerge with "the story."

And indeed, narrative revision has been the explicit aim of the Scholars' Initiative. As put by authors from the United States Institute for Peace, one of the supporting institutions, the project is "Explaining the Yugoslav Catastrophe: The Quest for a Common Narrative": "This

Scholars' Initiative aims to contribute to the peace building process in the Balkans by forging a single, multi-faceted narrative comprehensible to all." Aside from the political importance of the project, its ambition and optimism, what caught my attention were the centrality of narrative theory to the Scholars' Initiative (SI) mission, and the apparent absence of any systematic consideration of narrative as a problem in itself. The construction of the project seemed to take for granted that historical methodology alone—transparent, rigorous, systematic handling of evidence to the standard of the modern research university—would naturally issue in that chronological, logically articulated, coherent yet comprehensive artifact we know as the successful and convincing historical narrative: disinterested, intelligible, plausible, and persuasive.

And the SI project has done its work; nearly all of the teams have issued reports and results are expected to be published soon.[22] But every team charged with a particularly sensitive topic repeatedly stalled at the point of writing their report in narrative form. Project teams' progress toward their reports suggests that the formal and theoretical problems inherent in narrative construction became nodes of conflict among the team scholars. One of the project scholars, Gale Stokes, a member of Team 3, "Fate of Minorities," has noted that no one had considered production of the "disinterested narrative" a matter of formal or theoretical complication, or tried to foresee the problems posed by narrative itself. "As you can imagine, it has proven to be extremely difficult, if not impossible, to produce such narratives, especially since most (not all) of the participants from the region are anything but disinterested. They see the narratives they and their colleagues construct for their own people as playing a fundamental role in their nation's self-conception."[23] One of the most important of the team researchers, charged with writing the report expressly on whether the peoples of ex-Yugoslavia could live together with their contradictory narratives of ethnic identity, had given up entirely, "simply providing the conventional narratives of each of the main national groups involved in the wars," with no effort to reconcile or combine or replace them. The report of Team 4 on "Ethnic Cleansing and War Crimes, 1991–1995" labors painfully, and bravely, over disputed definitions of basic terms such as *ethnic cleansing* and *genocide* and has notable trouble deploying active verbs, always a symptom of narrative distress. The status report emailed from Charles Ingrao on February 25,

2007, noted that the Scholars' Initiative is withholding the draft of the report on "Kosovo Under Milosevic" from the review process "during the current crisis and media frenzy over Kosovo's future" to protect the writers from "undue pressure from partisans on both sides."

What is it about narrative that makes it the emotional fulcrum of conflict, and so often between peoples who inhabit the same governable space? If history is the discourse of the real, narrative is the formal voice of persuasion, group authentication, and deep recalcitrant conviction. In a review article examining ten books on the Bosnian war and the breakup of Yugoslavia, "MetaBosnia: Narratives of the Bosnian War," David Campbell brings Hayden White's analysis of narrative to bear on "the narrativizing strategies of ostensibly objectivist works dealing with the Bosnian War" in a political science mode, quite a novel analysis in 1998. After systematically comparing ten accounts of the events of August 1990 to April 1992 (covering political debates about Bosnia's future in the collapsing Yugoslavia up to the beginning of warfare in Sarajevo), Campbell affirms that White's analysis is both accurate and useful in current, real-world terms. "Those events," he concludes in agreement with White," which attain that status by being emplotted in the first place, can be narrated in different ways (or overlooked entirely), often to support contradictory conclusions. The consequence of that, uncomfortable though it may be, is that a recourse to the historical record will not by itself resolve the issue of which is better or worse."[24] More than this generalized insight, however, serious attention to narrative theory (documented in his footnotes) gives Campbell the critical instruments to scrutinize the very concept of an event, the processes of emplotment, perspectival causal logic, and, perhaps most importantly, the concept of ethnic identity.

One could wish that the Scholars' Initiative teams had undertaken the same course of readings to gain a little critical control over narrative meltdown because the concluding Scholars' Initiative report by Team 11, titled with affecting candor, "Living Together or Hating One Another," finally confronts the inciting power of narrative in justifying ethnic violence, citing narrative directly seventeen times and implicitly many more throughout the report. The authors recognize that deconstructing the cynical complicity of political and media elites who reawakened and popularized long dormant ethnic/victim narratives to make violence in Bosnia and Kosovo historically "inevitable" is sadly not enough to erase these nationalist histories when "challenging psychological and sociological patterns that are often of long duration." Narrative form, with its mnemonic and reality-conjuring force, forges a strong link between large-scale national entities (however empirically ungrounded or "imagined," as we often say) and personal identity.

Narrative has become the key mode of explanation for every area of conflict in the Mideast. *New York Times* reporter Robert Worth, writing about Iraq, quotes a Princeton expert, Michael Doran, on this general phenomenon: "In the Middle East, as in the Balkans and Ireland, suppressed religious and ethnic groups have a kind of film playing in their minds of their own oppression. . . . In moments of political disruption they are ready to add another scene to the pre-existing narrative." The reporter adds that Iraqi Shiites, suppressed under Saddam Hussein, "carry a narrative of massacre and oppression that dates back to the founding of their religion."[25] Obviously enough, narrative is rapidly becoming a catchall phrase, faddishly invoked, often without much depth. But its cultural function as the one form addressed to public and collective life that exposes the deep wish Hayden White has asked us to recognize as its profound source is understood by the most serious students. In an essay in volume three of *Time and Narrative*, Paul Ricoeur describes the circumstance when believers invest a national narrative with their deepest desires, inviting certain "epoch-making" events to "generate feelings of considerable ethical intensity, whether this be fervent commemoration or some manifestation of loathing." History becomes, not a rationally provisional explanation of events, but a form charged with the emotions of veneration and victimhood.[26]

Commentary on the Israel/Palestinian conflict that casts the conflict explicitly in narrative terms is endemic to the historical and political debate. A notable element is that everyone, not only academics, reaches for this instrument. A former Israeli chief of staff, in the midst of explaining his views on withdrawing from the Golan, explained to a reporter: "This is a clash between the two narratives, the Jewish and the Arab, in the endurance of the two societies."[27] The journalist quoting him interjected an angry commentary: "Narrative is a postmodern term that stresses relativity and subjectivity. In the history of the nations there is no absolute truth—except, of course, the Palestinian truth. It is important to reiterate and state that the life story of the Israeli nation in the land of Israel . . . is neither myth nor relative truth. They, according to every historical sociological parameter, are absolute truth, not narrative." Nowhere, in my reading, is *narrative* so fraught a concept and practice as among Israelis and Palestinians. In a 2003 study of the practical implications of the Palestinians' "right of return," the Palestinian Center for Policy and Survey Research in Ramallah concluded that Palestinians demand acceptance of this right as the centerpiece of their story of victimization and expulsion, but that they would not act on it if it were granted. The director of the center said: "Once the Palestinian narrative is assured, then the tactical issue of where they will go becomes easy to approach. . . . Everybody wants the emotional question addressed." This is far from the conclusion suggested by Ahmad H. Sa'di in his movingly detailed essay "Catastrophe, Memory and Identity: Al-Nakbah as a Component of Palestinian Identity." "The question of identity among Palestinians," Sa'di writes, "has become intimately connected to the 'restoration of the individual's subjectivity,' that is, a national narrative has been constructed through life stories, documents, and viewpoints of individuals." Sa'di describes a national life in which treasured house keys that fit no houses have become fixed in psychic life as "a symbol for the return."[28]

The tough and fair-minded joint Israeli-Palestinian website Bitter lemons.org has devoted two long issues, in 2005 and 2006, to the problem of conflicting narratives, with authors citing the Serbia-Kosovo and China-Taiwan conflicts as similar instances of people creating "historical narratives to explain attachment to land [and] integrate specific geographical regions into historical-religious narratives."[29] The political issue they examine is whether the land can be divided without altering the narrative of either side; conclusions are ambivalent and painful.

A deep sophistication about narrative pervades Israeli and Palestinian political and intellectual life; no one on either side of this divide seems to require convincing that history is inconceivable without narrative, and narrative is informed by ideology in the broad sense. Again quoting White: "The endowment of past events with meanings and values [is] relevant to the promotion of political and social programs in the present for which historians write. For narrativization has to do with the problematic of action, whether action is considered to be possible or impossible, a good thing or a bad thing, a burden or a gift of the gods, of fate, or of history."[30]

One of the most fascinating narrative experiments is the high school textbook *Learning Each Other's Historical Narrative: Palestinians and Israelis* (2003 draft available in English), created by a committee of Israeli and Palestinian history teachers, a five-year project of Peace Research Institute in the Middle East (PRIME). This ambitious work, aimed at developing a tentative degree of mutual recognition in teenagers in the region, gave up on working out a single narrative as unrealistic.[31] The book provides the Israeli narrative running down the left, the Palestinian narrative on the right, and a blank column in the middle for students' writing. The authors cover three events: the Balfour Declaration, the 1948 war, and the 1987 Intifada (truly Ricoeur's "epoch-making events"). The stark facts of what is really involved in narrative construction stare out right from the first page: the problem of beginnings. Beginnings, as narrative theory alerts us, are not natural occurrences. Aristotle's *Poetics* is our originary text for this—beginnings are logically determined, depending on the teleology of your plot. The Israeli version starts with Zionism, the Jewish national movement of the nineteenth century, Theodor Herzl, and the political organization he founded. Historical context is supplied by European developments, such as nationalist movements, anti-Semitism, and so forth.

The Palestinian narrative begins with Napoleon and his fanciful proposal in 1799 for a Jewish state: "the first post-Renaissance expression of cooperation between a colonialist power and the Jewish people." In this narrative, Zionism is portrayed as the ready instrument of European imperialism, an overwhelming force (British, not French in the end) employing the Jews to displace and colonize the Palestinian lands. This incommensurate quality is not merely one of dates, one that can be debated in historical terms. It is a deeper matter of narrative agency—the intentional and motive force of historical change—and the conception of the position of narrative protagonist. The protagonist of the Israeli narrative is the Jews, as leading individuals and groups. They are the agents of their historical destiny, acting with and against forces in the larger historical surround. In the Palestinian version, nearly all agency is given to major European powers imposing their late imperialist ambitions on a small people whose victimization is inevitable, given the unequal force of their opponent. The Jews in this version lose their protagonist status, and become the willing tool of imperialist masters. The differences separating these stories are profound. To analyze them in narrative terms, as well as historical-archival terms, is not a trivial occupation.

Deep Wells of Narrative Power: Telling the Self

Discussions of nationalist narratives, and indeed, all larger-scale historical narrative inevitably devolve back to the structure of individual identity, and that structure is increasingly acknowledged to be narrative in form. Constituting and maintaining the integrated sense of self over time is the work of narrative at the level of the individual mind, involving acts of highlighting and suppression to sustain coherent identity, the work of memory and forgetting, the hermeneutics of experience. Narratives of collective power and narratives of individual integrity are bound together at their roots since both can be theorized in terms of serial sequencing, foregrounding and suppression, selection of motifs of meaning, the assignment of agency, and, finally, causal responsibility. As an instrument of coherence and meaning reaching from the deepest interiority of the self outward to and beyond the boundaries of the sovereign nation, narrative, this deceptively formal and dispassionate area of literary theory, has immense carrying power. The relation of narrative to the work of the mind—conscious, unconscious, dreamwork—is not a new insight. Psychoanalysis has been working out the transformational relations between experience and narrative ever since Freud and Breuer's pathbreaking *Studies on Hysteria* in 1895, but in recent decades narrative has taken its mainstream place in the academic psychology of the self.

The compelling work of Dan P. McAdams, to name a frequently cited and highly respected psychologist, attracted many research psychologists interested in the study of personality and the concept of the self to examine the processes and formal elements of narrative as central to their project. His important 1993 book, *The Stories We Live By: Personal Myths and the Making of the Self*, summarizes a decade of research and theory by himself and many others, and nonspecialists can usefully consult his 1996 article, "Personality, Modernity, and the Storied Self: A Contemporary Framework for Studying Persons."[32] The breadth and depth of research that places narrative at the center of personal identity is nicely displayed in Jefferson A. Singer's survey of the field in 2004: "In a quiet but consistent way, a new subdiscipline of personality psychology—narrative identity research—has emerged." Only gradually becoming distinct from its overlap with other areas of psychology and the other humanities, "now, however, it is clear that there is a body of midcareer and younger empirical researchers who place narrative identity at the center of personality."[33] From a historian theorist's perspective, the imbrication of narrative with nearly every area of humane study is testimony to its importance, and I note with great interest that the research psychologists routinely cite philosophers (Ricoeur references William James often) and even psychoanalysts, an unexpected rapprochement. McAdams's coedited anthology *Identity and Story: Creating Self in Narrative*[34] offers a selection of ongoing mainstream research as of 2006; the title reveals the central theme. This is a densely populated field of psychology now, with lively disputes and research models, but unified in the core insight that narrative formulation (as a series of interiorized operations within a commonly legible form) is indispensable to human self-awareness and sense of coherence. Personal narrative is always understood by academic psychologists as psychosocial: the life story is "jointly authored by the person and his or her defining culture."[35] Narrative is how the individual finds a location in history.

The psychic work narrative does at the core of personal identity—an insight shared by psychoanalysts and research psychologists, and by Hayden White—anchors the persuasive force of narrative in the public sphere. Narratives are layered, from the interior of the self out to local and public collectivities, and the effect of narrative in maintaining identity may be the engine of its power in the public realm. "Telling one's story" has become the equivalent of advocating and justifying the point of view of the narrative protagonist, and thus taking the protagonist position is a serious and political act. Storyness is argument. Nonetheless, parallel, contradictory, self-justifying narratives do not advance understanding, in the political or intellectual sense. But when narratives carry the burden of national and ethnic identity, it is hard to see what a correction might look like, how it might take root.

The most impressive thing about the near-universal adoption of "narrative" as a central principle of understanding in so many areas of human concern is that it is regarded as equally powerful at every scale, from the most inward and individual conceptions of selfhood and identity outwards, layer by layer, through small relational areas, social institutions, group identity and ethnic histories, national histories—especially those that exist in conflicting temporal parallels (our Israeli/Palestinian, Albanian/Serbian examples). The public and social impact of narrative is intense because narrative goes "all the way down" in psychic organization. At the same time, the authority of public uses of narrative (in national self-assertions, political explanations of, say, Islam and the West) enhances the weight of the more personal and small-scale deployments of narrative—in a continuing feedback loop of self-authorizations.

History, in terms offered by Hayden White, is a "discourse of the real." And the questions he poses about this verbal artifact, balanced between "the discursive" construct and "the real" past, are exactly the ones we have to take to the political battlefield of narrative: it may seem too obvious for statement, but crucial and expanding areas of the post-postmodern world have circled back to where Hayden White first drew our attention, to the buried procedures that reveal *how* narratives are constructed, not merely the acknowledgement *that* they are. The question he recognized implicit in every narrative is still *the* question: "What wish is enacted, what desire is gratified, by the fantasy that real events are properly represented when they can be shown to display the formal coherency of a story? In the enigma of this wish, this desire, we catch a glimpse of the cultural function of narrativizing discourse in general."[36]

It is disconcerting but deeply enlightening that the most defenselessly traditional, even naively humanist of the artifacts made from language—narrative—is proving to be the most resilient. Endlessly deconstructed, disassembled to expose the wish-fulfillment inner workings of human agency and order, debunked in its claims to picture reality, narrative form proves both eerily elastic and tenacious in its grip on human purposes. The unillusioned yet unresisting embrace of narrative may prove the center of the post-postmodern stance.

Notes

1. A select sample of enduring interest in the history/fiction question and the problems posed to the integrity of the discipline by postmodern insights should include: Kuisma Korhonen, ed., *Tropes for the Past: Hayden White and the History/Literature Debate* (Amsterdam: Rodopi, 2006), the very interesting proceedings of a conference held in Finland; David Carr, Thomas R. Flynn, and Rudolf A. Makkreel, eds., *The Ethics of History* (Evanston, IL: Northwestern University Press, 2004), which engages issues of integrity and moral reponsibility in the

wake of postmodernism; Ann Curthoys and John Docker, *Is History Fiction?* (Ann Arbor: University of Michigan Press, 2005) for a viewpoint grounded in specifically Australian historical conflicts.

2. Michael Roth, review of *Sublime Historical Experience*, by Frank Ankersmit, *History and Theory* 46 (2007): p. 66.

3. Lauro Martines, review of *Changing Patrons*, by Jill Burke, *Times Literary Supplement*, February 25, 2005. "To read a document in an innocently empirical key is to want to take terms such as 'love' and 'friendship' at face value, when in fact they were notoriously rhetorical. . . . Texts might not be what they seemed."

4. Elizabeth A. Clark, *History, Theory, Text: Historians and the Linguistic Turn* (Cambridge, MA: Harvard University Press, 2004), p. ix.

5. Boaz Shoshan, *The Poetics of Islamic Historiography: Deconstructing Tabari* (Leiden, Neth.: Brill Publishers, 2004), p. 25.

6. Robert M. Stein, "Literary Criticism and the Evidence for History," in *Writing Medieval History*, ed. Nancy Partner (London: Hodder Arnold, 2005), p. 75.

7. Ibid.

8. John Warren succinctly describes the role of Richard Evans as an expert witness during the 2000 libel case brought by Holocaust denier David Irving against American academic Deborah Lipstadt. "The Rankean Tradition in British Historiography, 1840 to 1950," in *Writing History: Theory and Practice*, eds. Stefan Berger, Heiko Feldner, and Kevin Passmore (London: Hodder Arnold, 2003), pp. 23–25. In the trial, all concerned, including David Irving, agreed on a definition of history along strict empiricist lines, and Evans successfully testified that Irving passed off deliberate and fraudulent distortions cunningly disguised as objective history. Postmodernism and deconstruction, which are alternatives of emplotment, were never at issue in this trial.

9. William Safire, "Narrative: The New Story of Story," On Language, *New York Times Magazine*, December 5, 2004.

10. Geoffrey Garin, quoted in Robin Toner, "For 'Don't Ask, Don't Tell,' Split on Party Lines," *New York Times*, June 8, 2007.

11. Michiko Kakutani, "The Politics of Prose," *New York Times*, April 22, 2007.

12. Hayden White, "The Value of Narrativity in the Representation of Reality," *The Content of the Form* (Baltimore: Johns Hopkins University Press, 1987), p. 1.

13. White quotes Barthes. "Value of Narrativity," p. 1.

14. Ibid., p. 2.

15. Ginia Bellafante, "The Frenchwoman, in All Her Moods," *New York Times*, March 5, 2004.

16. Michael Kimmelman, "Racing to Keep Up with the Newest," *New York Times*, November 19, 2004.

17. Arthur Lubow, "Re-Moderning," *New York Times Magazine*, October 3, 2004.

18. Howard Gardner, *Changing Minds: The Art and Science of Changing Our Own and Other People's Minds* (Cambridge, MA: Harvard Business School Press, 2004).

19. "Living in the world, where the world is that of late modernity, involves various distinctive tensions on the level of the self. We can analyse these most easily by understanding them as dilemmas which, on one level or another, have to be resolved in order to preserve a coherent narrative of self-identity." Anthony Giddens, *Modernity and Self-Identity: Self and Society in the Late Modern Age* (Stanford, CA: Stanford University Press, 1991), p. 187.

20. Galen Strawson, "A Fallacy of Our Age," *Times Literary Supplement*, October 15, 2004, in which he vehemently insists that the formal structure of his own life is episodic.

21. Descriptions of the Scholars' Initiative project can be found online. Ylli Bajraktari and Daniel Serwer, "Explaining the Yugoslav Catastrophe: The Quest for a Common Narrative," U.S. Institute of Peace, http://www.usip.org/pubs/usipeace_briefings/2006/0105_narrative.html; the original prospectus with the list of international scholars and team assignments, "The Scholars Initiative Prospectus," is also available. "The Scholars' Initiative: Confronting the Yugoslav Controversies, 2001–2005," Department of History, Purdue University, http://www.cla.purdue.edu/history/facstaff/Ingrao/si/scholarsprospectus.htm.

22. Until the book publication, the SI team reports are available online at "The Scholars' Initiative: Confronting the Yugoslav Controversies," Department of History, Purdue University, http://www.cla.purdue.edu/academic/history/facstaff/Ingrao/si/scholars.htm.

23. Private communication with team member.

24. David Campbell, "MetaBosnia: Narratives of the Bosnian War," *Review of International Studies* 24 (1998), p. 263.

25. Robert Worth, "In Iraq, a Tug of War over the Truth," *New York Times*, April 24, 2005.

26. Paul Ricoeur, "The Interweaving of History and Fiction," *Time and Narrative* (Chicago: University of Chicago Press, 1988), 3: p. 187. This essay is essential reading for Ricoeur's views on the psychological grounds for the imbrication of history and fiction at the level of collective narratives.

27. Chief of Staff Moshe Ya'alon, quoted in *Ha'aretz*, online edition, August 13, 2004.

28. Ahmad H. Sa'di, "Catastrophe, Memory and Identity: Al Nakbah as a Component of Palestinian Identity," *Israel Studies* 7, no. 2 (2002), pp. 175–98.

29. Yossi Alpher, "Geography Is Doable, History Isn't," bitterlemons.org, May 23, 2005, http://www.bitterlemons.org/previous/bl230505ed17.html#isr1. The entire issue of September 4, 2006, is also given to the subject of "Narratives Revisited."

30. Hayden White, "Historical Discourse and Literary Writing," *Tropes for the Past*, p. 30.

31. The homepage of Peace Research Institute in the Middle East (PRIME) is http://www.vispo.com/PRIME/. A downloadable PDF of the two-narratives textbook *Learning Each Other's Historical Narrative* is available through the website of the public radio program *Speaking of Faith*: http://speakingoffaith .publicradio.org/programs/twonarratives/adwan-textbook.shtml. Dan Bar-On and Sami Adwan explain the textbook and their pedagogical approach in "The Psychology of Better Dialogue Between Two Separate but Interdependent Narratives," *Israeli and Palestinian Narratives of Conflict: History's Double Helix*, ed. Robert I. Rotberg (Bloomington: Indiana University Press, 2006), pp. 205–24.

32. Dan P. McAdams, *The Stories We Live By: Personal Myths and the Making of the Self* (New York: William Morrow, 1993); "Personality, Modernity, and the Storied Self: A Contemporary Framework for Studying Persons," *Psychological Inquiry* 7 (1996), pp. 295–321.

33. Jefferson A. Singer, "Narrative Identity and Meaning Making Across the Adult Lifespan: An Introduction," *Journal of Personality* 72, no. 3 (2004), pp. 437–59, offers a survey of this field with extensive bibliography.

34. Dan P. McAdams, Ruthellen Josselson, and Amia Lieblich, eds., *Identity and Story: Creating Self in Narrative* (Washington, DC: American Psychological Association, 2006).

35. Dan P. McAdams, "Personality, Modernity," p. 307.

36. Hayden White, "Value of Narrativity," p. 4.

5

"Nobody Does It Better"

RADICAL HISTORY AND HAYDEN WHITE

Keith Jenkins

I want to begin this essay for Hayden White—an essay inconceivable without White and therefore indebted to him—by sketching out, in its very much longer first part, what I take to be the necessary conditions of possibility for the production of a radical history—by which I mean a history that, from the point of view of the current "state of the situation," is deemed to be of little or no significance. What do I need to be able to think this kind of history, and what are some of the consequences of doing so? And in part two, I want to explain how I see all of this relating back to White.

Part One

Without further preliminaries, then, let me re-pose the question governing this first part: what are the necessary conditions of possibility for the production of a radical history? And here I want to take a step back so that I can identify as my starting point certain *ontological* presuppositions which, acting as *axioms*, will then allow me to build a history thereon, axioms and the resultant history both being, on this occasion, presented in tabular form (and thus somewhat skeletally, impressionistically).

(1) I take as my originary axiom the existence of matter, of materiality, of "actuality." I take it that the "stuff" we call, for example, the

world, the universe, etc., is really out there and is therefore not the product of my current mental state. Of course I cannot prove this; I cannot get out of my head to check if there is something outside of it, but my working premise is that there is. In that sense I'm a *realist*, but a realist of a certain kind; namely, a *transcendental realist*—by which I mean that not only does such stuff exist (and has existed previously and will exist in the future), but that it transcends each and every attempt in each and every social formation to reduce it to their inhabitants' experiences, vocabularies, lexicons, abstractions, such that they might think that they really do *know* it. For it seems apparent that the actuality of "existence" skips free of every (definitive) anthropomorphism. Yet at the same time, such transcendental realism does not commit me to *metaphysical realism* (namely, that we can know the way things are independent of the way we access them). Rather, my type of realism commits me to precisely the opposite. Insofar as we can present examples of our intuitions via various representations, such intuitions/representations cannot escape the exact circumstances of their production; cannot shrug off the pressure of time and chance and so are thus *radically* contingent (in this instance, *radically* meaning forever irreducible to definitive meanings). In other words I hold the view (with Richard Rorty) that while the "world" is "out there," *meanings* are not; that while the world is "out there," *truths* are not, since meanings and truths are in sentences and sentences are not "out there."[1] There is therefore a radical break—an *ontological* break—between the "actuality" of the world (all that "stuff") and so-called reality, such reality being created/constituted by our human discourses which are "about" but which do not knowingly correspond to that to which they "refer." Indeed, it is these discourses—broadly construed—which alone *make* the world variously meaning-full, and we know of no other common reality than that thus constituted.

(2) This reduction of any "knowledge" we "may think we have" of the world (past, present, future) to the contingencies of knowledge production, distribution, reception, etc., means—as already noted but now rearticulated slightly—that we can never have access to the actualities of "stuff" plain, pure. That such "worlds" as ours are always just that, ours, and are thus *inescapably* human, *inescapably* meaning here, that just as giraffes or eagles have giraffe and eagle worlds—have their own species-

bound "readings" of the stuff of actuality, never cognizant of human readings of the same phenomena—so, locked up in our own human readings, we have no access to giraffe and eagle "reality." Nor is there some form of neutral actuality/reality that offers a way of adjudicating between different species' readings in the hope of finding a trans-species "real reality." Thus we human animals ("just one more species doing its best") are indeed just doing our best to pragmatically live out a life unknown to other species and which is for all of us—both them and us—ultimately unfathomable.

(3) Such irreducibility of the actuality of the stuff of our "worded world" to our human sensations, experiences, concepts, categories, schemas, analogies, whereby we try to transform our "experiences" of the "concrete" into the "concrete in thought"; the inadequacy of every representation to fully capture the objects "subjectified" by our gaze (to gain subject-object identity; full presence, etc.), means that, when carrying out our meaning-making operations, we cannot but become (on the back of our transcendental realism) *intersubjective idealists*; namely, that it is we who make our actuality "real" by endowing attributes to stuff which thus realizes "it." This is a way of still thinking of "actuality"—after all these years—along the lines of the old Kantian "thing-in-itself"; as that ungraspable *excess* which thwarts ("for all we know") all our efforts to make things identical to us; the same as us. I therefore hold, axiomatically, that the stuff of existence exceeds our every limit, transverses all our boundaries, escapes our most definitive closures, making both our experiential actions and our thoughts unremittingly and inescapably *open*: ludic, aleatory, heuristic, and thus, once again, radically contingent. And here we might recall some recent and well-known formulations of this excess: Albert Camus' absurd, the sublime of Jean-François Lyotard and White, Alain Badiou's multiples, Jacques Lacan's Real, Jacques Derrida's undecidables, Julia Kristeva's semiotic, Jean Baudrillard's symbolic-semiotic spiral. Of course, we must not for a moment think of such formulations as ever being adequate to the excess. For the excess, the *sublime*, is not a delimited object or thing; it is not something which we knowingly "lack" and which, if found, would allow us to fulfill our (sometime) human desire for completion, closure, totality. For the sublime is forever unpresentable, is something unable to ever be historicized, is precisely nonontolo-

gizable—otherwise it just wouldn't be sublime—and is therefore just a further dimension of our human imagination which posits that beyond our every closure there lurks an "undoing outside," which, despite all our attempts to disavow or negate or just plain forget, hauntingly persists to remind us that beyond all the "somethings" we have made out of "nothing" (making "something out of nothing" is the story of our lives), is the sense of that (constitutive) nothing that can spell *ruin* for even our very best *representations*. Thus to my growing list of axioms—to my transcendental realism, intersubjective idealism, and the undoing sublime—I add *radical antirepresentationalism* (which, in a nutshell and following Paul de Man, can be put like this: that it is not a priori certain that language functions according to principles that are those, or are like those, of the phenomenal world. And that it is, therefore, not a priori certain that language is a reliable source of information about anything but itself). To this antirepresentationalism, I want to add a certain type of nominalism, a (metaphorical) naming process, that, because of its unavoidable *violence*, forcefully welds together the ontological (and the ontic) to the political, thus to what is axiomatically just one expression of the (power) political: *history*. In articulating this interconnection, I have found it useful to think of this production of meaning as having (after various suggestions by Jacques Derrida) *three* levels of violence.

(4) To make (to realize) a meaning, to bring meaning into the world, is ultimately an act of violence—a violence of "writing" that can be called *first-level violence*. Because there is no one-to-one natural correspondence between word and world, no literal entailment of signifier to signifier and thence to the putative signified and thence to the putative referent, then to get the actuality of the world into a "language" it never asked to be put in is to always establish both a power and a metaphorical relationship (that tree as if it really was a tree, that past as if it really was history). Yet, accurate as this is, Derrida thinks that the notion of a metaphorical relationship still runs the risk of carrying (naïve) realist overtones, in that it may suggest that there is (already) a meaningful "reality," some solid ground(ing), to which the sign-system refers—albeit figuratively. But obviously there isn't. Consequently, the founding concepts of meaning are instances not of metaphor generally but the (metaphorical) trope of *catachresis*: a violent production of meaning, an imposition, an abuse. Derrida:

I have always tried to expose the way in which philosophy is literary, not so much because it is metaphor but because it is *catachresis*. The term metaphor implies a relation to an original "property" of "meaning," a "proper" sense to which it indirectly or equivocally refers, whereas *catachresis* is a violent production of meaning, an abuse which refers to no exterior or proper norm.[2]

Yet, while this violent call to meaning is, of course, a necessary one if any meanings are to be produced at all—since this violent imposition is the very condition of the possibility of meaning—Derrida is concerned to show how this naming process can never achieve what it would like to achieve; namely, literal, full presence. And for him it is precisely *différance*, as the irreducible tension (aporia) between what he calls the "idealized transcendental gesture" and the necessity of empirical inscription, which is the site of its unavoidable undoing.

Now, how can this undoing be developed in what is termed the level of *secondary violence*; well, *différance* again says it all. The argument goes thus.

For Derrida, every sign wants to say what it "really" means. This is the sign's motivation; the idealized gesture of the (quasi) transcendental—to achieve full presence and so forth. Yet, for the sign to operate as a sign it must be irreducible to one context, it must be repeatable (albeit always slightly differently) in other contexts (*iterable*), otherwise it just wouldn't be a sign. Consequently, the necessity of empirical inscription guarantees the logical impossibility of the purity of the transcendental gesture. Nevertheless, the "myth" of the transcendental (universals, absolutes . . .) remains the animating force behind the signs of, say, Justice, Law, Ethics, or History, such that it is here that the aporetic tension inevitably resides. For while the originary violence of the sign enables us to think the transcendental gesture, that gesture is never realizable at the empirical level. Consequently, Justice or Law or Ethics or History are always only accessible at the level of the empirical/iterable (as justices, laws, ethics, histories . . .) and yet are irreducible to them. Historical discourse then (now concentrating on "history") cannot ever escape indeterminacy; cannot escape *différance*; of being always both the idealized gesture *and* iterable—that is, being always *open* to new inscriptions, meanings, to interminable redescriptions. The fulfillment of any idealized gesture is thus permanently delayed; will always be "to come" yet will never arrive: there is no "last instance," no "last word," no closure, no "final solution." We

shall never know what History/history "really is"—that will remain a secret, like the name and the face of God. Its putative aim—the truth-full
reconstruction of the past—is thus an impossible "myth," yet one which
continuously energizes historians' productions. We shall, courtesy of *différance*, never know what the nature of history is any more than we shall
know The Law, Justice, Ethics, or God; we shall never know the past "in
and for itself"; for its "own sake."

Now, it is precisely this "fact" (and if there is a fact, this is it) that
Derrida thinks we have tried to forget; to disavow. And it is this refusal
to remember the violent, contingent, and thus arbitrary relationship of
words and things in favor of literal truths, permanent categories, invariable essences, and nonrelativistic ethics, that goes under the name of *secondary violence*—the violence of forgetting.

This "mind-world" of secondary violence—of "realism," of repre-
sentationalism, of "real" ethical imperatives—is the one most of us habitually inhabit: this is our "reality," this is what we "take for granted."
And it is therefore precisely the *unreality* of these realities which Derrida
and others wish us to recall by deconstructing via *différance* those pro-
tective, fictive shelters of secondary violence which, if I can put it this
way, the overwhelming thrust of the Western tradition erected as barriers
against "the other(s)" (modernity and the modern nation-state being the
swan song of this tradition). I mean, all those "infinite fixes," those rigid
designators, those binary oppositions, those various/sometime white,
ethnic, gendered, onto-theological fantasies which, embodied in phal-
lologocentric articulations, have included amongst their vehicles numer-
ous histories, not least those finding sometime expression in uppercase
(metanarrative) and lowercase (certaintist/academic/professional) forms.
Derrida, as I read him—along with other radical post-structuralist/post-
modern historians—is concerned to remove all and every remaining,
privileging carapace insofar as they have tried (and try) to help legitimate
reasons excusing acts of *third-level violence*; that is, the everyday empirical
violence of exclusion, rape, murder, war, genocide. At which point, the
deconstructionist drive works *backwards* from third- to first-level violence
. . . for it can now be shown that level three violence is not of a *necessary*
kind, but is just the arbitrary outcome of its catachretic founding, thus
opening it up—de-realizing reality—to "alternative realities" which could
be—which *ought* to be—explicitly liberating, empowering, and uncom-

promisingly emancipating for those people needing these things: most of us. This is not to say that any such "new reality" will not be "arbitrary," will not be another simulacrum, but the deconstructionist hope is that this world might be a better one than the one we inhabit now. This is a hope for a "lesser violent" world based on the interminable revisions of its *axioms*, an endlessly "open" world that, recognizing its undecidability, its provisionality, refuses all closures. Ernesto Laclau has seen the unavoidability of this better than most:

> The metaphysical (logocentric) discourse of the West is coming to an end, and philosophy in its twilight has performed a last service for us in the deconstruction of its own terrain. Let us think, for instance, of Derrida's undecidables. Once undecidability has reached the ground itself—once the organisation of a certain camp is governed by a hegemonic decision—hegemonic because it is not objectively determined, because different decisions were also possible—then the realm of philosophy comes to an end and the realm of politics begins. This realm will be inhabited by a different type of discourse . . . which . . . constructs the world on the "grounds" of radical undecidability.[3]

This is the sort of politics the radical historian is committed to.

(5) And so I come now to some of the details of that radical history which might (possibly) be used to help realize such emancipating goals by *building* on the above set of "open" axioms a sort of *superstructural* history that might transform and supersede the "normal" historians' "traditional calling" by responding to a call that comes not from the past at all but directly from ethics, from politics. Radical historians, unlike "normal" ones, don't go to work to understand the past on it own terms and for its own sake; radical historians don't work on behalf of the people who lived in the past: they work for us.

So to the question of how to proceed to the establishment of the necessary conditions for the production of such a radical history, my answer, on this occasion, is *dialectically*. That is to say that I want to show, initially, how the conditions of possibility for a closed, empirical/epistemologically striving *nonradical* history—for a history that attempts to establish assured historical knowledge, understanding, and meaning—*cannot* ever be met: this acts as my *thesis*. Of course, traditional historians of whatever stripe—the majority of the history profession, say—are not unaware of some of the factors that deny them surety; they intuit that their type of history has epistemological (and/or even scientific) ambitions it lacks the means to deliver. But more often than not it is "business as usual," as such troubling thoughts are brushed under the carpet or, if raised to the level of consciousness, are articulated as "problems" to solve, "challenges" to overcome, and "difficulties" to work through, as they "come to terms with the past." And it is my argument—my *antithesis*—that such limits and difficulties are not seen by radical historians as problems at all but as *opportunities* for newness. Radical historians thus turn the weaknesses of "proper history" into strengths, celebrate the fact that historians' representations (including their own) are *always* failed representations, that historians qua historians always get the past wrong, and that it is these "facts" which become the basis for a new *synthesis* which, discarding the desire for closure, builds uncertainly on uncertainty. At which point old (modernist) empirical/epistemologically striving histories in whatever case—histories that can never achieve closure nor prevent interminable openness—hopefully "drop out of the conversation" as radical (postmodern) histories take their place. There is no need for any nostalgia here—modernist histories have had their day in the sun—and thus there is no need to keep "a foot in both camps" in some middle-ground, conserving consensus: we can all become thoroughly postmodern.

* * *

So let me now give some substance to the above argument, beginning by outlining my *thesis*, that is, by sketching out the irremovable obstacles to the establishment of any empirical/epistemological history of closure. And let me retabulate as I work through *six* relevant areas.

(1) First there is the problematicizing contamination—the interpretive bulk—of the historian as author. Frank Ankersmit sets the scene and triggers a train of thought. Ankersmit:

We have historical writing in order to compensate for the absence of the past. So whereas in the case of pictorial and political representation the represented has a logical priority to its representation, in the case of historical representation the reverse is the case, namely, that the represented—that is, the past—depends for its (onto)logical status on its representation. No representation, no past.[4]

No representation, no past: exactly. And because such representations by no means come from nowhere, then it is the "writers" of history, historians (and those acting as if they were historians), who have a prior "logical priority": no representation, no history is (tautologically) "correct," as is, no representer, no representation.

Representers—historians—come in all shapes and sizes to the production of the historicized past, but none come innocently. Historians are affected by all kinds of suasive desires and material everyday pressures that are not left behind when they enter the study—by ambitions, jealousies, careerist aspirations; by institutionalization, duplicities, and disavowals; by niggling worries, acts of gratitude and support and various incompetencies—that cannot avoid unevenly, singularly, influencing and conditioning the practices and the products of the author-historian. History is a contaminated discourse that cannot be purified of the tensions and ambiguities—never fully knowable—of situation, circumstance, authorization, legitimation, play. Any "genealogy of history," as Sande Cohen puts it, by any half-thorough account, must demonstrate such "mixed origins," which no appeal to the archive, the sources, the data, the facts and objectivity, can negate or transcend.[5] These are the circumstances that variously and immeasurably infuse the historians' texts with life, and that, while not ignoring the empirical/epistemological components of historicizations, are underdetermined by them.

(2) In which context the next question is, what, more precisely, is these historians' referent and its status? Could it literally be the past per se? Well, no, since that no longer exists. Moreover, even if it did, (the *idea* of) that past is far too complicated to become a fixed object of inquiry. For there is never a solid, "real" past that acts as the common/neutral past for everyone—any more than there is a common/neutral time it exists "in." Rather, many different levels of many pasts and many presents and many perspectival "timings of time," congeal and become unstuck, sometimes rapidly sometimes slowly, and these interrelationships affect how we choose, as Cohen puts it, to initiate, to accept, to reject the data of experience, interpreting and assessing inner and outer relations. Present habits and memories, continues Cohen,

incessantly weave themselves into degrees of pastness in the form of powerful memories mixed with obsessions blended with attempts to self-distract, joined with new projects of forgetting, so that there is no neutral present's relation to the past—as. Remember that the present "is" no more objectively nor subjectively real than the past, as both are embroiled in the other in terms of actualization in any present . . . we are constantly dismantling and assembling the present; we are constantly dissembling the present to have a different effect/affect of and with the past.[6]

No stable referent here then.

So can the historian's referent be the *traces* of the past, the (always already historicized) archive, as widely construed as one wishes? Well, no. Because although historians refer to the archive and to, say, the documents therein and the "facts" that may be generated out of them in terms of singular statements that "correspond" to singular or clusters of singular "evidential sources," and though they *reference* these things copiously in footnotes, these things are still not their *referent*.

So what can it be? And the answer is simply that historians' referent is "nothing" but the product of their *inferences* based upon their existential (personal, ethical, public, ideological) condition, their previous/current "dealing" in the field, their modes of prefiguration which work up the "material" they have to make it into an object capable of analysis, and their constitutive "research" concerns, theses, and so on, which, in never-stable interconnections, *cause* some of the traces they find/produce to become activated as relevant sources and thence as *evidence* for any arguments they happen to be running. (The "past itself" doesn't have in it any arguments or problems that historians solve . . . only historians have arguments, as they seek to establish their readings over others.) And that on these bases, they then *infer* a past—either simple or complex—which now *fits* their data, their position, their inferences. And this inferential process *cannot* work in reverse, no matter how much pleading to the contrary. For historians cannot *know* the past—especially that part of it which they are putatively "finding" for the first time as they seek the holy grail of "originality"—and then search for the sources to correspond to it, thus confirming it as "knowledge." Rather, the process is that of using "this and that" from which a past to conform to "this and that" is inferred. This inference, now the historicized past, which constitutes the figural "content" of their texts to which they refer . . . , *this* is their *referent*, a referent let us note and underline, which is "always in thought": no one can knowingly ignore Roland Barthes' possessive strictures on this.[7]

(3) But note now some further aspect of the epistemic status of this referent. Note *four* things. Note, *first* of all, that this is a referent that cannot ever have the status of truth or definitiveness—it is only an inference after all—and it cannot be objective, either. For not only is it self-referencing, but other self-referencers (historians) going to, say, the same archives and working on even the same traces/sources, can and do infer very different pasts; indeed, history (as historiography) is composed of such "interpretive differences" that no appeal to the facts as other historicizations (inferences) can close down. And, of course, lurking in this area is the old fact-value problematic which ensures that, whatever the inferred relationship between phenomena and meaning, that relationship is never entailed: "the past" can be read and "made to mean" any way you like.

Note, *second*, the fact that inferences are always arguments means, again, that truth cannot ever come into it.[8] For as we all know, arguments are never true or false; arguments can only be valid or invalid, so that, no matter how many times "forgetful" historians slip the notion of an argument "that's true" into their "discussions," a true argument, like another old favorite, the true interpretation, is an oxymoron. Note, *third*, that because the historian's referent is inferential then the kinds of things inferred—structures, processes, trends, watersheds, statistical runs, influences, movements, explanations, meanings—were never actually there in the first place, or at least, not in the way Lord Nelson's flagship HMS *Victory* was once there. This historicized past is therefore a past which (as Hayden White puts it after Michael Oakeshott) no one ever experienced while it was in the process of taking shape, that no one ever observed, and which exists *now* only in the minds of, and the texts created by, historians and those acting *as if* they were historians. There is thus, as Carolyn Steedman has put it, "a double nothingness" in the writing of history. History is about something that never did happen in the way in which it comes to be represented (the happening exists in the telling, in the text), and it is made of materials (the inferences) that are also not there—in the archive or anywhere else.[9] Jacques Rancière has made the same point: "There is history because there is an absence . . . [and] the status of history depends on the treatment of this two-fold absence of the "thing itself" that is no longer there [the past is past] and that never was . . . because it never was such that it was [and is] told."[10] And note *fourthly* and finally, that the *logic* of inference is the logic of *probability*, which is to say that the historian's logic is not that of the *syllogism* (although syllogistic reasoning can appear in parts of the historian's text), but rather the logic of the *enthymeme*, a form of logic which cannot lead to definitive conclusions—and thus closure—but can only be to the occasion for the expression of an "undecidable decision," an aporetic choice. For enthymemes always involve a calculation of probabilities and a judgment, which leaves things open so that one can always argue to the contrary: "both sides of the case." Consequently, history as a probable/possible reading—and this is the status of *all* histories—is always neither rigorously true or rigorously false; at best it can have to recommend it "a certain appearance in its favour." This, a measure of the shortfall of any epistemological claims for histories, is as good as it gets.

(4) On this account, history has all the elements that fulfill the classic criteria for something to be of a rhetorical kind, namely, a method "to invent subjects and arguments, to organize discourse, and to make good judgements,"[11] and is therefore the type of phenomenon Aristotle called *illusio*, which, because it deals with things contingent and opaque, can only be demonstrated or "proved." On this reasoning history cannot ever be a science. For since history has neither a definitive object of inquiry (the "past" looked at "this way and that way" may be imagined but definitive examples of it cannot be presented), nor any definitive (universal) method of inquiry, then such a discourse, as Martin Davies has put it, "belongs properly to the realm of rhetoric," since this is of a kind of discourse that, "not dealing with "any one definite class of objects" is "merely a faculty for furnishing arguments." Moreover, since history and politics also have an instrumental, ideological intention, their aim is rhetorical: they are concerned to "discover the real and apparent means of persuasion."[12]

Since history, then, deals only with contingencies (accidental facts, antecedent possibilities, metonymic extrapolations. . .) and proceeds by means of enthymemes (rhetorical induction) that can only provide a lesser standard of proof than "logic" offers, then history will remain interminably open, always waiting for the next interlocutor to arrive. One always comes along.

(5) Which means, still pursuing this line of thought, that as *illusio*, as inferential acts of the imagination, historical representations and

consciousness (of this and that) are both fictive (that is, fabricated, made up, fashioned, *fictio*) and, as the product of rhetorical devices and stylistic figures, of an *aesthetic* kind. Such aesthetic figures are not, of course, subject to epistemological checks at the level of the text: an aesthetic cannot answer to epistemology. Of course, as already noted, empirical/epistemological elements can and do (once things have been "put under a description") operate at the level of singular statements and so on, but a discourse with a story to tell in the form of a *narratio* is always a manifestation of that mixture of the "found" (the sources, etc.) and the imagined (the inferences) wherein, between these two unstable poles, one is always in a radically indeterminate "middle range." This is indeed a past as much imagined as found or, more precisely I think, *more* imagined than found: the aesthetic overdetermines the "empirical." Always.

And the radical historian likes this overdetermination, likes the essentially aesthetic nature of *all* histories. For it is not, incidentally, as if there are some histories (say modernist ones) which really are of an empirical/epistemological kind "all the way down" and that these can be set against aesthetic histories (say postmodern ones). Rather, the point is that all histories—just to be histories—always have been and always will be of an aesthetic type; all histories are of the type the radical/postmodern historian raises to the level of consciousness: rhetorical/aesthetic histories are the only game in town. Thus, logically speaking, no empirical/epistemological histories, and no empirical/epistemological historians, have ever existed on the face of the earth. Traditional historians of this type are generally quite proud and normally not at all defensive when they are called "empirical historians," indeed, many insist on being so called. But in fact no such specimen has ever been found and it beggars belief to think that they could "ever have been imagined." R.I.P.

(6) And so I come directly to the area which Hayden White has pretty much made his own over the last forty years or so: narrativity. To be sure, right from the start White has been much criticized by various history establishments across the left-right ideological spectrum—what do you expect if you insist history is a kind of fiction-making?—and many historians and some theorists continue to critique, disavow, or just plain ignore him. There are some very silly people around. And of course, I am aware of some of these critiques, just as I am aware that White has made some (minor) adjustments to his position over the years. And I rec-

ognize that White isn't—nor would want to be—the closing/last word on anything. Nevertheless, all that said, I think the radical historian can subscribe—I subscribe—*entirely* to White's decisionist/impositionist/singular/relativistic position on narrativity. Thus I take it as read, for example, "that no given set of events figure forth apodictically the kind of meanings with which stories provide them . . . no one and nothing *lives* a story" (*Tropics of Discourse*); that "the meaning, form, or coherence of events, whether real or imaginary ones, is a function of their narrativism" (*Figural Realism*); that "one must face the fact that when it comes to apprehending the historical record, there are no grounds found in it for preferring one way of construing its meaning over another" (*The Content of the Form*); that the only grounds for choosing one perspective on history rather than another are ultimately aesthetic and ethical/political: "the aged Kant was right, in short, we are free to conceive history as we please just as we are free to make of it what we will" (*Metahistory*). And I sign up to all these axioms, just as I sign up to most of the detail whereby White establishes the *metahistorical* nature of *all* history productions vis-à-vis the ubiquity of tropes, emplotments, argumentative governing, and ideological positioning; I mean, can you imagine a history that is not troped, not emplotted, not governed by argumentation and not suasively/ideologically intended? Could one exist? Now that *is* a rhetorical question.

And I subscribe to all of this because I also sign up to what I think of as White's radical "philosophy of history." That the past is sublime in its "whole" and problematic in its parts; that at the level of meaning (not truth but *meaning*) historical narratives are inexpungeably singular/relativistic; that skepticism about historical knowledge/meaning is a necessary counter to dogmas everywhere; that "the past" has no legitimate gatekeepers who can tell us what we can and cannot do with it (least of all academic historians); that no one owns the past or has a monopoly on how to appropriate it; that the interminable openness of the past to countless readings should be celebrated and democratized in the hope that we might, disobediently, seriously entertain those creative historical "distortions offered by minds capable of looking at the past with the same seriousness as ourselves but with different affective and intellectual orientations." Collectively, these practices should alert us to the conserving nature of now-preeminent narrations that tidily lock up events to keep them from being radically relocated, and which absorb experimentation in the name of a fake pluralism; and, further, that the essence of a radical history is its future-orientated politico/ethical thrust. White:

> I take ethics to be about the difference between what is (or was) the case and what ought to be (or ought to have been) the case in some department of human comportment, thought, or belief [opening] up a space in which "something has to be done." This is quite different from morality that, on the basis of some dogmatism, insists on telling us what we *must and must not do* in a given situation of choice. The historical past is "ethical" in that its subject matter (violence, loss, absence, the event, death) arouses in us the kind of ambivalent feelings, about ourselves as well as the "other," that appear in situations requiring choice and engagement in existentially determining ways.[13]

And this existentialism, this "humanism" with a performative rather than an essentialist subject—an old topos in White's work—is also invoked in the cause of permanent openness. Recalling Camus's having once written that in trying to find out whether or not life had to have a meaning to be lived and his conclusion that "it will be lived all the better if it has no meaning," White comments that "we might amend the statement to read: it will be lived all the better if it has no single meaning but many different ones."[14]

And I think, finally, that radical historians should always wear these kind of sentiments where White has always worn his: openly, explicitly, on his sleeve. White cannot have the last word for radical historians—for his is not the only voice that *ought* to be heard. But I think he deserves to have the first.

* * *

Now, history as I have presented it here could be seen—from an "orthodox" perspective—as being in pretty bad shape; it's difficult to imagine how this particular Humpty Dumpty could ever be put together again. At the "top" of my "open" axioms, it has contaminated writers, an object of inquiry they can neither access nor definitively present; it has a referent that is inferred and therefore imagined, which is another way of saying that given that inferences constitute history then history is imagined. Moreover, it has no definitive, shared method; rather, it is a mode of discourse of a rhetorical kind, a product of argumentation and figuration: an aesthetic *illusio*. In its presentation as *narratio* history has to have—simply to be a narrative—all the elements common to narrative per se. In other words, it has to be troped and emplotted and sustained by argumentation;

its articulation depends on textual poetics, rhetorical devices and figures, compositional strategies, intertextual readings, variable/contingent theories and methods and personal theses, which are expressed by, and expressive of, the singular circumstances of the author. None of these things are "found" in the past, none are discoverable in the famous "archive," but these are the conditional elements of any history. This is the way history just is for all of us . . . these are "its necessary conditions of possibility." And this condition is not *denied* but *accepted* willingly and reworked by radical historians. Radical historians *like* this history; they can live with it, use it, experiment with it, and, insofar as we still need histories at this point in time, direct it towards emancipation and liberation. (By which I mean the making possible of that which is considered impossible; to put an end to consensus.) And of course, radical historians recognize that history (historiography) just is impossible to close down, not just "once and for all," but at all. A history of this kind—and these are some of its consequences—means the end, surely, of every metanarrative edifice and of all those academic histories of an empirical/epistemologically striving type: toward both of these genres we must have that incredulity Lyotard reserved for metanarratives, as well as working in opposition to all those who would work to prevent what, in the end, radical historians like: the fact that historicizations of the past can be anything you want them to be. This raises, of course, all kinds of dangers; it's always a risk, always a chance, to exist without something like foundations: some future historicization may well be monstrous. But it's not, I'm afraid, the case that this is a "risk worth taking" *as if* it were an option; it's a risk that is unavoidable: we have come, let's hope for better rather than worse, to the end of the illusion of the possibility of closure in such a manner that it seems incredible not only that (to reuse one of White's epigrams again) such histories have been imagined in the past but that they have actually been found. Radical historians hope that—insofar as we might *need* histories in the future at all, which is not obvious—such absurdities will not be repeated in the future even as farce, and certainly not as tragedy.

Part Two

I now come to what I hope by this point is obviously yet just another rhetorical question: what has all of this got to do with Hayden

White? For the answer is simple: *everything*. To be sure, in the above argument I have occasionally had in mind influences gleaned from what are by now old favorites, including Karl Marx, Friedrich Nietzsche, R. G. Collingwood, Louis Althusser, Roland Barthes, Michel Foucault, Jean-François Lyotard, Jacques Derrida, Richard Rorty, Ernesto Laclau, Jean Baudrillard, Alain Badiou, and others, as well as midterm or newer ones, such as Frank Ankersmit, Arthur Danto, Elizabeth Ermarth, Judith Butler, Sande Cohen, and Martin Davies, a few of whom I have referenced. But the point is that I "got into" most of these people because of Hayden. By this I don't mean that he introduced me to or helped me to think better or differently about things, but that he has been involved in my very formation—he figures as *the* point of departure for my thinking about history; my subsequent journey remains indebted to him. For it was Hayden who, almost single-handedly, turned me from the old Marxist I once was to the post-Marxist I think I may have become, and from the old normal/empirical/modernist historian I was by "training," into the postmodern person I would like to be. Of course, it's not his fault, nor anyone else's, that I have turned out the way I have . . . a popularizer of postmodern history . . . and I don't expect Hayden to necessarily agree with anything I have written under the influence—however attenuated—of his own brilliant writings, including this paper! No. All I am saying is that he occupies a special place in my thinking, and I want to write just two final paragraphs on this.

I first read Hayden's 1973 text *Metahistory* in the mid 1970s and I didn't understand it. I'm ashamed to admit that I neglected him until the early 1980s, when I bought a copy of *Tropics of Discourse* (1978), after which I went back to *Metahistory*, rereading it through the later volume of essays. After that, Hayden became my critical guide through the types of history that then constituted the "historical theory" field, a field that, compared to Hayden's work, seemed thin, myopic, sterile, and, often, just plain dull. Indeed, Hayden's theorizing—coupled with the fact that he seemed to say everything so unerringly "right" and in a style that was at once so analytically powerful and so memorably epigrammatic (such that looking over his texts now I can hardly read them since they are so underlined and contain so many marginal comments); these texts were so different from anything else I had read that they just seemed to come from nowhere. Accordingly, Hayden's theorizations became my touchstone, a

way of looking that gained increased momentum with my further reading of his various books and papers as they appeared. I've never looked
back, nor have I really looked elsewhere; my thinking about Hayden's
texts fused with other reading such that there is a sense in which "reading
White" has taken on the mantle of a Badiou-like *Event*; an immanent,
transformative break after which things just never ran the same, and
to which I have remained faithful; an act of fidelity to a certain "truth"
which, like all fidelities, necessitates reflexive, critical development but
which has only served to strengthen my original commitment. Why not
say it: Hayden is an intellectual hero of mine.

The final paragraph. When I first read Hayden—over thirty years
ago now—I never thought that I would meet him. But over the years—
on his occasional visits to London, at various conferences in Europe and
England, over the telephone and, more lately, via email, I have got to
know him a little. And on every occasion when we have met (even when
rebuking me for "falling asleep" while on a panel), he has been unfail-
ingly kind and supportive. A complex mixture of laid-back modesty and
forceful assertiveness with more than an edge, a man who doesn't suffer fools gladly and yet who is incredibly generous to his often far from
generous critics (*many* of whom are very foolish indeed). There is a moment—I relate it somewhat anecdotally—that has stayed in my mind in a
way that typifies Hayden for me. When passing through London in 1997,
he agreed to an interview. Published in 1998 in a slightly edited form in
Literature and History as "A Conversation with Hayden White," our discussion, which lasted for about three hours, was finally brought to a close
when I asked him about criticisms of his work: was he happy to live with
them, even the unjust ones? And his reply was as follows:

My attitude about the books and articles I have written is that you write them,
you send them out and if people can use the stuff that's fine. If they want to
use it in a distorted form, if they want to adapt it, let them do it. That's what
intellectual work is all about, if they don't like it, let them reject it, do it better.
Collingwood used to say, "I don't engage in polemics." He used to say, *if you
don't like my ideas do them better.* It's no good getting angry about things, these
are ideas which we are trying out in as interesting a way as we can. And I agree
with that.[15]

And I just want to conclude by saying that actually, for me, "nobody does
it better . . ."

Notes

1. Richard Rorty, *Contingency, Irony, and Solidarity* (Cambridge: Cambridge University Press, 1989), 5.

2. Richard Kearney, *States of Mind* (Manchester: Manchester University Press, 1995), 172.

3. Ernesto Laclau, *Emancipations* (London: Verso, 1996), 123.

4. Frank Ankersmit, "'Presence' and Myth," *History and Theory* 45:3 (2006): 328.

5. Sande Cohen, "The 'Use and Abuse of History' According to Jean-Francois Lyotard," *Parallax* 6:4 (2000): 100.

6. Cohen, "The 'Use and Abuse of History,'" 248–49.

7. Roland Barthes, "The Discourse of History," in: *The Postmodern History Reader*, ed. Keith Jenkins (London: Routledge, 1997), 120–23.

8. For a brilliant essay on argumentation, see Geoffrey Bennington, "For the Sake of Argument (Up to a Point)," in: *Arguing with Derrida*, ed. Simon Glendinning (Oxford: Blackwell, 2001), 34–56 (with a reply by Derrida).

9. Carolyn Steedman, *Dust. The Archive and Cultural History* (Manchester: Manchester University Press, 2001), 153–4.

10. Jacques Rancière, *The Names of History: On The Poetics of Knowledge* (Minneapolis: University of Minnesota Press, 1992), 63.

11. Wendy Olmsted, *Rhetoric. An Historical Introduction* (Oxford: Blackwell, 2006), 1.

12. Martin L. Davies, *Historics* (London: Routledge, 2006), 55.

13. Hayden White, "The Public Relevance of Historical Studies: A Reply to Dirk Moses," *History and Theory* 44:3 (2006): 338.

14. Hayden White, *Tropics of Discourse* (Baltimore: Johns Hopkins University Press, 1978), 50.

15. Keith Jenkins, "A Conversation With Hayden White," *Literature and History* 7:1 (1998): 82.

6

Metahistory as *Anabasis*

Andrew Baird

As readers of this book will undoubtedly already know, Hayden
White's work in and on *Metahistory* is pathbreaking, influential, and controversial, and has as such been recapitulated, interpreted, lauded, and
criticized extensively. I don't know that my long engagement with it has
produced any insights that have not already been brought to our attention by other readers and scholars, but, of course, the occasion demands
that I throw in my two cents. I will try to acquit myself by offering some
comments about the relationship between *Metahistory* and *anabasis*. Long
familiar as the title of Xenophon's account of the tribulations of a Greek
mercenary force lost in Persia, *anabasis* has recently been appropriated by
Alain Badiou "as a possible support for meditation on our century":

> In the trajectory it names, anabasis leaves undecided the parts respectively al-
> lotted to disciplined invention and uncertain wandering. In so doing, it con-
> stitutes a disjunctive synthesis of will and wandering. After all, the Greek word
> already attests to this undecidability, since the verb αναβαυειν ["to anabase,"
> as it were] means both 'to embark' and 'to return'. There is no doubt that this
> semantic pairing suits a century that ceaselessly asks itself whether it is an end
> or a beginning.[1]

In *Le Siècle*, Badiou tackles a range of issues that could be considered metahistorical. As the just-cited passage suggests, he addresses the
impossibility of deciding whether the century was an end or a beginning.
Badiou grapples with the question of whether we can do without, or move

beyond, the type of thinking about history that relies on beginnings and ends, even though we recognize that this type of thinking is highly susceptible to irony. These issues, however important, are a little too broad to be addressed here; I am proposing to take Badiou's comments on anabasis as a "possible support for meditation" on a more limited question, which I think has been asked several times over the past thirty years with reference to the work of Hayden White: is metahistory a beginning or an end? In other words, does metahistory lead to new ways of thinking about or "doing" history, or is it mainly a demystification or debunking of the claims that have been made for the way history has been thought about or "done" over a certain period? I am not sure that it is possible to answer this question, but I am sure that in order to think about it and what is at stake in it, we are going to have to think about irony. The wager of this essay is that the idea or figure of anabasis, as it is presented by Badiou, might help us to come to terms with Hayden White's irony, which seems to be the most challenging aspect of his work—for its detractors as well as its admirers.

Irony and the Burden of History
in Nietzsche and Badiou

It is worth remembering that White characterizes his own approach as "meta-ironical"; that is to say, his work takes a (self-conscious or reflexive) ironic approach to the (naïve) irony of the "disciplined" historical consciousness that is the object of its critical analysis. The key question—one that has been raised repeatedly in the reception of metahistorical work—is whether meta-irony, the ironization of irony, can help to resolve or ameliorate the existential or ontological predicament that irony discloses, which we might as well call, given the occasion, "the burden of history."[2]

After Nietzsche, we can understand this predicament as a tension or conflict between History and Life. In the second *Unfashionable Observation*, Nietzsche presents this predicament as follows:

Thus the animal lives *ahistorically*, for it disappears entirely into the present, like a number that leaves no remainder; it does not know how to dissemble, conceals nothing, and it appears in each and every moment as exactly what it is, and so cannot help but be honest. The human being, by contrast, braces himself against the great and ever-greater burden of the past; it weighs him down or bends him over, hampers his gait as an invisible and obscure load that he can pretend to disown, and that he is only too happy to disown when he is among his fellow human beings in order to arouse their envy.[3]

Nietzsche observes that people, unlike animals, are afflicted by memory and their experience of time's passage; to the extent that happiness is possible for human beings, it is a product of forgetting: of being, for at least a short time, entirely within the present moment. Nietzsche posits an opposition between memory and forgetting, which is paralleled by an opposition between historical sensibility and action. Memory and historical sensibility are negative, and forgetting and action positive, but it is not within the power of human beings to move entirely into the realm of forgetting and action; such a move would eliminate the distinction between humans and animals.

When it is admitted that the tension between memory and forgetting, or between historical rumination and what Nietzsche terms "life," is a constitutive feature of human existence, and impossible to resolve in favor of one pole or the other, then the question of the best possible balance or combination of the two poles arises, almost inevitably:

In order to determine the degree and thereby establish the limit beyond which the past must be forgotten if it is not to become the grave digger of the present, we would have to know exactly how great the shaping power of a human being, a people, a culture is; by shaping power I mean that power to develop its own singular character out of itself, to shape and assimilate what is past and alien, to heal wounds, to replace what has been lost, to recreate broken forms out of itself alone.[4]

The problem, of course, is that the weight of the past has already been described by Nietzsche as "invisible, obscure." To the extent that this "burden of history" is something Althusser might call a "real condition of existence," it will never be possible to "determine the degree" to which it affects the present, or to measure "exactly" the shaping power of a human being, people, or culture. Nietzsche does not suggest that such a final or universal accounting is possible, and points instead to the wide variation in the level of "plasticity" that can be found by making comparisons between individuals, peoples, or cultures.

The tension between memory and forgetting, rumination and action, history and "life," or determinism and voluntarism is not resoluble through reference to the "real"—this has been concluded before. The impossibility of demonstrating the correct combination of history and life is an essentially ironic insight, and is, of course, susceptible to all the criticisms that are made regarding irony's debilitating influence on action. Reflection on the tension between history and life is a way of "binding" anxiety provoked by the enigma of historicality, and the development of this type of reflection, from a variety of perspectives, is one of the central functions of "culture." The way in which the enigma is described, and the proper balance between "history" and "life" that is advocated on the basis of these provisional descriptions, is of paramount political importance. To put it simply, an approach that suggests that no action is possible or desirable is likely to benefit whatever order is presently established, while an approach that suggests that action is desirable and possible is likely to threaten the current order, if widely adopted. "Realism," as it pertains to politics, concerns the possibility of effective action; this is why political debate hinges not only on the desirability of or need for change, but also on whether the prospects of successfully achieving change are "realistic."

If one accepts or departs from the idea that "historicality" (being-in-time, with others) is an ontological condition of all human being, then one must eventually confront questions about how much and what types of "consciousness" or "knowledge" of History in one's relationship to it are possible. This avenue of reflection eventually encounters the issue of the proper role of historical consciousness (is there a "proper" role, and if so, how can it be discerned?) in "making history." Are there forms of historical knowledge, or modes of historical consciousness, that "serve Life," that assist people in confronting the present task of making the future? Or is historical consciousness, in the end, a diversion from or burden on this confrontation of History and Life? Every answer to these questions is susceptible to irony, but the questions themselves are unavoidable, particularly in the aftermath of human-made catastrophes that were brought about, to no small degree, by the passions, projects, and programs of the last century. As Badiou demonstrates in *Le Siècle*, these enterprises, despite their variety, constitute a sort of unity insofar as they were all understood by those who initiated and pursued them as heroic confrontations with History.

One way of understanding the task that Badiou undertakes in *Le Siècle* is as an attempt to grasp the twentieth century as a massive effort to resolve or overcome the predicament of historicality. As the book's title suggests, Badiou's text presents a critical reflection on the problem of the unity of the past century. What was the twentieth century, in philosophical terms? For Badiou, the philosophical question is not what happened, but what was thought, and more precisely, what was thought in the twentieth century that was not thought in the nineteenth century. Badiou argues that the most important of these thoughts pertained to History, and Man's relationship to it: how did the twentieth century understand its relationship to History, and how did these understandings shape the century's trajectory?[5]

For Badiou, the unifying idea of the century is the project of creating a New Man. In the thought of the twentieth century, as compared to that of the nineteenth, the relative priority and the locus of agency in the "Man/History" dyad are reversed. Whereas it was generally believed in the nineteenth century (the "golden age" of History) that History would carry Man forward, in the twentieth Man tried to take charge of History and redirect it. Badiou introduces the phrase "the passion for the real" as a way of describing the century's governing attitude, its zeitgeist. With this phrase, Badiou tries to capture the extent to which the affect associated with the desire for the "new," for a different future, is displaced from the task of envisioning the "new" onto the task of preparing for it, clearing its place. Imagining a better future and attempting to realize it are tasks that go together, but they are not equivalent, and the tragedy of the "passion for the real" that gripped the century is that it equated the creation of the new with the destruction of the old, and pursued the negative task with such a frenzied vigor that it undermined the possibility of the positive. Badiou addresses the relationship between destruction and creation in the desire for the "definitive" in the following passage:

In every instance we can see that this longing for the definitive is realized as the beyond of a destruction. The new man is the destruction of the old man. Perpetual peace is achieved through the destruction of old wars by total war. By means of an integral formalization, the monument of completed science destroys the old scientific institutions. Modern art brings the relative universe of representation to ruin. A fundamental couple is at work here, that of destruction and the definitive. Once again, this is a non-dialectical couple, a disjunctive synthesis. That is because destruction does not produce the definitive, which means that we are faced with two very distinct tasks: to destroy the old, and to create the new.[6]

The problem of creating "the new" has been confronted in virtually every field of human endeavor; it is often described as the problem of the "modern." How are we to understand the "novelty" of the new, or the "modernity" of the modern if we want to move beyond a simple apprehension of the facticity of change (in which the "new" or "modern" is whatever prevails today that can be distinguished from what prevailed in the past)? In characterizing the relationship between destruction and creation (of the "definitive") as a "disjunctive synthesis," Badiou is pointing to what we might be tempted to identify as the fundamental predicament of historicality: History seems to depend on the destruction of the past and the drive for the "new" as a condition of its vitality, its "movement," but it is impossible to imagine the product of this "movement" in terms that are other than "historical."[7] Whether the new is understood as the recuperation of an "authentic" origin that has been lost or obscured, or as the product of another historical process that will be initiated out of the ruins of the old, the project of its creation remains caught within history. This recognition of the disjunctive synthesis of ending and beginning, destruction and creation, recognition of error and revelation of truth—this undecidability—is in the end what we call irony.

Metahistory, *Parabasis,* and "The Ironist's Cage"

Even in the context of a book on Hayden White, some further remarks to clarify my use of the term "metahistory" are in order. For heuristic purposes, I will say that I understand metahistory to be a critical counter-discourse that pursues a "second-order" reflection on history. As White suggests in "The Historical Text as Literary Artifact," this type of second-order reflection on history can be understood as a critical history of history as a discipline:

In order to write the history of any given scholarly discipline, or even of a science, one must be prepared to ask questions *about* it of a sort that do not have to be asked in the practice *of* it. One must try to get behind or beneath the presuppositions which sustain a given type of inquiry and ask the questions that can be begged in its practice in the interest of determining why this type of inquiry has been designed to solve the problems it characteristically tries to solve. This is what metahistory seeks to do.[8]

Metahistory asks questions about history that are not asked in the practice of it, but nevertheless need to be asked. Particularly in the years immediately following the publication of *Metahistory* (the book), the types of questions that metahistory (the field) asked tended to involve the status of the historical text as a "literary artifact," "a sign system," "a verbal structure in the form of a narrative prose discourse." As critique, metahistory takes as its object the discipline of history's "reluctance to consider historical narratives as what they most manifestly are: verbal *fictions* [my emphasis], the contents of which are as much *invented* as *found* and the forms of which have more in common with their counterparts in literature than they have with those in the sciences."[9]

To treat histories as "fictions that are as much invented as found" is to treat them as "products" of the historian's labor in the present. Histories are also products of a discipline that shapes and constrains the historian's labor in ways that can themselves be situated and historicized, and shown to be the result of contingent choices that have no necessary relationship or grounding in the past reality that is the putative object of the discourse. The reluctance of history to address the reliance of its discourse on figurative language, or to acknowledge the role of the present in the invention of a past that it pretended to discover, is understandable, insofar as engagement with these issues calls into question, and limits, the claims that can be made for professional historical representations as "knowledge," and in doing so threatens the autonomy and prestige of the discipline that makes these claims.

When White states that histories—like other fictions—depend on figuration to produce whatever meanings, or meaning-effects, they can be said to produce, he is acknowledging a predicament, not arguing for that predicament's desirability. This distinction has often eluded the most vociferous critics of White's work. Nevertheless, once the indissoluble ties that bind historical representation to figuration are recognized, there follows an obligation to consider or assess the ability of language to grasp, capture, adequately reflect "reality" (the extra-linguistic, the material, the natural, the self, etc.). A vast body of work in semiotics, philosophy, and literary theory—work on which metahistory draws and to which it contributes—suggests that figuration is unable to bridge securely or with finality the gap between reality and the linguistic representations of it we are able to produce; the recognition of this difference, this nonequivalence, of linguistic representations and the extra-linguistic objects (experiences, events, practices, or structures) they purport to represent, is what is called *irony*. It is notoriously difficult to define Irony, but White provides a fine summary of in the following passage from *Metahistory*:

It can be seen immediately that Irony is in one sense metatropological, for it is deployed in the self-conscious awareness of the possible misuse of figurative language. Irony presupposes the occupation of a "realistic" perspective on reality, from which a nonfigurative representation of the world of experience might be provided. Irony thus represents a stage of consciousness in which the problematical nature of language itself has become recognized. It points to the potential foolishness of all linguistic characterizations of reality as much as to the absurdity of the beliefs it parodies. It is therefore "dialectical," as Kenneth Burke has noted, though not so much in its apprehension of the process of the world as in its apprehension of the capacity of language to obscure more than it clarifies in any act of verbal figuration. In Irony, figurative language folds back upon itself and brings its own potentialities for distorting perception under question . . .

The trope of Irony, then, provides a linguistic paradigm of a mode of thought which is radically self-critical with respect not only to a given characterization of the world of experience but also to the very effort to capture adequately the truth of things in language. It is, in short, a model of the linguistic protocol in which skepticism in thought and relativism in ethics are conventionally expressed.[10]

Because irony exposes an unbridgeable gap between the world and our representations of it, it can be used "negatively" to challenge the adequacy of any strategy of representation to the task it seeks to accomplish. Irony is particularly useful in undermining the beliefs and prescriptions of others, but it does not itself provide a ground upon which to base positive alternatives. Irony's negative power makes it particularly effective in "tactical" applications, but problems arise when one tries to make the move from "tactics" to "strategy," from a "negative" critical position to the "positive" articulation of an alternative to what has been criticized. White's statement continues:

Existentially projected into a full-blown world view, Irony would appear to be transideological. Irony can be used *tactically* for defense of either Liberal or Conservative ideological positions, depending on whether the Ironist is speaking against established social forms or against "utopian" reformers seeking to change the status quo. And it can be used offensively by the Anarchist and the Radical, to pillory the ideas of their Liberal and Conservative opponents. But, as the basis of a world view, Irony tends to dissolve all belief in the possibility of positive political actions. In its apprehension of the essential folly or absurdity of the human condition, it tends to engender belief in the "madness" of civilization itself and to inspire a Mandarin-like disdain for those seeking to grasp the nature of social reality in either science or art.[11]

Much has been made, in the reception of White's work, of the risks associated with the ironic perspective, and of the skepticism and relativism it is said to engender. Irony is held to be dangerous and irresponsible, insofar as it deprives political action of a basis in truth or knowledge, and indeed, seems to question the possibility of a "truth" or "knowledge" that would be distinguishable or free from association with "belief," "ideology," or "mystification." Again, to argue, as White does, that history's dependence on figurative language denies that discipline a firm epistemological basis or ground is to say nothing about the *desirability* of foundations—it is simply to deny that, in the case of history, they are there. But even sympathetic, reflective, theoretically sophisticated readers of White, readers that otherwise accept his view of the role of figurative language in conditioning historical representation, tend to express reservations regarding the status of irony in his work. In the end, these reservations involve not the validity of White's analyses, or his motivations in pursuing them, but of the unknown, risky "political" consequences of an ironic skepticism about the possibility of distinguishing between "history" and "ideology."

Michael Roth (a noted intellectual historian and now president of Wesleyan University) is a former student of White's, and the essay devoted to White's work in his book *The Ironist's Cage* is admirable both for its lucidity and its fairness.[12] In this essay, Roth begins by acknowledging White's recognition of irony's potential to engender both a debilitating skepticism and the concomitant temptation to retreat from practical engagement with problems that are not made less "real" by the provisionality of our attempts to grasp them.[13] Roth notes that White's stated aim is to turn irony against itself in the interest of "unburdening" historical consciousness of a discipline that limits the freedom of individuals and groups to develop relationships to their pasts that support the "making of history" in the present, for the future. Metahistory aims to produce freedom; however, Roth suggests that the value of that freedom might itself be called into question by the ironic mode of its production:

White's own use of tropes was meant to move us "beyond irony" by showing us the moral, political, and aesthetic choices that remained open to us. Once we understood that it was we who construct our narratives out of the past, the appeal to history should become not a constraint on freedom but one of the ways in which we could choose to give meaning to our lives. But if we are "always already" embedded in an arbitrary figure of speech, where was the place from which we made our choices?

Here we reach the limits of White's ongoing project; so far, he has had very little to say about how such choices are made. This choosing seems to be beyond rhetoric, although we would never know about it but for its rhetorical expressions. As a critic of these expressions, White's own rhetoric leads us to the questions of why we turn to history in the first place. What do we want from the past, and what shall we do with our history once we understand that it can no longer function as a court of appeal? White leads us to these questions, but he also carefully avoids them. Perhaps he cannot do otherwise given the position he has created for himself as a critic of history writing.[14]

White's work seems to provide Roth the paradigm for the predicament that gives *The Ironist's Cage* its title. In the introduction to the book, Roth raises the issue more assertively than he does in the chapter on White:

Foucault, Rorty, and White certainly share the view that all knowledge is constrained by the paradigm, episteme, or simply, the culture of the knower. This is no more than saying that knowledge is constrained by, since it is expressed in, language, or that it is dependent on the knower's historical context. The dream of escaping from this constraint into "genuine" knowledge is one of the objects of their critical perspectives on modern philosophy and theory. However, the acceptance of the constraints of one's own historical situation becomes increasingly problematic as one becomes more critical of one's own historical situation—that is, as one regards these constraints as illegitimate (but from where does one regard them?) . . . In contemporary cultural criticism this problem results in what I call the ironist's cage, the prison of cultural critics who realize that they have no position from which to make their criticism. The desire to be politically radical and still be intellectually sophisticated has led many contemporary critics into the ironist's cage.[15]

It seems to me that Roth's "ironist's cage" is another way of describing the predicament of historicality, the "disjunctive synthesis" between destruction and creation that constrains and recuperates any effort to imagine and achieve a "new" History (or in this case, history). As Roth indicates, White's efforts are primarily focused on the task of "un-binding" or "destruction"; to the extent that White discusses what could be created out of this process, his vision conforms, more or less, to the possible trajectories that Badiou identifies. On one hand, the "new" history might be understood as a "return," to the more expansive and dynamic conception of historiography's possible forms and purposes that prevailed during the "golden age" of the nineteenth century. On the other hand, the "new" history cannot be a simple restoration of a past "authenticity," and so White points to the possibility of a renewed vitality for a historiography that would take its inspiration from "modern" science and literature. Overall, White is reluctant to delineate a positive or "definitive" vision of the history he would like to see created.

With the image of "the ironist's cage," Roth is questioning the value of a critique that will not or cannot articulate an alternative position that would be, as Badiou puts it, "definitive." We are approaching the crux of the issue I want to address by way of a consideration of anabasis. White suggests that "meta-irony" can provide "the grounds for a rejection of Irony itself," and that this rejection liberates or unbinds the historical imagination. Without the identification of a possible position for critique that would be "beyond irony," or the affirmation of any criteria for preferring one approach to the past over another, does this freedom represent an escape from the "ironist's cage," or simply a confinement that is more conscious of itself? In the continuation of the passage cited above, Roth presents Paul de Man's discussion of irony as evidence of irony's irredeemability:

Paul de Man perhaps knew the contours of this confinement ("the ironist's cage") better than most.

"Our description of irony seems to have reached a provisional conclusion. The act of irony, as we now understand it, reveals the existence of a temporality that is definitely not organic, in that it relates to its source only in terms of distance and difference and allows for no end, for no totality. Irony divides the flow of temporal experience into a past that is pure mystification and a future that remains harassed forever by a lapse into the inauthentic. It can know this inauthenticity but can never overcome it. It can only repeat it and restate it on an increasingly conscious level, but it remains endlessly caught in the impossibility of making this knowledge applicable to the empirical world. It dissolves in the narrowing spiral of a linguistic sign that becomes more and more remote from its meaning, and it can find no escape from this spiral."

Irony, de Man emphasizes, reveals a "truly temporal predicament." One can, like de Man, relish this seemingly complex spiral, this "permanent para-basis." But the effort to display one's knowledge of it (to show that one is on an "increasingly conscious level") while still connecting to the political world leads much of contemporary cultural criticism to rattle the bars of the ironist's cage.[16]

Now, I assume that some of my readers will be familiar with Paul de Man's treatment of Irony in "The Rhetoric of Temporality" and "The Concept of Irony," and will as such be beginning to see what all of this has to do with *anabasis*. Roth's passage alludes to one of the touchstones for de Man's discussion of Irony: Schlegel's definition of it as "permanent *parabasis*." In the context of a novel or a play, *parabasis* refers to the inter-ruption of a narrative by the "intrusion of a self-conscious narrator." Para-basis reveals the disjuncture between the events being narrated and the narration itself, and generally can be said to present an ironic perspective on the gap between the narrative's intent and its actual meaning. Instead of introducing a positive element of historical fact into the fictional nar-ration of the novel, parabasis indicates the impossibility of resolving the problem of what is to be considered fiction and what fact by denying the possibility of a reconciliation between the world of language and the em-pirical world; the implied positivity of the narrator's self-consciousness is always contained within, and undone by, the negativity of the text. Para-basis in the novel exemplifies irony's general temporal structure in that it displays a repetition of duplication, disruption, and doubt that never reaches a final synthesis or positivity. De Man argues, after Schlegel, that the intrusion of a self-conscious narrator in parabasis introduces an ir-recuperable disruption; the interruption can be sustained and redoubled (until a point of exhaustion or madness), but it cannot close the rift it opens.

Parabasis is a break, an interruption, a departure from a mystified state that presumes the identity or equivalence of a representation and the real state of affairs it purports to represent. But is it "permanent"? Yes, in the sense that it is irrevocable: parabasis is like a sort of biblical "fall," as the prior state of mystification cannot be restored. No, or maybe not, in the sense that the spiraling movement of self-consciousness that it sets in motion is not perpetual, but eventually comes to a halt in exhaus-tion or a *relapse into mystification*. For De Man, *parabasis* is a moment (or series of moments, when sustained) within a temporal sequence: first, there is mystification or naïveté; then, there is the ironic intervention that exposes this mystification; this parabasis can be sustained, irony can become more and more conscious, until it ends in madness, exhaustion, or a relapse into mystification. It is unclear to me, from my own reading of de Man, whether it is fair to say as Roth does that de Man "relishes" sustained parabasis and the increasing awareness it engenders of man's "temporal predicament." It is fair to say, I think, that whereas de Man is concerned in "The Rhetoric of Temporality" with assessing Irony's ability to render an "authentic experience" of this temporal predicament, Roth is concerned with whether an ironic perspective on history can itself be limited, after its negative power is deployed. Everything hinges, it seems to me, on how we understand the relationship between the state of mystification that is the point of departure for the subject of parabasis and the one to which the subject returns, or relapses.

With respect to the criterion of "authenticity" that concerns de Man, the original and relapsed state of mystification may well be equivalent. This is not to say, however, that they are equivalent in all respects. Can we imagine better and worse "states of mystification"? Can they be assessed according to criteria other than their ability to represent man's "authentic temporal predicament"? To say that irony is negative, critical, destructive, and that sustained, redoubled, "meta" irony only engenders more negativity, is to say that irony will never, left to its own devices, lead to a positive ground; it does not preclude the subsequent creation or invention of positivity. To say that whatever positivity might follow "after irony" is inevitably a "relapse into mystification" is to say nothing about the desirability of this state, in comparison to the starting point. From this standpoint, irony is a risk, a wager on the "undecidable possibility" that the future holds.

Hayden White's work, and metahistory generally, have the merit of taking up the question of "the point of historical consciousness"; it has insisted on the importance of critical reflection on the relationship between History and Life. It has pursued this critical reflection through the analysis of the ways in which this relationship is construed, explicitly and implicitly, in professional historical discourse. But the question that remains to be addressed is: Does metahistory improve our ability to negotiate Nietzsche's tension between History and Life? Does metahistory "lead" anywhere, if the critical insights it provides are irrecuperably negative? Does an ironic approach that is increasingly conscious of itself lead us out of "the ironist's cage" and toward a situation in which historical consciousness can play a vital, positive role in "public discourse" and life, or does it lead us further into the cage, thereby precluding a practical engagement with a present historical conjuncture? What can we make of the "freedom" that a metahistorical approach to history provides? In what remains of this essay, I want to suggest that the figure of *anabasis* can help us frame an understanding of metahistory as a critical movement that creates the undecidable possibility of a better future.

Anabasis

At this point, I want to circle back to the first section's brief discussion of *Le Siècle*, simply to suggest that Badiou, too, is struggling against the bars of Roth's "ironist's cage." Badiou's reflection on the passions of the twentieth century is of course aimed at illuminating where we are today and what it is possible to hope for and to do in the wake of the twentieth century. It should be noted that while Badiou's position on these questions can only be categorized as ironic, it is hardly a passive or satisfied irony. While Badiou is straightforward in his recognition of the terrible price paid by millions in the attempt to create the new, and acknowledges that these efforts must largely be assessed as catastrophic failures, he seems to retain some sympathy or admiration for the goals and passions that animated these efforts, even though they led to disaster and defeat. Badiou heaps scorn on what he calls the "restoration" of a market-driven, "security-oriented" consensus that follows upon the failure of the grand, or grandiose, projects of the twentieth century, but is unable to endorse any new project for the twenty-first.

If Badiou is unable to offer a positive proposal on the type of philosophy of history that would be appropriate for our present conjuncture, that could help the twenty-first century move beyond or rise above the failures and catastrophes wrought by the visions of History that animated the twentieth, he does offer us the figure of anabasis. If anabasis provides us with a way of considering the way that movements or journeys that begin in the desire for the new tend to become, after their departure, attempts to return, it also provides us with a way of thinking about the value of what goes on between the advance and the retreat, between the leaving and the returning, between the point of departure and the des-

tination. Against the altogether understandable tendency to view resignation or voluntarism as the only responses to our abandonment to the
predicament of historicality, the figure of anabasis suggests that a "disciplined invention" provides a minimal hope, an *undecidable possibility*, of a
better future within history.

In the chapter of *Le Siècle* titled "Anabasis," Badiou tells us that:

We can extract three points concerning what, at first glance, characterizes the
movement named "anabasis."

(a) Xenophon describes the collapse of the order that gave meaning to the
collective presence of the Greeks at the heart of Persia. After Cunaxa, the Greeks
find themselves brutally deprived of any reason for being where they are. They
are nothing now but foreigners in a hostile country. At the root of anabasis lies
something like a principle of lostness.

(b) The Greeks have only themselves, their own will and discipline, to rely
on. Having gone there at another's behest, in a position of obedience and paid
service, they suddenly find themselves left to their own devices, forced, as it
were, to invent their destiny.

(c) It is imperative that the Greeks find something new. Their march
through Persia, towards the sea, follows no pre-existing path and corresponds
to no previous orientation. It cannot even be a straightforward return home,
since it invents its path without knowing whether it really is the path of return.
Anabasis is the free invention of a wandering that *will have been* a return, a return that did not exist as a return-route prior to the wandering.[17]

Badiou uses Xenophon's account of the march of the "ten thousand" as
a starting point for his understanding of 'Anabasis' as a figure. In the
aftermath of their defeat at Cunaxa, the ten thousand find themselves in
dire circumstances: they are lost, "out of place and outside the law," abandoned to their own resources of invention. The predicament into which
the mercenaries are thrown is reminiscent of the one de Man describes
as afflicting the ironic subject trapped in parabasis, but it differs because
the mercenaries are not paralyzed by reflection—they move. Although
no outside authority or obligation prevents them from reflecting on their
predicament, the mercenaries make the free choice to "accept a discipline," and this discipline might be understood simply as an acceptance
of their present "abandonment," and a concomitant commitment to move
forward together, toward "home" (*vers "chez eux"*).

Anabasis is an open-ended, nondialectical, nonteleological movement. It is the "disjunctive synthesis," in exiled wandering, of departure

and return. It is a response to abandonment—an attempt to persevere, survive, and overcome, in the absence of an orientation that would delineate how these goals would be possible. It should be understood as a sort of active "homelessness," a state in which the security and repose represented by "the home" lie behind, in an inaccessible past, or ahead, in an uncertain future. In this respect, *the temporal structure of anabasis seems comparable to that of irony as mystification/parabasis/exhaustion or relapse.* But whereas for de Man's ironic subject, the gap between the self and the world, the subject of language and the empirical self, will never be bridged, for the subject of anabasis, a re/finding "home" is not an impossibility, but rather an undecidable possibility, and this hope can be pursued tactically, if not strategically.

In suggesting that anabasis is essentially "tactical," I am alluding to the distinction between "strategy" and "tactics" that is elaborated by Michel de Certeau in *The Practice of Everyday Life.* Certeau's treatment of this distinction strikes me as eminently relevant to both the understanding of anabasis that I am trying to develop here, and to the relationship I am trying to establish between anabasis and metahistory, so I am going to reproduce it here:

I call a "strategy" the calculus of force-relationships which becomes possible when a subject of will and power (a proprietor, an enterprise, a city, a scientific institution) can be isolated from an "environment." A strategy assumes a place that can be circumscribed as *proper* (*propre*) and thus serve as the basis for generating relations with an exterior distinct from it (competitors, adversaries, "clienteles," "targets," or "objects" of research). Political, economic, and scientific rationality has been constructed on this strategic model.

I call a "tactic," on the other hand, a calculus which cannot count on a "proper" (a spatial or institutional localization), nor thus on a borderline distinguishing the other as a visible totality. The place of a tactic belongs to the other. A tactic insinuates itself into the other's place, fragmentarily, without taking it over in its entirety, without being able to keep it at a distance. It has at its disposal no base where it can capitalize on its advantages, prepare its expansion, and secure independence with respect to circumstances. The "proper" is a victory of space over time. On the contrary, because it does not have a place, a tactic depends on time—it is always on the watch for opportunities that must be seized "on the wing." Whatever it wins, it does not keep. It must constantly manipulate events in order to turn them into "opportunities."

. . . In this respect, the difference corresponds to two historical options regarding action and security (options that moreover have more to do with constraints than with possibilities): strategies pin their hopes on the resistance that the establishment of a place offers to the erosion of time; tactics on a clever utilization of time, of the opportunities it presents and also of the play that it introduces into the foundations of power. Even if the methods practiced by the everyday art of war never present themselves in such a clear form, it nevertheless remains the case that the two ways of acting can be distinguished according to whether they bet on place or on time.[18]

Badiou says that Xenophon narrates the movement of the mercenaries toward "home"; to understand *Anabasis*, we need to read "home" not as the factitious point of departure, but instead in the sense that Certeau ascribes to the "place" of the subject. For the subject of *Anabasis*, a subject that is exiled or "out of place," the prospect of being "at home" is an aspirational ideal that cannot be envisioned without reference to experience, but is not equivalent or reducible to whatever factical experience of "home" may have preceded the march. It is worth noting that the ten thousand are a mercenary force; they have no necessary tie to "Greece" or even to their cities or regions of origin. The translator's introduction to *Anabasis* points out that a mercenary force of this size constituted a historical novelty. The size of the force assembled, considered in juxtaposition to the ill-fated, ill-conceived objective set before it, suggests that the motivation for Panhellenic adventurism in Persia was not simply the conquest of territory, but also the displacement of a potentially destabilizing social element: poor, underemployed mercenaries wandering the streets threatened the order of the city-states. In short, to describe "a return home (*chez eux*)" as the goal of the mercenaries is fair, to the degree that "home" is equated to safety and respite; however, the mercenaries' attitude toward their goal is somewhat more complicated when one considers that the place from which they departed may have sent them away, and may be ambivalent about their return, and that this ambivalence may have motivated their enlistment to wander in the first place.

As a counterpoint to the acknowledgement of the ten thousand's dogged determination to escape Persia and return to Greece, it is worth noting some "utopian" moments during the *Anabasis*. There is a sense in which the band itself, in the midst of its engagement with the task of survival, becomes something like a "home" for its members, a kind of moving city-state in which the individuals feel integrated, rather than abjected. Xenophon discusses at a couple of points the possibility that the ten thousand will stop trying to make it back to Greece, and will instead stay in Persia and found a new city on a particularly propitious site. That "home" is a vision of fullness or satisfaction, an aspiration for a place of rest, that is variously imagined as a vanished past or an uncertain, utopian future, does not prevent the ten thousand from continuing in their search for the sea. "Home" should not be understood as an "actually existing" place, although its existence is not an impossibility. Rather, it is an undecidable possibility whose realization has to be characterized with the future anterior.

Conclusion

I think these comments on strategy/tactics, space/time, and the anteriority of "home" provide a useful counterpoint to Roth's concern about the "position" or "place" of metahistorical critique. To use a vocabulary of exile and itinerancy to describe the position of the critic is by now commonplace, even a cliché. And yet, it seems apt to describe Hayden White's work and the metahistorical movement as an *anabasis*, a deliberate or self-imposed exile from the discipline of history. To stay in a "place," to enjoy the security and the position it provides, is to accept its authority, its self-justification, the rules and limitations it places on the activities that transpire within it. Metahistory is unable to accept the limitations that the discipline of history demands as its conditions of residence; metahistory refuses proscription and bounding of historical representation on the basis of standards of realism and responsibility whose grounds are contingent, and are themselves historical and historicizable but are too rarely the object of critical reflection or defense. It *is* possible to pursue a path of critique without pursuing *the definitive*, without having, from the moment of departure, a vision of the ultimate destination in mind. It is enough to ask the question: where is the discipline of history in the confrontation with History, the attempts to "make history" (or "end" it) that are unfolding all around us?

Thinking about metahistory as anabasis reframes the problem of irony by situating it within a movement. This movement can be thought of as the departure from the security of a "place" into an open-ended wandering, one whose "discipline" is the refusal to occupy a position for the sake of having a position, or to accept a positivity one believes to be false. Instead, it is, as Certeau puts it, "a wager on time," a reliance on tactics, that holds out for the undecidable possibility of a "return" to a better home, or the establishment of a utopia.

As is well known, the climax of Xenophon's *Anabasis* is the sighting of the sea. For the ten thousand, the view of the sea retrospectively imbues their long journey, their wandering, with the meaning of a return. Their "disciplined invention" of a path that might be a return comes to an end, both as "discipline" and "invention," and becomes something more definite, a tracing of the coastline to their home. I would have liked to conclude this text with, if not a description of the sea, at least a whiff of salty air. In my inability to provide this, I take some comfort from the notion that in acknowledging that though I would love to see it, the sea is for me out of sight, I am at least staying true to the example of my teacher Hayden White, who has taught me that the desire for a conclusion should not be misrecognized as a guarantee of its validity.

Notes

1. Alain Badiou, *Le Siècle* (Paris: Editions du Seuil, 2005). Translated by Alberto Toscano as *The Century* (London: Polity Press, 2007), 82–83. All references are to Toscano's translation.

2. There is, of course, quite a body of work addressing White's "meta-irony" and its implications. See, for example, Herman Paul, "An Ironic Battle Against Irony: Epistemological and Ideological Irony in Hayden White's Philosophy of History," in *Tropes for the Past: Hayden White and the History/Literature Debate*, ed. Kuisma Korhonen (Amsterdam: Rodopi, 2006); Ewa Domańska, "Hayden White: Beyond Irony" *History and Theory* 37 (May 1998): 173–81; A. Dirk Moses, "Hayden White, Traumatic Nationalism, and the Public Role of History," *History and Theory* 44 (October 2005): 311–32.

3. Friedrich Wilhelm Nietzsche, *Unfashionable Observations*, vol. 2 of *Works*, trans. Richard T. Gray (Stanford, CA: Stanford University Press, 1995), 88–89.

4. Ibid., 89.

5. In *Le Siècle* Badiou identifies Nietzsche as the nineteenth-century thinker who frames in advance the problem of the twentieth century: the paradoxical tension within the concept of Life between a vital continuity with the past and a voluntarist zeal to throw off that past to create a new future. Badiou, *Le Siècle*, 16.

6. Badiou, *Le Siècle*, 36.

7. In his famous essay "Literary History and Literary Modernity," Paul de Man provides what is still, in my view, an unsurpassed diagnosis of this predica-

ment. See Paul de Man, *Blindness and Insight* (Minneapolis: University of Minnesota Press, 1983), 142–66.

8. Hayden White, *Tropics of Discourse* (Baltimore: Johns Hopkins University Press, 1978), 81.

9. Ibid., 82.

10. Hayden White, *Metahistory: The Historical Imagination in Nineteenth-Century Europe* (Baltimore: Johns Hopkins University Press, 1973), 37.

11. White, *Metahistory*, 38.

12. Michael Roth, *The Ironist's Cage: Memory, Trauma, and the Construction of History* (New York: Columbia University Press, 1995), 144–45.

13. In the preface to *Metahistory*, White states:

> It may not go unnoticed that this book is itself cast in an Ironic mode. But the Irony which informs it is a conscious one, and it therefore represents a turning of the Ironic consciousness against Irony itself. If it succeeds in establishing that the skepticism and pessimism of so much of contemporary historical thinking have their origins in an Ironic frame of mind, and that this frame of mind in turn is merely one of a number of possible postures that one may assume before this historical record, it will have provided some of the grounds for a rejection of Irony itself. And the way will have been partially cleared for the reconstitution of history as a form of intellectual activity which is at once poetic, scientific, and philosophical in its concerns—as it was during history's golden age in the nineteenth century. (White, *Metahistory*, xii)

14. Roth, *The Ironist's Cage*, 142, 145.

15. Ibid., 7.

16. Ibid., 8. The de Man passage is from "The Rhetoric of Temporality" in *Blindness and Insight* (Minneapolis: University of Minnesota Press, 1983), 222.

17. Badiou, *Le Siècle*, 82.

18. Michel de Certeau, *The Practice of Everyday Life* (Berkeley: University of California Press, 1984), 19, 38–39.

7

History: Myth and Narrative

A CODA FOR ROLAND BARTHES
AND HAYDEN WHITE

Stephen Bann

What I propose to do in this chapter is to look at the significant interconnections between two of the most influential recent commentators on historiography and myth in the Western tradition. By "recent," I am extending the inquiry back over roughly half a century to cover that remarkable phase of intellectual renewal that took place in Europe and North America in the 1960s and 1970s, with French critical practice at least initially at its epicenter. Both Roland Barthes and Hayden White have, in their very different ways, contributed massively to the critical reexamination of the intrinsic and extrinsic conditions of historical discourse, and, in so doing, have raised the crucial question of the relationship of history to myth. It could well be concluded that this is about all that can be said usefully about the kinship between them, because their subject matter is evidently so different, and their intellectual profiles appear to be so unlike one another. Obviously, I disagree with this judgment. In order to distinguish what they hold in common, and where they remain distinctive, I believe it is necessary to start with some quite humdrum accounting of history of ideas. The problem with the past half-century of critical practice is that, at present, it is inevitably seen *en bloc*. To put the matter in Barthes' terms, criticism has turned into *doxa*, a litany of familiar concepts often repeated and so worn thin by the process of repetition. To open up some of the fissures and fault lines in the "bloc" can only be a positive thing.

There is one important factor in this reexamination of intellectual crosscurrents that I should stress from the start. As far as I know, Roland Barthes never expressed an opinion on—or indeed, showed signs of having read—the major work which established Hayden White's career and contributed a new and highly controversial term to the tired debate about historiography and philosophy of history: that is, *Metahistory*, subtitled *The Historical Imagination in Nineteenth-Century Europe*, first published in 1973. Barthes died in 1980, and in the works of his last years he was not ostensibly concerned with historical discourse. I say "ostensibly," because (as I hope to show) there is in effect a very telling reference to historical experience in his last and, in many ways, still most contemporary book, *La Chambre claire* (published in English as *Camera Lucida*), which was published in the year of his death. Barthes was probably not much aware, if at all, of the contentious reception of *Metahistory* in the Anglo-Saxon historical world. There was no French translation of the work, and indeed there has subsequently been what one is tempted to call a general embargo on White's work in the world of French publishing—which contrasts with the attention paid to it by (for example) German historians of historiography and Italian specialists of Giambattista Vico.

By contrast, the debt of White to Barthes has been freely acknowledged on a number of occasions. In a published conversation with the Polish scholar Ewa Domańska that dates from 1993, White stated, after a brief discussion of his contacts with Michel Foucault: "But the thinker dearest to me is Barthes, definitely."[1] The point is then further elaborated a few lines on, in a surprisingly frank fashion: "Someone like Barthes, when he writes a little essay, 'The Discourse of History,' suddenly shows you things that my whole book [that is, *Metahistory*] could not convincingly display." What could be added to this acknowledgment, in my judgment, is the point that White had probably not seen the essay in question, which was published several years before but in a rather obscure location, when he wrote *Metahistory*. In all events, it does not appear in his bibliography. So any question of interaction with Barthes' work has to be seen not in relation to this early, talismanic work, but over White's development as a whole. This is the type of issue that seems to me important in assessing the joint contributions of the two authors. It leads me to begin by making a chronological survey of the two careers in parallel, but not necessarily in harmony, with one another. I shall insert as a medium term my own personal role as a kind of litmus paper testifying to the reception of these two sequences of work over four decades.

Barthes, of course, acquired his international reputation as a literary critic in the 1960s, and the precipitating factor was no doubt his study of Racine, published in 1963, which created a furious debate in France around the concept of "New Criticism." As with all such intellectual squabbles, the antagonism extended from the writings to cover a more general cleavage between the old guard of the Paris universities and the new voices of the École des hautes études, which was played out (somewhat improbably) on the international stage. I can well remember a confrontation of the two camps at the Institut français in London around ten years later, when the Sorbonnards exclusively wore dark blue suits and *cheveux en brosse* (crew cuts), while the new critics were in gray tweed jackets and sported more luxuriant hairstyles. There was no difficulty in discovering to which camp Barthes belonged!

The Anglo-Saxon world took little account of Raymond Picard and his polemic against New Criticism titled *Nouvelle critique—Nouvelle imposture*, but it warmed to Barthes' criticism. As it did so, it also discovered his earlier writings of the 1950s, when he had played a decisive role as a commentator on contemporary mass culture. His extraordinary collection *Mythologies*, consisting of brilliant individual analyses of such diverse phenomena as "steak and chips," the brain of Einstein, and the new Citroen Déesse, was initially published in 1957. Before that, however, Barthes had already demonstrated a deep interest in the linguistic aspect of historical writing. His first book of all, *Le Degré zéro de l'écriture*, which dealt with the attempt of the French revolutionary journalists to establish a language free from the figures of rhetoric, had been published in 1953. His second book, which appeared in 1954, and alone of his major works had to wait until after his death for a translation into English, was a study for the popular Le Seuil series Écrivains de toujours of the French historian Jules Michelet.

The very fact that Barthes had selected, for a series predominantly devoted to men of letters in the conventional sense, the most challenging historical writer of the previous century, says a great deal about his early preoccupation with the "discourse of history." The special format of the series—involving a large proportion of quoted texts, and a series of generic questions—enabled him to foreground the main philosophical and literary influences on Michelet's work. First among the "influences" listed came, as might be expected, the eighteenth-century Neapolitan Giambattista Vico. This credit was finessed by a further, more specific comment a few pages later: "The young Michelet had inherited two schemas: History-as-Plant (Herder), and History-as-Spiral (Vico). In the *Introduction à l'histoire universelle* (1831), he adds the image of History-as-Synthesis."

It comes as hardly a surprise that this study of Michelet is indeed included in the bibliography of White's *Metahistory*. However, it is included, oddly enough, without a date of publication and, more significantly, White's chapter "Michelet: Historical Realism as Romance" does not involve any allusions to Barthes' writing on the subject. The reason for this apparent omission can doubtless be explained in the context of the long introduction to *Metahistory*, subtitled "The Poetics of History," which was written after the main body of the text, but presented its most striking and contentious claims to attention. Here White explains in a note which credits as his main resource the literary theory of Northrop Frye and Kenneth Burke: "I have also profited from a reading of the French Structuralist critics: Lucien Goldmann, Roland Barthes, Michel Foucault, and Jacques Derrida. I should like to stress, however, that I regard the latter as being, in general, captives of the tropological strategies of interpretation in the same way that their nineteenth-century counterparts were."[2] He then adduces the particular example of Foucault, making a valuable point to which I shall return. The inescapable conclusion is that Barthes figures hardly at all in White's *Metahistory*, except as a generic structuralist, and that his special commitment to the analysis of historiography, and the relation between history and myth, has not yet been appreciated.

The whole issue of "structuralism"—in relation to Barthes and White in the first place and in relation to wider issues bearing on history and myth—needs some preliminary comment. We have to distinguish, for the purposes of the argument, the practice of structuralist analysis as it emerged in the 1960s and 1970s, and the wider perspective on structuralism that developed, after a certain stage, through the shift to what will finally be known as "post-structuralism," and is based on an acknowledgment and repudiation of the earlier phase. To put my own oar in here, I published in 1966 what was certainly one of the first English translations of Barthes' essays: "The Activity of Structuralism," from

1963. At this time, I was coeditor of a "little magazine" specializing in poetry and the visual arts, and the note that I appended to the translation credited Barthes with providing "a new model for the relationship of the artist, the work and the world, which is relevant to much contemporary literature and art." After struggling through the disciplinary thickets of "intellectual history" and "history of historiography" in my PhD thesis, completed in 1967, I finally saw the light and published my own first structuralist analysis of historiography in an issue of *20th Century Studies*, which appeared in 1970. The analysis examined three nineteenth-century French historians of whom the third, Michelet, had written in a letter of his cyclical relationship to his predecessors, and so put into my head the concept of a "cycle in historical discourse." My opening remarks in the article were broadly addressed to Barthes' study of Michelet, but my analytic tools came directly from Lévi-Strauss, whose *Le cru et le cuit*, published in 1964, was still for me the last word in structuralist methodology. Like White at this stage, I was still unaware of Barthes' 1967 essay "The Discourse of History."[3]

The general point that I am making from this autobiographical insertion is that "structuralism" initially functioned simply as a tool kit for doing new things with old, and often neglected, texts. The ideological rim around the critical practice was rarely evident, or regarded as at all important in practical terms, despite (or perhaps because of) the intense and continuing geopolitical crisis of the 1960s. In retrospect, White has glossed *Metahistory* by agreeing that it was indeed "basically . . . structuralist."[4] It was, purely and simply, a "study of nineteenth-century historical writing" that borrowed the tools of literary theory, and in particular applied the notion of "emplotment" borrowed from the criticism of Northrop Frye. Where White discussed, and raised objections to, the methods of so-called French structuralists like Foucault, this was because, in his view, they had misrecognised the status of the tools that were needed for the job. Or rather, they had failed to recognize that, in many cases, their analysis was simply masking with unnecessary subtlety the type of analytic distinction that could be made much more palpable by applying the broad generic concepts of "comedy" and "tragedy" as used by Frye—or indeed the array of tropes ordered in diachronic sequence by Vico: metaphor, metonymy, synecdoche, and irony. White's defense was at the time, and so remained, a justification on the purely practical level of "tools for the job." Structural analysis was justified simply because it had never been employed in the context of historiography. Significantly, this produced a major misreading of the political and ideological import of *Metahistory*. To quote from the Domańska interview:

> I always regarded myself as a kind of Marxist . . . The Marxists in my own country and abroad, for example Mogilnitsky in Russia, say: "This is formalism." I say: "Yes, it is formalist." In my introduction, I said: "My method is formalist!" Why? Because, I think, no one had ever done a formalist analysis of the historian's text.[5]

The slide from "structuralism" to "formalism" implied in this quotation, and the introduction of a Russian interlocutor, bring in a number of interesting questions. Roman Jakobson, whom White explicitly links with Lévi-Strauss as "leading exponents of the tropological conception of nonscientific discourse" in the introduction to *Metahistory*, had in a famous essay from the revolutionary period compared the conventional literary critic to a detective who, when a murder has been committed, proceeds to arrest everyone in the area. Jakobson stood by the concept of *literaturnost*: the literariness of literature, as opposed to its inexhaustible social, cultural, and historical associations. To say that *Metahistory* proposed a similarly radical reduction of the scope of historiographical analysis would be at least part of the truth. Russian Formalism had been given a second breath of life by the rise of structuralism in the 1960s, and was making new headway throughout the early 1970s. Such a judgment on the scope of historiographical analysis also helps to explain the sense of scandal in the reception of *Metahistory* by historians, who interpreted the strategy as a unilateral decision to efface the boundary line between history and literature—to subordinate fact to the blandishments of fiction. This misunderstanding has indeed continued to dog White, though it must be acknowledged that he gives as good as he gets. I quote again from the Domańska interview:

> [Carlo] Ginzburg thinks I am a fascist. He is also naïve in many respects. He thinks that my conception of history is like that of Croce, that is subjectivist, and that I think you can manipulate the facts for aesthetic effect. I think that one can do so, and although Ginzburg thinks you ought not to do that, in my view, he himself does it quite often.[6]

Rather than follow up this heated debate over *Metahistory*'s supposed defection from history—which might involve, for example, the more moderate complaints of Arnaldo Momigliano—I think it may be more useful to think of what readers of the work actually took from it in a positive light. For example, Susan Crane has given an excellent, historically situated account of how she, as a student in graduate school in the 1980s, reacted to the stimulus of *Metahistory*:

> I read [White] as a prejudiced individual, whose intellectual affinities inclined her towards the postmodern, relativist, anti-universalist, alterity-sensitive, multivalent aspects of texts. I did not assume that White was instructing me in the way I should read other histories. Rather, I read White as I have read many texts, ever since I read Nietzsche: on the premise of "do as I do, not as I say." Hayden White had articulated his own way of reading history. I wanted to do the same, and what I would take from *Metahistory* was its prompting to question the status of written history as a genre.[7]

This is, I believe, a fair index of how *Metahistory* contributed to the general furtherance of humanistic studies—not, as some of the wilder critics have implied, encouraging a generation of Holocaust deniers, but (as in Crane's case) inspiring some of the best recent writing on the development of historical consciousness of nineteenth-century Germany. My own experience, as a member of an earlier generation, may also be worth mentioning here. My reading of *Metahistory* shortly after its publication obviously led to an exchange of articles, and then an invitation to visit the Center for the Humanities at Wesleyan University, where White was director. It was from his article "Foucault Decoded," first published in *History and Theory* in 1973, that I learned more about the revisionist view of Foucault mentioned briefly in the introduction to *Metahistory*: that is to say, the idea that the epistemic categories used by Foucault to distinguish periods in *Les Mots et les choses* amounted in effect to "formalizations of the tropes."[8] It was this insight that helped me to develop what still ranks as my most frequently translated and republished essay, "Poetics of the Museum," first aired in seminars at Wesleyan and Princeton in 1976, and appearing in 1978 in the journal that had supported White's inquiries from 1965 on, *History and Theory*.[9]

The reference to White's continuing publications in *History and Theory* also serves as a warning not to fetishize *Metahistory* in the sense of making all roads lead in its direction. This will of course be made clear when I return to discussing White's more recent career in the light of the later work of Barthes. But it is also evident in relation to the role that this unique journal played in the 1960s and 1970s in jumpstarting the virtually moribund fields of history of historiography and philosophy of history. In 1965 *History and Theory* had published White's article "The Burden of History," where he attacked the historian's claim to stand on "an epistemologically neutral middle ground between art and science."[10] It was a practical demonstration of the stance taken in this article that, having operated for some years as a professional historian of the Middle Ages, he should then have shifted his area of inquiry to the historical status of history as a discipline, not avoiding its modern discontents.

This new concern, indeed, brought him face to face with the formidable task of characterizing the literary operations of the historiographical text. Undoubtedly, the philosophers associated with *History and Theory* prompted questions that were relevant to this objective. In the Domańska interview, he adduces the example of Louis Mink, who "pointed out that, if you took each of the sentences of a history and . . . ask about the truth-value of each one, you might come out with—say—fifteen true, fifteen false. But . . . it is not the same thing as asking about the truth-value of the whole." White fully agrees with this proposition in the interview, and also freely admits apropos of Mink's conclusion: "Metahistory does not give an adequate account of the 'whole' work. It tried to, but of course it failed."[11] Parenthetically, I would suggest that this recognition could be said in a certain degree to have shaped the later development of White's enquiries. This never involved repudiating the method of *Metahistory*, let alone making the attempt to go over the same vast area once again with more sophisticated tools. It did, however, lead to a continual refinement of his linguistic and rhetorical analysis, which was surely in part a response to his greater awareness of the work of Barthes.

I will return to this issue of growing awareness at various stages of this essay. For the moment, I can give one obvious example, because it surfaces in the Domańska interview, bringing up the inevitable issue of the relevance of Hegelian dialectic to anyone considering himself to be "a kind of Marxist." White answers the objection that Vico attempts to "reduce logic to rhetoric" with the categorical statement that practical thinking (and indeed literary composition) does not take the form of the syllogism, but that of the "enthymeme."[12] Here he is surely echoing the feline subtlety with which Barthes insinuates in "The Discourse of History" that "rational, or syllogistic" discourse is not a feature of historical discourse—historical discourse, rather, is "enthymematic," that is, the "case of syllogisms which are approximate, or incomplete." To illustrate this point that argument in history characteristically takes the form of rhetorical rather than logical demonstration, Barthes chooses an amusing extract from Michelet, thus paraphrased:

(1) To distract the people from revolt, it is necessary to occupy them; (2) now, the best way to do that is to throw them a man; (3) so, the princes chose old Aubriot.[13]

QED—or not, as the case may be! This, I would suggest, is the kind of lapidary observation to which White is referring when he maintains that Barthes "suddenly shows you things that my whole book could not convincingly display."

What I hope to have presented in the foregoing argument is a deliberately ragged account of the relationship between the two major critical theorists concerned with rhetorical models of history in the second half of the past century. It is a relationship that has to be extrapolated in the case of Barthes, who touched on so many of the issues close to White's concerns, but never directly engaged with his work. In White's case, as I have argued, Barthes' major essay was probably unknown to him when he wrote his most influential book, and his great admiration for Barthes in particular developed during the more recent phases of his writing. For Barthes, Vico's thought is important because it is a major ingredient in the idiosyncratic mix of intellectual affiliations that makes up Michelet, who was one of Barthes' first objects of study and no doubt a pointer to his own extraordinarily diverse future production as a writer. In White's case, however, Vico is deeply anchored in the successive phases of his development. It is almost as if Vico offered a historical justification for the crucial decision to abandon the search for syllogistic logic and the Hegelian dialectic. Despite White's ready response to the accusation of being a formalist, it is clear that he wished to align himself with the singular contribution of the Neapolitan thinker for whom, in his own words, "the theory of metaphorical transformation serves as the model for a theory of the autotransformation of human consciousness in history."[14]

I would like to take the comparison a little further by looking at the very different connotations that the notion of "mythology" holds for Barthes and White, and particularly by touching on the role of the image in communicating the operations of myth in mass society. This angle by no means exhausts the significance of both these thinkers for our own period, and it privileges the contribution of Barthes, who as a major theorist of the image has already delivered his complete body of work, over White, who is still advancing though along rather different lines. But I know that White, like myself, has contributed to a debate about Melancholy as a disciplinary attribute of the art historian, which appeared in the *Art Bulletin* in March 2007.[15] Without speculating on his response (which I have not yet seen), I believe I can see our lines of argument as tending in the same direction.

First of all, to examine mythology in White's work, it is helpful to view White's interest in Vico essentially as a way of grounding rhetorical analysis in the historical development of ideas. This would be in the double sense that Vico's mode of explanation linked history and rhetoric in an indissoluble bond, and also that Vico was an emblematic figure in the history of thought, whose principle of the "verum ipsum factum" anticipated the rise of sciences which deal with the world of cultural and social artifacts: anthropology, sociology, and psychology among them. The essay on Vico in *Tropics of Discourse*, published in 1976, just three years after *Metahistory*, is a powerful exegesis of the main themes of the "New Science." And it arguably represents a crucial advance over the type of tropological analysis that had determined the structure of *Metahistory*. For in *Metahistory*, the tropes of metaphor, synecdoche, metonymy, and irony were employed with great insight and virtuosity to characterize the differences between historians and philosophers of history like Ranke, Michelet, Tocqueville, Burckhardt, and Croce. But there was no attempt to analyze the way in which such a "poetic logic" was operating diachronically within an overall historical scheme. Nor was there any attention paid to the extent to which rhetorical features observable in the discourse of such writers might have reflected the prevalent methods of teaching of language and rhetoric in the period.

The essay of 1976, by contrast, sought to establish the diachronic character of Vico's "poetic logic," and indeed located it as the major dividend of his approach to culture. For Vico did not simply (to repeat White's words) demonstrate how a "theory of metaphorical transformation" might serve as the model for "a theory of the autotransformation of human consciousness in history." He also drew attention to the specific role of irony in that transformative process. Again, in White's words: "Irony represents a stage in the evolution of consciousness in which language itself has become an object of reflection."[16] Irony, or "double vision" as it can be termed in this context, concatenates a true and a false meaning in one single utterance or expression. But, in Vico's case, it does so in such a way as to escape from traditional forms of binary or dialectical logic. To quote White again, "[Vico] reverses the relationship between the components of ironic consciousness so that the false is seen, not to oppose the true, but to be combined with it as a necessary stage in the attainment of the whole truth."[17]

This is not the only instance where White has fruitfully dwelt upon aspects of Vico's "poetic logic" and brought them into focus in such a way that they become extremely useful tools for current critical analysis. In the case of "irony," I can vouch for my own considerable indebtedness to White's treatment of the concept—which is amply demonstrated by the fact that the German scholar Wolfgang Ernst's recent essay on my work adopts as its title: "Let There Be Irony."[18] Other tropological strategies related to Vico have also proved fruitful in White's later writings, as I shall suggest. But for the moment I want to focus particularly upon the notion of "irony," as it offers the possibility of a direct and illuminating comparison with Barthes.

Myth is a term that rarely appears in White's work, no doubt because in its Vichian transformation it is omnipresent. In other words, he avoids using the term to the extent that it is associated with mere fables, or allegories that have been devised to interpret the human condition. Vico has taught us, as he argues, that the relationship between language and the world of things is not merely a reflexive one. Indeed the operation of the poetic tropes through the course of history in itself supplies the evidence for a continuous and necessary mediation between words and things.

Other theorists working in the period when *Metahistory* was published were of course not so reluctant to fasten upon myth as a key term governing a cluster of concepts anchored within the development of modern linguistics. Lévi-Strauss, whose well-known pronouncement that "myth is a form of speech" was greatly influential in dispelling the naïve notion of myth as fiction, also rehabilitated the term to form part of the key triad in the opening overture to *Le Cru et le cuit* (1964). In keeping with this musical analogy, the virtuoso anthropologist developed the theme of a cyclical progression of linguistic functions modeled upon

Jakobson's distinctions among the "metalinguistic," the "referential," and the "poetic." Rebaptizing these functions as the code, the message, and the myth, Lévi-Strauss then suggested that we might well employ the three terms to designate the structural relationship between major composers: "Bach and Stravinsky [as] musicians of the "code," Beethoven— and indeed Ravel—as musicians of the "message," Wagner and Debussy as musicians of the "myth."[19]

I should mention here that I hijacked this triadic motif for my own initial structuralist analysis of historiography published in 1970. Taking my authorization from Michelet's view that he and his predecessors in French historiography formed a "kind of cycle," I applied the cyclical scheme as Lévi-Strauss had interpreted in the case of the composers. So Michelet himself was designated as a historian of the "myth," according to Jakobson's principle that his work was coded "from the basis of elements which are already in the order of the récit."[20] To go into this aspect in further detail would take me away from this chapter's main argument. It can surely be recognized, however, that this concept of the "mythic" function runs in some ways parallel to White's reading of Vico, in which "irony" contains and subsumes antagonistic data. The concept of "myth" in Michelet is being used to designate a form of historical writing that does not negate and thus supplant its predecessors, but incorporates previously coded elements in a fertile, but unresolved, tension.

Of course, Roland Barthes had devised his own category of "Mythologies" in 1957, several years before the appearance of *Le Cru et le cuit*. It should be emphasized that, three years after publishing his *Michelet*, Barthes had established himself as a Brechtian social critic concerned to expose the hollowness and bad faith that lay beneath in the social codings of the French Fifth Republic. These "mythologies" brought together in 1957 ranged from acute but relatively affectionate appraisals of such French institutions as "steak and chips," and the new Citroën, to corrosive attacks on the subterfuges of bourgeois humanism as in the damning analysis of the so-called Great Family of Man exemplified in a prestigious international exhibition of photographs. Barthes excoriates the pretension of photography to disclose the "human condition," precisely through the process evacuating its history. As he puts it: "Yes, these are facts of nature, universal facts. But if one removes History from them, there is nothing more to be said about them . . . The failure of photography seems to me flagrant in this connection: to reproduce birth or death tells us, literally, nothing."[21]

It is significant that Barthes is at his most creatively suspicious when photographs are concerned, because this attitude heralds a lifelong preoccupation with the havoc that photography can cause to a well-intentioned Brechtian posture of aesthetic distancing. For photography is all too often the vehicle of an insinuating naturalism. As he later explains in the essay "Rhetoric of the Image" from 1964, naturalism sneaks in when our guard is down and catches us before we can summon up our critical defenses, insidiously persuading us that, because an advertisement for pasta is garnished with market-fresh fruit colors and blazoned with the colors of the Italian flag, it promises a "real" gastronomic experience.

Barthes' first systematic attempt to analyze the linguistic structure of such undercover propaganda is, however, the example of the black soldier saluting the French flag, glimpsed on the front cover of *Paris Match*, which is the main feature of the essay on "Myth Today" incorporated as a conclusion to *Mythologies*. No one was ever allowed to see the original magazine image illustrated beside Barthes' text—and this was for good reason.[22] The original issue of *Paris Match* displays no flag, and the "black soldier" of whom he speaks is indeed little more than a cadet, appearing in a military spectacle called "Les Nuits de l'armée." This apparent misreading matters little, nonetheless, as Barthes' point is precisely that the "myth" catches on like wildfire in a contemporary urban arena, where a magazine idly picked up at the hairdresser's will communicate its second-order meaning in a flash, with no opportunity for further checking. The first-order signification of the black cadet's appearance in a military spectacle is transcended by a second-order signification, with the first signified becoming the signifier for a new meaning: that is, the myth of a French empire upon which the sun never sets. Barthes is writing at this point both as a critical observer of the last throes of the French postwar colonial debacle, before the final withdrawal from Algeria, and as a new convert to semiology. But the semiological model that he uses seems fairly mechanistic, and makes no allowance for the possibility of irony.

To some extent, a similar criticism could be directed at Barthes' essay "The Discourse of History," which was first published in French in 1967. In spite of the tremendous insights offered by this piece of analysis—to which I have already referred—the argument is marked (and possibly marred) by Barthes' consistent desire to exorcise the lure of the "real." It is notable that, where White takes confidence from his study of Vico to assert the integral role of "poetics," or rhetoric, in transforming the human world, Barthes in his early work habitually places rhetoric on the side of the enemy. In the case of "Myth Today," structural linguistics and semiology are offered as the neutral analytic tools that will hopefully dissolve the socially constructed meanings—though photography is a stumbling block precisely because of its resistance to such analysis. In "The Discourse of History," narrative is accused of putting up the same kind of resistance to rational analysis. It is difficult to see how such an approach could possibly be reconciled with the rhetorical focus of *Metahistory*. Barthes views the historical writers of the nineteenth century as being complicit with a kind of massive confidence trick, in so far as they "institute narration as the privileged signifier of the real." By way of opposition to this strategy, he concludes his essay with a barely disguised encomium to the French Annales school of historians, and what he welcomes as their revisionist strategy:

Narrative structure, which was originally developed within the cauldron of fiction (in myths and the first epics), becomes at once the sign and the proof of reality. In this connection, we can also understand how the relative lack of prominence (if not complete disappearance) of narration in the historical science of the present day, which seeks to talk of structures and not of chronologies, implies much more than a mere change in schools of thought. Historical narration is dying because the sign of History from now on is no longer the real, but the intelligible.[23]

No one can doubt the antithetical force of Barthes' argument in this essay. Equally no one—and surely not White—could in retrospect wholly assent to the proposition that narration was in the process of "disappearing" in the 1960s. Indeed, it would be plausible to see much of White's most engaging work up to the present day as being involved precisely with the persistence of narration, inflected as always by the tools of rhetoric. His essay "The Value of Narrativity in the Representation of Reality," first published in 1980, could be perceived as an attempt to situate a limit case of meaningful narrative, which takes the form of the dramatically lacunar medieval Annals of Saint Gall. Its objective is to reveal the narrative potential in what appears to be even the most vestigial metonymic series.[24] In his essay "Literary Theory and Historical Writing," first published in 1988, White goes on to suggest that the figure of synecdoche, "the dominant trope for 'grasping together,'" is the essential feature characterizing narrative. This "grasping together" should be regarded as a perennial feature of human creativity. "We do it in historical language when we wish to speak about continuities, transitions, and integrations. And we do it in literary language when we wish to write narrative novels, poems, or plays."[25]

I will return eventually to this important essay, where White's divergence from Barthes as well as his broader knowledge of Barthes' writings is most clearly indicated. Yet I should also mention that there is little point in questioning Barthes' quixotic faith in the triumph of the "intelligible," as it was expressed just a year before the epoch-making "May events" of 1968 in Paris. There is little point in doing so simply because Barthes himself later proved to be his own most eloquent critic. When I published the second translation into English of "The Discourse of History" in 1981, I also had to note the publication of *La Chambre claire* (*Camera Lucida*) in my translator's introduction, followed shortly after by Barthes' death, in the previous year.[26] It would be an oversimplification to argue that Barthes repudiates his earlier views on both photography and history in this final text. What he does do, however, is to place them in close conjunction, thus revealing a historical perspective bleakly devoid of the utopian aspirations that characterized his structuralist period. The relevant passage is a striking one:

A paradox: the same century invented History and Photography. But History is a form of memory fabricated from positive recipes, a purely intellectual discourse which abolishes mythic Time; and Photography is a sure testimony, but a fleeting one; to such an extent that, today, everything tends to prepare our species for an incapacity, which will soon be with us: an incapacity to conceive, either affectively or symbolically, of *duration*. . . .[27]

The analysis is compelling. Barthes is still anxious to maintain that History will be a "purely intellectual discourse which abolishes mythic time." Would the author of *Metahistory* have been ready to agree? Yet what appears most significant in the statement, and germane to the whole enterprise of what proved to be Barthes' most profound autobiographical work, is the subjective position that he adopts, historically, in relation to this "paradox." In speculating about the development of the "species," he is also tactfully excusing himself from the traumatic plight of losing all sense of "duration," that is, all sense of lived time. He is detaching himself, as the last man of myth, from the contemporary scene. The concluding sentence of this section makes the point incontrovertible: "And no doubt, the astonishment of saying 'That has been' will vanish, that as well. It has already vanished. I remain, I don't know why, one of its last witnesses . . . and this book is its archaic trace."

Curiously, that confession sets the scene for a comparison with Hayden White, which helps to explain why their views on the value of historical-mindedness are complementary, and do not ultimately exclude one another. Barthes recognizes himself as one of the latter-day beneficiaries of European bourgeois culture, and in his analysis, the predicament (and paradox) inherent in the destiny of the bourgeoisie is that it has invented the weapons that will ultimately destroy its illusion of permanence. White positions himself differently, on the outside looking in. From that point of view, the lure of tradition still appears (endlessly?) compelling. I quote from his interview with Domańska:

I would say that what I do stems from the fact that, as with most historians, the past has always been a problem for me. Growing up as a working-class person, who had no sense of tradition and for whom high culture was a kind of mystery, that I came to know through education, I found it fascinating that there were whole classes and groups of people who oriented themselves in terms of the memory of the provided tradition. That seems to be a mystery to me. And history was the same to me: to be a place you can examine, that relationship of the individual to the past. It seemed to me evident, the more I studied, that what historians produce are imaginative images of the past that have a function rather like the recall of the past events in one's own individual imagination. That is why I sometimes stressed the subtitle in [*Metahistory*]. Because to imagine something is to construct an image of it . . . What does it mean to experience history? What is a historical experience? . . . It has to be an imaginative creation. But real.[28]

It is perhaps this distancing of the self from the object of analysis that also enables White to diagnose and effectively resolve the issue that remains outstanding for Barthes. In the essay "Literary Theory and Historical Writing" from which I have already quoted, White showed himself to be well aware of the ultimate inconsistency of Barthes' project for modern historiography. Contrasting the Annales school's concern with the "intelligible" with the nineteenth-century adherence to narrative was an oversimplification, White recognized, born of a misreading of the antithetical character of modernist writing. In his view, "literary modernism did not so much reject narrativity, historicity, or even realism as explore the limits of their peculiarly nineteenth-century forms and expose the mutual complicity of these forms in the dominant discursive practices of high bourgeois culture."[29] On the other side, "literary modernism revealed new or forgotten potentialities of narrative discourse itself, potentialities for rendering intelligible the specifically modern experiences of time, historical consciousness, and social reality." This is a message that still comes across very powerfully today.

Notes

1. See Ewa Domańska, ed., *Encounters: Philosophy of History after Postmodernism* (Charlottesville: University Press of Virginia, 1998), p. 34.

2. Hayden White, *Metahistory: The Historical Imagination in Nineteenth-Century Europe* (Baltimore: Johns Hopkins University Press, 1973), p. 3.

3. See Stephen Bann, "A Cycle in Historical Discourse: Barante, Thierry, Michelet," *20th Century Studies* 3 (1970): 110–30.

4. Domańska, *Encounters*, p. 19.

5. Ibid.

6. Ibid., p. 16.

7. Susan A. Crane, "*Metahistory Received*," *Storia della Storiografia* 25 (1994): 52–53.

8. See Hayden White, "Foucault Decoded: Notes from Underground," republished in *Tropics of Discourse: Essays in Cultural Criticism* (Baltimore: Johns Hopkins University Press, 1978), pp. 230–60.

9. See Stephen Bann, "Historical Text and Historical Object: The Poetics of the Musée de Cluny," *History and Theory* 17:3 (1978): 251–66.

10. White, *Tropics of Discourse*, p. 27.

11. Domańska, *Encounters*, p. 25.

12. Ibid.

13. Roland Barthes, "The Discourse of History," trans. Stephen Bann, ed. Elinor Shaffer, *Comparative Criticism: A Year Book* (Cambridge: Cambridge University Press, 1981), 3:19 n. 11.

14. White, *Tropics of Discourse*, p. 205.

15. See "Response: Reasons to Be Cheerful," *Art Bulletin* 89 (March 2007): 1, 34–39.

16. White, *Tropics of Discourse*, p. 207.

17. Ibid., p. 216.

18. See Wolfgang Ernst, "Let There Be Irony: Cultural History and Media

Archaeology in Parallel Lines," in *About Stephen Bann*, ed. Deborah Cherry (Oxford: Blackwell, 2006), pp. 8–29.

19. Claude Lévi-Strauss, *Mythologiques: Le Cru et le cuit* (Paris: Plon, 1964), p. 38.

20. Bann, "A Cycle in Historical Discourse," p. 124.

21. Roland Barthes, *Mythologies*, trans. Annette Lavers (London: Jonathan Cape, 1972), p. 101.

22. This was, however, resourcefully located by Steve Baker, who made it the subject of an excellent article. See Steve Baker, "The Hell of Connotation," *Word & Image* 1:2 (1985), pp. 29–58.

23. Barthes, "The Discourse of History," p. 18.

24. Hayden White, "The Value of Narrativity in the Representation of Reality," in *The Content of the Form* (Baltimore: Johns Hopkins University Press, 1987), pp. 1–25.

25. Hayden White, "Literary Theory and Historical Writing," in *Figural Realism: Studies in the Mimesis Effect* (Baltimore: Johns Hopkins University Press, 1999), p. 21.

26. See my review of the work in *Times Literary Supplement*, 4050 (1980), p. 1301.

27. Quoted in Bann, introduction to Barthes, "The Discourse of History," pp. 5–6.

28. Domańska, *Encounters*, p. 35.

29. White, "Literary Theory and Historical Writing," p. 26.

PART THREE

DISCOURSE

Discourse, an Introduction

Frank Ankersmit

Since the days of Lucian in the second century, historians have worried about the problem of subjectivity. Specifically, they have been concerned about whether the historian could ever keep from projecting his own subjectivist moral and aesthetic prejudices onto the past itself. As long as the historian fails in this, elements of the subject (that is, the historian) will distort the nature of the object under investigation itself (that is, the past)—and "subjectivity" will be the both inevitable and regrettable outcome.

But the Hayden White of *Metahistory* completely upsets this well-known characteristic of the historian's predicament. In that book, the historian's moral and aesthetic convictions are considered wholly *ex aequo* with the exclusively cognitivist aspects of historical writing to which the objectivist had always wished to reduce the effort of the historian. For White, historical writing is always an attempt to get hold of the past, to get it into one's power, or, as he puts it, to "appropriate the past," and in this attempt the arsenal of moral and aesthetic considerations may prove as indispensable as those of cognitivism. It follows, by the way, that White is certainly not the skeptic or even irrationalist that he has often been decried as being: he does not in the least hold cognitivist rationality in contempt; he merely insists that cognitivism does not exhaust the arsenal of instruments we possess for making sense of the past. Morals and aesthetics are not to be seen as categories necessarily weakening our grasp of the world, but rather as the indispensable allies of cognitive Truth. White clearly agrees here with Hans-Georg Gadamer's attack on "the prejudice against prejudice" (*das Vorurteil gegen die Vorurteile*) that we have inherited from the Enlightenment.

In his contribution to this volume, David Harlan also takes White's rehabilitation of moral and aesthetic "prejudice" (to use Gadamer's terminology) as his point of departure. When doing so, he uses Oakeshott's dogmatic distinction between the "practical" and the "truly historical" approach to the past as his *repoussoir*. Obviously, the distinction is a variant of the venerable and well-known one between "subjectivist" historical writing ("practical history") and "objectivist" historical writing ("truly historical"). Somewhat surprisingly (because of his fierce attack on the Enlightenment from the perspective of Burkean conservatism), Oakeshott is wholly and unreservedly on the side of objectivism, and he defends the canonical rejection of "subjectivity." Harlan draws arguments from an impressive number of sources against Oakeshott's defense; he insists that such a rejection is at odds with what White had described as "the burden of history." We can never do away with that "burden" in the futile attempt to objectify the past and to reduce it to a reality without any impact on our contemporary selves.

Allan Megill further develops this argument by seeing in dialectics the antecedent of White's focus on the historical text. He argues that cognitive Truth is not all-decisive in dialectics, because dialectics always relates the claims of Truth to the moral and aesthetic *Umwelt* in which dialectical debate unfolds. Megill adds a fascinating dimension to this argument by applying it to White's own formation as a scholar. He relates White's penchant for dialectics to his teacher at Wayne State University, William Bossenbrook; he also paints an engaging picture of Bossenbrook, clearly suggesting what White must have inherited from him—both as a scholar and as a personality. Everyone ever having the pleasure of meeting White in person is sure to be struck by his personality and by the marvelous continuity between his writings and who he is. Megill's essay on White and his mentor Bossenbrook is especially revealing here.

Hans Kellner's essay continues Megill's argument about the dialectical character of White's historical theory. Dialectics denies that there are clear and fixed beginnings and endings: dialectics makes us look for a beginning preceding each beginning and for an ending going beyond all endings. If there are no proper beginnings and no proper endings, *explanation* is in difficulties as well. Explanation always relates a cause (beginning) to an effect (ending); hence, without beginnings and endings, the very notion of explanation will lose both its meaning and utility. Kellner correctly emphasizes that putting the most fundamental categories out of operation allows us to make sense of the world through the notion of the sublime, as it has been defined by eighteenth-century theoreticians of aesthetics such as Edmund Burke, Immanuel Kant, and Friedrich Schiller. Kellner illustrates his argument by quoting an intriguing passage from Michelet's *Histoire de la révolution française*, in which Michelet introduces an anonymous architect who had planned an impressive building for the cremation of the victims of Maximilien Robespierre's regime of terror and virtue. The premonition of Hitler's *Konzentrationslagern* (concentration camps) is so singularly powerful that we cannot avoid seeing here a "cause" (or rather a figure, as White would put it) of the terrors of the twentieth century (the fulfillment). So, what better illustration could be given of the futility of our conception of beginnings, endings, and of explanation, and hence, of the sublimity of historical reflection?

The sublime has its psychological counterpart in the notion of trauma: both have to do with events that effectively defy every attempt to make sense of them and to fit them into a world that is already familiar and accessible to us. If understood in this way, the notion of trauma is deeply embedded in White's historical theory, for already in *Metahistory* he was interested in those cases in which the great nineteenth-century historians escaped from the tropological grid he proposed there rather than in those in which they meekly followed it. Dominick LaCapra takes his point of departure here and compares the relevant aspects of White's writings with those by Jacques Lacan, Slavoj Žižek, and Alain Badiou. He pays special attention to White's account of the so-called middle voice, a discourse in which the subject of action is also its object (as in "I wash myself"). And then the question arises whether the middle voice might be the most appropriate linguistic instrument for overcoming trauma, because it seems particularly effective in bridging the gap between the self and what is alien to it, and hence in making traumatic experience accessible to us.

8

"The Burden of History"
Forty Years Later

David Harlan

> Each man and each woman of you I lead upon a knoll,
> My left hand hooking you round the waist,
> My right hand pointing to landscapes of continents and the public road.
> Not I, not any one else can travel that road for you,
> You must travel it for yourself.
> —Walt Whitman, "Song of Myself" (1855)

To whom or what are historians responsible? Edith Wyschogrod thinks our primary responsibilities are to the people who lived in the past, those for whom we presume to speak:

What is it that must precede the conveying of history? Must there not be the declaration of a double passion, an eros for the past and an ardor for the others in whose name there is a felt urgency to speak? To convey that-which-was in the light of this passion is to become a historian. Because the past is irrecoverable and the others in whose stead the historian speaks are dead, unknowable, she cannot hope that her passion will be reciprocated. To be a historian then is to accept the destiny of the spurned lover—to write, photograph, film, televise, archive, and stimulate the past not merely as its memory bank but as binding oneself by a promise to the dead to tell the truth about the past . . . without the necrophilia of the historian who gives herself to overcoming the past's passing into oblivion, there would be only the finality of death . . . the ethical referent goes all the way down."[1]

A "double passion" then, and a double commitment: to the dead and to the truth (or the eros that drives one's search for the truth).[2] Allan Megill also thinks the ethical referent goes all the way down: "I take the promise of truth to be ethically primary. Fundamentally, before anything else, the historian needs to be able to vouch for the truth of the history that he or she writes, just as the accountant needs to be able to vouch for the truth of the accounts that he or she presents."[3]

Arthur Danto has even argued that we don't really have a choice in the matter:

It is, of course, not altogether plain that truth is to be preferred to illusion, or certain that it will make us free. It is only that we have no choice in the matter once we achieve historical consciousness, for we cannot will falsehood or inconsistency. Obviously we will live differently in the present as our beliefs about the past are modified . . . It may not be a better or more felicitous present, but it is not as though we have a choice. For when the past is in doubt, a question mark blurs the present . . . The present is clear just when the relevant past is known.[4]

Finally, and most important for our purposes, most historians, academic historians anyway, tend to believe that the best way to fulfill these commitments—this "double passion"—is by hewing to what Megill calls "the professional standards that constitute the historical endeavor."[5] Like Megill, Hans Kellner thinks that it is only in the practice of these standards that we define ourselves as historians:

Ethos has its etymological origins in the local, in the "haunts" of a people. It is, shall we say, "the way we do things here," for any particular "we." Ethics is rhetorical ethos, the general opinion of the community. Because we belong to many different communities simultaneously, ethical problems only arise when we are uncertain which identity takes precedence. So we need to ask who we are when we are being historical, as opposed to being something else. . . . For historians are without question primarily members of a guild with tacit rules and knowledge that determine almost everything. . . . Truth is what we have when we have located ourselves in this identity.[6]

In the pages that follow I will argue that Hayden White's most important contribution—informing almost everything he has written, from "The Burden of History" in 1966 to "The Public Relevance of Historical Studies" in 2005—has been to point us in a very different direction, and that only now, at the beginning of the twenty-first century, are we coming to see both the importance and the urgency of that contribution. I

begin with a brief discussion of E. H. Carr's little classic, *What Is History?*
then move on to a slightly longer analysis of Michael Oakeshott's several
responses to Carr, particularly his famous essay—more of a manifesto,
really—"The Emergence of the History of Thought." All this in order
to provide a context in which to think about what is White's "Burden."
Published almost simultaneously with Oakeshott's essay, it is best read
as its classical counterpoint. For at the very moment that Oakeshott was
urging historians to elevate their discipline to the status of an autonomous professional discipline, White was calling on us "to preside over the
dissolution of history's claim to autonomy among the disciplines." I end
by explaining why it is that now, at the beginning of the twenty-first century, it is not Michael Oakeshott but Hayden White who hooks us round
the waist and points out the road we must travel.

Good Historians Have the Future in Their Bones.

Edward Hallett Carr published *What Is History?* in 1961.[7] Alun
Munslow wasn't far off the mark when, forty years later, he declared, "for
many today, *What Is History?* is the most influential book on historical
thinking published in Britain this [the twentieth] century."[8] But it was
an intensely controversial book at the time. Within a few months of its
publication, Michael Oakeshott had launched a stinging attack, dismissing Carr's argument as "inherently absurd" and Carr himself as "an old-
fashioned thinker nibbling at the edge of stale ideas."[9] Six years later, in
a then much-discussed but now nearly forgotten essay titled "The Emergence of the History of Thought" (1967), Oakeshott felt compelled to return to the issues Carr had raised. "Emergence" is a remarkable essay,
not only for the clarity and obvious sympathy with which Oakeshott described and then rejected Carr's position—without mentioning Carr by
name—but also because it appeared almost simultaneously with White's
pivotal essay, "The Burden of History."

Carr was an erudite man, a powerful polemicist and a confirmed
historicist for whom "the beliefs which we hold and the standards of judgment which we set up are simply part of history."[10] *What Is History?* is his
critique of the profession's "almost mystical belief in the objectivity and
supremacy of historical facts."[11] It is a brooding, haunted account that
reads as if it had been written under all the weight and pressure of what

Whitman once called "the terrible doubt of appearances."[12] Carr claimed that history could never be a science because it could never find an evaluative standard that transcended its subject matter, could never come up with a truly autonomous criterion of judgment that stood outside of or beyond history itself—what Thomas Nagel famously called "the view from nowhere."[13] "Historical facts" become historical facts only when some time-bound, date-stamped historian attaches her own particular significance to them by placing them in a narrative of her own, that is to say, only when she finds a way to describe the past which the past itself never knew.[14]

Rather than an objective science, Carr wanted us to think of history as a conversation between past and present—a continually evolving dialogue in which both the historian and her facts are constantly pressing up against one another, challenging and changing one another:

The historian starts with a provisional selection of facts and a provisional interpretation in the light of which that selection has been made—by others as well as by himself. As he works, both the interpretation and the selection and ordering of facts undergo subtle and perhaps partly unconscious changes through the reciprocal actions of one or the other. And this reciprocal action also involves reciprocity between present and past, since the historian is part of the present and the facts belong to the past. The historian and the facts of history are necessary to one another. The historian without his facts is rootless and futile; the facts without their historian are dead and meaningless. My first answer therefore to the question, 'What is history?' is that it is a continuous process of interaction between the historian and his facts, an unending dialogue between the present and the past. (35)

Celebrating the very practices Herbert Butterfield had condemned thirty years earlier in *The Whig Interpretation of History*, Carr insisted that it was "the dual and reciprocal function of history to promote our understanding of the past in the light of the present and of the present in the light of the past."[15] And since the present is shaped by our hopes for the future, history becomes a dialogue between "the events of the past and progressively emerging future ends."[16] Carr thought histories that attempted to evade this self-conscious shuttling between past and present were inevitably "dead and barren."[17]

We have become accustomed to reading Carr's *What Is History?* against Geoffrey Elton's *The Practice of History*, published six years later:

Carr the progressive, Elton the conservative; Carr the rubbery relativist, Elton the defender of truth.[18] And indeed, it is precisely when read against Elton's response that Carr's historicism, his understanding of history as an ever-evolving interrogation between past and present, seems so freshly perceptive and immediately relevant, even now, forty-some years after *What Is History?* first appeared. Oakeshott focused all his wit and fury on this issue when he wrote "The Emergence of the History of Thought" in 1967.

Oakeshott had first visited these issues in the 1930s; he returned to them in a 1951 commentary on Butterfield's *The Whig Interpretation of History* and again ten years later in his initial review of *What Is History?* But it was not until "The Emergence" in 1967 that his thoughts really took wing.[19] In *Experience and Its Modes* (1933), he had distinguished "the historical past" from what he called "the practical past." By the latter he meant the past we create in order to make "valid practical beliefs about the present and the future, about the world in general."[20]

Wherever the past is merely that which preceded the present, that from which the present has grown, wherever the significance of the past lies in the fact that it has been influential in deciding the present and the future fortunes of men, wherever the present is sought in the past, and wherever the past is regarded as merely a refuge from the present—the past involved is a practical, not a historical past.[21] If the "practical past" is "naïve"—at one point he even suggests that it "may arise from some dark deficiency of the imagination"—the "historical past" arises from impersonal interest and disinterested curiosity:[22]

The past for history [is] the past as the historian is accustomed to see it. And this past may be distinguished at once (distinguished from the practical past and from all other pasts) as the past for its own sake. History is the past for the sake of the past. What the historian is interested in is a dead past, a past unlike the present. . . . He is concerned with the past as past, and with each moment of the past in so far as it is unlike any other moment.[23]

Where the "practical past" is the past as prologue, the "historical past" is "the past for its own sake," a "dead past," a past stripped of any connection to present or future. Needless to say, this is not the kind of past that comes knocking on your door at two o'clock in the morning, a past that roars like a furnace or hurls Hebraic judgments; it's not a past of midnight meditations on the saving power of remorse and regret; this is not a past that might ease our gnawing sorrows or steady our skittery compass. That kind of past—a normative past, a past that might be used for moral reflection—is completely alien to Oakeshott's notion of a "truly historical past"—and to the professionalization of historical study that it made possible.[24]

But that was in 1933; when Oakeshott returned to these issues thirty-four years later, in "The Emergence of the History of Thought" (1967), his notion of the practical past had changed in subtle but important ways. It still has the same outlines and essential elements he had ascribed to it earlier, it is still "a hindrance and obstacle" to the emerging profes-sionalization of historical studies, the chrysalis from which "a genuinely historical concern with the intellectual past" was even then struggling to free itself.[25] But the hard-edged antipathy that marked his earlier pro-nouncements has given way to a deeper, more sympathetic understand-ing of the practical past. He now seems to recognize, as Nietzsche once said, that "history belongs above all to the man . . . who needs models, teachers, comforters and cannot find them among his contemporaries."[26] We make our peace with death not by understanding it, Oakeshott ad-mits, but "in the recollection that other and better men have passed that way. Xerxes did die, and so must I."[27] Rather than "some dark de-ficiency of the imagination," the practical past has become our primary means of locating ourselves in time, even "the condition of all human self-consciousness."[28]

What is most interesting about Oakeshott's reappraisal of the prac-tical past is his unexpectedly sympathetic treatment of the ways in which earlier thinkers had evoked just this notion of the past in order to rede-fine themselves. For example, he is much taken with the way Aristotle, in Book I of the *Physics*, created an intellectual inheritance for himself:

This past evoked by Aristotle is composed of the ideas of those only whom he understood to be his intellectual forebears . . . And he uses those ideas as a means of identifying his own engagement, which thus becomes a passage in an inquiry which he did not begin and will not end. . . . It may be recognized as Aristotle locating himself, identifying himself and his own enterprise by evoking an intellectual past, an epic of physical speculation, to which he as a physicist claims to belong.[29]

The seventeenth-century Baconians did pretty much the same thing: never quite able to get over the disgrace of having been born in an "intellectual hovel"—the cultural compost of the Dark Ages—they redefined themselves and their philosophical-scientific achievements by choosing a different cultural inheritance, constructing a different pantheon of predecessors for themselves.[30]

But for all his sympathetic understanding of the uses of the "practical past," Oakeshott still regarded this sort of thing as "intellectual legend-making," one of those praetorian practices from which history would have to extricate itself—Oakeshott uses the word "surmount"—if it were to complete the process of professionalization and finally take its place in the new post-war world of the social sciences and the multiversities.

Oakeshott was trying to distinguish a "genuinely historical concern with the intellectual past" from the "naïve interest in the past which any man whose main interest is in the present might be expected to show." Only by freeing itself from the grip of the present and formulating its own seemingly disinterested approach to the past could history claim its rightful place as a truly autonomous discipline, with its own specialized modes of notation and representation.[31] Paul Franco, Oakeshott's most sympathetic and insightful biographer, claims that Oakeshott's attempt to extricate professional history from its Whiggish past "represents one of the most profound treatments of history in the twentieth century."[32] Perhaps.[33] Certainly the wedge Oakeshott drove between the "practical" and the "truly historical" was precisely what the process of professionalization required as it shifted into high gear in the 1960s.[34] Certainly it was Oakeshott's distinction that allowed academic history to establish itself as the sole authority over what counted as "history" and what did not; it would be professors of the "truly historical" who would pass judgment on how and why the past was invoked—and police those outlying practitioners of the "practical past" who continued to write as if history were still one of our primary modes of moral reflection. As White later explained:

The distinction between "the historical past" and "the practical past" was necessary for establishing history's status as a (special) kind of scientific discipline, a discipline purified by the elimination of futuristic concerns, on the one hand, and excluded from making moral and aesthetic, not to mention political and social, judgments on the present, on the other. At the same time, professional historical inquiry, in the main or orthodox line of its development, set itself up as judge and arbiter of "practical" history.[35]

But what's more interesting for our purposes is that just a few months before Oakeshott's essay appeared, Hayden White had published "The Burden of History."

At the very moment that Oakeshott was working to transform history into an autonomous, self-authenticating, and rigorously professional discipline, White was calling on historians "to preside over the dissolution of history's claim to autonomy among the disciplines."[36] White thought history had no way of knowing that was uniquely its own, and that every attempt to come up with one had only divided history against itself and deepened the discipline's isolation, driving it further and further away from the insights and interests of the larger intellectual community.[37] And where Oakeshott insisted that historians must isolate the past, quarantine it from the present, pin it down, study it for its own sake—"What the historian is interested in is a dead past, a past unlike the present"—White argued that history's only value lies in the relationship it constructs between past and present, that its only meaning lies in the temporal dimension it brings to our understanding of the present.[38] As William Faulkner famously remarked, "The past is never dead. In fact, it's not even past."[39] Whatever moral clarity the historian may claim, whatever street-level epiphanies and small-scale consolations she may offer, she offers to the present, as White explained in "The Burden of History":

Anyone who studies the past as 'an end in itself' must appear as either an antiquarian, fleeing from the problems of the present into a purely personal past, or a kind of cultural necrophile, that is, one who finds in the dead and dying a value he can never find in the living. The contemporary historian has to establish the value of the study of the past, not as 'an end in itself' but as a way of providing perspectives on the present that contribute to the solutions to problems peculiar to our own time.[40]

It was not altogether surprising that White would call on the rising generation of historians, the men and women who were entering the profession in the late 1960s and early 1970s, to abandon history's quest for a truly historical method of its own and set about redefining historical studies "on a basis that will make them consonant with the aims and purposes of the intellectual community at large."[41] Nothing even remotely like that happened, of course. On the contrary, the professionalization of historical studies was just then embarking on its most spectacular expansion ever.

In the forty years since Hayden White wrote "The Burden of History," Western historical thought has achieved worldwide hegemony.[42] The central beliefs and assumptions, the mental habits and institutional procedures Oakeshott had described—especially the distinction between the "practical past" and the "historical past"—have become the basis for what the British historian Peter Burke recently described as "a global community of professional historians with similar if not identical standards of practice."[43] So what are we to make of "The Burden of History" after all these years? Were White's hopes completely misplaced? Or was he perhaps thinking half a century ahead of his time?[44]

The Contestations of Faculties

In his introductory remarks about Peter Burke's essay "Western Historical Thinking in a Global Perspective—10 Theses," the German historian Jörn Rüsen pointed out that professional history's achievement of global hegemony has come at precisely the moment when popular history—historical novels, films, and comics, Web sites, museums, and so on—is staging its most dramatic comeback ever. This is the "practical" history Oakeshott had hoped to bury, of course, and as Rüsen exclaimed, it has returned "with a vengeance."[45] We see it in the United States especially. One could argue that Americans are more intensely interested in history now than they've ever been. Most of the museums in this country were built in the last quarter-century and they're packed with visitors, day after day, week after week. The Holocaust Museum in Washington, D.C., has become a major tourist destination, with long lines snaking around the block and people standing in line for hours on end. An account recently published in the *American Historical Review* claims that the Holocaust Museum and others like it account for fully two-thirds of all the museums in the United States. "It is no stretch, except perhaps for our professional egos, to suppose that museums actually deliver more history, more effectively, more of the time, to more people than historians do."[46] The same thing is happening with historical films: Hollywood used to make two or three big-budget historical dramas a decade; now they turn out three or four a year, many of them very good movies by any standard. Even historical documentaries are reaching a mass audience, as the remarkable career of Ken Burns so richly demonstrates. Indeed, a career like

Burns's would have been inconceivable twenty years ago. And historical fiction has become immensely popular; you'd have to go all the way back to the first half of the nineteenth century to find a time when Americans read historical novels as eagerly as they do now. *Cold Mountain* (1997), a dense, five-hundred-page historical novel set in the backwoods of North Carolina during the autumn of 1864, was the most commercially success-ful novel in recent memory.[47] When it won the National Book Award in 1997, it edged out historical novels by such well-known writers as Caleb Carr, Don DeLillo, and Thomas Pynchon. And there were more the fol-lowing spring, by some of the best writers in the country: Russell Banks, T. C. Boyle, Peter Carey, Charles Johnson, Elmore Leonard, Jane Smiley, Gore Vidal, and others. Six of the last thirteen National Book Awards and seven of the last thirteen National Book Critics Circle Awards have gone to historical novels. Even historical comics are enjoying a renaissance, Art Spiegelman's *Maus* being only the best known of a growing genre. And the same thing is happening in the United Kingdom and Europe, across the same wide range of genres and with the same surprising intensity.[48] As the Princeton historian Sean Wilentz recently pointed out, we now find ourselves in the middle of popular history's "new golden age."[49]

We academic historians haven't known quite what to make of all this. We are delighted to see so many people turning to the past, of course, but we tend to think that most of the films they're watching and the novels they're reading (to say nothing of the comics) are little more than historical melodramas, long on misty nostalgia but short on critical analysis. The professional journals do review historical films occasionally, though with a growing sense of professional and intellectual inadequacy. As the editor of the *American Historical Review* (*AHR*) recently explained, "our reviewers have usually been historians with little training or exper-tise in film studies and often with little interest in the medium other than as moviegoers." Given which, they tend to concentrate on the historical accuracy of the films they review and ignore everything else—"some-thing which those with a deep interest in film are quick to point out."[50] In May of 2006 Robert Schneider, the editor of the *AHR*, announced a temporary suspension of film reviews, for the reasons mentioned above. As of April 2007, the *AHR* had not published a film review for over two years. Historical novels? The mainline historical journals almost never re-view them, a 1998 *AHR* forum on Margaret Atwood's novel *Alias Grace* being the only significant exception. On the rare occasion when they do, the reviewers they choose tend to be practicing historians with little or no knowledge of literary criticism. So, like their colleagues doing film reviews, they rarely venture beyond the most obvious questions of factual accuracy. As James Goodman recently explained,

Historians are not, by and large, interested in what most interests novelists: the sound of words, imagery, the shape of the story, voice. They approach fiction no differently than they approach history, discussing what the novelist got right and what he or she got wrong, the analytic ends but not the literary means, the content but not the form.[51]

Sean Wilentz recently wrote a cover essay for the *New Republic* titled "America Made Easy: McCulloch, Adams, and the Decline of Popular History."[52] It was an odd title, because Wilentz wasn't worried about the decline of popular history so much as its re-emergence: historical amateurs flooding the country with Hollywood docudramas and comic books posing as history books.[53] As Wilentz sees it, most of these new histories are little more than a sticky-sweet compound of cheap sentimentalism and soppy-eyed spectacle: appreciative rather than critical, descriptive rather than analytical, reassuring rather than demanding—and worst of all, intellectually debilitating. It is a fashionable and pleasing history that does little more than regurgitate and reconfirm the petty platitudes and self-serving mythologies of the dominant culture—in other words, precisely what Oakeshott dismissed as "practical" history.[54] We may be witnessing "a new golden age of historical popularization," but Wilentz thinks that golden age has produced little more than a vacant lot heaped with rubbish.[55]

Perhaps. But if academic history hopes to avoid what looks more and more like a terminal estrangement from the larger intellectual community, if it hopes to have a hand in shaping historical consciousness in the years to come, it will have to negotiate some terms of accommodation with the rising influence of popular history. For it is in the yet-to-be-defined relationship between academic history, with its self-isolating professional pretensions, and the proliferation of popular histories, in virtually every developed country of the world, that the past—or rather, our various and mutually canceling pasts—will be shaped and defined. The history of history through the end of the twentieth century may indeed be a narrative describing the rise of academic history to global hegemony, but if the profession hopes to survive as something more than a priestly cult of declining relevance, it will have to make the history of history through the first decades of the twenty-*first* century something different: a narrative of the periodic and various accommodations that local academic communities have managed to forge with the popular—what Oakeshott used to call the "practical"—historical cultures that surround them.

In the increasingly urgent necessity of coming to terms with popular, nonacademic history, we begin to see the real importance of what Hayden White has been trying to tell us all these years. From "The Burden of History" in 1966, with its call to "reestablish the dignity of historical studies on a basis that will make them consonant with the aims and purposes of the intellectual community at large," to "The Public Relevance of Historical Studies" in 2005, with its call for "a return to the intimate relationship [History] once had with art, poetry, rhetoric, and ethical reflection prior to professionalization," Hayden White, more than anyone else in the field, has been urging us to come to terms with the various and varied forms of historical representation bubbling up all around us.[56] Nothing like that happened in the mid-1960s, of course; indeed, the profession turned its face in the opposite direction. But things are different this time around: the new popular history is proliferating far too rapidly, has saturated the surrounding culture far too thoroughly, and has become far too prominent for academic historians to continue ignoring it. And its practitioners are making increasingly sophisticated claims to intellectual legitimacy, claims that can no longer be dismissed with the sort of smug and sweeping contempt with which Sean Wilentz dismissed them. After all, it's academic historians who are in danger of becoming a priestly caste, not those untenured laymen doing history outside the cast-iron boundaries of the discipline.

The future of academic history depends, to a very large degree, on the shifting accommodations it manages to forge with the growing, increasingly heterogeneous and divergent communities of practitioners who are writing, drawing, filming, producing, archiving, and exhibiting history outside the walls of the academy. Dipesh Chakrabarty, the University of Chicago historian, has given us a glimpse of what this coming "contestation of faculties" may look like:

To the degree that the media and other institutions of popular culture today (such as films, television, internet, museums, and so on) challenge the hegemony of the university as the producer and disseminator of research and knowledge by setting up parallel institutions that, socially speaking, serve the same function with respect to the past, narratives about the past will have many different sources authorizing them. In the contestation of faculties that takes place in the cultural turmoil of mass-democracies . . . universities may very well seek different kinds of accommodation with popular culture in different social and national contexts. Out of that process may emerge a global culture of professional history that will not be identical all over the world."[57]

A Map of the Historian's
Rapidly Expanding Territories

We historians like to think of ourselves as "practitioners," members of a first-order discipline engaged in the professional production of original and reliable knowledge about the past.[58] We assume that our most important responsibility is to convey this professionally certified knowledge to our undergraduates, and the techniques for producing it to our graduate students—in other words, we are there to teach them how to read and write academic history. A new and in many ways a more vibrant history is being produced outside the walls of the academy, by novelists, memoirists, autobiographers, comic book authors, filmmakers, curators, and the like. If we intend to meet the challenge of this new history—which is to say, after all, that if we wish our students to develop historical imaginations that are personally sustaining, socially relevant, and politically engaged—we must teach them to be thoughtful, critical, reflective, resourceful readers of all the forms in which their society represents the past to itself. Academic history is one of those forms, of course, but it is only one, and for most of the history-consuming public, *and for most of our undergraduates*, it is neither the most interesting nor the most important.

What we need now is a map of our rapidly expanding area of responsibility. Such a map would, first and most obviously, identify the major forms of historical representation, both established and emerging, and explain the advantages, limitations, and responsibilities peculiar to each one. Second, it would, hopefully, describe the codes and conventions that govern representation and evaluation in each of these realms—thereby reminding us of what we already know but too often forget: that the criteria for evaluating any representation of the past must be both media-specific and genre-specific. We simply do not have a set of meta-criteria that we can apply to any and every form of historical representation. The criteria we have developed for evaluating written history, for example, do not work very well when it comes to evaluating history-on-film, as Robert Schneider's explanation of why the *American Historical Review* has suspended film reviews so vividly demonstrates. Like every other realm of historical representation, history-on-film will have to develop its own criteria for determining what counts as good history and what does not.[59]

Finally, such a map would help us understand the relationships *between* a culture's various modes of historical representation. How, for example, should we understand the different forms of meaning and understanding generated by Oliver Stone's film *Nixon* (1995) and David Greenberg's book *Nixon's Shadow: The History of the Image* (2003). Both offer informative and insightful accounts of the man and his presidency, but they have very different things to tell us about those subjects, and they tell us in very different ways. What can we learn from the one that we can't learn from the other? And more generally, what can we learn from historical films that we cannot learn from historical novels or historical monographs? And how should we conceptualize the relationship between them? History-on-film is obviously more than a supplement to written history. As the historian and film critic Robert Rosenstone once put it, film stands *adjacent* to written history, at a location whose coordinates are yet to be specified.[60] A map of the historians' rapidly expanding territories would help us specify those coordinates—that is, the map would delineate and describe the relationships between the culture's primary modes of historical representation.

And with this we finally arrive at the heart of the matter. If our students are to become thoughtful, critical, and resourceful readers of the past in a culture whose forms of historical representation are becoming ever more varied, dispersed, and eclectic, they will have to become adept at finding their way between competing but equally valid truth claims made in distinct and often divergent modes of representation. It is not so much a commitment to the dead that they need, or even to the truth; what they need now are the skills of the *bricoleur*. They must become sophisticated multimedia ragpickers, quick, shrewd, witty readers of all the forms in which their culture represents the past, shuttling back and forth, to and fro, cutting and pasting, weaving and reweaving interpretive webs of their own devising. For only thus can they hope to develop a historical imagination that is morally coherent and politically effective—a historical imagination that can help them say, "This is how we mean to live but do not yet live; this is what we mean to value but do not yet value."[61]

Notes

1. Edith Wyschogrod, *An Ethics of Remembering: History, Heterology, and the Nameless Other* (Chicago: University of Chicago Press, 1998), xi, 22. Note that E. P. Thompson had said much the same thing nearly a half-century ago:

> I am seeking to rescue the poor stockinger, the Luddite cropper, the 'obsolete' hand-loom weaver, the 'utopian' artisan, and even the deluded follower of Joanna Southcott from the enormous condescension of posterity. Their crafts and traditions may have been dying. Their hostility to the new industrialism may have been backward-looking. Their communitarian ideals may have been fantasies. Their insurrectionary conspiracies may have been foolhardy. But they lived through these times of acute social disturbance, and we did not. E. P. Thompson, *The Making of the English Working Class* (New York: Victor Gollancz, 1963), 12–13.

Observe also that this notion of indebtedness has always been contested, at least since the early nineteenth century: "The exponents of realistic historicism—Hegel, Balzac, and Tocqueville, to take representatives from philosophy, the novel, and historiography respectively—agreed that the task of the historian was less to remind men of their obligation to the past than to force upon them an awareness of how the past could be used to effect an ethically responsible transition from present to future." Hayden White, "The Burden of History," *History and Theory* 5:2 (1966): 132.

2. For an eloquent exploration of "the paradox that, on the one hand, there is no straightforward way to match our propositions about events with events themselves, yet, on the other hand, the historian is justified in claiming she can tell the truth," see Wyschogrod, *An Ethics of Remembering*, 3. For an interesting discussion of the relation of truth and being in a culture of information, see ibid., 108ff. For a critical response to Wyschogrod, see Allan Megill, "Some Aspects of the Ethics of History: Reflections on Edith Wyschogrod's *An Ethics of Remembering*," in *The Ethics of History*, ed. David Carr, Thomas R. Flynn, and Rudolf A. Makkreel (Evanston, IL: Northwestern University Press, 2004), 45–75.

3. Allan Megill, "Some Aspects of the Ethics of History," 49. "The guiding idea," as Frank Ankersmit recently explained, "is that the historian should be

a mere mirror of the past. As Lucianus himself argued: 'the historian should resemble a clear, well-polished and reliable mirror, rendering the images of the past exactly how it has perceived them and without changing anything as to their forms and colour. What the historian must tell us is independent of his arbitrary preferences; the events of the past have always been there, they have happened already and have to be recounted.'" Ankersmit, "The Ethics of History: From the Double Binds of (Moral) Meaning to Experience," *History and Theory*, 43 (December 2004): 84–102. Postmodernism has pretty much demolished this classical notion of objectivity, of course (see Brian Fay's introduction to *The Ethics of History* and Hans Kellner's review of same), though see Carr's much earlier discussion of "truth" as a function of what he calls the "reciprocal" exchange between past and present (for example, in Carr, *What Is History?* [New York: Random House, 1961], 175ff.). Thomas Nagel probably put our present position as succinctly as anyone has: "if truth is our aim, we must be resigned to achieving it to a very limited extent, and without certainty." Thomas Nagel, *The View From Nowhere* (New York: Oxford University Press, 1986), 10.

4. Arthur Danto, *Narration and Knowledge* (New York: Columbia University Press, 1985), 341. All of which is, of course, not to suggest that the past is given, if for no other reason than because, as Danto so eloquently demonstrated in his *Analytical Philosophy of History*, the past will always be differently described because its relation to the present is constantly changing.

5. Allan Megill, "Some Aspects of the Ethics of History," 45–75.

6. My emphasis. Hans Kellner, Review of *The Ethics of History*, by David Carr, Thomas R. Flynn, and Rudolf A. Makkreel, ed., *CLIO* 35:2 (Spring 2006): 263.

7. This subheading is taken from E. H. Carr, as quoted by Michael Oakeshott, *What Is History?* The original passage reads, "Good historians, I suspect, whether they think about it or not, have the future in their bones." E. H. Carr, *What Is History?* 143.

8. See Munslow's review of the new edition of *What Is History?* in *History in Focus*, 2 (Autumn 2001), available online at http://www.history.ac.uk/ihr/Focus/Whatishistory/carr1.html.

9. Oakeshott, "What Is History?" reprinted in Oakeshott, *What Is History? And Other Essays*, 319, 332.

10. Carr, *What Is History?* 109, 159.

11. Ibid., 98. Outside the discipline of history, Carr is known, somewhat paradoxically, as a "realist." Indeed, one commentator even goes so far as to claim that "E. H. Carr is undoubtedly the doyen of English realism in international relations, to the extent that he has become emblematic, almost a caricature, of that tendency." See David Boucher's review of *E. H. Carr and International Relations: A Duty to Lie*, by Charles Jones, *American Political Science Review* 93:4 (December, 1999): 1020.

12. Walt Whitman, *Poetry and Prose*, ed. Justin Kaplan (New York: Library of America College Edition, 1996), 274–75: "Of the terrible doubt of appearances, / Of the uncertainty, after all, that we may be deluded, / That may-be reliance and hope are all but speculations after all."

13. Carr, *What Is History?* 159. Note, however, that Carr did consider history to be one of the social sciences. See, for example, ibid., 158.

14. Carr, *What Is History?* 159; Richard Rorty, *Contingency, Irony, and Solidarity* (Cambridge: Cambridge University Press, 1989), 29.

15. Ibid., 166.

16. Ibid.

17. Ibid., 141. Butterfield famously condemned "the tendency in many historians . . . to emphasize certain principles of progress in the past and to produce a story which is a ratification if not the glorification of the present." He thought "the study of the past with one eye, so to speak, upon the present is the source of all sins and sophistries in history. . . . It is the very sum and definition of all errors of historical inference. . . . It is the essence of what we mean by the word 'unhistorical.'" Herbert Butterfield, *The Whig Interpretation of History* (1931; repr. New York: Norton, 1965), v, 31–32.

18. "Currently the field is held by two books published thirty or more years ago by the British historians Edward Hallett Carr and Sir Geoffrey Elton." Richard J. Evans, *In Defense of History* (New York: Norton, 1999), 1.

19. Some scholars have argued that Oakeshott's philosophy of history does not cohere until "Three Essays on History" in 1983. See, for example, Paul Franco, *Michael Oakeshott: An Introduction* (New Haven, CT: Yale University Press, 2004), 140.

20. Oakeshott, *Experience and Its Modes* (Cambridge University Press: Cambridge, 1966), 104–05.

21. Ibid., 103.

22. Ibid., 104-105; Oakeshott, "The Whig Interpretation of History" (1951) in *What Is History? And Other Essays* (Charlottesville, VA: Imprint Academic, 2004), 220.

23. Oakeshott, *Experience and Its Modes*, 106. Heidegger, of course, would have denied any distinction between a practical and a historical past. For Heidegger, Habermas, Rorty, and others, Oakeshott's "practical past" is the only past we can possibly have, the past as part of what Heidegger calls *Lebenswelt* and Habermas calls "lifeworld," the informal background of culturally grounded understandings, competences, practices, and attitudes that make us "lifeworldly" (Habermas's term). On Heidegger's notion of *Liebenswelt* see Jürgen Habermas, *The Philosophical Discipline of Modernity: Twelve Lectures*, trans. Frederick G. Lawrence (Cambridge, MA: MIT Press, 1998), 143–60; on Habermas's own understanding of "lifeworld," see ibid., 298–327. For an interesting discussion of Habermas's notion of "lifeworld," see Omid A. Payrow Shabani, *Democracy,*

Power, and Legitimacy: The Critical Theory of Jürgen Habermas (Toronto: University of Toronto Press, 2003), 84–96.

24. Oakeshott, *Experience and Its Modes*, 103.

25. Oakeshott thought that "a genuinely historical concern" with the past "may be observed to be emerging during the nineteenth-century and, in some respects, may be said not yet to have got very far." Oakeshott, *What Is History? And Other Essays*, 365. "The intellectual past had to be released from its servitude" to the practical past. Ibid., 369.

26. Friedrich Nietzsche, *Untimely Meditations*, ed. Daniel Breazeale (Cambridge: Cambridge University Press, 2004), 67.

27. Oakeshott, *What Is History? And Other Essays*, 349.

28. Ibid., 346. These ideas are most fully developed in Oakeshott's *On History and Other Essays* (Oxford: Blackwell, 1983).

29. Oakeshott, *What Is History?* 351.

30. Ibid., 359.

31. As Luke O'Sullivan explained, "In *On History* as in *Experience and Its Modes* Oakeshott aims to present historical understanding as *sui generis* and entirely distinct from the modes of understanding found in practical life or science, or for that matter, philosophy." Luke O'Sullivan, *Oakeshott on History* (Exeter, UK: Imprint Academic, 2003), 221.

32. Paul Franco, *Michael Oakeshott: An Introduction* (New Haven, CT: Yale University Press, 2004), 140. See also Paul Franco, *Hegel's Philosophy of Freedom* (New Haven, CT: Yale University Press, 2002), 346–48. Oakeshott's "Three Essays on History" was first published in Oakeshott, *On History and Other Essays* (London: Blackwell, 1983).

33. Note, however, that because Oakeshott has most often been thought of as a Thatcherite conservative, his reputation has to some extent risen and fallen with the political tides.

34. It was, by the way, a highly gendered distinction, one which stigmatized the "practical" as soft, naïve, etc. and the "truly historical" held up as trained, efficient, and hard-headed.

35. White, "The Public Relevance of Historical Studies: A Reply to Dirk Moses," *History and Theory* 44 (October 2005): 334.

36. White, "The Burden of History," 112. For White's most recent comments on Oakeshott, see White, "The Public Relevance of Historical Studies," 334–35.

37. White, "The Burden of History," 124.

38. Ibid., 132.

39. Faulkner, in his 1951 novel, *Requiem for a Nun*, as reprinted in *Faulkner: Novels, 1942–1954* (New York: Library of America, 1994), 535. Oakeshott is generally thought of as a conservative, both culturally and politically (he was an outspoken supporter of Margaret Thatcher in the 1980s). It is unusual to see a conservative urging such a complete break with the past—though maybe not so

strange in Oakeshott's case because his mentor Herbert Butterfield had urged us to the same repudiation. For whatever reason, Butterfield and Oakeshott forgot what Faulkner never forgot: that every present is deeply rooted in the past, indeed, that the present is haunted by a past that defies every attempt to renovate or extirpate it, a past that continues to replicate itself in the minds of the living, over and over again, world without end. In his novel *Pylon* (1935) Faulkner has his narrator remark, "only the moment, the instant [dead]: the substance itself not only not dead, not complete, but in its very insoluble enigma of human folly and blundering possessing a futile and tragic immortality." *William Faulkner: Novels, 1930–35*, ed. Joseph Blotner and Noel Polk (New York: Literary Classics of the United States, 1985), 832.

40. White, "The Burden of History," 125.

41. Ibid., 124.

42. Peter Burke, "Western Historical Thinking in a Global Perspective—10 Theses," in *Western Historical Thinking: An Intercultural Debate*, ed. Jörn Rüsen (New York: Berghahn Books, 2002), 15–30.

43. Burke, "Western Historical Thinking," 17.

44. White thinks—and has always thought—that professional historiography has been absolutely central to Western civilization's sense of its own cultural superiority. As early as 1973 he had argued that "the historical consciousness on which Western man has prided himself since the beginning of the nineteenth-century may be little more than a theoretical basis for the ideological position from which Western civilization views its relationship not only to cultures and civilizations preceding it but also to those contemporary with it in time and contiguous with it in space. In short, it is possible to view historical consciousness as a specifically Western prejudice by which the presumed superiority of modern industrial society can be retroactively substantiated." White, *Metahistory*, 2.

45. Jörn Rüsen, preface to *Western Historical Thinking: An Intercultural Debate*, ed. Jörn Rüsen (New York: Berghahn Books, 2002), particularly vii. But see also xii, where Rüsen acknowledges the emergence of "other cultural, but non-academic, practices of 'sense formation' as being equally important forms of human orientation and self-understanding (in their general function not much different from the efforts of academic thought itself)."

46. Randolph Starn, "A Historian's Brief Guide to New Museum Studies," *American Historical Review* 110:1 (February 2005): 68.

47. Bruce Cook, "Peeps Into the Past," *Washington Post*, July 18, 1999, X4.

48. Richard Evans, "How History Became Popular Again," *New Statesman*, February 12, 2001, 25–27.

49. Sean Wilentz, "America Made Easy: McCulloch, Adams, and the Decline of Popular History," *New Republic* 225:1 (July 2, 2001): 36.

50. Robert A. Schneider, "On Film Reviews in the *AHR*," *Perspectives*, May 2006, http://www.historians.org/Perspectives/issues/2006/0605/0605aha2.cfm.

51. James Goodman, review of *Novel History: Historians and Novelists Confront America's Past (and Each Other)*, by Mark C. Carnes, ed., *American Historical Review* 107:2 (April 2002): 502.

52. Wilentz, "America Made Easy," 35–40.

53. By "decline," he actually meant that while popular history has indeed staged a remarkable return, its *quality* has declined.

54. Oakeshott, "The Emergence of the History of Thought," in *What Is History?* (see note 8), 365.

55. There are doubters, of course: Brian Fay, the longtime editor of *History and Theory*, thinks these "unconventional histories" have the capacity to both deepen academic history and extend its reach. But among mainstream academic historians, he and others who share his sensibility comprise a distinct minority.

56. White, "The Burden of History," 124; White, "The Public Relevance of Historical Studies," 335. I don't mean that this is the *only* thing he has been trying to tell us. In the years that followed "The Burden of History" (1966), White developed a rigorously formalist model of the historical imagination. He still thought of historical accounts as acts of the moral imagination, but he now argued that the imagination itself is structured and governed by an underlying set of mental categories that are both a priori and universal. This was the understanding of historical imagination that underlay and informed *Metahistory* (1973), *Tropics of Discourse* (1978), and *The Content of the Form* (1987). (Though see F. R. Ankersmit's very different interpretation in his *Historical Representation* [Stanford: Stanford University Press, 2002]). What gave White's account such vivid life and made it so deeply interesting was the tension between his humanist insistence on the freedom of the imagination and his structuralist insistence that acts of the imagination are governed by "the deep structures" of human consciousness. In the late 1980s and early 1990s, however, he began moving away from what was by then a rather antiquated formalism. In 1992 he published an elusive and widely misunderstood essay titled "Historical Emplotment and the Problem of Truth" in *Probing the Limits of Representation: Nazism and the "Final Solution,"* ed. Saul Friedlander (Cambridge, MA: Harvard University Press, 1992), 37–53. In that essay White returned to his earlier conviction that historical writing is essentially a form of moral reflection, a way of coming to terms with ourselves, a means of dealing with "the blind impress" that history has stamped on our foreheads. This is the Hayden White who once wrote that "the moral implications of the human sciences will never be perceived until the faculty of the will is reinstated in theory" (White, introduction to *Tropics of Discourse*, 23); it is the Hayden White who used to insist that stories about the past constitute the most basic unifying structures of the self, and that rethinking the past is a way of rethinking ourselves and reordering our values (Ralph Cohen, ed., *The Future of Literary Theory*, xvii). And see White, "Writing in the Middle-Voice," *Stanford Literary Review* 9 (1992). On redescribing ourselves by redescribing our

past, see Hayden White, "What Is a Historical System?" in *Biology, History and Natural Philosophy*, ed. Allen D. Breck and Wolfgang Yourgrau (New York: Plenum Press, 1972), especially his discussion of what he calls "retrospective ancestral substitution."

57. Dipesh Chakrabarty, "A Global and Multicultural 'Discipline of History'?" *History and Theory* 45:1 (2006): 109.

58. I have borrowed the distinction between "first-order disciplines" and "second-order disciplines" from Mortimer J. Adler, "Philosophy's Past," in *The Four Dimensions of Philosophy* (New York: Macmillan, 1993). Adler writes that "first-order disciplines" employ a common methodology to produce empirical knowledge about a specifically defined subject matter. "Second-order disciplines" concern themselves with the critical examination of concepts, methods, and assumptions used by first-order disciplines. That's not to say that they presume to *resolve* disputes within first-order disciplines so much as to *midwife* them (The analogy is Socrates' as as recounted by Plato in *The Theaetetus*: "The god constrains me to play the part of midwife to others, but does not allow me to have a family myself." *The Theaetetus of Plato*, translated by F. A. Paley [London: George Bell and Sons, 1875], 16. A marvelous image that Socrates embellishes on this and the following page.).

59. For an interesting progress report on precisely this project, see Robert Rosenstone, *History on Film/Film on History* (London: Longman, 2006), and the special issue of *Rethinking History* 11:4 (December 2007) which includes commentaries on Rosenstone's book by Robert Burgoyne, Vivian Bickford-Smith, Leen Engelen, and Guy Westwell.

60. I am indebted to Robert Rosenstone for this formulation, as for so many other insights. See Rosenstone's important statement "The Historical Film as Real History," *Film-Historia* 1:1 (1995), especially 21–22. For a popular expression of the idea that film and video *are*, in fact, replacing the written text, see Sven Birkerts, *The Gutenberg Elegies: The Fate of Reading in an Electronic Age* (Boston: Faber and Faber, 1994). For a deeper, more compelling (and enthusiastic) analysis by a partisan of what he interprets as the "video revolution," see Steven Johnson, *Interface Culture: How New Technology Transforms the Way We Create and Communicate* (San Francisco: Harper Edge, 1997).

61. I have borrowed these words from Michael Walzer, *The Company of Critics* (New York: Basic, 1988), 230.

9

The Rhetorical Dialectic
of Hayden White

Allan Megill

In this chapter I first describe Hayden White's distinctive modus operandi as a historian and cultural critic, and then I offer an explanation as to why he operates in this way. My central concern, however, goes beyond the critical task of saying what White has done and why he has done it, for ultimately I am interested in what we can learn, for our own practice as scholars and critics, from White's work.

The first of White's books to achieve widespread attention was *Metahistory* (1973), which was followed by three essay collections: *Tropics of Discourse* (1978), *The Content of the Form* (1987), and *Figural Realism* (1999).[1] These books manifest a common way of dealing with the burden of cultural knowledge. The basic problem that White seeks to address is how we are to assimilate a cultural inheritance that confronts neophytes as something almost completely foreign. This problem was present to White as early as his undergraduate years at Detroit City College, later named Wayne University and now Wayne State, which he attended in 1947–51 and where he was an instructor in 1955–56 and 1957–58. At Wayne he came into the orbit of a charismatic teacher, William J. Bossenbrook, who introduced him to the cultural history of the West and gave him the beginnings of a solution to the problem that this new knowledge created.

I

For the moment I leave aside the cultural and educational environment within which White grew up, in order to look instead at one chapter of *Figural Realism*. Although it is not among White's most striking or original writings, I focus on it because it offers an especially clear view of his most characteristic way of arguing, which I call "rhetorical dialectic." Rhetorical dialectic has two aspects. The rhetorical aspect involves a willingness on the part of the arguer to work with (and remain within) "mere opinion." The dialectical aspect involves a predilection for arguments that entertain an opposition between two different positions that are assumed to be antithetical to each other.

Qua dialectician, White is akin to two of his intellectual heroes, Hegel and Marx. But he is a follower of neither, for the rhetorical aspect is the more distinctive aspect of his work. In dialectic in its "pure" form, abstracted from rhetoric, there is a movement from scientific disagreement to a resolution of that disagreement "at a higher level," with the previously contending positions superseded. An elegant instance of "pure" dialectic is the debate, analyzed by Marx in 1844, between David Ricardo and Jean-Baptiste Say as to whether commodities have a "natural price." Ricardo held that they do and Say that they do not. Marx raised the debate to what he saw as its higher level by arguing that we need to go beyond the market, and thus beyond the notion that made the debate possible—price.[2] In contrast, in White's rhetorical dialectic there is no presumption of a higher level. Instead, the initial terms of the debate remain in place, even while the rhetorical dialectician (or dialectical rhetorician) recognizes that they have no ultimate validity. As dialectician, the rhetorical dialectician is as critical a critic as can be imagined. But as rhetorician, he refuses to believe that criticism can offer us words to live by. In short, the dialectical rhetorician puts to use terms in whose ultimate validity he does not believe. This allows him to continue speaking.

Consider the chapter of *Figural Realism* about the literary theorist Erich Auerbach, "Auerbach's Literary History: Figural Causation and Modernist Historicism."[3] Here White focuses on the concept of literary history as it emerges from Auerbach's great *Mimesis: The Representation of Reality in Western Literature.*[4] The details of Auerbach's argument need not detain us, for we are mainly interested in how White argues. White begins by evoking the literary critic Fredric Jameson's claim that the task of literary history today is not to "elaborate some achieved and lifelike simulacrum of its supposed object" [namely, literary history itself], but rather to "produce" the "concept" of literary history (87).[5] White also notes that Jameson sees *Mimesis* as engaged in this very task.

A more conventional scholar than White would ask whether it is *true* that the task of literary history is to "to 'produce'" the "concept" of literary history. But instead of investigating the truth of the claim, White "follow[s] out the line of thought" that Jameson proposes. Fundamental to rhetoric is a reliance on the (mere) plausibility of claims. If one's audience already accepts the truth of a claim or can be persuaded to do so, it is unnecessary to probe further. The plausibility of Jameson's claim that the task of literary history is to produce the concept of literary history is sufficient warrant for working out the implications of that view—whether or not the claim is true.

Accepting the notion of a "concept" of literary history, White suggests in short order that the concept is "peculiarly aesthetic" and that its aesthetic character is centrally tied up with "figurality." Indeed, White proposes that in *Mimesis* the "specific content of the history of Western literary realism is shown to consist in the figure of 'figurality' itself," and that this figurality is "fulfilled" in the notion that the task of literature is to represent reality realistically.[6] White constructs the beginning of his dialectic by plucking plausible claims from Jameson and Auerbach. Offering homage to both (but especially to Auerbach), White operates within the domain of epideictic rhetoric, the rhetoric of praise and blame. It is "no accident," as White might say, that his Auerbach chapter was first published in a book devoted to Auerbach's legacy; we might think of it as a belated funeral oration.[7] Indeed, White's work in general shows a heavy bias toward the praise side of epideictic rhetoric.

Whatever the roots of White's bias toward praise (an innately sunny disposition? a feeling that it is tiresome to discuss at length writers to whom one is badly disposed?), his chosen stance solves a problem that is potentially crippling for the dialectician: that of making a beginning. Strict dialectic demands a scientifically grounded beginning. As Hegel, the greatest modern dialectician, once wrote, in philosophy we "can assume nothing and assert nothing dogmatically; nor can we accept the assertions and assumptions of others. And yet we must make a beginning: and a beginning . . . makes an assumption, or rather is an assumption. It seems as if it were impossible to make a beginning at all."⁸ Because rhetoric, unlike philosophy, is comfortable with claims that are merely plausible (that is, that are only *possibly* true), it relieves the pressure to be foundational and thus makes beginning easier. Dialectic encourages beginning with oppositions as a basis for exploration.

But the text's movement is only partly dialectical, for the dialectical rhetorician's rhetorical commitment affects the entire dialectical movement. *Dialectic* in its classic sense wants to resolve contradictions, because the law of noncontradiction leads it to see the continuing persistence of contradiction as illogical. Accordingly, a strict dialectician would seek to resolve Auerbach's antithesis between the figural and the literal. In contrast, White reflects on the complexities of fulfillment itself (88–100). He is thought-provoking and stimulating, particularly when he evokes the notion of a *historical* fulfillment. In a relatively brief essay White gives us a richer understanding of the various concepts involved—figurality, realism, promise, fulfillment—and of Auerbach's *Mimesis*, which he finds analogous, in its "modernist style," to Virginia Woolf's *To the Lighthouse* (100). One is tempted to reread *Mimesis* in the light of White's comments, for he prompts us to see that book as itself an instance of rhetorical dialectic. But White engages in no "fundamental" examination of *Mimesis* or of the categories central to it. In fact, he finds irrelevant the very idea of a foundation.

In this essay White enters into a complex and perhaps unfamiliar discourse without becoming entangled in it. The approach eases entry into such discourses by, first, putting into abeyance the question of the truth of the discourse, and, second, by offering a way of structuring discussion of it. White follows a similar method in many other writings. For example, in another chapter of *Figural Realism*, "Freud's Tropology of Dreaming," he juxtaposes Freud's dream theory and the theory of tropes as articulated by "post-Renaissance rhetoricians" without ever addressing the question of the adequacy of these theories.⁹ In yet another chapter, "Formalist and Contextualist Strategies in Historical Explanation," he explores the conventional contrast between formalism and contextualism, not resolving its tensions but only suggesting "that there is no such thing as a specifically historical approach to the study of history but that there is a variety of such approaches."[10] And in a widely noticed 1980 paper, "The Value of Narrativity in the Representation of Reality," reprinted as the first chapter of *The Content of the Form*, he explores the tensions between narrative and narration viewed as "panglobal facts of culture" and their status as specific modes or genres of representation.[11]

As already noted, Hegel held that beginnings in philosophy must be nondogmatic, nonhypothetical, noncontingent, and universally justified. Although these demands might seem impossible to satisfy, Hegel did make a beginning, on the basis of which he constructed a number of wide-ranging cultural syntheses, notably his phenomenology of spirit and his philosophical histories of politics, art, religion, science, and philosophy. Hegel aimed to restore a measure of unity and coherence to people's ways of thinking in the wake of the French Revolution. As one student of Hegelianism, John E. Toews, has emphasized, Hegelian philosophy can be interpreted as "a titanic attempt to reconstruct a convincing consciousness of cultural integration . . . in a historical context in which traditional modes of integration had lost their experiential viability."[12] For a brief historical moment, which did not go beyond the early 1840s, some members of the cultural elite in Germany were persuaded by Hegelianism—albeit a Hegelianism split into different, warring camps. Hegel's aspiration toward synthesis and the failure of the proposed synthesis were hardly unique to him; on the contrary, many prominent nineteenth-century thinkers entertained the same aspiration toward systematic comprehensiveness, with similarly disappointing results.[13]

Two of White's earliest scholarly articles focus on the search for historical synthesis. Published in 1957 and 1958, they examine the philosophy of history of the English Catholic historian Christopher Dawson, the account of historical thinking offered by the philosopher R. G. Collingwood, and the narrative of world history offered by the erstwhile diplomatic historian Arnold Toynbee.[14] Toynbee and Dawson were exceptions among English historians, for both attempted to articulate comprehensive visions of the historical process. At this stage in his career White held that the best approach to comprehending history (in the two senses of *comprehending*, namely, *understanding* something, and grasping it *as a whole*) was to be found in the "idealist" approach to history offered by Collingwood and by the Italian philosopher Benedetto Croce. White makes this claim most clearly in a 1963 article, where he describes Croce as having seen that "the great world-views of the late nineteenth century were all based on *partial* visions of the world and were slaves to metaphors provided by those partial visions." According to White, Croce's solution to the problem of seeing history as a whole was "to frame a concept of history that would depend upon no single metaphor for its characterization but would point to a level of being so complex as to defy equation with any analogue in nature, technics, or pure thought."[15] In his 1958 article White detected a similar concern for totality in Collingwood.[16]

White never claimed that Croce or Collingwood, let alone Dawson and Toynbee, had *succeeded* in their synthesizing projects. The rhetorical dialectic that later became White's explicit mode of intellectual operation attempted to address the problem explicitly noted by Hegel, that of making a beginning, and the related problem of comprehensiveness.[17] White often indicates that he is concerned with beginnings alone. Rhetorical dialectic allows one to begin *without shame*—that is, without the shame of appearing to mistake mere commonplaces for apodictically justified truths. In another chapter of *Figural Realism*, "The Modernist Event" (first published in 1996), he begins by observing that "it is a commonplace of contemporary criticism that modernist literature and, by extension, modernist art in general dissolves the trinity of event, character, and plot which still provided the staple both of the nineteenth-century realist novel and of that historiography from which nineteenth-century literature derived its model of realism" (66). He then reflects on this commonplace, not in order to determine whether it is true but in order to explore one of its implications, namely, that "the dissolution of the event undermines a founding presupposition of Western realism: the opposition between fact and fiction" (66).

White's method of dialectical reflection on commonplaces entered his work around the mid-1960s. An important landmark is his 1966 essay, "The Burden of History," in which he reflected on the widespread commonplace that historiography is a combination of art and science.[18] To be sure, one finds something akin to the method of reflecting on commonplaces even earlier, in his 1958 article, "Pontius of Cluny, the *Curia Romana*, and the End of Gregorianism in Rome," where he notes that

scholarly opinion is generally agreed that the order of Cluny reached its apogee during the abbacy of St. Hugh . . . and began its decline as a result of the misrule of his successor, Pontius of Melgueil. . . . It is the purpose of this article to subject the accepted view of Pontius' career to scrutiny and to present an alternative interpretation of the known facts. (195)[19]

However, there is a crucial difference between White's approach in "Pontius of Cluny" and his approach in his later work. Writing on Cluny, White purported to be offering an interpretation of what *really was the case* in the twelfth century. The same is true of his dissertation, completed at the University of Michigan in 1955, wherein he depicts an opposition between two types of papal "leadership ideals"—a "bureaucratic" ideal, launched by Gregory VII and carried to an extreme by Urban II, and a "charismatic" ideal, which was embodied in ascetic monasticism.[20] In contrast, in his later writing White's overwhelming focus is on interpreting interpretation itself.

II

What could have motivated White's shift from seeking to make claims about history *wie es eigentlich gewesen* to engaging in a dialectical-rhetorical interpretation of interpretation? It is helpful to have some grasp of White's social and educational roots. White was born in 1928 in a small town, Martin, Tennessee, ten miles south of the Kentucky border in an area devoted to the growing of food crops and cotton. He began life as a Southerner in what was one of the most impoverished parts of the South during the Depression.[21] In 1936 the family migrated to Detroit, driven by economic necessity. Thanks to the automobile industry, Detroit had grown from being the thirteenth largest U.S. city in 1900 to fourth largest in 1920, and it maintained this position through the 1940 census. Although economic activity in Detroit remained depressed, White's father managed to obtain work in the automobile factories, where Hayden, too, worked while a high school student (by that time World War II had turned Detroit into a boomtown). Yet the family maintained its ties to Martin: in fact, White took his senior year of secondary school at Fulton High School in Fulton, Kentucky, just across the Tennessee-Kentucky border from Martin.[22]

White's early years thus involved moving between what Marx and Engels called the "idiocy of the countryside" and a city that was raucous, multi-ethnic, and conflict-laden. In the preface to a *Festschrift* for his former teacher at Wayne State, William J. Bossenbrook, White, writing in the late 1960s, offered a negative judgment on "the cultural and social wasteland of Detroit during the Depression." According to White, he and his fellow students found in Bossenbrook "our introduction to the world of intellect; in fact, he *was* that world. More: he permitted us to believe that we could become a part of it on the basis of our intellectual abilities alone."[23] White poses a dialectical opposition that he overstates for epideictic effect: cultural wasteland (Detroit) vs. enlightenment (Bossenbrook).[24] But the opposition is not *greatly* overstated. On the one hand, White surely registers the subjective experience of a young man from a respectable but economically strapped family of former Southern sharecroppers that had migrated to the center of American capitalism. On the other hand, Detroit's political and economic elite had long been eager to raise the level of the area's public schools, for in their eyes education was crucial for Americanizing the immigrant tide that populated the metropolis. For this reason, at the beginning of the 1930s the Detroit public school system was remarkably good—although its academic quality declined ever after.[25] The pinnacle of Detroit's public education system was Detroit City College, which played a similar role in Detroit that City College played in New York in the same period. In 1933, Detroit City College and other academic units amalgamated and acquired a new name, Wayne University (after the county in which Detroit is located).

At Wayne, White obtained the real beginnings of his education. On graduating from high school, he enrolled in the U. S. Navy's "V5" officer-training program for aviators. The training program was combined with attendance at college, and in 1947 White enrolled at Wayne. A bright young man of higher socio-economic standing would most likely have attended an elite private college or, failing that, the University of Michigan, forty miles away in Ann Arbor. Wayne University attracted a high proportion of working- and lower-middle-class students, since the cost was low and students could save money by continuing to live with their families. An extremely high proportion of Wayne students were surely children of parents who had not finished secondary school. Many were children of immigrants from Europe. But although—or perhaps because—Wayne was not a socially elite school, like CCNY it had many intellectually engaged students. Also, many students were politically engaged. Given the important role that the United Auto Workers played in Detroit in the 1930s and 1940s, it is unsurprising that Wayne had a strong non-Communist Left ambiance.[26]

I turn now to focus on William Bossenbrook's approach to teaching and scholarship and on its relation to White's intellectual style and calling. William John Bossenbrook (1897–1984) had a tremendous impact on White and on a number of other bright students who attended Wayne from the late 1930s to the late 1950s. Strikingly, the two most original historical theorists to emerge in the United States, White himself and Arthur C. Danto, were both Bossenbrook students. In fact, Danto wrote in the preface to his *Analytical Philosophy of History* (1965) that Bossenbrook's

courses in history . . . awakened me, and a whole generation of students, to the world of intellect. His lectures were the most stimulating I ever audited, and I should have devoted my life to the study of history as a result of them were it not for the discovery that they were unique.[27]

White's rhetorical dialectic is best understood as a modification of Bossenbrook's approach to cultural history and to liberal-arts education generally, an approach that—as we shall see below—was rooted in the Calvinist tradition within which Bossenbrook was raised. Although Bossenbrook's published work never achieved renown or even much notice in the community of historians, he had local fame at Wayne as an energetic and charismatic lecturer. The character of his lectures can be inferred from reports by people who experienced them and from supplementary evidence in his published writings. In 1993, responding to a question from Ewa Domańska, Danto declared that Bossenbrook's classes "are impossible to describe, but one felt that nothing was irrelevant and that he saw everything somehow connected with everything else."[28] Statements by two of Bossenbrook's younger colleagues, Goldwin Smith and Richard Miles, convey some sense of Bossenbrook's aura in the classroom. In a lecture delivered in 1970–71, Smith declared that

when Professor Bossenbrook talked about the trade routes to the East you could almost see the sails of the great spice ships and hear the camels grunt by the wells of Trebizond. You saw, or almost saw, the ceiling of the Sistine Chapel being painted and felt the agony and genius of the creator. You almost saw Thomas Becket murdered in the gloom of a vast cathedral.[29]

And in "reminiscences of Wayne" written in the late 1990s, Miles noted that Bossenbrook

> was described as unbelievably dramatic in the classroom, moving about all the time, striding up the aisles, crouching before the students, and attacking the blackboard with explanatory hieroglyphic marks, lines, and swirls of the moment. I often entered a classroom after he had held forth, to find the chalk dust thick and the board indecipherable, but I was told that it all had dramatic meaning to the students.[30]

In short, Bossenbrook had all the hallmarks of a master rhetorician, skilled at attracting and holding the attention of students. But his lectures were more than exercises in dramatization. In fact, it is clear from his biography and writings that they were part of an attempt on his part to engage in a work of democratic orientation and uplift. It is highly significant that Bossenbrook came out of the Christian Reformed Church (CRC), a small ethnic and religious community with a strong presence in Wisconsin and western Michigan. He was born in 1897 in Waupun, Wisconsin, the only son of a father, Aart Bossenbroek (1864–1940) who, having migrated from the Netherlands to the United States as a boy, became a successful local businessman. Aart, his parents, and his siblings first came to the United States in 1874 from the rural community of Elspeet, Gelderland, but returned to the Netherlands after only a year in the United States. In 1881, after the father died, the mother came back to the United States, accompanied by five boys, including Aart. The family settled first in Alto, a community six miles outside Waupun that in 1880 had 1,400 residents (three-quarters of them Dutch), moved for a year to Grand Rapids, Michigan, where the boys did factory work, and then returned to Alto, where they went to work on a farm. Clearly, the widow and her children found a support network among their fellow Dutch immigrants. Soon after 1885, the family joined the Alto Christian Reformed Church. After a failed first marriage that produced a daughter born in 1886, Aart married again in 1895. In spite of his early divorce, rare in the CRC community, Aart seems to have stayed in good standing with his church; much later, in 1935, he was one of the founders and supporters of the Waupun CRC.[31]

Founded in the mid-nineteenth century by Dutch immigrants to the United States, the Christian Reformed Church was part of a movement, also evident in the old country, toward rescuing Dutch Calvinism from liberal Protestantism. Three of William Bossenbrook's first cousins became CRC ministers and a nephew became a minister and prominent figure in the other small Dutch Calvinist denomination in North America, the Reformed Church in America (also known as the Dutch Reformed Church).[32] In 1912, at the age of 15, Bossenbrook himself was sent to the CRC's college in Grand Rapids, now known as Calvin College. At that time it was a preparatory school and junior college—and theological seminary—that did not yet offer the bachelor's degree. Bossenbrook studied at Calvin College for seven years, from 1912 to 1919, completing four years of secondary school and three of college. In 1919–20 he did his final year of college at the University of Michigan, which granted him a B.A. After teaching high school in Chicago in 1920–23, he undertook graduate work in history at the University of Chicago, obtaining his master's in 1925. This allowed him to obtain an instructorship in history at Washington State University, in Pullman, Washington. In 1931 he returned to Michigan on being hired by Detroit City College. His personnel record indicates a desire on his part to be located closer to his family; he was, after all, the only son of aged parents.[33] In Detroit Bossenbrook was thrust into a social order very different from the town and small-city environments of Waupun, Grand Rapids, and Pullman.

Calvin College was Bossenbrook's central point of contact with the intellectual aspects of Calvinism.[34] Influential faculty members at the college were attracted to the thought of the Dutch journalist, educational innovator, politician, statesman, and theologian Abraham Kuyper (1837–1920). Kuyper is perhaps most widely known for having founded, in 1880, the Free University of Amsterdam, and for having served, in 1901–1905, as minister-president of the Netherlands. But in the United States his greatest influence, mediated largely through his L. P. Stone Lectures delivered at Princeton Theological Seminary in 1898–99, was theological. In this work and elsewhere, Kuyper propounded "Neo-Calvinism," which construed Calvinism beyond a set of theological views, as a "life system."[35] Denying that any kind of theoretical thought can be neutral, he held that all thinking and practice are shaped by worldviews, and that the understanding of all spheres of life ought to be shaped by the Christian worldview. Elaborating on the doctrine of "common grace," Kuyper held, among other things, that the interest of Christians in the works of non-Christian scholars is justified, because by God's bestowal of grace, "the treasures of philosophic light" can emerge even among pagans and infidels.[36] Thus Neo-Calvinism insisted that Christians should strive to attain a comprehensive understanding of the world, and this included an understanding of the world of non-Christian scholarship. As Kuyper put it, "a Calvinist who seeks God" takes it as his task "to open to view both the order of creation, and the 'common grace' of the God he adores, in nature and its wondrous character, in the production of human industry, in the life of mankind, in sociology and in the history of the human race."[37]

We know what courses Bossenbrook took in his years at Calvin College, and from which professors.[38] He studied most extensively with Barend K. Kuiper (1877–1961), who was Calvin College's professor of history in 1900–1903 and then again in 1907–18. From Kuiper, Bossenbrook took a two-year preparatory school sequence in both History and Civics in academic years 1912–13 and 1913–14. He then took Political Economy from Kuiper in 1916–17 and Sociology in 1917–18. In 1917–18 he took Kuiper's course "The Revolutionary Period in Europe," the "main object" of which was "a critical study of the principles underlying the French Revolution."[39] In 1903–1907 B. K. Kuiper had spent time at the Free University of Amsterdam (and also at Heidelberg and Erlangen). The eldest son of an influential Dutch-immigrant CRC minister, Klaas Kuiper, who was one of Abraham Kuyper's most effective disciples, B. K. Kuiper went to a public high school in Chicago and obtained a B.A. from the University of Chicago in 1900. B. K. Kuiper was a committed Kuyperian, who as early as 1903 wrote a little book, *The Proposed Calvinistic College at Grand Rapids*, where he argued for a college that would be an "intellectual center" within which Calvinism would radiate light on all subjects.[40] Kuiper was also a brilliant (although erratic) lecturer, whose style must have influenced Bossenbrook. Moreover, Kuiper's course on Modern History would have had "as Kuyperian a focus as possible—the French Revolution, which served for Kuyper as the pivotal entré of the 'antithetical principle' [that is, antithetical to the Christian/Calvinist principle] on the world stage."[41]

Bossenbrook also studied Philosophy, as well as the History of Education, with Johannes Broene, another Kuyper-friendly professor. The Kuyperian impulse at Calvin was manifested in an emphasis on comprehending the earth and the heavens and everything within them and on seeing the world as marked by a conflict between the opposing principles of the Revolution and of Calvinism. And Bossenbrook could not have escaped the college's insistence—as stated in the *Calvin College Yearbook 1917–18*—that *"all* the class work, *all* the student's intellectual, emotional and imaginative activities shall be permeated with the spirit and teaching of Christianity [emphasis added]."[42]

In Bossenbrook's work four elements remained of the Kuyperian view: an insistence on trying to understand the world as a totality; a tendency to think in terms of dialectical oppositions; an insistence that academic study must address the problems of present-day life; and an ethical concern with confronting the present degraded condition of the world. Bossenbrook's commitment on these points underlies his involvement in a two-volume *History of Western Civilization* that he and various colleagues (primarily in the Wayne history department) produced in 1939–40.[43] In 1,498 pages, *A History of Western Civilization* attempts to give students an introduction to the whole of the "Western" experience as seen from the standpoint of the present.

In their preface to the first volume, Bossenbrook and a colleague, Rolf Johannesen, make it clear that the authors aimed to highlight "the dominant aspirations or ideals" of each period, or those that "are most significant for the present" (1: v). In the preface to the second volume, which surveys Western history from the seventeenth century to the recent outbreak of "a new holocaust of war," Bossenbrook (now the only listed preface author), asserts that:

The authors of this survey have been concerned especially with presenting contemporary Western civilization as a *dynamic totality*. . . . The preliminary introduction seeks to portray the general physiognomy of contemporary Western civilization as it differed from other civilizations. An introduction to each section presents an interpretation of a period of this civilization, indicating its *coherent* character and tying the subsequent chapters into a *meaningful whole*. Synoptic chronological tables provide a summary of the main movements and events of a period. (2: v; emphasis added)[44]

The attractiveness of such a comprehensive vision to the kind of student that Bossenbrook and his colleagues hoped to encounter at Wayne is easy to imagine. Such a student was a stranger to the higher spheres of culture but was nonetheless eager to learn. *A History of Western Civilization* aimed to give such students an overview of the history of the West that would help them make sense of a present marked by economic crisis, social conflict, and war. And yet from an epistemological point of view, Bossenbrook's project was questionable. How does one *know* which past "aspirations and ideals" are "most significant for the present"? Indeed, how does one know that there is such a thing as "Western civilization," let alone Western civilization considered as a "dynamic totality"? Bossenbrook's epistemological assumptions, although they might pass muster in an undergraduate classroom, were to prove incapable of doing so within the context of professional historical scholarship. Both the aspirations and the unresolved problems of Bossenbrook's scholarship are manifest in his only major published scholarly work, *The German Mind* (1961).[45] *The German Mind* attempts to address an issue much debated by historians in the post–World War II period, the so-called "German problem." Bossenbrook begins the book by posing what he calls "the key question of the 'German problem,'" namely, "why the Germans have not been 'integrated' into the Western community of values" (vii). Bossenbrook's question presupposes the thesis of German exceptionalism, which David Blackbourn and Geoff Eley harshly criticized in the 1980s in their influential *The Peculiarities of German History*.[46]

However, Bossenbrook's adherence to a "paradigm" that many later historians rejected does not invalidate *The German Mind*. Rather, the book raises difficulties for itself of an epistemological and also an ontological character. Bossenbrook centers the book on large dialectical abstractions that were and are foreign to the thinking of the vast majority of historians. For example, he declares that *The German Mind* "is based on the assumption that the Germans and the French have played the chief dialectical roles in the formation of the European community of values" (vii). But what justifies the claim that "the Germans" and "the French" are coherent and persisting entities, let alone the claim that they are "dialectically" related? What is worse, Bossenbrook's focus of attention is not even "the Germans," but a higher abstraction, "the German mind."[47] And where, exactly, is the historian to find "the European community of values"? Bossenbrook tells us that *The German Mind* was "originally intended as part of a general history of the Germans proposed by Professor Allan Nevins" (vii), a well-known historian at Columbia University.[48] Nevins must have anticipated a "normal" work of history, but that is not what Bossenbrook produced. More clearly than in his outline of *Western Civilization*, Bossenbrook reveals in *The German Mind* an idealist ontology that most historians at the time (and now) would regard as evidentially unsupportable.

Many of the details in *The German Mind* are fascinating, from Bossenbrook's discussion of handwriting in the Middle Ages to his evoking of such figures of modernity as Friedrich Nietzsche, Oswald Spengler, Ludwig Klages, Karl Jaspers, and Martin Heidegger. The book's combination of breadth and interesting detail helps us see how Bossenbrook achieved renown as a lecturer to undergraduates. But Bossenbrook does not offer anything like a defensible historical explanation of National Socialism, nor even an adequate descriptive-narrative history of Germany. Rather, he portrays three "moments" in a history of absolute spirit: from a sacred *ordo* to the freedom of faith (800–1600); from a cosmic order to the creativity of the spirit (1600–1850); and from historicism to "technical existenz" (1850–1950). These moments amount to three successive manifestations of dialectical conflict in an essentially theological story. In Bossenbrook's words, "this book is concerned mainly with the impact of the process of secularization on the German mind" (10). Bossenbrook offers a theologically inflected philosophy of history, with Nazism interpreted as the unfortunate outcome of "the technological revolution" unleashed by secularization, which acted upon the Nazi leaders without their being "fully aware" of it (447). *The German Mind* passed all but unnoticed by Bossenbrook's fellow historians: in fact, it was not reviewed in any major historical journal.[49]

III

White, Bossenbrook's student, emulated Bossenbrook—and went beyond him. It is noteworthy that White is one of only two people who, Bossenbrook writes, had "read the manuscript [of *The German Mind*] and gave me many suggestions for its improvement" (viii). In the early stages of his career—up to *Metahistory*—White attempted, like Bossenbrook, to offer a unified and comprehensive vision of the world for the practical and existential benefit of students. In the early 1960s (if not already in the 1950s), White took on the task of editing a book series, of which six volumes were published, which aimed to cover "Major Traditions of World

Civilization." White wrote one of these volumes, *The Greco-Roman Tradition*, which, like *Metahistory*, was published in 1973.[50]

White's solution to the problem of "covering" two large civilizations in the course of 150 pages was in the spirit of Bossenbrook's work. The solution involved two moves: an *interpretive* move, and an *essentializing* move. *The Greco-Roman Tradition* is interpretive in two senses. First, it is largely cast as a response to others' interpretations: White refers repeatedly to previous, named commentators, such as Arnold Toynbee, with whom he takes issue, as well as to what is "conventionally" or "often" or "sometimes" "said" or "suggested" or "taught" about classical civilization.[51] Second, it is interpretive in the sense that White emphasizes the *present-day significance* of the Greco-Roman tradition: thus he tells us early on that "historical thinking" attempts "to make sense of the present by reflection on its relation to various parts of the past" (8). (These two senses of interpretation are akin in their emphasis on the *meaning* of the past: in the first instance, its meaning for previous interpreters; in the second, its meaning for us, now.)

In his focus on interpretation White was following Bossenbrook. Bossenbrook showed his preference for the interpretation of previous interpretation as early as his master's thesis at the University of Chicago, "The Interpretation of the Italian Renaissance" (1925); continued along this track by writing his doctoral dissertation on "Justus Moeser as an Historian" (1932); and persisted in the same direction in *The German Mind*, the introduction of which addresses "The Interpretation of German History" (1–11). Bossenbrook's mentor at Chicago, the medieval historian James Westfall Thompson, had a strong secondary interest in the history of historiography, which became Bossenbrook's primary interest.[52] We have of course already seen that Bossenbrook was also interpretive in the different sense of emphasizing the present-day significance of the past.

White's essentializing move is in tension with his interpretive move. But first we need to get a better idea of what is involved in essentialization, and this is more visible in Bossenbrook's work than in White's. Again and again Bossenbrook claimed to offer *the* spirit or essence (and not merely *an* interpretation) of such and such a historical object. For example, again and again (and not only in *The German Mind*), he employed typologizing labels to which he appeared to grant an essential, and not merely an interpretive, reality. For example, in his introduction to a short anthology on nationalism published in 1965, he suggests that twentieth-century conditions would "bring about great changes in its [nationalism's] essential character."[53] Similarly, the syllabus of his graduate course on "Modern Historiography" (1952 version) is replete with dialectically related types that one suspects were given an essentialist twist: Rationalism and Enlightenment, Romanticism and Liberalism, Realism and Positivism, Impressionism and Expressionism.[54]

The early Hayden White was also addicted to essentialization. In his article "Romanticism, Historicism, and Realism" in the Bossenbrook Festschrift, he treats these three labels, all capitalized, as if they were substantive entities.[55] White makes a similar essentializing move in *The Greco-Roman Tradition*, the initial chapter of which is entitled "The Essence of Classicism." By essentializing, and thus by making it possible to exclude everything not connected to the *essence* of Greco-Roman culture among the myriad available facts about ancient Greece and Rome, White was able to offer in a mere 158 pages an account of "the Greco-Roman tradition" that could purport to be coherent.

But there are two problems with essentialization. First, most historians find it hard to take seriously work that blithely passes over the various objections and counterarguments—the "buts" and "no, it was not quite like that" and "you have completely ignored X, Y, and Z"—that dominate the culture of academic life. Second, there is a theoretical problem, for the interpretive move (which is implicit in any insistence on "the uses of history") makes the historical object relative to the standpoint of the interpreter. Interpretation is contrary to the notion that there is an object (for example, "classicism") that has an essence of its own. There is a contradiction here—perhaps even a *dialectical* contradiction. It is hardly surprising that White made the turn, discussed in the first part of this chapter, to a *rhetorical*, and thus nonessentialist, dialectic.

White's "rhetorization" of Bossenbrook—with the focus of attention shifting from mysterious essences (such as "the German mind") to the commonplaces of discourse—allowed him to escape the epistemological objections to which Bossenbrook was vulnerable. To be sure, White himself has sometimes been accused of denying the distinction between truth and fiction, thus of making it impossible for adherents of his view to counter false claims about the past.[56] But while White's work characteristically involves a juxtaposing of "mere" commonplaces, this is not a denial on his part of the truth/falsehood distinction. White has chosen the path of a rhetorical critic, but he has never said that rhetorical criticism makes up the entire scholarly enterprise. In any case, White's approach is both rhetorical and dialectical, which means, among other things, that he is concerned with saying true—that is, argumentatively justified—things about commonplaces.

IV

We are left with the question as to what benefits we might gain from White's rhetorical dialectic. I want to point out two benefits in particular. The first has to do with issues of coherence—and incoherence. Sixty and more years ago, Bossenbrook and his colleagues at Wayne University were acutely conscious of the problem of coherence, no doubt because, unlike the privileged historians teaching at Yale, Harvard, Princeton, and similar institutions in that period, they could not rely on the authority of a mandarinically authorized conception of the coherence of history. Because Bossenbrook was the inheritor of a Neo-Calvinist concern for practicing one's vocation to ethically good ends, he insisted that historians should strive to impart to their students a single, coherent conception of history—for this, he thought, would help them orient their lives in a confusing time.

We know full well that the historical monographs that most historians write will not cumulate into anything like a coherent picture of the past and its significance. Rather, we are faced by a vast collection of disparates. The young Hayden White shared the unifying impulse that led Bossenbrook to produce, with his colleagues, *A History of Western Civilization*. Over time, however, White's commitment to coherence, which underlay his book series Major Traditions of World Civilization, changed its shape. By 1970, when the two-volume textbook *An Intellectual History of Western Europe*, coauthored with Willson Coates, appeared, there was no more talk of essences.[57] And in his breakthrough book, *Metahistory*, the whole point is to suggest that many *different* ways of finding coherence in the past are possible.

The implications extend well beyond the sphere of historical scholarship. The potentially wider uses of a rhetorical dialectic are perhaps most evident in times of cultural multiplicity and epistemological uncertainty, such as our own. For example, the multiplicity of cultural expressions at the present moment is enormous, and the task of "making sense of it all" utterly intimidating. There are real risks of intellectual paralysis, of throwing up one's hands in despair. A rhetorical dialectic, proceeding by way of categories that are *imposed* on the body of cultural material, but imposed in an exploratory and provisional way, offers us one way of trying to make global sense of that material. A rhetorical dialectician never claims to have access to absolute truth. As a dialectician, she knows that she must go in search of coherence, because dialectical argument works on the basis of contradiction, and without some measure of commonality contradiction never appears. Yet, as a rhetorician, she also knows that the chances of reaching absolute truth, about coherence or anything else, are slim. This has implications of a profound sort for the way we live both our public and our private lives.

My second point has to do with issues of evidence. There exist hotly disputed questions of public policy, having to do with war, the environment, ethnic conflict, and other issues, which cannot be resolved by an appeal to evidence, either because the evidence is hidden and is likely to remain so for some time, or because the issues are such that no appeal to evidence alone will resolve them. Historians and critics of the present might well regard themselves as stymied by the evidential situation and as obliged to sit and wait—for ten or twenty or a hundred years—until an adequately interlinked body of evidence becomes available and until enough of the consequences of present action have worked themselves out that these consequences can be used to cast light on what for now is a mystery. But even while lacking adequate access to an archive, the *contemporary* historian—appearing in the guise of a critic of the present and of the recent past—has the option of analyzing the (dialectically) opposing discourses of justification that the participants in present-day debate (rhetorically) offer.

The rhetorical analysis of claims in the present to well-grounded truth, combined with the dialectical analysis of the present's rhetorical commonplaces, could be considered a strategy *faute de mieux*, made necessary by the absence of a well-organized and accessible archive and by the uncertainty of outcomes. Putting into abeyance the question of the Truth or Justice of the various claims being made (for example, for and against such and such a war, or such and such an environmental policy, or concerning the "right to exist" of such and such a state), the rhetorical dialectician would instead focus on the consistency of the claims being made and on the possible implications of their full unfolding. Such an approach can, I believe, be taught to students, in such a way that they can carry it with them in their public lives. It is a matter of a critical rhetoric, able to reveal the nakedness of positions that cannot stand the light of day, and yet able also to promote conversation and debate, by dint of never claiming to know *absolutely* what the Truth actually is or where Justice is actually to be found.

Notes

1. Hayden White, *Metahistory: The Historical Imagination in Nineteenth-Century Europe* (Baltimore: Johns Hopkins University Press, 1973); *Tropics of Discourse: Essays in Cultural Criticism* (Baltimore: Johns Hopkins University Press, 1978); *The Content of the Form: Narrative Discourse and Historical Representation* (Baltimore: Johns Hopkins University Press, 1987); *Figural Realism: Studies in the Mimesis Effect* (Baltimore: Johns Hopkins University Press, 1999).

2. Allan Megill, *Karl Marx: The Burden of Reason (Why Marx Rejected Politics and the Market)* (Lanham, MD: Rowman & Littlefield, 2002), 168–71.

3. White, *Figural Realism*, 87–100.

4. Erich Auerbach, *Mimesis: The Representation of Reality in Western Literature*, trans. Willard R. Trask (Princeton: Princeton University Press, 1953).

5. White quotes Fredric Jameson, *The Political Unconscious: Narrative as a Socially Symbolic Act* (Ithaca, NY: Cornell University Press, 1981), 12.

6. White, *Figural Realism*, 87. In chapter 7, "Choosing a Past: Figure and Fulfilment," of his 2006 University of Groningen dissertation, Hendrik Jan [Herman] Paul offers a thorough account of White's application of the notions of figure and fulfillment to historiography. Hendrik Jan Paul, "Masks of Meaning: Existentialist Humanism in Hayden White's Philosophy of History" (PhD diss., Rijksuniversiteit Groningen: 2006). I am indebted to Herman Paul both for his fine dissertation and for an illuminating e-mail correspondence concerning White's background.

7. Seth Lerer, ed., *Literary History and the Challenge of Philology: The Legacy of Erich Auerbach* (Stanford: Stanford University Press, 1996).

8. G. W. F. Hegel, introduction to *Logic, Being Part One of the Encyclopedia of the Philosophical Sciences*, trans. William Wallace (Oxford University Press: Oxford, 1975), 3.

9. White, *Figural Realism*, 101–125; quotation at 105.

10. Ibid., 43–65; quotation at 65.

11. White, *The Content of the Form*, 1–25; quotation at 1.

12. John Edward Toews, *Hegelianism: The Path Toward Dialectical Humanism, 1805–1841* (Cambridge: Cambridge University Press, 1980), 4.

13. Maurice Mandelbaum, *History, Man, and Reason: A Study in Nineteenth-Century Thought* (Baltimore, MD: Johns Hopkins University Press, 1971) offers perhaps the most comprehensive study of the search for synthesis in nineteenth-century European thought.

14. White, "Collingwood and Toynbee: Transitions in English Historical Thought," *English Miscellany* 8 (1957): 147–78; and "Religion, Culture and Western Civilization in Christopher Dawson's Idea of History," *English Miscellany* 9 (1958): 247–87.

15. Hayden V. White, "The Abiding Relevance of Croce's Idea of History," *Journal of Modern History* 35 (1963): 109–124; quotation at 115.

16. He praised Collingwood for having attempted to "raise historical thought" to the dignity of a form of thought that "contained implicitly the artistic, religious and scientific moments," but which "transcended their limitations by seeing the world as a totality." White, "Religion, Culture, and Western Civilization," 261.

17. White's most widely noted work, *Metahistory*, is an extended ironic commentary on the failure of eight of the greatest thinkers of the nineteenth century to achieve the comprehensive view that the first of them, Hegel, so adamantly sought.

18. Hayden V. White, "The Burden of History," *History and Theory* 5 (1966): 111–34; rpr. as chapter 1 of White, *Tropics of Discourse*, 27–80.

19. Hayden V. White, "Pontius of Cluny, the *Curia Romana* and the End of Gregorianism in Rome," *Church History* 27 (1958): 195–219, quoted at 195.

20. Hayden V. White, "The Conflict of Papal Leadership Ideals from Gregory VII to St. Bernard of Clairvaux with Special Reference to the Schism of 1130" (PhD diss., University of Michigan, 1955). I rely here on Herman Paul's discussion of White's dissertation in Paul, "A Weberian Medievalist: Hayden White in the 1950s," *Rethinking History* 12 (2008), supplementing my own notes on White's dissertation, which I read in 1993. White's second and final article in his original field of academic specialization likewise claims to be about the realia of medieval history: White, "The Gregorian Ideal and Saint Bernard of Clairvaux," *Journal of the History of Ideas* 21 (1960): 321–48.

21. White's very name reveals his Southern roots. The preservation of a family name by converting it into a first name is an offshoot of the patriarchalism that once suffused Southern society. The "V." in his name is also interesting, since there is no middle name for which it stands. Rather, it marks an attempt to *evoke* a name of high cultural status, that of Virgil, without being so forward as to actually *speak* it. In naming their child with such an "empty but potent" signifier, White's parents appear to have manifested both respect for high cul-

ture and shame at their lack of it. (On lower-middle-class cultural insecurity, see Rita Felski, "Nothing to Declare: Identity, Shame and the Lower Middle Class," *PMLA* 115 [2000]: 33–45; quotation at 36).

22. For city population rankings, see Campbell Gibson, "Population of the 100 Largest Cities and Other Urban Places in the United States: 1790 to 1990," prepared by the Population Division, U.S. Bureau of the Census (Washington, DC: June 1998), http://www.census.gov/population/www/documentation/twps0027.html. In the 1950 census Detroit fell to sixth place among U.S. cities, and in the 1990 census to seventh. For personal details I rely on a 1993 interview with White.

23. Hayden V. White, ed., preface to *The Uses of History: Essays in Intellectual and Social History Presented to William J. Bossenbrook* (Detroit: Wayne State University Press, 1968), 10.

24. In my characterization below of the cultural experiences that Detroit, Wayne University, and Bossenbrook offered, I rely on communications from 1993 with White, Ralph Giesey, and Martin Havran, who were students at Wayne University from 1943 until the early 1950s, as well as on a letter of August 12, 1993, from Richard D. Miles, who arrived at Wayne as a history instructor in 1948.

25. The economic situation of the period—and its effects on the Detroit school system—are well recounted by Jeffrey Mirel, *The Rise and Fall of an Urban School System: Detroit, 1907–81* (Ann Arbor: University of Michigan Press, 1993), especially chapters 3 and 4.

26. In communications with me, both Giesey and White remarked on the political orientation of Wayne students. Several informants also noted the large proportion of Jewish students. On the economic, social, industrial, and political situation in Detroit, see Nelson Lichtenstein, *The Most Dangerous Man in Detroit: Walter Reuther and the Fate of American Labor* (New York: Basic Books, 1995). On Wayne University, see Leslie L. Hanawalt, *A Place of Light: The History of Wayne State University* (Detroit: Wayne State University Press, 1968); and Henry V. Bohm and Paul J. Pentecost, eds., *Reminiscences of Wayne: Memoirs of Some Faculty and Staff Members of Wayne State University* (n.p., 2000), especially the editors' introduction and the essay by Richard D. Miles, i–iv, 1–14.

27. Arthur C. Danto, *Analytical Philosophy of History* (New York: Columbia University Press, 1965), xvi. Danto elaborates on this comment in an interview with Ewa Domańska, in Domańska, ed., *Encounters: Philosophy of History after Postmodernism* (Charlottesville: University Press of Virginia, 1998), 166–67, 176.

28. Domańska, ed., *Encounters*, 166.

29. Goldwin Smith, "The Gates of Excellence," in *The Professor and the Public*, ed. Goldwin Smith (Detroit: Wayne State University Press, 1972), 27.

30. Richard Miles, in *Reminiscences of Wayne*, 9.

31. For information on Bossenbrook's family, I rely on a "Bossenbroek Ge-

nealogie" downloaded from the Web in early 2007 (http://theodeweerd.tripod
.com, no longer available), and on information supplied in e-mail exchanges
with Roland E. Bossenbroek of El Cajon, California, also in early 2007. Roland
Bossenbroek reports that the "Bossenbroek Genealogie" was compiled by Revs.
Harold and Leonard Bossenbroek.

32. The curator of archives at Calvin College, Richard H. Harms, alerted me
to Bossenbrook's clerical cousins. Herman Paul informed me of the ecclesiasti-
cal career of Bossenbrook's nephew, Albertus G. Bossenbroek.

33. I am deeply grateful to Professor James D. Bratt of Calvin College, who
identified and copied documents in the Calvin College archives relevant to
Bossenbrook and composed a detailed e-mail, dated April 3, 2007, interpreting
what he had found. Other information was supplied in 1993 by Patricia Bart-
kowski of the Walter P. Reuther Library at Wayne State University.

34. Harry Boonstra, *Our School: Calvin College and the Christian Reformed
Church* (Grand Rapids, MI: Eerdmans, 2001), provides a useful brief introduction to the history of Calvin College. See also John J. Timmerman, *Promises to
Keep: A Centennial History of Calvin College* (Grand Rapids, MI: Calvin College
and Seminary, with William B. Eerdmans Publishing Company, 1975).

35. Abraham Kuyper, *Calvinism: Six Lectures Delivered in the Theological Seminary at Princeton* (New York: Fleming H. Revell, 1899). See especially
Kuyper's first lecture, "Calvinism a Life-System," 1–45, and his fourth, "Calvinism and Science," 143–88. Peter S. Heslam offers a sympathetic overview
of Kuyper's thought as articulated in his Stone lectures, in Heslam, *Creating
a Christian Worldview: Abraham Kuyper's Lectures on Calvinism* (Grand Rapids, MI: Eerdmans, 1998). See also *Abraham Kuyper: A Centennial Reader*, ed.
James D. Bratt (Grand Rapids, MI: Eerdmans, 1998); and James D. Bratt, *Dutch
Calvinism in Modern America: A History of a Conservative Subculture* (Grand
Rapids, MI: Eerdmans, 1984), especially chapter 2, "Abraham Kuyper and Neo-
Calvinism," 14–33.

36. On common grace, see Kuyper, *Calvinism: Six Lectures*, 162–65; quotation at 165. On the relation of common grace to science, see Heslam, *Creating a
Christian Worldview*, 120–23.

37. Kuyper, *Calvinism: Six Lectures*, 165. Kuyper had already declared in
his lecture delivered at the founding of the Free University of Amsterdam that
"There is not an inch in the whole estate of our human existence, of which
Christ, who is Sovereign over all, does not proclaim: 'It is Mine.'" Boonstra, *Our
School*, 4, quoting Abraham Kuyper, *Souvereiniteit in Eigen Kring* (Amsterdam:
Kruyt, 1880), 35.

38. Bossenbrook's official transcript indicates which courses he took when,
and the grades achieved. The yearbooks of the Theological School and Calvin
College for 1912–13 through 1918–19 give much information about the college's
curriculum.

39. *Yearbook of the Theological School and Calvin College 1917–18*, 20. Information about B. K. Kuiper has come to me from James Bratt, Richard Harms, and Herman Paul, as well as from Boonstra, *Our School*, and Timmerman, *Promises to Keep*.

40. Timmerman, *Promises to Keep*, 35–36.

41. Bratt, e-mail of April 3, 2007. Timmerman comments on Kuiper's lecturing—and sometimes erratic behavior—in *Promises to Keep*, 35–38.

42. *Yearbook of the Theological School and Calvin College 1917–18*, quoted in Boonstra, *Our School*, 35.

43. William J. Bossenbrook and Rolf Johannesen, *A History of Western Civilization*, vol. 1, *Foundations of Western Civilization* (Boston: D. C. Heath, 1939); William J. Bossenbrook, *A History of Western Civilization*, vol. 2, *Development of Contemporary Civilization* (Boston: D. C. Heath, 1940).

44. Pursuing a similar line, Bossenbrook and his colleague Raymond C. Miller coauthored the 5,000-word essay "The Introductory Course in History: A Declaration of Independence," where they claim (in words that sound like Bossenbrook more than Miller) that "any age and any period must be viewed as part of a cultural totality, for the description of which the historian must have some sort of theory (call it a philosophy of history if you like) which will relate the culture to the totality of man's development." See Raymond C. Miller and William J. Bossenbrook, "The Introductory Course in History: A Declaration of Independence" (Faculty Publications Collection, University Archives, Wayne State University), 6. This undated, privately printed essay was accessioned by the Wayne University archives in September 1941, according to a date stamp on its first page. I am indebted to Brecque Keith, university archivist at Wayne State, for her assistance.

45. William J. Bossenbrook, *The German Mind* (Detroit: Wayne State University Press, 1961). Bossenbrook never published his 1932 Chicago PhD dissertation, "Justus Moeser as an Historian," although a brief spin-off from the dissertation appeared as "Justus Möser's Approach to History" in *Medieval and Historiographical Essays in Honor of James Westfall Thompson*, ed. James Lea Cate and Eugene N. Anderson (Chicago: University of Chicago Press, 1938), 397–422. Also in 1938, an offprint of this chapter appeared (between hard covers) as a "Private Edition, Distributed by the University of Chicago Libraries"; misleadingly, some library catalogues classify it as a book.

46. David Blackbourn and Geoff Eley, *The Peculiarities of German History: Bourgeois Society and Politics in Nineteenth-Century Germany* (Oxford: Oxford University Press, 1984).

47. Bossenbrook's interpreting of German history in terms of disembodied ideas echoes Abraham Kuyper's insistence that, in Bratt's words, "the determinative forces of reality were not external or material but the ultimate commitment of the heart of man, his 'life-principle'. . . . every nation, every civilization was

simply the elaboration of a principle or of the conflict of principles. Therefore history was explicable as the development of ruling ideas." Bratt, *Dutch Calvinism in Modern America*, 17. Kuyper's most explicit discussion of the progression of history occurs in his *Calvinism: Six Lectures*, 32–40.

48. Nevins was coeditor, with Louis M. Hacker, of *The United States and Its Place in World Affairs 1918–1943* (Boston: D. C. Heath, 1943), to which Bossenbrook contributed the first two chapters, "Democratic Principles and Group Values in Western Society" and "Revolutionary Ideologies between Two Wars," 3–27.

49. It *was* reviewed by Herman Weill in *The Historian* 24 (1962): 235–37. *The Historian* is the journal of Phi Alpha Theta, an undergraduate honors society for history majors. It was also reviewed by a Detroit resident, Samuel I. Shuman, in *Archiv für Rechts- und Sozialphilosophie* 48 (1962): 433. The book also appeared in a German translation: no doubt its emphasis on German *Geist* gave it an audience in some quarters. See William J. Bossenbrook, *Geschichte des deutschen Geistes*, trans. Georg Hincha (Gütersloh: Mohn, 1963).

50. Hayden V. White, *The Greco-Roman Tradition* (New York: Harper & Row, 1973). The other volumes in the series were John B. Christopher, *The Islamic Tradition* (1972), Milton Covensky, *The Ancient Near Eastern Tradition* (1966), J. H. Hexter, *The Judaeo-Christian Tradition* (1966), Dean Arthur Miller, *The Byzantine Tradition* (1967), and John Weiss, *The Fascist Tradition: Radical Right-Wing Extremism in Modern Europe* (1967), all published by Harper & Row. Hexter aside, the authors were White's colleagues at his first two teaching posts, at Wayne (Covensky, Weiss) and then at the University of Rochester (Christopher, Miller). White thus continued the Bossenbrook tradition of undertaking collaborative work with colleagues.

Note also that the series echoes a reference that Bossenbrook makes in the preface to the second volume of *A History of Western Civilization* to "such cultural totalities as the ancient Oriental, the Graeco-Roman, and the medieval Christian" that had laid "the foundations of contemporary Western civilization" (2: xvii). Bossenbrook was himself echoing, in a secularized key, Abraham Kuyper's insistence that "the five stadia of Babylonian-Egyptian, Greek Roman, Islamitic, Romanistic and Calvinistic civilization" make up "the broad stream of the development of our race," which has now culminated in the "fundamental antithesis" between "the energy of Calvinism" and "its caricature in the French Revolution" (*Lectures on Calvinism*, 36–37). I do not know whether White was aware of the Neo-Calvinist background of his book series.

51. White, *The Greco-Roman Tradition*, 1, 7–8, 14, 33–34, 61, 67–68, 74, 77, 117, and passim.

52. James Westfall Thompson, with the collaboration of Bernard J. Holm, *A History of Historical Writing*, 2 vols. (New York: Macmillan, 1942). Like Bossen-

brook, Thompson (1869–1941) was born into the Calvinist persuasion: he was the son of a Reformed Church in America minister in Pella, Iowa.

53. William J. Bossenbrook, introduction to *Mid-Twentieth Century Nationalism*, ed. William J. Bossenbrook (Detroit: Wayne State University Press, 1965), 5. Bossenbrook's own essay, "German Nationalism and Fragmentation," 15–32, emphasizes the dialectical relation between unifying and fragmenting tendencies in nationalism.

54. William Bossenbrook, "Modern Historiography Syllabus" (Department of History, Wayne University, 1952). From a copy of the syllabus in my possession (given to me by Professor Martin Havran).

55. Hayden V. White, "Romanticism, Historicism, and Realism: Toward a Period Concept for Early 19th Century Intellectual History," in *The Uses of History*, 45–58. White also treats these categories dialectically: in his first page and a half he poses oppositions between Historicism and Realism, between searching for the mutual influences between them and studying their formal similarities and differences, and between the approaches to Historicism and Realism of Georg Lukács and Erich Auerbach.

56. Carlo Ginzburg, "Just One Witness," in *Probing the Limits of Representation: Nazism and the 'Final Solution,'* ed. Saul Friedlander (Cambridge, MA: Harvard University Press, 1992), 82–96; Georg G. Iggers, "Historiography between Scholarship and Poetry: Reflections on Hayden White's Approach to Historiography," *Rethinking History* 4 (2000): 373–90.

57. In this work the authors place "the vast body of raw materials generally known as the history of ideas" *beyond interpretation* (or rather, beyond "capricious manipulation by the intellectual historian"). At the same time, they never claim to know what this body of materials *essentially* means. See Hayden V. White, Willson Coates, and J. Salwyn Schapiro, *The Emergence of Liberal Humanism: An Intellectual History of Western Europe*, vol. 1, *From the Italian Renaissance to the French Revolution* (New York: McGraw-Hill, 1966); and Hayden V. White and Willson Coates, *The Ordeal of Liberal Humanism: An Intellectual History of Western Europe*, vol. 2, *Since the French Revolution* (New York: McGraw-Hill, 1970). See Coates's and White's preface to vol. 1, v–vi.

10

Does the Sublime Price Explanation
Out of the Historical Marketplace?

Hans Kellner

When Hayden White published "The Politics of Historical Interpretation: Discipline and De-sublimation" in *Critical Inquiry* twenty-five
years ago, he, the arch-modernist, took hold of a central concept of the
developing postmodern discourse and made it his own. The author of
Metahistory took the concept of the sublime, put forth at the end of the
previous decade by Jean-François Lyotard as the defining concept of the
"postmodern condition," and made of it, or rather of the beautiful/sub-
lime binary, a defining perspective on historiographical development
in the nineteenth century. White noted that the rhetorical dominance
of historical meaning meant that the past "could be made to bear as
many meanings as wit and rhetorical talent could impose upon it,"[1] and
that this threatened human self-understanding with an absurdist ("abderitic," in Kant's words) indeterminacy that needed to be disciplined.
This discipline consisted of a "rigorous de-rhetoricization,"[2] and, as
White had already indicated in *Metahistory*, a "tendency of historiographers within the main line of the professional convention of the nineteenth century to regard *formalistic characterizations of the historical field*
and *narrative representations of its process* as the appropriate way to write
'history.'"[3]

This anti-rhetorical narrative formalization qua disciplining of
proper historical practice eliminated from responsible consideration the
possibility that history may in fact be a chaos, an abderitic, intrinsically

formless thing. In other words, for the emerging discipline of professional history, the past could no longer be represented aesthetically in the mode that Kant called "sublime" in the *Critique of Judgment*. Banishing the historical sublime closed off many pre-modern debates. Its reopening in a postmodern register would suggest new questions, because the sublime had always been a threat to naming and to explanation, and naming and explanation are exactly how history sells its products, packaging human events.

Because the sublime is not an attribute of anything to be found in the world, except perhaps in the individual sensibility, discussions of the topic tend to be occasions of persuasion. I am required to define what the sublime represents for me, generalize that (against all logic) and identify examples of it, then convince you that you also find it where I do. This is what I shall try to do here, because the discourse of the sublime is an active rhetorical device. Even more than the beautiful, it requires an audience. What I want to do here is to present a version of the historical sublime, note the sense in which the sublime is a substitute or placeholder for explanation within existing systems of understanding. By postponing (or figuring the postponement of) a discourse of understanding, the historical sublime, which is our intuition of this postponement, helps to free us from the present, not through bondage to the past, but in anticipation of a future that cannot be anticipated. What is priced out of the market by the sublime is not explanation as such, but confidence that our terms of explanation are final ones.

David Punter, coming from a very different position from Hayden White's, has placed the sublime in the arena of the crisis of representation brought on by the Revolution of 1789. The crisis of representation had its political side—who can stand for (and speak for) another—as well as its discursive, indeed rhetorical, side—how to confront the failure of all the old Augustan figures of proportion, limits, and boundaries. As Punter lists them: "resemblance, analogy, sympathy, imitation, emulation, order, degree."[4] This was then the repertoire of historical explanations, and in fact remains a pretty good version of it. These figures seemed useless to some Englishmen of the late eighteenth century, presumably because the French Revolution with which they were forcefully confronted was an event without precedent, so that analogical appeals to the past could not restore the fractured relationship of the individual ego and the enormity of events. This disparity between ego and the forces of history, as well as the absence of any language through which the history could speak for the ego, created that sense of paranoia so widely encountered in romantic literature, and in many histories.

Hyperbole became the redemptive figure. Its gestures of excess indicate that the explanatory structures of analogy are challenged, that compromises will not hold, and that incommensurability marks the broken relations of individual and history. The social contract of genre is destroyed by the great hybrid texts of that time, whose hyperbole of form and matter "are immense Gothic bridges between the universe of discourse and forces of history."[5] The discontinuity and interruption of authority in France is due to a broken genre contract. Henceforth, a multiple array of discourses will seek a unifying fiction that can limit and control the explosive multiplicity unleashed by historical forces. And these multiple texts—the sort of thing that Linda Orr has called the "omni-genre"—have become the mark of the literary for our time. Here we arrive at the sublime, a discourse and practice well prepared and elaborated by the end of the eighteenth century. Punter chooses the figure of the marketplace to describe the effects of the sublime in its function as a negotiator for the individual confronting history. "Yet in that very ideological gesture, we can also sense a reversed contour: of the sublime as precisely that rearguard code which is necessary to neutralise, through a 'pricing out of the market,' the threat to the universe of what can be said among classically educated men and women."[6]

Hyperbole works in two directions: it validates a move beyond the regulative limits, which specify relationships between the given components of a system, into a world of "gigantism and miniaturization."[7] To put this into discursive terms, we might say that the grammatical and syntactic levels have been abandoned in favor of the semantic level (gigantism) and the lexical level (miniaturization).[8] Yet it is precisely in these middle levels of discourse—grammar and syntax—where "responsible" explanation, or beautiful explanation, to borrow the eighteenth-century term, takes place. This is clearly why Kant identifies the beautiful as the symbol of the morally good and the sociable. In noting that we can move above the sensible to the explanatory (via analogy) and that others can share this intelligibility, we are "ennobled."[9] Kant's illustration of this beautiful intelligibility is political:

Thus a monarchical state is represented by a living body if it is governed by national laws, and by a mere machine (like a hand mill) if governed by an individual absolute will; but in both cases only symbolically. For between a despotic state and a hand mill there is, to be sure, no similarity; but there is a similarity in the rules according to which we reflect upon these two things and their causality.[10]

In other words, at the grammatical level there may be no similarity between state and mill (no common topics), but at the syntactic level, intelligibility and causality become apparent, making of us intuitively complete people. So at least a certain form of explanation is to be found there; we might say that it is at these levels of discourse, the grammatical and syntactic, that the beautiful resides.

The asocial, genre-busting, hybrid form of the sublime is at the semantic level, where the very intelligibility of intelligibility itself is at stake in a gigantic opening up to interpretation and loss of control. It is equally to be experienced, however, at the lexical level, where the terms and units of discourse (and thus, of the world) are at stake, and the basic elements may vanish or simply appear. Since the stability of these levels of discourse is central to intelligibility, this is the "pricing out of the market" that Punter refers to. The social terms of intelligibility, which we might call the genre contract of explanation, are put up for bids, and the starting tender is hyperbolically high.

Punter, we noted, specified that it was classically trained individuals of the Old Regime whose grasp of the world was shaken by the new discourse regime. But this disruption of the situation at the end of the eighteenth century sounds very much like what was described in the late twentieth century by Jean-François Lyotard. In his familiar account of what he called the postmodern condition, Lyotard claimed that consensus is no longer the goal of discourse. Consensus presumes that the rules of the game are stable, and, he maintains, they are not. Lyotard's version of the postmodern describes it as an event (noticeable) that is not yet an event (because although noticeable, it is not imaginable). The "what was that?" is postmodern because it cannot yet be made into part of the story that governs meaning (which is to say, part of the narrative that marks its own situation of enunciation as modernity). The postmodern event has happened, yet hasn't happened yet. As a noticeable physical event, it is a presence, what Giorgio Agamben calls the "whatever." But as a social unit, part of what can be known and named (and thus explained), the event exceeds the existing possibilities. It is not an innovation, because anything seen as new exists already within the system that can distinguish new from old. It is rather what Lyotard called a *paralogy*, an incommensurable, unexplainable move that may (or may not) change the game itself. And if it does, of course, it will be part of the new game (or narrative). It will be modern. So the postmodern precedes the modern, and it evokes the sublime in the Kantian sense precisely because it is a matter of understanding, like both the Faustian "always not yet," and the Heideggerian "always already."

From this "condition," as Lyotard called it, several conclusions might be drawn with implications for historical discourse. One, which we attribute to Jean Baudrillard, sees the sublime postponement of meaning as an endless stream of substitutes, a "precession"—not a procession—of simulacra. The "great trauma" of the period, our period still, is the decline, not of credible metanarratives, as Lyotard has it, but of "strong referentials."[11] Baudrillard finds this in the perfect accuracy with which the cinema imitates the past. But, he implies, this imitation is limited to a merely grammatical, or tactical, level: "In the absence of a real *syntax* of meaning, one has nothing but the *tactical* values of a group in which are admirably combined, for example, the CIA as a mythological machine that does everything, Robert Redford as polyvalent star, social relations as a necessary reference to history, technical virtuosity as a necessary reference to cinema."[12] Baudrillard cites a demonic, terroristic sublime, in which the real that is flawlessly reproduced turns out to have no priority over the copies, which do not proceed from it, but rather precede it, a "precession of simulacra." Without "strong referentials"—and here we are reminded of what Punter wrote about the failure of the Augustan figures of analogy—we are given an anestheticized past which will "preferably be the one immediately preceding our 'irreferential' era."[13] This era is fetishized to cover up the great trauma in a way similar to the fetishization attendant to the other great trauma, the discovery of sexual difference. Hence, the omnipresent references to fascism, not least in discussions of the historical sublime. If the real is always already there as a copy, why not observe the most recent copy, since it will also seem most real? Fetishization will eliminate the need to explain it—it is so vivid, after all—but in any case, explanation is rather beside the point in a world of simulacra.

Lyotard rejects this because he believes in time, and thus in change. The postmodern sublime erupts and is noticed, but cannot be named or placed in any existing narrative, that is, any explanatory system.[14] It remains as a placeholder (Lyotard does not use the word, although his nemesis Habermas does, to make the opposite point) in anticipation of a subsequent move in the game of discourse, which will afford it a position in a new system, and which will of course be modern.[15]

To make all this a bit more clear, I would like to consider two historical texts that deal with the dead. One, by Jules Michelet, addresses an unusual problem in urban sanitation during a time of mass executions. The other, by Robert Conquest, denotes the enormity of slaughter during a similar era. Yet, clearly, they do not have the same sort of impact. Enormity has nothing to do with the sublime in these examples: Conquest is chronicling vast murders under Stalin; Michelet is, among other things, noting how little the size of the carnage matters to human agents, compared to the symbolism.

First, Conquest. Where is the sublime in this detailed reconstruction of horror?

The cellars of the Lubyanka [the headquarters of the Soviet Union's People's Commissariat of Internal Affairs, or NKVD] were really a sort of basement divided into a number of rooms off corridors. Later on, in the ordinary routine, the condemned handed in their clothes in one of these rooms and changed into white underclothes only. They were then taken to the death cell and shot in the back of the neck with a TT eight-shot automatic. A doctor then signed the death certificate, the last document to be put in their files, and the tarpaulin on the floor was taken away to be cleaned by a woman specially employed for that purpose. (Execution with the small-bore pistol is not, as might seem, very humane. Of the 9,432 corpses exhumed at Vinnista, 6,360 had needed a second shot; 78, a third shot.)[16]

And so forth.

The final official document in important cases, he writes, was a note to the "sanitary-burial" service of the NKVD to take a certain number of corpses to a crematorium. The less important went to the enormous mass graves. "One prisoner was employed to whitewash the walls of the cells of executed prisoners immediately after they were taken to the NKVD headquarters for execution. This was to cover the names that they had scratched on the walls."[17]

Conquest's version in *The Great Terror* has nothing sublime about it. He presents, as best he can, the thing itself; its millions of dead are calculable, however many they are. The regime is over, its meaning (for Conquest, at least) is fairly clear. He quotes a poem by a bright young English Communist; the topic is the Purges: "Nothing is ever born without screaming and blood." And, of Stalin, "Only in constant action was his constant certainty found." Young John Cornford, the author of these lines, died in Spain, and illustrates Conquest's argument "that not even high intelligence and a sensitive spirit are of any help once the facts of a situation are deduced from a political theory, rather than vice versa."[18] This, as far as I can see, is a warning tale for the future, without any sense that the future will speak back with another set of rules for understanding.

Toward the end of his *History of the French Revolution*, in the midst of recounting the height of the Terror, Michelet pauses in his political history to tell a concurrent story about the cemeteries of Paris, or "the cemeteries of the Terror," as he calls them. The topic, he noted, was a sad one, but one that Michelet felt obligated to address because "history wants it."[19] Moreover, this information, brought to Michelet's attention by the archivists, had been absolutely unknown until this presentation. In early 1793, the guillotine proceeded with its work: whether sixty heads per day, or forty or thirty hardly mattered. Paris was blasé, accustomed to death. Then, in February, complaints began about the danger to the public health of so many corpses in the cemeteries.

These complaints were novel. The far-larger massacres under the monarchy had never stirred anxiety. Elements like summer heat would become a factor, but the same fears were expressed regardless of season or district. They were a "general feature of the popular imagination."[20] The section of La Madeleine was the first to complain, as early as February; by the end of the month, interments began at Monceau—with Georges Danton, Camille and Lucile Desmoulins, and Pierre Gaspard Chaumette, whose corpses were first laid out at La Madeleine and later moved in secret. But complaints persisted wherever the bodies were buried (and a number of different spots were used). The chapter recounts the desperate search for burial space acceptable to local residents, the bodies hauled through the streets all summer, interments and reinterments, quicklime treatments, bubbling putrefaction, and ongoing protests. Then, the protests, couched in the Enlightenment language of concerns for public health, ended, as suddenly as they began. Michelet can proceed to narrate Thermidor.

But first, Michelet adds the following passage:

An architect, undoubtedly inspired by these memories, imagined a monument for the combustion of the dead that would have simplified everything. His plan was truly one to capture the imagination. Imagine a vast, open, circular portico. From one pillar to the next, so many arcades, and under each one is an urn which contains the ashes. At the center, a large pyramid, that smoked at the top and at the four corners. Immense chemical apparatus, that shortened the proceedings of nature, without disgust, without horror, this could take an entire nation, if necessary, and transmit it, by a pure flame, from the sickly, stormy, dirty condition we call life to peaceful state of definitive repose.

He had this idea after the Terror and proposed it in the year VII, in anticipation, no doubt, of the immense, coming increase in the Empire of Death. What matter the twelve hundred guillotined of these two months (from Prairial to Thermidor) in the presence of the prodigious destructions with which the nineteenth century begins?[21]

The forgotten document Michelet describes, brought to his attention by some unnamed archivist, epitomizes for me the historical sublime. As usual with Michelet, the placement of this digression on the cemetery problem—an issue which vanished as quickly as it had arisen—delays the inevitable arrival in his narrative of Thermidor, which in effect ends his history; the episode adds a certain commentary to the whole story of the Revolution as Empire of Death. This much, I think, is writerly craft. The further digression within the digression, however, goes farther. The plan for a mass crematorium is not contemporary with the events of summer 1793, so it is further craft (that is, intention) that he shows in placing the tale in this chapter. (Strategic placement is one of Michelet's characteristic and most effective devices.) And he tells us his ironic purpose. The great uproar over the disposal of bodies in '93, this unfocused but powerful concern for the dead of the Terror, seems a quaint bit of nostalgia when seen in the light of the ensuing slaughter; Michelet adds a note pointing out that the total number of those guillotined during the whole Revolution was one-fortieth of the dead in one Napoleonic battle, Moscow.

Certainly this irony cannot be sublime, if only because it is a trope of analogy, a trope which foregrounds our human failure to respond rationally to the proportions of historical slaughter. But the plan for the "monument for the combustion of the dead," so clean and whatever is the opposite of horrible, is where I begin to sense the historical sublime. It begins, to be sure, in the ironies of the beauty and efficiency of the structure ("sans dégout, sans horreur"), rather like the humane guillotine itself, but takes this irony straight into a hyperbolic gigantism. "An entire nation, if necessary" could be blessedly conveyed from the miseries of life to the restfulness of a "repos définitif." What could make such an event necessary? Michelet wants to compare the revolutionary expenditure of life and the concern it aroused with the mass slaughter of the Empire, and its absence of concern. The tale of the cemeteries is figured by the crematorium, fulfilled and clarified by the reality of later events. From the point of view of eighteenth-century theory (and Michelet was a child of the eighteenth century—Schiller's essays on the sublime were both written in the decade in which Michelet was born), the tale of the cemeteries can be read as a sublime reminder of the "bizarre savagery" and "evil fatality" of history, at least when contemplated from the standpoint of free and noble minds. As Schiller put it: "Then away with falsely construed forebearance and vapidly effeminate taste which cast a veil over the solemn face of necessity and, in order to curry favor with the senses, counterfeit a harmony between good fortune and good behavior of which no trace is to be found in the actual world. Let us stand face to face with the evil fatality."[22]

This is sublime, but it is not the sublime I have in mind. For who can read the Michelet passage today without adding much that the author did not know? This reader, at least, stopped at the paragraph of the monument, read it again and again, amazed. The future seems to be right there—the universal feast of death, as Thomas Mann called World War I, and the Holocaust. What was for Michelet a figure of the nineteenth-century slaughter became for me a sublime figure—more sublime because its completion (for me) was not part of the text. (I don't read Nostradamus, but aren't we all a bit unnerved by a premonition?) Because it escapes the simple singularity of the event—as compared with Conquest, who offers a generalized maxim about ideology as explanation—explanation becomes highly problematic. The Terror, the battle of Moscow, the Holocaust, and all the rest—what sort of explanation could encompass them, except an allusion to nature itself and its sublime awfulness?

The paragraph about the "monument for the combustion of the dead" was a *placeholder*. To Michelet, it was an ironically placed figure linking the events of the Terror—even farcical ones such as the problems of disposing of corpses—with the disasters of his own lifetime. The responsible historical reader must limit its historical meaning, its meaning as an artifact as well as a history, to the fulfilled figure. Michelet *intended* this, and no more. But a reader who chooses a different protocol, whom Schiller might call a "simply free observer"("*bloss freie Betrachter*"), finds it an *un*fulfilled figure in its mid-nineteenth-century context. It is "what will have happened," a "future anterior," as Lyotard puts it, and a *post-modern* intervention. Michelet's contemporary reader would not recognize it as such, would not know what to do with it in the sense I have suggested. His repertoire of possible fulfillments for this figure seems meager to us at the start of the twentieth-first century. The figure held a place for our reading, our sublime disquiet. As an unfulfilled figure, it is sublime—but how can we speak of an unfulfilled figure? Can a figure be recognized at all without some sense of having already been fulfilled? The answer is clearly no. Nothing appears to us historically until it has been rendered meaningful by a corresponding event. The monument struck Michelet as meaningful only in light of subsequent events (with which it had no causal relationship).[23]

Now I will briefly turn to Kant's contribution to the discourse of the sublime, which may be said to embody the entire Copernican Revolution of his philosophy.[24] The sublime is a form of alienation in which man projects his Infinity as a moral creature onto an external object, then cowers as that object returns to him as sublime. The object is constituted by the self-awareness of the subject (an insight used to some effect by Hegel, Feuerbach, and Marx), so nothing is sublime in itself. It is only made sublime by our moral sense of freedom, but we forget this in the face of our sublime creation and imagine ourselves helpless before it. So, as Schiller comments, without the sublime, we forget our dignity and remain strangers to the sphere of action. It is our creation.

I have made this digression to clarify my remarks here. The historical sublime is NOT the characteristic of any category of events. Although we can predict at a particular moment what an audience of similar people might apprehend as sublime, the sublime object is constituted by their feeling, not vice versa. So what was the status of the non-yet-constituted sublime event? I have called it a *placeholder* and positioned the constitution of the sublime in Lyotard's terms. It is a figure that appears as figure only at the moment of its fulfillment. The sublime comes with the realization that it existed through time waiting for its objectivity to be born, like the "monument for the combustion of the dead," which is fulfilled, not in the death machinery of the twentieth century, but rather as a place in our moral imaginations. And as we contemplate its existence, we intuit the possibility of our own existence as truly historical—that is, as objects with meaning not within our own scope, but dependent upon the sensitivity of moral ages which we cannot imagine. Varieties of this notion of the sublime are to be found in the eighteenth century and in its undisputed champion of sublimity, Homer. But most of all, in Virgil, the poet of the historical sublime.

Thomas Gray's "Elegy Written in a Country Churchyard" (1743) strikes me as the essential discussion of the unfulfilled sublime figure, presented as an elegiac awareness of historical possibilities that were never fulfilled.

> Some village Hampden that with dauntless breast
> The little tyrant of the fields withstood;
> Some mute inglorious Milton here may rest,
> Some Cromwell guiltless of his country's blood.

And on and on. Their "lot forbade" glory. Half a century before the French Revolution, and before the elaborate theorizing of the eighteenth-century discourse of the sublime, these lines still offer the miniaturizing hyperbole that Punter describes, and a sense of postponed fulfillment, even if it is only the poet's notice. They lay in their graves, placeholders, waiting for these lines to be written.

Gray's sublime is elegiac, but I do find a tragic unfulfilled figure in the *Iliad*, Book 6, where Helen tells Hector:

> You bear such a burden
> For my wanton ways and Paris' witlessness.
> Zeus has placed this evil fate on us so that
> In time to come poets will sing of us.[25]

This makes of Helen one of the most fulfilled of all the unfulfilled figures. (She is unfulfilled because she can see no purpose to the suffering she has caused; her fulfillment, which she intuits here, is the future these sufferings will produce as "song.") Homer suggests that the meaning of their lives is not present to them, that they are tragic placeholders, sublime, waiting for the poet. Or the historian, perhaps, since it is surely wrong to read these lines as a proleptic vision of a concept of literature that did not exist. One of the future versions of Helen that calls our attention to her tragic figuration is Gorgias's "Encomium for Helen." In this classic piece of sophistic argument, Gorgias strips away all her fulfillments (all guilts placed on her by the poets) in her defense, leaving almost nothing remaining. She is thus disfigured, a pure figure in an absurd world, innocent in her complete dehumanization.

If this is too literary, let me refer to what Frank Ankersmit has written of Tocqueville, because I think it is a perfect example of what I mean. Ankersmit sees Tocqueville's sense that democracy, and the long historical process that led to it, is sublime, a source of pain more than pleasure.[26] He feared democracy, because it would lead to equality at the expense of that liberty which he most prized as an aristocrat. At the same time, he emphasized his awareness of his limited human and historical condition, compared to that of the "Creator and Preserver of man." "What seems to me decay is thus in his eyes progress; what pains me is acceptable to Him."[27] Elsewhere I have written about Tocqueville as a postmodern historian, a judgment that must seem like a jest, but was not quite meant as such.[28] His intuition was that there is a way of knowing that is absolutely particularistic and has no need of essentialisms of any kind, but that this knowledge is unavailable to humanity, dependent on a language that lumps things together and so is always in error. Further, Tocqueville imagines an entity that knows what all figural placeholders are, as it were, waiting for. He understands that the only sort of being that could meet the postmodern criteria of knowledge would be God, and, unlike most of us, he has no hesitation in pointing this out.

Although it is not difficult to understand the basis of his objections, I do not agree with Christopher Norris that the sublime deprives thought of its critical power, that it is "a privileged trope for everything that teases philosophy out of thought."[29] If the philosophy and critique that he misses in the sublime are only expressions of a confidence that the present has a right to control the past, and that the intuition of possible futures and our inability to imagine them are failures of nerve, then he may be correct. But if we cannot imagine the future, we can intuit our inability itself (especially in what Ankersmit calls our "Age of Unintended Consequences"). To be sure, the historical sublime moves beyond the grammar and syntax of events to open up areas that escape the rules of current understanding, but this does not mean that understanding is impossible. It may serve as a placeholder for some future way of knowing, in which it will stand as a fulfilled figure. In Book 8 of the *Aeneid*, Aeneas stares in amazement at the shield his mother Venus gave to him, covered as it was with the future history of Rome. He stares, understanding nothing, except what we must call a sense of the historical sublime. But Virgil and his contemporary readers understood the shield very well; it was their historical world, and all the figures were fulfilled in Augustus. Again and again, Virgil presents the hero facing the future, always without recognition or understanding. This is a reminder that our place in time makes us in a sense placeholders for some future time that will make sense of what is for us sublimely mysterious. So we can read this passage as the fulfillment of another sort of figure, not available to Virgil—what Kant called "the rules according to which we reflect."[30] The "monument for the combustion of the dead" figured for us by Michelet does the same thing, as does democracy for Tocqueville, who posits not only a future humanity, but also a postmodern deity, to remedy his time- and class-bound limits. So if the sublime does price explanation out of the market, by pointing to some goods as having a value that cannot yet be imagined, it also makes for us another market, a market of historical reflection, where a different currency prevails.

My discussion of the historical sublime up to now will surely seem too narrow, miniaturized by its focus on the example from Michelet, who is as unique as a historian can be. So, in order to invoke the hyperbolic sublime, I want to extend my notion in a way that is far too broad—gigantism. And so I suggest that every reflection on the past that takes into account the historicity of the observer has about it, if only for a brief moment, something of the sublime. By "the historicity of the observer" I do not mean our sense of ourselves as characters in a historical account, creatures of our time, which is as solid as any other time. Instead, I mean a sense of our life-world as an unfulfilled figure, open to a future that may itself never be fulfilled, in the sense of having a stable meaning.

Every historical account is a beautification, inventing form (through conceptual grammar and syntax) for a part of the past. But historical reflection moves beyond form to the enormity of the past, and more particularly, the future, the unknown that will determine and fulfill the figures of the past, and give them a meaning—perhaps the ash that is unavailable to us. Our reflections will become written accounts, indentured to language and its forms. So the sublime will inevitably become beautiful, and, in Lyotard's familiar terms, the postmodern will become modern.

This is surely not too miniaturized to reflect upon. And Hayden White is the figure who made these reflections possible.

Notes

1. Hayden White, "The Politics of Historical Interpretation: Discipline and De-sublimation," in *The Content of the Form* (Baltimore: Johns Hopkins University Press, 1978), 65.

2. Ibid.

3. Hayden White, *Metahistory: the Historical Imagination in Nineteenth-Century Europe* (Baltimore: Johns Hopkins University Press, 1973), 275.

4. David Punter, *The Romantic Unconscious: A Study in Narcissism and Patriarchy* (New York: New York University Press, 1990), 25.

5. Ibid., 27.

6. Ibid.

7. Ibid., 25.

8. White, *Metahistory*, 65. White's discussion of the linguistic levels (lexical, grammatical, syntactic, and semantic) in *Metahistory* (274–76) remains extraordinarily suggestive.

9. Immanuel Kant, *Critique of Judgment*, trans. J. H. Bernard (New York: Haffner, 1951), 199.

10. Ibid., 198.

11. Jean Baudrillard, *Simulacra and Simulation*, trans. S. F. Glaser (Ann Arbor: University of Michigan Press, 1994), 43.

12. Ibid., 46.

13. Ibid., 44.

14. Jean-François Lyotard, *The Postmodern Condition: A Report on Knowledge*, trans. G. Bennington and B. Massumi (Minneapolis: University of Minnesota Press, 1984), 77–82.

15. Habermas has written that philosophy itself must stand today as a placeholder (*Platzhalter*, translated as "stand-in"), and accept the modesty that befits that situation. Unlike Lyotard, though, he is quite confident that he knows what place philosophy is holding: "empirical theories with strong universal claims." In other words, the future will look very much like the present as a system of legitimation. The philosophical placeholder cannot be a paralogy, because "marked down in price, the venerable transcendental and dialectical modes of justification may still come in handy." Jürgen Habermas, "Philosophy as Stand-In and Interpreter," in *After Philosophy: End or Transformation?* ed. Kenneth Baynes, James Bohman, and Thomas McztCarthy (Cambridge, MA: MIT Press, 1987), 310.

16. Robert Conquest, *The Great Terror: A Reassessment* (Oxford: Oxford University Press, 1990), 287–88.

17. Ibid.

18. Ibid., 463.

19. Jules Michelet, *Histoire de la Révolution Française* (Paris: Bibliothèque de la Pléiade, 1939), 1081.

20. Ibid.

21. Ibid., 1086–87, my translation.

22. Friedrich Von Schiller, *Two Essays: On the Sublime and Naive and Sentimental Poetry*, trans. Julius A. Elias (New York: Ungar, 1966), 209.

23. This retrospective constitution of the figure by its fulfillment corresponds to White's discussion of choosing ancestors, which I noted in the introduction to this book.

24. Yirmiyahu Yovel, *Kant and the Philosophy of History* (Princeton: Princeton University Press, 1980), 131.

25. Homer, *Iliad*, trans. Stanley Lombardo (Indianapolis and Cambridge: Hackett, 1997), 6.2: 373–76.

26. F. R. Ankersmit, *Aesthetic Politics: Political Philosophy Beyond Fact and Value* (Stanford: Stanford University Press, 1996), 336.

27. Alexis de Tocqueville, *Democracy in America*, trans. G. Lawrence, ed. J. P. Mayer (New York: Anchor, 1969), 704.

28. Hans Kellner, "Postmodern History and Tocqueville's God," in *Swiat historii*, ed. Wojchiech Wrzosek (Poznan, Poland: Instytut Historii UAM, 1998), 251.

29. Christopher Norris, *What's Wrong With Postmodernism: Critical Theory and the Ends of Philosophy* (Baltimore: Johns Hopkins University Press, 1990), 11.

30. Kant, *Critique*, 198.

11

History Beyond the Pleasure Principle?

Dominick LaCapra

For Freud, beyond the pleasure principle lay the repetition compulsion, the death drive, and especially trauma—what Lacan addressed in terms of the "real" as a traumatizing excess that may be the ambivalent source of ecstatic, perhaps sadomasochistic, jouissance. How can historiography recognize and give a responsive account of such forces that have played a notable role in history without simply identifying history with trauma or transferentially enacting compulsive repetition or some variant of excess (all-consuming negativity, inconsolable melancholy, endless mourning, an indiscriminate aesthetic of the sublime, or the affirmation of apocalyptic desire, transcendent acts of grace, or blank utopian hope)? Can it in any significant way assist in the attempt to work through post-traumatic symptoms, even disclose ways of averting or countering trauma and traumatizing violence as perhaps the most excessive modalities of excess, while not denying their role or holding out the false promise of simply transcending them or achieving a deceptive state of therapeutic "cure," closure, or full identity?

Such questions, which are active in my recent work, also inform the present essay, including its relation to the work of Hayden White. Responses to the intersection of history and critical theory must intervene in the historical discipline in informed and cogent but flexible, noncodifiable ways that address its current configuration and try to point it in more desirable directions.[1] Such interventions would be attuned to the dimensions of historiography that are not confined to the present but that themselves have a longer history and a possible future in that they continue to pose thought-provoking questions over time. Indeed, they would also make one mindful of the interaction between the historical and transhistorical forces that affect the historian—forces that may even question the possibilities of the historical enterprise and indicate the manner in which the historian, like others, is internally challenged by what has been figured in terms of the "transhistorically" (or structurally) traumatic, the dangerous supplement, the "extimate" other, the disorientingly uncanny—that which leaves residues and remainders that set limits to a history of meaning in that they cannot be fully mastered or integrated meaningfully into a historicized narrative or interpretive account.[2] Conversely, however, a break or event (in Alain Badiou's sense) may in some sense be a creation ex nihilo that is forged on the edge of an indeterminacy or void (a "madness" of sorts), but possibly traumatic indeterminacies or voids are themselves situated historically in changing ways that may be elucidated.

It is significant that the interest in figures such as Giorgio Agamben, Alain Badiou, and Slavoj Žižek came about unpredictably and quite suddenly but can nonetheless be situated and contextualized within limits. And it is noteworthy that all three are in a significant sense unhistorical (or at times counterhistorical) thinkers who at best rely on very sweeping historical categories (such as modernity or "post-Auschwitz"), and they often subordinate history to the transhistorical or even the universal, at most referring or alluding to specific historical phenomena to illustrate transhistorical forces (such as the Lacanian real [in Žižek] or abjection, *homo sacer*, mere life, and the state of exception [in Agamben]). History is not one of Badiou's four areas of ontological concern (those areas are science, art, politics, and love). For him mathematics seems more philosophically important than history, and set theory is tantamount to fundamental ontology.[3] The complex relation between the transhistorical and the historical is obviated or reductively construed in such approaches, along with the challenge of working out a mutually questioning interaction between historiography and theory.[4]

I would open a parenthesis to note that Žižek has objected in the following terms to an earlier version of my contention that he tends to subordinate the historical to, if not collapse it into, the transhistorical:

This also enables us to answer Dominick la Capra's [*sic*] reproach according to which, the Lacanian notion of lack conflates two levels that have to be kept apart: the purely formal "ontological" lack constitutive of the symbolic order as such, and the particular traumatic experiences (exemplarily: holocaust) which could also NOT have occurred—particular historical catastrophes like the holocaust thus seem to be "legitimized" as directly grounded in the fundamental trauma that pertains to the very human existence. . . . . Against this misunderstanding, one should emphasize that the quasi-transcendental lack and particular traumas are linked in a negative way: far from being just the last link in the continuous chain of traumatic encounters that reaches back to the "symbolic castration," catastrophes like the holocaust are contingent (and, as such, avoidable) events which occur as the final result of the endeavours to OBFUSCATE the quasi-transcendental constitutive lack.[5]

I agree with Žižek's critique of a one-dimensional, un-self-critical historicism and his important supplementary point that a historical trauma should not be seen as the last link in a chain leading back to the transhistorical. But I take issue with the manner in which he formulates the argument I make in "Trauma, Absence, Loss."[6] I distinguish analytically between transhistorical absence (or void) and historical losses or lacks, but do not see the transhistorical as purely formal or argue that the two levels have to be kept apart. In fact, I argue that in empirical cases, the two will be imbricated but that the analytic distinction is still important because it resists the collapse of the transhistorical and the historical, which subordinates the one to the other and leads either to confusion or to a deceptive explanation of one in terms of the other. (Also deceptive is the *opposite* of Žižek's tendency: the contextualizing explanation of everything transhistorical, for example, dimensions of anxiety, in terms of particular historical circumstances or situations.) I do not assert that an explanatory venture necessarily has legitimizing functions, although, as Žižek's comment itself indicates, it may always be read or misread in that manner. Still, Žižek's rejoinder, I think, actually supports the view of him as, in significant ways, an unhistorical thinker or at least a thinker for whom history is in a very subordinate if not derivative position.[7]

   Historical trauma may to some extent be prompted by an avoidance of an encounter or engagement with transhistorical trauma (or the Lacanian "real"). But such an encounter is never unmediated, and historical traumas have to be understood in nonderivative terms, thus not construed simply as radical contingencies. Moreover, transhistorical trauma is better figured as an absence or void than as a (constitutive) lack, even though confusion or misprision may induce an unsettling if not traumatizing experience (or fantasy) of transhistorical absence (most notably, the absence of absolute foundations or of full community and unity with the other) as a lack—indeed induce the feeling that one has lost or lacks what one could not possibly ever have or have had. (Conversely, not experiencing transhistorical absence as a lack or loss may not eliminate all traumatizing potential but may nonetheless facilitate an experience of that absence or void as an affirmative opening to possible futures, including [as Nietzsche saw] an invitation to improvisation.)

While one may undertake historically traumatizing activities in order to obfuscate or avoid anxiety and vulnerability, attendant on transhistorical trauma, by projecting the source of anxiety and vulnerability onto scapegoats, the opposite is also possible. In other words, one may traumatize others and risk traumatization oneself in order to enact or act out (rather than work through or live with) transhistorical trauma and the "death drive," compulsively engaging in traumatizing, often violent scenes and even thereby attaining a sublime sense of transcendence. Heinrich Himmler's own fascination and repulsion in the face of gloriously extreme and unheard-of transgression, which surfaces in his oft-quoted Posen speech, could be read in such terms. One could even, albeit implausibly, see Himmler and other elite Nazi perpetrators as obeying a higher call and undertaking genocide for a pure, honor-bound sense of duty and a refusal to betray Hitler, despite their own personal desire to act otherwise ethically, hence becoming similar, in their own unconditional *actus purus*, to the Princesse de Clèves in Žižek's reading of her "heroic" action. (This conception of the SS and their killing operations is in fact suggested in Jonathan Littell's novel, *Les Bienveillantes*.)[8]

Anything other than psychosis may be interpreted as in some way an obfuscation (if not "gentrification") of the putative "transhistorical constitutive lack." The historical as well as ethicopolitical problem is to specify the nature, validity, and implications of the "obfuscation." Construing something as an obfuscation of the transhistorical is not sufficient for an analysis or understanding of the historical in its specificity and singularity. To believe that such a construction is sufficient would make very short shrift of historiography and might well accord with a sweepingly apocalyptic or postapocalyptic politics that takes itself as engaging directly with the traumatic real.[9] In any event, the broader problem is how to articulate the complex, variable relations between the transhistorical and the historical. The assertion that historical catastrophes come about through an avoidance or obfuscation of the transhistorical does not properly address these relations—this assertion situates history vis-à-vis the real in a position analogous to that of divertissement in Pascal's conception of the anxiety-ridden relation to the *Deus Absconditus*.

In Žižek, who shares with Agamben and Badiou a pronounced antinomian strain, stressing grace transcending (but not necessarily transgressing) the "dead letter" of the law, there is also an ascetic insistence on law, voided of an "obscene superego supplement" or bonus of pleasure, as necessary to control monstrous excess. Here a seemingly extreme leftism merges with an extreme conservatism reminiscent of theologians for whom the radical evil of "man" requires strict and even cruel normative strictures. As the old saw has it, *les extrêmes se touchent*, and a Bakhtinian notion of the desirability of a viably alternating rhythm of social life (ordinary obedience to the law relieved by periodic, legitimated, carnivalesque transgression) is firmly rejected in favor of a strict Pauline (or Kantian) insistence on adherence to a decathected law, stripped of its "obscene superego supplement," and sustained by the hope of transcendent acts of grace.[10] Thus Žižek can offer the totally speculative, implausible interpretation of the acts of refuseniks in Israel, refusing to fight in the occupied territories, not only as a move away from seeing Palestinians as Agamben's homo sacer toward a vision of them as Judaeo-Christian neighbors (what happens to Islam here?), but also as designating the miraculous moment in which eternal justice momentarily appears in the temporal sphere of empirical reality"—in effect as acts of transcendent grace conflated with (or incarnated in) this-worldly miracles.[11]

The initiatives of such recent figures as Agamben, Badiou, Santner, and Žižek pose challenges to historians attempting to rethink history in ways that make the admittedly tension-laden attempt both to connect with problems deemed significant in professional historiography as well as insistently to relate historical inquiry to work in other disciplines and to larger social and political issues. One way to define the desirable, historically pertinent intervention is as an essayistic attempt (*essai*) to make available for critical inquiry the often-unexamined assumptions informing a practice. Moreover, one or another critical theory (Foucauldian genealogy, Derridean deconstruction, Frankfurt school *Kritik*, Freudian or Lacanian psychoanalysis) would not simply be "applied" to historical material that is reprocessed unilaterally in its terms. These orientations, including psychoanalysis, are, from the approach I am proposing, to be taken as critical theories (not simply as therapeutic techniques, methodologies convertible into research procedures, or cutting-edge sources of insight). Rather, there would be a mutually thought-provoking relation between historical understanding and critical theory that would sensitize the historian to issues that are otherwise avoided or underconceptualized and enable him or her to explore questions of cross-disciplinary significance. (In this exercise, theory would be contrasted with habitus in the sense of critically unself-reflective practices and assumptions.)

No one has been more important than Hayden White in criticizing the limitations of unself-reflective practice and of a narrow and self-sufficient "conventional" research paradigm, which reaches its extreme form in positivism. But he has at times been tempted by its opposite number or even its "flip side": radical constructivism (at times open to a sublime notion of creation ex nihilo that may seem almost miraculous). In the latter perspective, referential statements making truth claims apply at best only to events and are of restricted, perhaps even marginal, significance. By contrast, performative factors—at times radically creative, figurative, aesthetic, rhetorical, ideological, ethical, and political—are essential. Factors or forces (not involving truth claims) that "construct" structures—stories, plots, arguments, interpretations, explanations—in which referential statements are embedded and take on meaning and significance are central. Radical constructivism often restricts itself to a strategy of reversal in its critique of positivism, which is useful in bringing out the limitations of a documentary or restricted research model of historical understanding. In comparison, radical constructivism's significant twist (or reversal of the binary relation) is that the disimplicated subject, in full creative, existential freedom, presumably imposes meaning and constructs the object ex nihilo on epistemological and political levels, a radical break with the past that brings with it a sublime elevation of the human subject to the quasi-transcendental heights of an "endower" of meaning. With this sublime elevation comes the simultaneous reduction of the object or other to raw material, unprocessed record, or mere life. (One obvious problem here is the implication of this perspective for other-than-human animals and the rest of nature.) As White himself at times seems to sense, the limitations of a strategy of reversal indicate the need to articulate problems and relations in a significantly different manner that is encompassed neither by a restricted research model, however refurbished in putatively post-linguistic or post-cultural terms, nor by its radical constructivist reversal.[12] Indeed, a self-sufficient research model and radical constructivism tend to converge in foreclosing the knotty question of the relation between the historical and the transhistorical. Gone is the need for responsive understanding and the attempt to work through one's "transferential" implication in the object of study, and with it the tendency to repeat, rather than critically reinscribe or respond to (in a sense, repeat with a significant, at times decisive difference), forces active in it.

Revisionist initiatives or perhaps gestures of restoration may in certain cases invite returns to earlier forms of documentary or self-sufficient research models, even though they present themselves as moves beyond radical constructivism, which is construed in cultural and linguistic turns. Such initiatives are apparent in Gabrielle Spiegel's introduction to the book she edited, *Practicing History: New Directions in Historical Writing after the Linguistic Turn*,[13] which runs parallel to the editors' introduction to *Beyond the Cultural Turn*, by Lynn Hunt and Victoria E. Bonnell.[14] In "valorizing once again a fundamentally and deeply ingrained historicist posture" (25), Spiegel herself adopts from the German sociologist Andreas Reckwitz the oxymoronic term "Practice Theory" as a name for the "new directions" she advocates in the historical discipline. Practice Theory is manifestly directed against attempts to rethink history in ways indebted to the work of Hayden White. Yet Practice Theory is itself an undertaking that, while uneven and misleading as a general theory, may well have application to the important areas it privileges, once its more dubious dimensions are removed. Indeed, it may harbor possibilities that those related to it (whether by themselves or by its advocates) ignore or avoid.

Most evidently, Practice Theory marks a putative move beyond radical constructivism, at least in the the cultural and linguistic turns which Spiegel tends to conflate. Plausibly enough, it rejects the idea that all of social life and history are the products of discourse, but it retains a so-called weak or attenuated notion of discourse (25) as playing a role in society and culture. It also rejects an identification of discourse with language, particularly in a structural-Saussurian sense, as well as textualism, understood in Geertzian (rather than Derridean) terms, as the idea that all of sociocultural existence and experience may be understood and read as text-analogues, especially as narratives. One limitation in the un-objectionable (if unsurprising) idea that not all social life may be reduced to discourse or language is that it may obviate sustained inquiry into the role of the complex, non-intuitive workings of language in history, a subject which was of concern to those, like White, whose association with the linguistic turn was more than a half-hearted pirouette.

I would note that Spiegel, in her appraisal of current historiography, joins others in the perception of a recent turn not so much to the history of, say, language or discourse in rhetorical, religious, philosophical, and poetic traditions, but instead from social to cultural history in a broad and somewhat vague sense. And she shares their apprehensions concerning why this putative shift has occurred. For example, Jay Winter writes with an assurance that indicates the extent to which he believes he is simply stating conventional wisdom about recent tendencies in historiography:

Cultural history is in the ascendancy these days, occupying a position which the sub-discipline of social history enjoyed in the 1960s and 70s. The French and Germans have no trouble eliding the two, and have done so for decades. But in the Anglo-Saxon world, the shift from one to the other has been palpable. The British Social History Society's journal *Social History* was renamed *Cultural and Social History* in 2004. The study of working-class movements and social and de-mographic structures, so fruitful in an earlier generation, is now out of fashion. Instead of learning about "the making of the working class" in a host of nations and towns, students are more likely to focus on the memory of past events, and especially traumatic ones.

Winter continues:

Since remembrance varies radically among different groups, the emphasis in such studies is more about multi-vocality and fragmentation than on linear historical narratives such as class formation and class conflict. Why this shift from social to cultural history has occurred is a complex question, touching on the eclipse of the transformational politics of the 1960s, the loss of faith in social scientific models in historical study, the influence of trends in critical theory, and the emergence in the 1970s and after of trans-disciplinary studies of the witness as the essential voice of historical narratives.[15]

As one of the shape-shifters with an interest in problems of memory, multivocality, trauma, and witnessing—as in his own way Winter (as well as White) is—I would not press too hard on his formulations. But

I would note that the title change of the journal he mentions would indicate an "Anglo-Saxon" desire to combine cultural and social history, and that rather than an eclipse or loss of faith, one might refer to a more critical approach to social-scientific models, and a revised conception of the role of culture in political life (affirmed in the 1960s and by Winter himself in his insistence on the importance of political culture). Moreover, the role of critical theory is not simply a question of trendiness; the witness's voice, and the very status of the witness, along with memory and trauma, are hotly contested issues across the disciplines. In any case, Winter's assertions have parallels in Spiegel's introductory essay, and her sense of what is to be done is worth analyzing, even if its prevalence cannot simply be assumed.

What then does Practice Theory defend or postulate as a truly historicist alternative to the linguistic and cultural turns? Here one is on theoretically shaky ground, for as Spiegel observes: "'Practice Theory' as such has scarcely attained the status of a viable 'theory' in any real sense of the word." And it hardly seems to point in new directions in that "the accent it places on the historically generated and always contingent nature of structures of culture returns historiography to its age-old concern with processes, agents, change, and transformation, while demanding the kind of empirically grounded research into the particularities of social and cultural conditions with which historians are by training and tradition most comfortable." Moreover, "as a form of historical reasoning that focuses on the selective cultural organization of experience 'Practice Theory' seems sufficiently capacious to accommodate a host of revisionist impulses, whose ultimate configuration remains to be realized" (25–26). It nonetheless could be argued that Practice Theory, as envisaged by Spiegel, is very close to Hunt and Bonnell's formulation advocating a return to a supposedly reconceptualized social history that emphasizes experience and practice, including routinized bodily techniques that are untheorized and inculcated in disciplinary formations—in general, what Bourdieu termed *habitus* (14, 19).[16] It also seems to advocate a restoration of empiricist historicism that, as itself a habitus or craftlike practice stressing "know-how," emulates (or transferentially replicates) its largely atheoretical objects of study. Its clearest, and perhaps most significant, field of application is in *Alltagsgeschichte* or what Michel de Certeau termed the *Practice of Everyday Life*—a field in which much noteworthy work has indeed been done recently.[17] But its occasionally bewildering array of ill-assorted and divergent formulations (presumably including "some of the most powerful insights of poststructuralism," which it simultaneously seems to disavow) may, I think, facilitate a return to conventional practices, including the unargued, ad hoc appropriation of concepts or discursive strategies as fuzzy tools in a heteroclite "tool-kit" adapted to established problems and procedures.

More precisely, what does Practice Theory underplay or omit? It pays scant attention to earlier initiatives that were at times misconstrued in terms of restricted linguistic or cultural turns but in reality attempted to rethink culture in terms of signifying practices that raised the problem of the possibilities and limits of meaning, and did not unproblematically see culture or society exclusively in terms of codes, narratives, or discursive structures. Here John Toews's influential article on the "linguistic turn"—which remains a key reference some twenty years after its publication, even for those affirming "new directions"—had the limitations of its remarkable virtues. For it was perhaps too influential in the masterful way it stylized and prefigured historians' understandings of theoretical initiatives and, however unintentionally, may have offered historians a seeming shortcut to understanding complex texts or problems, while diverting attention from specific articulations that did not fit its own Hegelian-phenomenological insistence on construing developments in terms of a triadic structure involving language, meaning, and experience—with privileged experience as a largely unexplained remainder that might even be seen as an upbeat, untraumatic analogue of the Lacanian real.[18] In any event, Practice Theory, in Spiegel's formulation, does not address the crucial problem of the relation of practices to ideology, understood not narrowly as systematic "theory" or rationalistic philosophy but in terms of the problem of subject formation, involving not only discourse (in some restricted sense), but also self-presentation, justification, prejudice, fantasy, affect, and experience that is not reducible to immaculate perception. In addition, a reductive historicism simply excludes the problem of articulating relations between the historical and the transhistorical. Further, Practice Theory does not face up to the intricacies and demands of critical analysis of texts, uses of language, and modes of discourse, including the complexities of reading and interpretation which, while not exhaustive of society and culture, do (as White insisted) demand differential, theoretically informed attention and cannot simply be reduced to the social contexts that inform or constrain them.

In addition, Practice Theory sidesteps the issue of the implication of the observer in the observed (or what may be termed the transferential relation), and, with it, the need for a responsive understanding of the object of study which cannot be totally objectified and may even raise problems for one's own prereflective disciplinary habitus or unexamined assumptions. It also marginalizes, brackets, or even excludes the type of intellectual history for which the preceding questions have been vital—the type of intellectual history (advocated by White) that has been a primary conduit for the introduction into the historical discipline both of sustained inquiry into the problem of language as a signifying practice, as well as critical theories addressed to assumptions and orientations. Practice Theory tends to shift attention from such problems to insufficiently rethought social history and social science approaches that emphasize methodology, while downplaying self-critical theoretical questions. It also tends not to consider psychoanalysis as a crucial form of critical theory that bears on the relation between the observer and the observed and that has been very significant in its mutual articulation with other critical theories, stemming both from tendencies of the Frankfurt school (in the work of Adorno and Habermas) and from poststructuralist and deconstructive developments. Thus, particularly in the terms Spiegel offers, Practice Theory promises much but it also downplays or misconstrues a great deal. I would note that one could not make this statement about certain figures to whom Practice Theory presumably looks.[19]

Here I would make special mention of Michel de Certeau, whose notion of practice challenged overly restricted humanist assumptions and was not presented as an alternative to psychoanalysis, poststructuralism, or intellectual history. Certeau's work, along with that of others (perhaps Derrida's most forcefully) would also indicate that any pure binary opposition between theory and habitus is dubious, for theory is never a fully self-reflective, masterful metalanguage, and habitus as a totally prereflective experience or phenomenon is itself a reflective myth. Indeed the affirmation of habitus, either as a disposition or as an object of study, typically comes with a resistance to theory or at least certain forms of theory but may itself be "theorized" in very abstract terms, as in Bourdieu. In the volume Spiegel edits, Andreas Reckwitz, in his defense of the study of habitus-like practice, makes the questionable assertion that Practice Theory, despite its seeming diffuseness, provides a "basic vocabulary" that "amounts to a novel picture of the social and of human agency" (247). A leitmotif of Certeau's approach was the effort to undercut a confining conception of social and of human agency and to explore the notion of practice in a way that might jeopardize the postulation of any criterion that would establish a sharp divide or gap between the human and the animal—at times even the plant. In terms reminiscent of Derrida, Certeau clearly asserted that "the question at hand [in *The Practice of Everyday Life*] concerns . . . an operational logic whose models may go as far back as the age-old ruses of fishes and insects that disguise or transform themselves in order to survive, and which has in any case been concealed by the form of rationality currently dominant in Western Culture" (xi). He even ventured to say that "many everyday practices (talking, reading, moving about, shopping, cooking, etc.) are tactical in character" and may be related to "the immemorial intelligence displayed in the tricks and imitations of plants and fishes. From the depths of the ocean to the streets of modern megalopolises, there is a continuity and permanence in these tactics" (xix–xx). If taken seriously, such an approach would indeed introduce what might be called "new perspectives" in history and related areas. It might even assist in the elaboration of a conception of critical thought as a practice that is distinctive but also related to other practices.

The caveats I have put forward about Practice Theory, insofar as it marks an unproblematic return to a restricted if not one-dimensional historicism, centered on social history and social science, may also indicate that constructivism, even in its radical form, continues to be relevant in the often sharply etched, discomfiting challenges it poses and the way it provokes rethinking and rearticulating historical inquiry. Despite its important power of provocation, it also tends to assume or assert an excessively narrow humanism or anthropocentrism, in terms of which all meaning and value are derivatives of specifically human endowment, projection, or will. And it becomes misleading when it takes the valid notion that there are structural similarities between historiography and art or literature and exaggerates them, at times to the point of identity between them, hence downplaying the role (as well as the difficulty) of research and truth claims in historiography. The question of how to relate history and art or literature in a nonreductive manner, neither seeing the work of art merely as a historical document nor converting historiography itself into a work of art, is a complex issue that calls for inquiry, reflection, and rearticulation. At present, this question also requires attention to recent attempts to effect a more or less unmediated, "postsecular" combination of melancholic immersion in lost, stranded, or ruined objects and chance occurrences, miraculous encounters, epiphanic openings, messianic longings, or events of grace.[20] There has even been an important tendency in modern culture and thought to transfigure trauma into the occasion for sublimity (or jouissance). In the sublime, the excess attendant on trauma becomes an uncanny source of elation or ecstasy. Even extremely destructive events may become occasions of negative sublimity or displaced sacralization.[21] They may also give rise to what may be termed founding or foundational traumas—traumas that are commemorated and paradoxically become the valorized or intensely cathected basis of identity for an individual or a group.[22]

I think the prevalent resistance to the very concept of working-through derives both from a limited if not stereotypical understanding of it as a form of closure, therapeutic cure, or even turning the page of the past and from a related valorization of melancholia, inconsolable attachment to lost (at times transfigured into sublime) objects, and even a belief, as in Žižek, that at the very core of the human is a monstrously inhuman excess or death drive that renders all working-through a deceptive form of obfuscation, evasion, or "gentrification." (One may recall here Žižek's moving self-image [in *Žižek!*, the excellent film directed by Astra Taylor] as an energized void resonating with quantum theory.) There may even be a tendency to identify radicalism with extremism, going to an implosive or explosive limit that bursts apart all existing intellectual and practical formations, and looks toward a blank utopia related to grace, the miraculous, and the transcendent.[23]

One may acknowledge the significance of "inhuman," uncanny excess (or the Lacanian real) as well as of an enigmatic dimension (or unconscious) in humans without dismissing or undervaluing the role of processes that counter the unlimited play of excess and are related to intimately interacting thought and practice, including the crucial role of institutional transformation. One should not become fixated on the concept of working-through, and it is of course possible to appeal to other conceptualizations in making comparable arguments. But the concept of working-through has had a very restricted role in academic appeals to psychoanalysis, and it stands in need of the type of elaboration that only dialogue and debate can give it. Such elaboration may indicate alternatives to a compulsive return to aporia and paradox that has carried over from deconstruction into trauma theory. The point here is not to deny the role of aporia or paradox, but to seek ways of negotiating double binds without simply postulating and endlessly reiterating their terminal or interminable nature. Working-through is a form of negotiating problems that is not tantamount to repression, denial, or obfuscation. And it may occur in many processes and practices, both in narrative and other genres (the essay, the poem, ritual, dance, music, and so forth). In general, working-through is an articulatory practice with political dimensions: to the extent one works through trauma and its symptoms on both personal and sociocultural levels, one is able to distinguish between past and present and to recall in memory that something happened to one (or one's people) back then, while realizing that one is living here and now with openings to the future.[24]

An attempt to work over and through problems may also enable a differential approach to the aesthetic of the sublime (and its possibly displaced relations with the sacred) that neither dismisses it nor remains uncritically within its frame of reference. Such an attempt does not signal total critical distance, full emancipation, or complete mastery of problems, including one's sometimes haunting implication in, if not possession by, the past. Nor does it imply that there is a pure opposition between past and present or that acting-out—whether for the traumatized or for those empathetically relating to them—can be fully transcended towards a state of closure or full ego-identity (as a professional historian or in terms of any other delimited identity). And it should not induce the conflation of subject positions (for example, with everyone becoming a victim and survivor). But it does mean that processes of articulation crucial to working-through may counteract both unchecked identifications and the symptomatic force of the repetition compulsion, whereby the past not only haunts but intrusively erupts in the present and is compulsively relived or reenacted, however inappropriate or politically disastrous its scenarios, and however much it may be conducive to endless cycles of violence. Such processes may also enable victims not to be overwhelmed by a single identity that preempts all others and blocks access to possible futures.

Processes of working-through, including mourning and modes of critical thought and practice, involve the possibility of making variable, complex distinctions—not dichotomous binary oppositions—that are recognized as problematic but still function as limits, bases of judgment, and resistances to the blurring of distinctions. (The latter states may indeed occur in trauma or in compulsively acting out posttraumatic conditions.) In general, perhaps the best way to understand the complex, ongoing process of working-through is as the attempt to work out counterforces to acting-out, the repetition compulsion, and denial—an attempt that, to be in any measure effective, must combine psychic "work" on the self with larger sociopolitical and cultural processes. Hence, for example, mourning should not be reduced to individual grieving but seen as a social practice, indeed, in some sense a critically tested ritual process, with political dimensions; one may undertake the difficult effort to divest psychically and politically from an abusive authority figure who merits sustained critique, not mourning.

One begins investigation already inserted in an ongoing historical process, and may attempt to acquire some transformative perspective or critical purchase towards it; a crucial aspect of this positioning is the problem of the implication of the observer in the observed, what in psychoanalytic terms is treated as transference. Transference indicates that one begins inquiry in medias res (or what White might term a "middle-voiced" position), which one engages in various ways.[25] A basic sense of transference is the tendency to reenact performatively, in one's own discourse or relations, processes active in the object of study. This transference occurs whether one recognizes it or not, and the problem is in coming to terms with it in various combinations of acting-out, working-over, and working-through. Indeed, to the extent one does not explicitly engage transferential implications, one tends blindly to act them out, living a habitus run amok, engaging in destructive behavior, or at the very least becoming involved in performative contradictions.[26] Working-through offers the possibility of enacting variations that may be decisive enough to bring about effective change, including transformations analogous to conversion experiences that, within the context of working-through, are not bolts from the blue or radically transcendent, aleatory acts of grace.

Can historiography participate, at least in limited ways, in the complex, self-questioning process of working through the past? This may be possible, especially on collective levels, notably in the effort to critically examine and monitor memory, counteract compulsive repetition, elaborate viable distinctions, disclose unrealized possibilities in the past, problematize by historicizing the present, and open possible—and possibly more desirable—futures.[27] Simultaneously, however, it may lessen one's enjoyment of symptoms and apocalyptic or postapocalyptic hope in miracles, messianic acts of grace, or blank utopias. Such a view does not imply a simplistic "Enlightenment" faith or an equally simplistic understanding of secularization as the opposite of the religious or as the culmination of a linear, teleological process of "modernization." Instead, it leads to the question of intricate, nonlinear displacements, repetitions, and variations in the complex interaction of the secular and the "religious." It also induces a critical inquiry into the recent notion of the "postsecular" which may be deceptive in that it, like the seemingly endless host of "post" terms (including *posthistoire*, with which the universalizing, dehistoricized, at times radically transcendent impetus of prevalent uses of the "postsecular" seems implicitly bound up), implies a linear temporality that it simultaneously denies. But the notion of the postsecular has a possibly fruitful role as an invitation to critical inquiry into unexamined assumptions, especially those wherein working-through itself is (mis)conceived as the secure attainment of secular maturity (Kant's *Mündigkeit*), which is complacently assumed to resolve or even transcend problems related to religion, the sacred, sacrifice, transcendence, and so forth.

Like working-through itself, any process of achieving secular "maturity" must be repeatedly undertaken or worked (and jokingly played) out in a self-questioning manner. It should also raise the critical question of the limitations of anthropocentric humanism (and certain anthropocentric posthumanisms), as well as the possible dimensions of religion that have complex displacements in secularity (including notions of human creation [and endowment of the world or the past with meaning] as well as of the "real" as comparable to a willfully arbitrary, demonic *Deus Absconditus*). But one may also raise the question of possible aspects of "religion," in all its complexity and multidimensionality, which may be rearticulated in a critical framework.[28] Here I would not look to political theology, however seemingly deconstructed, or to a "psychotheology of everyday life"—tendencies that retain doctrinaire dimensions (for example, the postulation of Lacan or Žižek as the unquestioned authority or even the "subject-supposed-to-know") and the uncritical treatment of objects of inquiry as sacred texts whose typically ahistorical, decontextualized exegesis will yield insight if not truth.[29] In a tentative and self-questioning manner, however, I would rather point in the direction of both fallible notions of belief and commitment, involving trust, and possible forms of critical thought and practice, crucially including carnivalized ones, that resist victimization (prominent in sacrificialism) and instead help generate articulations for transitional points in life (for example, with respect to mourning as a critically informed process of working-through losses of legitimately valorized [not all] others).

The broadest question here is the insertion of the human, as well as any form of the postsecular or posthuman, in a nonanthropocentric relational network that includes other animals and the rest of nature—a relational network that would itself indicate the need for historically and situationally overcoming certain existing institutionalized forms (prominently including runaway capitalism that excessively constrains and impoverishes many to allow for multiple excesses in some). Such a network would also limit human (and posthuman) assertion that is typically legitimized by a decisive criterion or gap separating the human from the animal along with nature in general (reducing the latter to a bizarre combination of raw material or mere life and quasi-sacrificial victim). This relational network, obviously requiring ecologically aware elaboration, would give a different valence to Hayden White's own notion of a middle voice, here genuinely situated in medias res, and indicate that his valuable initiatives might fruitfully be supplemented by an appeal both to a more expansive, nonanthropocentric (as well as other than theological) frame of reference and to a revised, insistently critical-theoretical understanding of psychoanalytic concepts (trauma, transference, repetition, the unconscious, acting-out, working-over, working-through, and so forth). The orientation I am suggesting further attests to the power of provocation that Hayden White's thought has continued to have across the disciplines.

Notes

1. This issue was of concern to Hayden White, as indicated in his recent "Afterword: Manifesto Time," in *Manifestos for History*, ed. Keith Jenkins, Sue

Morgan, and Alun Munslow (London: Routledge, 2007), 220–33. Although I go for the most part in different directions in the present essay, for lines of argument that supplement or parallel formulations here, see my contribution to *Manifestos for History*, "Resisting and Apocalypse and Rethinking History," 160–78, as well as my recent books, notably *Writing History, Writing Trauma* (Baltimore: Johns Hopkins University Press, 2001); and *History in Transit: Experience, Identity, Critical Theory* (Ithaca: Cornell University Press, 2004). See also my "Tropisms of Intellectual History," *Rethinking History* 8 (2004): 499–529, and the responses to it in the same volume by Ernst van Alphen, Carolyn J. Dean, Allan Megill, and Michael Roth.

2. Derrida's deconstructive reading of Foucault's history of madness might in certain respects be taken as paradigmatic with reference to these questions. In Foucault himself, despite some inconsistency in usage, unreason [*déraison*] would seem to be the transhistorical force, and madness [*folie*] its reduced modern form or figuration. Derrida asks whether the project of writing the history of madness itself—or rather unreason—is mad and whether one can write only a history of one or more of its figures or figurations over time, including madness in a more specifically modern sense. See Derrida's "Cogito and History of Madness," in *Writing and Difference*, trans. Alan Bass (1967; Chicago: University of Chicago Press, 1978), 31–63; as well as my "Rereading Foucault's 'History of Madness'" in *History and Reading: Tocqueville, Foucault, French Studies* (Toronto: University of Toronto Press, 2000), 123–68.

3. Badiou sees himself as an insistently secular (anti)philosopher. But his conception of the secular is problematic, especially when he invokes notions of grace, and his exemplar of the radical militant is Saint Paul (one is tempted to add *als Erzieher*). He very much remains a classical philosopher in his unhistorical universalism and his sharp opposition between the human and the animal via an appeal to "thought." See, for example, his *Saint Paul: The Foundation of Universalism*, trans. Ray Brassier (1997; Stanford: Stanford University Press, 2003); and *Manifesto for Philosophy*, trans. and ed. Norman Madarasz (Albany: State University of New York Press, 1999).

4. The relation between the transhistorical and the universal is problematic, and I am tempted to argue that what is asserted as universal (notably some kind of foundational or originary trauma or, in Judith Butler, the closely related notion of the formation of subjectivity on the basis of a constitutive melancholy) is at best transhistorical or repeated (at times compulsively) in given traditions, such as dimensions of Christianity and Judaism. See Butler, *The Psychic Life of Power: Theories in Subjection* (Stanford: Stanford University Press, 1997), esp. 197–98. See also my more nuanced discussion of this aspect of Butler's thought in *Writing History, Writing Trauma*, 72–74.

5. Lacan.com, "Death's Merciless Love," http://www.lacan.com/zizek-love .htm, 19n (accessed October 27, 2008).

6. A version of this essay is included as chapter 2 of *Writing History, Writing Trauma*.

7. Certain tendencies prominent in the influential work of Giorgio Agamben, Alain Badiou, Eric L. Santner, and Slavoj Žižek might even be seen as threatening to undermine the very historical "consciousness," with its relation to critique, that Hayden White did so much to elucidate and defend. Witness White's recent assertion:

> Critique means, as Jameson says, 'Always historicize!' but not in the conventional way of the professional historian, that is to say, not as a way of providing an event with a past from which it must have derived, but rather as a way of restoring events to their presents, to their living relations with their conditions of possibility. But more: it means treating the present as well as the past as history, as a condition adequate to its possibility but also as something belonging to history—which is to say, as something worthy of being overcome and escaped from—that links critique to a particular kind of modernism or feeling of modernity characteristic of our time. (Hayden White, "Afterword: Manifesto Time," *Manifestos for History*, 225)

I see processes of working through problems as intimately related to the historical attempt to understand and overcome, without simply transcending, aspects of the past. I would further note that figures such as Agamben, Badiou, Santner, and Žižek do not share White's humanism, and White's work is not a reference point for them. But I think their seeming posthumanism remains anthropocentric in that their concerns are fixated on the human and its relation to the theological or the "postsecular," and they assume or insist on the radical difference or divide between the human and the animal. In Santner, the divide is conceived in terms of the role of trauma, signifying stress, and "cringing" abjection in the human—all of which are reminiscent of notions of original (or originary) sin (and fallenness)—also evoked by certain elaborations of the Lacanian real and (in Žižek) of distinctive "inhuman," all-too-human, monstrous excess. See Santer, *On Creaturely Life: Rilke/Benjamin/Sebald* (Chicago: University of Chicago Press, 2006). See also Slavoj Žižek, Eric L. Santner, and Kenneth Reinhard, *The Neighbor: Three Inquiries in Political Theology* (Chicago: University of Chicago Press, 2005). Santner's notion of "signifying stress" gives a semiotic twist to anxiety.

8. Paris: Gallimard, 2006.

9. See the defense of such an antihistoricist (as well as unhistorical), seemingly unmediated engagement with the "real," as well as of Žižek's thought in general, in Paul Eisenstein, *Traumatic Encounters: Holocaust Representation and the Hegelian Subject* (Albany: State University Press of New York, 2003).

10. See, for example, *The Puppet and the Dwarf: The Perverse Core of Christianity* (Cambridge, MA: MIT Press, 2003), 113. To use an older terminology

(which Žižek would probably reject), one says "yes" with the body but a saving "no" with the spirit in confronting *la condition humaine* that is essentially a Kafkaesque horror film in which relief comes only from radically other incursions of grace and "love."

11. *Welcome to the Desert of the Real* (London: Verso, 2002), 116. How Hayden White, who has a strong but existentially humanist utopian impulse, would respond to the kind of quasi-theological or "postsecular" apocalyptic utopianism in Agamben, Badiou, and Žižek is a matter one would like to see him address, for has not, to my knowledge, provided sustained commentary on their thought, despite its significance on the current critical scene. This currency is evident in the more recent work of Santner, who attempts to "triangulate" their thinking and relate it (along with that of such figures as Walter Benjamin, Franz Rosenzweig, and Freud) to the tradition of German-Jewish, putatively "psycho-theological" thought.

12. This sense of needing a significantly different articulation of problems is perhaps most acute in White's reflections on the Holocaust and other extreme or limit events. See "Historical Emplotment and the Problem of Truth," in *Probing the Limits of Representation: Nazism and the Final Solution*, ed. Saul Friedlander (Cambridge, MA: Harvard University Press, 1992), 37–53. This text was reprinted in *Figural Realism: Studies in the Mimesis Effect* (Baltimore: Johns Hopkins University Press, 1999), 27–42.

13. New York: Routledge, 2005. There are only a few references to White in this book, and the one by Spiegel is rather dismissive, incoherently amalgamating, and perhaps mimetically related to the kind of practice she strains to describe:

> How does the historian write up [*sic*] the multi-dimensional, semi-coherent, semi-articulate dynamics of practice in the face of traditionally felt needs to represent the past in some kind of narrative logic and/or form of emplotment, a not insignificant problem when one remembers the origins of linguistic turn historiography in the narrativist schools of White, LaCapra, Kellner, Ankersmit, and the like, who argued that *no* historical account is possible without some form of troping or emplotment? (23)

14. Berkeley: University of California Press, 1999.

15. Jay Winter, "Got the T-Shirt," review of *The Culture of the Europeans: From 1800 to the Present*, by Donald Sassoon, *TLS*, no. 5416 (January 19, 2007), 4.

16. Isabel V. Hull's recent book could be read as both avoiding theory and instantiating "practice theory," while dismissing, with respect to her object of study, the relevance of ideology (understood narrowly as tantamount to systematic "theory" or philosophy). See her *Absolute Destruction: Military Culture and the Practices of War in Imperial Germany* (Ithaca: Cornell University Press, 2005). What is not explored in the book is the role of ideology in a broader, subject-forming sense (for example, involving more or less fantasized images of

the fighting man as a virile if not sublime combatant who proves himself in battle).

17. *The Practice of Everyday Life* (1980; Berkeley: University of California Press, 1984).

18. John Toews, "Intellectual History after the Linguistic Turn: The Autonomy of Meaning and the Irreducibility of Experience," *American Historical Review* 92 (1987): 879–907. See my discussion of the essay in *History and Reading: Tocqueville, Foucault, French Studies* (Toronto: University of Toronto Press, 2000), 56–62. Toews provides a generous but reductive reading of my *History & Criticism* (Ithaca: Cornell University Press, 1985) and especially my *Rethinking Intellectual History: Language, Texts, Contexts* (Ithaca: Cornell University Press, 1983). In both books, my analysis invokes Bakhtin as well as Derrida, is critical of a restricted Saussurian-structural approach, and emphasizes the role of signifying practices, including language in use or "practice" (*langage* in contradistinction to the *langue/parole* binary). I raise the problem of the relation among "levels" or dimensions of culture (elite, popular, and mass) and, especially in *Rethinking Intellectual History*, reiterate the importance of what was indeed important for Hayden White but not prominent in historiography at the time: a close, critical reading, along with the problematic contextualization, of significant texts involving problems of language or, more broadly, signification not reducible to codes, narratives, or structures, although obviously not simply ignoring their role. I do, however, suggest that language understood not as autonomous or self-referential "discourse" but as an institution and a practice might be paradigmatic of other institutions and practices. In later work the scope of concern is broadened, and the question of the relation of texts and contexts, including the limitations of an exclusive focus on canons, is stressed. See, for example, *Representing the Holocaust: History, Theory, Trauma* (Ithaca: Cornell University Press, 1994), chap. 1. For an attempt at a critical analysis of the concept of experience in its multiple dimensions, see my *History in Transit*, chap. 1.

19. In his ambitious *Formations of the Secular: Christianity, Islam, Modernity* (Chicago: University of Chicago Press, 2003), Talal Asad employs a Foucauldian notion of embodied practice that he links to habitus, although the relation of habitus-like practice to critical theory is unclear. This includes the role of critical theories as themselves self-critical practices embodied in traditions and the manner in which such theories need not be totalizing or foundational but instead involve the questioning of assumptions in ways in which Asad himself engages.

20. In *On Creaturely Life: Rilke/Benjamin/Sebald*, Eric L. Santner develops and valorizes this view of the work of W. G. Sebald, which he relates to that of others, including Kafka and Anselm Kiefer. See also "Miracles Happen: Benjamin, Rosenzweig, Freud, and the Matter of the Neighbor," in *The Neighbor*, 76–133. On the question of *Trauer* (mourning) and melancholy in Sebald, see Mary Cosgrove, "Melancholy Competitions: W. G. Sebald reads Günther Grass

and Wolfgang Hildesheimer," *German Life and Letters* 59 (2006): 217–32. Cosgrove argues,

> melancholy resignation is the only "Trauer" discourse deemed suitable [by Sebald] for discussing the Jewish victims of the Holocaust. . . . Sebald's enormous success ensures that his subjectively valid position on the past has gained currency in some academic discourses, not always as an intriguing phenomenon within a specific context of taboos and prohibitions, but as a context-creating discourse in itself. It is his tendency to extrapolate from a single perspective on the past which should be critiqued, for it is highly problematic when applied to general interpretative frameworks, and invites undiscerning forms of identification. (232)

I would add that Sebald, in his mixed-genre writings, at times has his narrator-witness identify with Jewish victims, or confuse them with Germans (say, in bombed cities), rather than specifying the particular kind of loss, or at times "victimization," that may apply to certain Germans, particularly those (like himself) "born later" who find themselves within a freighted heritage which may generate in them confused feelings of "guilt."

21. For an elated response to the bombing of Hiroshima and Nagasaki, which at times resorts to a discourse of the sublime, see Georges Bataille's 1947 essay, "Concerning the Accounts Given by the Residents of Hiroshima," in *Trauma: Explorations in Memory*, ed. Cathy Caruth (Baltimore: Johns Hopkins University Press, 1995), 221–35. For an analysis and critique of Giorgio Agamben's turn to the sublime in his treatment of the Holocaust, and specifically the figure of the *Muselmann* (in his *Remnants of Auschwitz*), see my *History in Transit*, chap. 4.

22. For thought-provoking approaches to these problems, see F. R. Ankersmit, *Sublime Historical Experience* (Stanford: Stanford University Press, 2005); and David Simpson, *9/11: The Culture of Commemoration* (Chicago: University of Chicago Press, 2006).

23. See, for example, Žižek's contribution to *The Neighbor*, "Neighbors and Other Monsters: A Plea for Ethical Violence," 134–90.

24. An interesting question is the way music may be understood in terms of a problematic process of working through the past, for example, how jazz, the blues, and sorrow songs have different relations to one another and to African-American experience as well as to that of other oppressed groups.

25. I have noted elsewhere that in the academy there are transferential relations between inquirers (especially pronounced in the relations between professor and graduate student and at times between the scholar and his or her critics) and between inquirers and the past, its figures, and processes. See also my cautionary discussion of the notion of a middle voice in *Writing History, Writing Trauma*, 19–21. I am here attempting to indicate certain possibly fruitful aspects of the concept.

26. Among innumerable instances of performative contradiction due to un-

reflective repetition or acting out of problems one studies, one may point to the way René Girard, in his valuable studies of scapegoating and sacrifice, nonetheless tends to scapegoat those with whom he disagrees—a tendency that is extremely difficult to avoid.

27. Although he might use a different concept, Hayden White might well agree with this role for historiography, as is intimated in the quotation from him in footnote 7 above. For extensive discussions of acting-out and working-through, as they apply to historiography, see especially my *Representing the Holocaust: History, Theory, Trauma, History and Memory after Auschwitz* (Ithaca: Cornell University Press, 1998); *Writing History, Writing Trauma*; and *History in Transit: Experience, Identity, Critical Theory*. See also the convergent argument in Françoise Davoine and Jean-Max Gaudillière, *History Beyond Trauma: Whereof One Cannot Speak, Thereof One Cannot Stay Silent*, trans. Susan Fairfield (New York: Other Press, 2004), as well as Theodor Adorno's still relevant "The Meaning of Working Through the Past," in *Critical Models: Interventions and Catchwords*, trans. Henry W. Pickford (New York: Columbia University Press, 1998), 89–103.

28. For a careful inquiry into how little we know about the very concept of religion, as well as for a discussion of the various senses in which it may be taken, see Jacques Derrida, "Faith and Knowledge: The Two Sources of 'Religion' at the Limits of Reason Alone," in *Religion*, ed. Jacques Derrida and Gianni Vattimo (Stanford: Stanford University Press, 1998), 1–78.

29. For a contrasting approach, see Eric L. Santner, *On the Psychotheology of Everyday Life: Reflections on Freud and Rosenzweig* (Chicago: University of Chicago Press, 2001). On the back cover of this book, which owes much to his own thought, Žižek makes this ecstatic, apocalyptic, almost sacralizing pronouncement: "I wonder how many people will be aware, when taking this book into their hands, that they are holding one of the key texts of the last hundred years—that a new classic is being born, on a par with Heidegger and Wittgenstein. This book is much more than an intervention into current psychoanalytic-religious debates; Santner opens up a new way to reactualize the Judaeo-Christian legacy against the oncoming offensive of Western Buddhism, New Age wisdoms, and fake fundamentalisms."

PART FOUR

PRACTICE

Practice, an Introduction

Ewa Domańska

While in Part 1 of this volume the contributors discuss the philosophical dimensions of Hayden White's work, Part 4 focuses on his role as historian and cultural critic. Even if White himself rarely expresses his views on contemporary ethical and political issues in writing, his political opinions are widely known to those who participated in his lectures and seminars. In addition, as the essays in this section demonstrate, his theory and ideas are often treated as points of departure and reference in critical inquiries into various aspects of politics and ethics.

Part 4 begins with Verónica Tozzi's essay. She claims that a pragmatist reading of White's *Figural Realism* would help Argentines to come to terms with the difficulty of reaching an agreement regarding the history of Argentina's Malvinas War (1976–1983). Real historiographical problems are not factual, nor can they be unraveled in factual terms—the debate amongst Argentines on how to represent their recent past demonstrates this. For Tozzi, figural realism serves as a guide in the analysis of the relationship between different realistic representations of the same historical phenomena, approached as new, improved promises on how to reach better accounts of reality. The historical representation that fosters more research, the assignment of new meanings, even novel rewritings, can and should be deemed heuristically better.

In her "Primo Levi for the Present," Judith Butler remarks that the demands to counter revisionist histories prompted Primo Levi to ground his testimony of Auschwitz in transparent language and positivist claims about what actually happened. Following Hayden White, Butler asks whether the ability to tell such a story does not require a multiform use of rhetorical language, if only to convey emotional reality. Levi comes to realize that his own stories have a way of taking the place of memory, and this leads to a broader problem: do the stories "crystallize" and take on a life of their own? The crystallization of the story produces a conundrum for politics because revisionism must be adamantly opposed, and a language to convey the horrors of the Shoah must be found. Both pro- and anti-Israeli bodies make use of stories of the Shoah: this fact shifts the political problem to a new level. Butler asks whether we can preserve the insight that the account of the Shoah must be conveyed through rhetorical and figural means without accepting any of the instrumentalizations of the Shoah that take place within contemporary life. Discussing Primo Levi's work and exploring the question of what it means to give an account of oneself, Butler takes as a point of departure Hayden White's essay "Figural Realism in Witness Literature." She demonstrates how Levi's historical experience in the concentration camp provided the framework for his critique of Israeli state violence in the 1980s. Butler points out that Levi as a survivor objected to the "use" of the Shoah to justify wanton military destruction, but he also found that the public circulation of his rhetoric assisted anti-Semitism, at which point he became mute on the topic. Butler asks: are there critical alternatives to this impasse in the present day?

Richard Vann discusses White's role as historian. Vann recounts the early days of White's career and reminds us of the "proper" archival research White did in Rome while preparing his doctoral thesis on Bernard of Clairvaux and the papal schism of 1130. Tracing White's interest in R. G. Collingwood, Arnold Toynbee, Christopher Dawson, and later in the existential version of Marxism, Vann stresses that at that time White sought answers to social and moral issues that the analytical philosophy of history failed to provide. In particular, Vann examines the ideas, inspirations, and concerns that led White to write *Metahistory*. He focuses especially on two underappreciated essays published in the 1970s: "Wild Man" and "Noble Savage." This dialectical pair, as Vann terms it, illustrates White's belief that there is no absolute distinction between history and philosophy of history. Vann emphasizes the originality of White's

Metahistory when compared with other, traditional works on the history of historiography. His thorough re-examination of White's tropology and poetic approach to historiography leads Vann to conclude that there has always been tension between White's roles as historian and critic. White believes that "historical thinking" in contemporary Europe has sought to overcome the ironic perspective on history which dominates academic historiography, and his own historical writing is a significant contribution to this effort.

Ewa Domańska's essay discusses the crisis of the university and Hayden White's reaction to it. It focuses on an issue rarely addressed in scholarly essays on White: the ways in which his style and engagement as a teacher and mentor embody a desirable model of intellectual work. As was also pointed out in the essay by Allan Megill, White followed in the footsteps of his own former teacher at Wayne State College, William Bossenbrook. White thinks of himself first and foremost as a teacher, and his chief aim is to liberate his students and teach them how to rebel. Thus he approaches education as the practice of freedom. For him the faculty is not meant to be a "docile body," as proven by his leadership of the History of Consciousness program at UCSC, a place for interdisciplinary, critical, and "rebellious" work. Domańska compares White as a teacher to the mythical figure of Chiron, considered as an archetype of the mentor, guru, and leader.

12

Figuring the Malvinas War Experience

HEURISTIC AND HISTORY

AS AN UNFULFILLED PROMISE

Verónica Tozzi
Translated by Moira Pérez

Hayden White's work is an ineluctable theoretical instrument when facing the conflictive task of historizing our recent past. In 1982 Argentina underwent, for the first and last time in the twentieth century, an international armed conflict: *the Malvinas War.* This war, known in the United States as the Falklands War, took place under a military regime (1976–1983), which was the fifth act in the drama of interruptions to the country's democratic process, and the bloodiest in terms of human rights violations. The post-dictatorship period leaves all Argentines, whether professional historians or not, with the task of forging public memories for that period, whose grievous effects persist not only in the memory of those who have survived, but also in their descendants and in contemporaries not directly affected. Malvinas demands us to take responsibility for the experience of young people being recruited in order to win a war. The civil society understood the resulting defeat as the beginning of the end for the military regime; this equation was problematic, however, because it challenged us to build a just image of the armed conflict, without thereby legitimizing the regime's martial discourse.

In this work I will show that a pragmatist reading of White's Figural Realism will allow us to come to terms with the difficulty and even impossibility of reaching an agreement (a definitive version) regarding the history of this past—all of which does not imply silencing the debate. Past events and processes are known to us through diverse conflicting interpretations, leading me to assert that an approach to the history of any recent event or process will submerge us in the history of that event's history. If our study of the remote past plunges us into an interpretational pluralism that is most certainly contentious, it will be so much more so in relation to the recent past, where the voices of those actively involved join in as well. The lack of agreement should not distress us; on the contrary, it is an occasion to test our imagination as it offers new ways of thinking about the past, thus avoiding the blurring of such a painful memory. With this diagnosis in mind, I will suggest that in the conflictive encounter with our recent past, and from a pragmatist perspective, the historical representation that fosters more research, the assignment of new meanings, even novel rewritings, can and should be deemed heuristically better.[1] This hypothesis was inspired by the particular interpretation offered by White of Erich Auerbach's *Mimesis: The Representation of Reality in Western Literature*.[2]

I

April 2, 2007, is the twenty-fifth anniversary of the recovery, occupation, or invasion of the Malvinas Islands by an Argentine combined military force of 500 men (army, navy, and air force). The purpose of that military mission: recovering a territory that, according to our country's history, had been seized by the British 149 years before (1833).[3] The armed conflict with Great Britain, which lasted seventy-four days, was sadly unique for Argentines for three reasons: (1) it was the only international war in the twentieth century in which Argentina took part as the main opponent of one of the greatest world powers; (2) it reached a vast civil and military consent (exceptional in a country marked by military coups against constitutional democracies); (3) it involved 18- to 20-year-old civilian conscripts.[4]

Between June 14 and 16, 1982, Argentines heard a series of "Comunicados" (releases) from the "Estado Mayor Conjunto" (Joint General Staff of the Armed Forces) announcing a cease-fire in their Southern Atlantic operations (that is, a surrender).[5] The defeat annulled any short-term possibility of regaining possession of the islands through diplomacy;[6] however, it also intensified the crisis—both economic and financial—that the regime was going through. This, in its turn, hastened its fall by contrasting the leaders' perverse efficacy as a paramilitary force for internal repression with their total ineptitude as military professionals sustained by a large state budget.[7]

The retreat to the mainland is a story that deserves attention in itself. The return to Argentina is the beginning of another odyssey: one for the acknowledgment that nothing was in vain, for demands for reparations, for reinsertion in society as active citizens. Up until the defeat, no one seriously considered the possibility of questioning mandatory military service (that is, handing their sons over for about a year to be cared for and educated by military forces). After the defeat, we do not know whether those who were at Malvinas are "ex-soldiers," "chicos," "ex-combatant soldiers," "ex-combatants," or "veterans." These terms are not innocent: they struggle over how to tell the Malvinas war story, over the character of later commemorations; they struggle, finally, over how to remember those seventy-four days in which a country united in order to send its sons to death.[8]

II

What does it mean, then, for those concerned with recent history, to have the testimonies of those who endured an extreme experience such as a war taking place under a military regime and ending with a defeat? In the specific case of historical research, they play an epistemic role by giving us access, albeit not direct, to what happened, and a political role, as living demands for the voices of those affected to be heard. In the particular case of Malvinas ex-soldiers' experience, we are facing the kind of event we call *traumatic*, whose main trait lies in the open wounds handed down to the present and shamelessly intensified by the exhibition of an ambiguous temporality (because, in their proper sense, these events belong to the past—the war is over, the regime ended—but in a vivid experiential sense, they are present). This temporal ambiguity impels us to address certain difficulties peculiar to these events when figuring their history. On the one hand, despite having trustworthy information, it is impossible for us to reach an agreed understanding of events. On the

other hand, any approach to them must avoid slipping into a veiled closure of the event, an acquittal of perpetrators or the silencing of victims'
voices. I have chosen to name these several ways of forgetting—be it by
lack of representation, or by imposing a closing and redeeming representation—*limbo mnémico*.[9]

It has been considered crucial to grant these experiences of ambiguous temporality an "epistemic privilege" in order to settle conflicting representations.[10] However, as the war will show, this "epistemic privilege"
is part of the limbo mnémico. Considering testimony as the register of a
privileged and direct experience of facts is epistemically naïve, because it
neglects that the theoretical load of all experience veils the problematicity
of what it registers. It is reprehensible because it ignores that testimonial
reports are nothing but discursive or literary genres just like novels, tragedies, or comedies. Considering testimony as a veridical, uninterpreted
record of facts deprives witnesses of taking part in public debates on how
to convey meaning, how to understand, how to offer new questions on
what happened, and this is unacceptable.[11] Precisely in the Argentine
case, this limbo mnémico in which the experience of those who took part
in the operating theater has been submerged acquires an awkwardly original tone, due in part to the indecency of a society that went imperviously
from cheerful support to an intransigent repudiation. But the main reason for this strange tone is the reversal of the epistemic privilege usually
granted to the victim's experience. Assuming experience as unreviewable
and indisputable, instead of problematic, conflictive, and narratively or
theoretically constituted, makes it possible to avoid listening to or talking
with these ex-soldiers; the grief of defeat and the vindication of the feat
are evaded.[12]

Another usual way of avoiding the victims' burdensome request—legitimacy of the claim and impertinence of the historiographer's profession
regarding fidelity to individual experiences—aims at freeing historians
from it, by restricting this duty to the work of commemorators. In this
case, history and memory are distinguished in terms of their respective
commitments to truth and politics. However, when embarking on the
search for a meaning for the recent past, it is difficult, if not impossible, to
maintain this division of tasks. Hence Argentine historian Hugo Vezzetti's
stance in *Pasado y presente. Guerra, dictadura y sociedad en la Argentina*.[13]
In it, he refuses to satisfy the demands for a memory seen as a *reproductive*

representation, based upon an assumed epistemic privilege. Apart from the commonplaces that proliferate in it, social memory is also subject to conflict and struggles over meaning.[14] According to Vezzetti, the aim of our encounter with the recent past is "problematizing the past in such a way that it comes back to us as an interrogation on the conditions, actions and omissions of society itself."[15] However, according to the author, even though memory and history have an intricate and unavoidable relationship, history, unlike memory, maintains the necessary critical distance in order to be able to problematize what intends to settle dogmatically.

If the best social memory that a historian can help build is one that raises problems and interrogations, then the risk will be of producing a historical representation that leaves more closed answers than open questions. Having said this, the predilection for inquiry-generating representations is partly a political answer to the abandonment of the ideal of history as a tale of "the past just as it was"—a transcendental but unachievable end.[16] We must then go beyond Vezzetti, and conclude that there is no relevant difference between memory and history, because both share the same agenda when facing our recent past: raising inquiries and encouraging further research up to a point critical enough for it to be worthy of rewriting its history.[17] Only a "figural realistic" approach to the representation of the past that tests historical imagination in order for conflict not to be concealed, eludes those specific kinds of omissions by unveiling the obscured "epistemic privilege" and "limbo mnémico" plot.

III

White's work has been read by its critics at times as denying past existence to those events, persons, processes, groups, and institutions to which history refers. It has also been read as only granting them a linguistic existence, overlooking his warning about the difficult decisions that must be made regarding "what we are to call these phenomena, how we are to classify them, and what kinds of explanation we are to offer of them."[18] Thus, I believe "figural realism"[19] shows us how the thesis of history as a construction underscores the effort involved in reaching significantly realistic representations of the past. Such a task demands imagination within available linguistic conventions, for which there is no one way of satisfaction. The pending debate among Argentines on how to represent their recent past is a key example of the fact that real historiographical problems are not factual nor can they be unraveled in factual terms. Was the so-called Guerra Sucia (Dirty War) really a war, or was it just plain state terrorism? Are those detained and disappeared passive victims, or social activists? Should we portray the war's soldiers as victims of the regime, or as ex-combatants?[20] Additionally, far from its interpretations as promoting a paralyzing relativism, figural realism is rather a guide in the analysis of the relationships among different realistic representations of the same historical phenomena: not as a succession or coexistence of descriptions getting closer to the truth—albeit unsuccessfully—but rather as new, improved promises on how to reach better descriptions or accounts of reality. I shall now reconstruct the argumentation behind this conclusion.

White professes to have found in Auerbach's history of occidental literature[21] a concept of realism—"figural realism"—suitable not only for literary history, but also for history in general.[22] *Mimesis* describes how each form of realism has put forth, on the one hand, connections between events in order for them to be correctly represented, and, on the other hand, connections among these successive attempts at representation (the connection thus established is called "figural causation").[23] It is figuratively that Greco-Roman civilization and Italian Renaissance culture are connected, considering Greco-Roman civilization as pointing to the latter, and the Renaissance as a fulfillment or consummation of the former.[24] "But as a historical event, it remains open to retrospective appropriation by any later group that may choose it as the legitimating prototype of its own project of self-making."[25] More specifically, past events are retrospectively seen by some later group as *figures*, whereas successive events—to which they are related when seen from the present—are thought of as fulfillments of what was previously *figured*.

What draws me to back White, specifically to his appropriation of Auerbach via "figural realism," is the suggestion of three methodological prescriptions. First prescription: take representations of reality (either literary or historical) as suggestions for us to regard past events under another light. We are encouraged to adopt another perspective, and assured that from this new point of view, reality will be better seen. Second: these proposals always emerge from a certain context (disciplinary and/or political), and it is this context that legitimates the achieved meaning. Third: the different proposals sustain a figuralist connection, a symptom of methodological fertility.[26] To sum up, "figural realism" will allow us to explain, first of all, the relationship between historical representations of reality and reality itself; secondly, the relationship between a representation and its context; and finally, the relationships between successive representations themselves.

"Figural realism," then, elucidating the historical operation as a promise—renewed over and over again, but never accomplished—of realistically representing the past, explains why it is impossible, and beside the point, to achieve a definitive version of the past. In a pragmatist key, we often see scientific practice adopt certain theories *not* based upon their stronger conformity with events (which cannot be decided once and for all), *but* because they open new paths of inquiry. This kind of evaluation, identified as "heuristic evaluation" in studies of scientific theory production processes, offers an adequate approach to the understanding of historiography's controversial character.[27] My pragmatist view of "figural realism" allows us to acknowledge not only that past events' truth and meaning can only be known after their taking place (as Danto accurately pointed out), but also that what makes a representation truly meaningful is its heuristic value—that is, its ability to leave open questions about those events, to the point of making a return to them or a rewriting of their history worthwhile. Because the relationship between representations of the recent past and testimonies of those directly involved is the focus of this chapter, it is crucial to show how my own reconstruction of White's "figural realism" allows me to approach it in a more comprehensive way, both politically and epistemically.

IV

My first methodological appropriation—the relationship between representation and reality—allows us to legitimately speak of "figural realism," emphasizing that we do not just register facts, but we interrelate them meaningfully as well. This relationship is therefore a construction, since it says something new about them, and yet does not disclose all that could be said.[28] This approach suggests regarding events as hoping to eventually reach, in relation to other events, their full meaning, despite this aim not being achievable or even exactly definable.[29] An apparently isolated historical event can take on a new meaning when related to a subsequent one, which comes by as a promise of realizing its significance. Having said this, in our current debates regarding the recent past, testimonies—just like academic historical representation, journalistic research, literary and artistic representations—must be seen as suggestions of links between past events and subsequent ones, as if hoping to one day achieve their full significance. It is only in terms of a renewed promise of representing past experience from the present, that we can come to terms with the temporal ambiguity specific to post-traumatic experiences.

This drives us to the second methodological appropriation—pertaining to the relationship between representation and its context—since these suggestions or promises of new meanings are made from a certain perspective, and there is no objective or transcendent need to make them. Just as in the Renaissance reading of Greco-Roman culture, White notices, associations are not causal: there is no actual need to link both cultures. Neither are they genetic: their inclusion in a single historical sequence has no objective grounds. Lastly, they are not teleological: the aim—to produce an ultimate picture of facts—is never achieved.[30] However, this is not about rejecting the establishment of objective time sequences (be they causal or genetic). It only shows that the laying out of a certain line or sequence instead of any other is not an isolated task, but rather a decision taken from a certain perspective.

Again, testimonies, academic historical representations, literary and artistic representations, are all, as representations, appropriations of the past from a specific present, with its available linguistic and symbolic resources. At this time, I must clarify a few points in order to avoid common misunderstandings of White's statements on the public uses of history. These have been unjustifiably reduced to a simplistic version of linguistic cultural determinism: certain figurations necessarily legitimate certain policies. At the same time, it is assumed that his warning on the lack of factual criteria to cast testimonies off allows us to combine such extreme determinism with a certain "freedom" for historical agents and historians to manipulate linguistic resources available to them (a clearly inconsistent combination). This does not take into account, in the first place, that the production or concrete carrying out of actual effective images can only be evaluated retrospectively. The problem of understanding for whom history is written, "reading" society's demand, is also a matter of figuration, imagination, and criticism. It also does not take into account, secondly, the fact that White's considerations on the connection between the metahistory shared by historians and the public, implies that those who seize their past from their present do not do so ex nihilo or from mere introspection on their pre-theoretical experience. This is why a formalistic analysis of available—although not necessarily determining—cultural resources is necessary for the building of historical works. Thirdly and finally, taking over a group's public demand for representation is necessarily both a self-critical task—since whoever takes on this role must face decisions on how to make use of those resources—and a critical one—because dealing with demands does not imply slavishly meeting them or embracing the group's position.

Finally, the relation between successive and/or coexistent representations of facts directed at emphasizing different angles of them—our third methodological appropriation—is also enriched by "figural realism." That is, aspects emphasized by successive representations renovate those highlighted by previous ones, trying to fulfill promises not kept by their predecessors, thus renewing the promise of reaching a better representation. I must add that my pragmatist reading of figural realism is an adequate development of a notion suggested early on by White in *Metahistory*, where he confines his tropological analysis to cognitively responsible appropriations of the past—that is, those political proposals for future action which assume they must rely on history for their legitimacy.[31] Once again, this gives me an opportunity to reject some frequent misinterpretations of White, such as Dirk Moses's recent rephrasing: "national or ethnic mythologies are a legitimate use of the past insofar as they are an answer to the burden of history. Certainly, no amount of 'objective' historical scholarship can disprove them."[32] In his essay, Moses overlooks White's warning that, in matters of political or moral adequateness of our uses of the past, no precision in facts or evidence can help us, precisely because we are dealing with political or moral dissent. This does not imply that we should accept any political conclusion allegedly drawn from historical reconstructions.

White's much-questioned assertions that both Israelis and Palestinians are legitimate holders of truthful chronicles of humiliation and spoliation aim at emphasizing that a comparative recounting of each peoples' sufferings is not going to solve the problem. In other words, assuming the *factual under-determination* thesis in interpretations of the past does not imply silencing discussion and appealing to force. Much to the contrary, my reading of "figural realism" posits a preference criterion among historical representations that does not do away with their factual and political dimensions. It would support whichever interpretation encourages further research from a heuristic perspective, thus renewing the promise of a realistic representation of the past. Historians, witnesses, and commemorators all take part equally in this dialogical contest.

In tune with his discomfort regarding the value of testimony in terms of exclusive veritative criteria, White has promoted the disallowance of typical twentieth-century academic forms of historical writing.[33] In its attempt to represent extreme events in terms of political, economic, or social conditions—in order to show their expectedness within their context—professional historiography has obstructed its reinterpretation and rethinking—which could grant a meaning to the victim's experience as part of a larger context. White will likewise turn away from those who prefer to keep silent or reproduce survivors' testimonies.[34] True to his rule of finding instruments of historical understanding in literature, he suggests imitating modernist literary style or interior monologue as a way to avoid distorting the persistent experience of the victim's perplexity and senselessness concerning what happened. His affliction cannot have any meaning. However, if this tone of doubt and perplexity is not turned into concrete questions—inspiring us to go over them again and again, in order to dialogically think them in another way—we risk repeating the same mistake we are trying to avoid. The iterating monologue of traumatic experience that aims at cancelling typical historical questions—why it happened, how it was possible, etc.—is viewed as a remedy against perplexity-annulling answers. However, I believe it risks sinking it into oblivion, by not only not encouraging but also literally canceling historical rewriting—our only means of keeping those questions open which force us to revisit those events.

I do not suggest taking testimony as the record of an experience—that of having access to the happening of certain events—with the purpose of corroborating or rejecting specific representations. On the contrary, as advised by White, we should view testimony as a promise of representing reality. That is, facing the implicit or explicit suggestion of regarding that past in a certain way, trying to answer the questions born from the adoption of that proposal in our own research context, and—when possible—renewing the promise with a new representation proposal.

V

Malvinas is an excellent opportunity to show this approach's fecundity, by taking on the question—when imagining a representation of our recent past—of how to establish a dialogue with its surviving ex-soldiers, cast by society into liminality and indeterminacy. The rising Argentine democracy found any expressions vindicating the war or rejecting the "young victims of the régime" category absolutely unacceptable, because they were seen to unite them either with the military or with the seventies' revolutionary ideologies. We can now resume under a new light the question that initiated this work: How can the political agenda of historizing our present be faced, upon assuming the "figural realistic" nature of representations of the past? How should a historiography in agreement with these demands be or not be? Before undertaking the analysis of some concrete examples—recently produced in Argentina—of the seizing of the past, I would like to draw attention to Todorov's advice about historicizing war: that of returning to old—but inspiring—tragic stories.[35] Since tragic stories of the recent past abound in Argentina, it is crucial to assess their heuristic value. In order to do this, I shall briefly return to *Metahistory*, since it is in the analysis of Tocqueville's tragic view that my pragmatist reading of White takes shape.

Upon reflecting on the conservation of the past, Todorov points out that, although it is commonly said that History is written by winners, a part of the writing in the twentieth century has also been claimed for the defeated, the subdued, and the victims. This notwithstanding, faced with the need to understand the past, identifying with the victims or granting them epistemic privilege does not bestow on us extra merit—we are still with the good ones. What would a story look like, Todorov asks finally, whose author refused to take sides with either the hero or the victim? Neither the past as victimization—the losers' perspective—nor the past as triumph—the winners' perspective. Rather, the past as a tragedy. History, he adds, has a soft spot for severe events. In it, good and evil do not take shape unmixed, and only tragedy can show not only suffering and anguish, not only the absence of good—which can also be illustrated in victimization stories—but above all, its sheer impossibility.[36]

Paradoxically, in *Metahistory*[37] Hayden White had already pointed out that, of the four primary literary genres in nineteenth-century historiography—*Romance, Tragedy, Comedy,* and *Satire*—current historiography has opted exclusively for the last, driven by our time's ironical spirit (*trope*). Its appeal resides in its being the trope that guides the kind of thought conscious of language's limitations to access reality. To White, however, this alleged linguistic self-consciousness is as arrogant and ungrounded, because it is just as close to (and as far from) reality as the other three narratives. Strictly speaking, they are all forms of "realism." Why then does Todorov favor tragedy? On first sight, it would seem to uniquely avoid the limbo mnémico, not so much by trying to remedy or satisfy the victim's demands, but rather by serving as an antidote to a potential evil in ourselves. Tragedy, says Todorov, is the only way in which we can draw a lesson from history.

White conveys this idea by portraying tragedy as a drama of the fall albeit with an increase of consciousness. In tragedy, just as in comedy, there are occasional and partial reconciliations. In the former, however, they are rather resignations of men to their condition, which cannot be changed, but within which they can function: the *Great Mechanism* as Jan Kott referred to Shakespeare's Royal Tragedy series.[38] A paradigmatic example of historical realism as tragedy is the work of Alexis de Tocqueville, who stands out for his effort to sustain coherently—albeit unsuccessfully—this tragic view of history, inspired by the metonymic trope. This led him to look into the causal laws governing history's functioning as a social process, while committing him to a certain radicalism close to materialism. Even more noteworthy is the fact that he chose to analyze his recent past, portrayed in *Democracy in America* and in *The Old Régime and the Revolution*. In these two works, the viewpoint can be seen of someone who partakes in a process and must struggle to pull out of it in order to guess its general movement or direction. However, what renders Tocqueville's work more interesting and draws us back to it, according to White, is precisely the bewilderment stemming from the impossibility of reconciling his tragic vision (which he did not formally renounce, despite his deeply ironic sense of humor) with his refusal to unveil the laws of the social process, his persistent conservatism, and his disguised liberalism.[39] Tocqueville's greatness does not reside in fulfilling the task appointed by his tragic vision—unveiling the *Great Mechanism* and taking on a radical ideology. Rather, it lies in having avoided the presentation of a story of closure and fulfillment: his tragic realism was not without ambiguity—unacceptable in a tragic vision of history.[40] Tocqueville's historical analyses, White notes, are actually means to un-reify language, conveying a genuinely ironic stance. With its fractured vision of the present—its abandonment of certainties and truth—irony calls on sensible readers to give their own names to the past, choosing their future according to their interests and aspirations. It is ultimately Tocqueville's inclination towards—albeit not definitive endorsement of—irony that contributed to his building of a past with more questions than answers—the shortest path to limbo mnémico's elision. Perhaps Todorov, upon rejecting stories built on simplistic identifications with the hero or the victim, envisaged tragedy as the way to avoid them. However, in this genre, as Kott has pointed out concerning Shakespeare and his historical vision, History—the Great Mechanism, transcendent truth—is the main character, and this confidence in History is the worst perspective we can endorse if we wish to draw up the death certificate for our recent past. In this work's last section, I shall test my pragmatist reading of White's reflections with three remarkable attempts to represent Malvinas "experiences": a film, an "editing" work on testimonies seeking to narrate a battle without an omniscient narrative voice, and a historiographical-critical study on the representations of Malvinas.

VI

Tragic reenactments of our history, inspired by an identification with the victim and legitimated by an alleged epistemic privilege, persist in our country in views of the Malvinas War commonly held by Argentines—in this case, regarding its ex-soldiers. In his recent *De chicos a veteranos. Memorias argentinas de la guerra de Malvinas*, Guber identifies three views which have given shape to the ex-soldiers' image: a) that of military analysts from Britain and the United States, confined to emphasizing their role as untrained partakers of the conflict; b) that of Argentine military authors who support the conflict and aim at promoting portraits of the Argentines' patriotism and war anecdote heroic tales; c) that of ex-soldiers as victims of the regime's authoritarianism. The last is the image all Argentines helped build, enduring in most critical political circles interested in collecting testimonies of military abuse in the war scene as yet another example of their absolute dominion over civil society in general.[41]

In all three of them, "the chicos" are crystallized as tragic heroes in a the-atrical staging that traps them in the past and prevents them from inte-grating into the present and looking forward to the future. None of them, according to Guber, "manages to grasp the complexity of the soldiers' memory, since they do not fall either for heroism and patriotism, or for naivety, ignorance and obsequiousness or adulation. Rather, they tend to bring forth scenes and paths marked by the dilemma, contradiction and paradox of a war which very few Argentines experienced first-hand."[42]

A pathetic example of this victimizing image is provided by the much-advertised film *Iluminados por el fuego* (Blessed by Fire) directed by Tristán Bauer, 2005,[43] based on ex-soldier Edgardo Esteban's book, *Malvinas, diario del regreso*.[44] In it, Esteban's character, upon learning about one of his comrades' suicide, reenacts the experience he had gone through twenty years before. In one of its most remarkable scenes—given that the film was publicized as a war film, a novelty in the Argentine industry—a group of four Argentine soldiers is shown in Malvinas land preparing a typical battlefield ambush. The image announces the unprecedented sight: "Malvinas chicos engaged in man-to-man combat with British sol-diers." However, raised expectations are immediately disappointed. In the following scene, we see that there are no such British soldiers, but rather a flock of sheep. Soldiers throw themselves fully over one of the poor ani-mals to slaughter it, owing to one soldier's agrarian skills. The memory of active warriors in fierce combat in the Malvinas comes forth as something unrepresentable for these filmmakers.[45]

Towards its end, Bauer's film offers us another example of the unac-ceptable—the depriving of "los chicos" of their political voices. We gain this through the narration of the protagonist's suicidal companion. The latter's wife, trying hopelessly to make sense of the outcome, recalls with distress: "he was with the veterans[46] for some time, but then they ar-gued and he left." Now, all those questions, inevitable twenty years after the surrender (Why did he disagree? What do ex-soldiers disagree about? What are their reasons to vindicate the occupation or not?), were not even hinted at in the film. If we follow the filmmakers, that testimony would lead to nothing worth examining. By prejudging their experience as privileged and untouchable, the only way to reject their vision is not to listen, since listening is reduced to accepting and legitimating. But that prejudice is born from another one: that the best historical representation is the one eliminating all conflicts and reaching an agreement on the official version—on the whole, a death certificate for research on the event. Contrary to Todorov's wishes, in this tragedy there are no lessons to be learned, because there are no new questions to be posed.

One of the most striking dialogues with simple first-person war testimonies (as opposed to the spoliation of the "chicos" as military actors in the battlefield and as citizens with views on the conflict they endured) is *Partes de Guerra*.[47] The text is an assembly of testimonies from Argentine soldiers and officers sent to Darwin and Goose Green, protagonists of the operations known as Operación Rosario. The aim of the editing work is that testimonies "weave into an account, amongst many other possible ones, of Malvinas war."[48] The editors' influence seems to emerge only in the chapter titles: "The calling," "The wait," "First attacks," "The surrender," "The return," and so on. There is an apparent passiveness in the narrator, who would do nothing but place the diverse testimonies under each chapter. This leaves us readers in the role of spectators of an experience (war) alien to us. However, the suggestive gathering of voices does not leave us unaffected: it moves us, it touches us, it vexes us, and, above all, it raises doubts in us and forces us to take sides among them. Although the editing of the diverse testimonies gives shape to an account of the war, the voices narrating the same events are not neutral or homogenous. Soldiers and military describe their experiences and present their anecdotes within the context of their diverse social and cultural backgrounds. As readers, we are ultimately invited to take part in this concert of voices struggling to present the most meaningful version—and not only the one most truthful according to the facts—of the war's events. Even editors-narrators themselves feel tempted to pull away from those testimonies with which they "would not agree," immediately countering them with another that questions their political adequacy. The book moves us with its wide-ranging testimonies, without annulling discrepancies between the narratives—in fact, the testimonies stir up more questions than answers, ultimately.

In order to illustrate the superiority of a pragmatist reading of "figural realism," I shall end my contribution by applying it to a work we can unhesitatingly consider "historiographical." In *Las guerras por Malvinas*, Federico Lorenz provides another example of heuristic and figural usage of testimonies, by employing them in the context of trying to understand the specificity of the 1982 conflict. Lorenz is aware that the construction of war memories is subject to the conflict's post-hoc constructions, and hence refuses to reduce them to mere relivings.[49] In my opinion, this is only possible by regarding the ex-soldiers' claims as descriptions of their experiences of the conflict, yes, but the ex-soldiers should also be respected as expert voices and their texts as expert interpretations of their experiences.

Las guerras por Malvinas is a concrete representation proposal (promise): that of facing Malvinas accounts—whether testimonial or not—in such a way that (symbolic) resources for the construction of war narrations are unveiled.[50] This approach will have direct heuristic consequences, on an epistemic level (usually limited to historians) and on a political one (left to memory-related policies). According to Lorenz, this will allow, in the first place, a withdrawal from usual representations of war as yet another aspect of the regime's political manners: that is, Malvinas as another way of hiding the other conflict (the forced "disappearing" of people), and not in its specificity (an international conflict). In the second case—that of memory construction—it will facilitate seizing the monopoly over the construction of a Malvinas-specific discourse from right-wing circles and the military.[51] War and its protagonists will hence cease to oscillate between the victims' limbo and the timeless pantheon of national heroes and martyrs. Thus, the end of Lorenz's book appears as an appeal to the rewriting, from new perspectives, of *Las Guerras por Malvinas*.

In conclusion, if my reading of White's "figural realism" is correct, then the incorporation of testimonies into the discussion on how to configure Malvinas' image is an invitation at least for Argentines to critically restore a more fundamental question: why was Malvinas a dream of national unification? Challenging this question seems to leave a void in the hope of building an identity through a common account. But, if I am right, it would be preferable to fill that void with new questions.

Notes

1. This notion, addressed in section 3, is taken from Thomas Nickles, "Heuristic Appraisal: A Proposal," *Social Epistemology* 3, no. 3 (1989): 175–88.

2. Hayden White, "Auerbach's Literary Theory: Figural Causation and Modernist Historicism," in *Figural Realism: Studies in the Mimesis Effect* (Baltimore:

Johns Hopkins UP, 1999). It is important to point out that the term "rewriting" will not be used literally: it will here refer to the production of new versions of the past, not limited to academic historiography or written discourse (journalism or literature), but rather including films, installation art, memorials, among other things. A recent study on the subject can be found in Cecilia Macón, ed., *Trabajos de la Memoria. Arte y Ciudad en la Postdictadura Argentina* (Ladosur: Buenos Aires, 2006), particularly in Horacio Banega's article, "La memoria como fenómeno corporal."

3. Two outstanding journalistic approaches to the conflict's events are Oscar Cardoso, Ricardo Kirschbaum, and Eduardo van der Kooy, *Malvinas, La trama Secreta* (Buenos Aires: Sudamericana-Planeta, 1983); and Rodolfo Terragno, *Falklands* (Buenos Aires: Ediciones de La Flor, 2002).

4. Features pointed out by Rosana Guber, *De chicos a veteranos. Memorias Argentinas de la guerra de Malvinas* (Buenos Aires: Ides, 2004), 13. Since 1904, Argentina had compulsory military service for 21-year-old males. In 1973, recruitment was set at 18 years of age—the age of high school graduation and entrance into the labor market and/or college. Thus, soldiers on the mission were about 19 to 20 years of age at the time. In 1994, following a conscript's death as the result of his superior's abuse, constitutional president Carlos Saúl Menem decreed the end of conscription.

5. *Comunicados* 163 to 165. See Terragno, *Falklands*, 405–408.

6. In the eighties, the Malvinas had around 1,000 inhabitants called *kelpers*—sheep breeders without British citizenship, all working for the Falkland Islands Company (established 1846). At the time of the invasion, Great Britain evaluated its national priorities, and the sovereignty of the Falklands Islands ranked forty-eighth in importance (according to a 1981 interview with Lord Carrington by a Caracas newspaper). See Terragno, *Falklands*, 29–33.

7. After the defeat, the dimensions of the Argentine repression became visible: around 30,000 persons detained and "disappeared," following their illegal kidnapping and imprisonment in clandestine concentration camps—these events were exposed as clear examples of state terrorism. Regarding representation resources for transition, see Laura Cucchi, "Reconstruir la esfera pública. La justicia reparatoria como deliberación"; Nicolás Lavagnino, "¿Adónde van las transiciones?"; Cecilia Macón, "Ruptura como continuidad. La transición 30 años después"; and Mariela Schorr, "La transición a la democracia en la Argentina. La responsabilidad social en la reconstrucción democrática"; all in Cecilia Macón, ed., *Pensar la democracia, imaginar la transición (1976–2006)* (Ladosur: Buenos Aires, 2006).

8. There was no space in those days for dissident voices, no space for those mothers, mostly working class, who had nothing to rejoice at, what with their sons—in many cases part of the family's financial support—lost in some far away and mostly alien islands.

9. I analyzed this notion in my essay "Apuntes sobre Malvinas. Tragedia y *limbo mnémico* en el encuentro con el pasado reciente," in *Pensa la democracia*, 83–98. With the term *limbo mnémico* I am trying to christen an imaginary space inhabited by those uncomfortable memories.

10. In Verónica Tozzi, "El privilegio de la postergación. Dilemas en las nuevas epistemologías de la identidad," *Análisis Filosófico* 26, no. 2 (November 2005): 139–64; I discuss Satya Mohanty's recovery of "epistemic privilege" from postpositivist realism in *Literary Theory and the Claims of History: Postmodernism, Objectivity, Multicultural Politics* (Ithaca, NY: Cornell UP, 1997).

11. This conception derives from identifying testimony with its legal function (witness before a court), forcing witnesses—especially those who have been victims of violence—to reveal a private truth. See Hayden White, "Figural Realism in Witness Literature," *Parallax* 10, no. 1 (January–March 2004): 113–24; Leigh Gilmore, *The Limits of Autobiography, Trauma, and Testimony* (Ithaca, NY: Cornell UP, 2001); and Martin Kusch, "Testimony," in *Knowledge by Agreement* (Oxford: Oxford UP, 2002).

12. "Confronted with the victimization that emphasized their youth, veterans ventured different answers; however, their political stand on the war, their appeal to such resources as carrying [sic] uniforms and adopting military rhetoric, hindered the circulation of their accounts." Lorenz, *Las guerras*, 216.

13. Hugo Vezzetti, *Pasado y presente. Guerra, dictadura y sociedad en la Argentina* (Buenos Aires: Siglo XXI, 2002).

14. See ibid., 33–34.

15. Ibid., 34.

16. Other possible reactions would be either silence or giving up research, neither of them defended in Argentina in the case of the Malvinas. Concerning state terrorism crimes, on the contrary, there are still voices (from rightists mostly) calling for the record to be wiped clean, for a tabula rasa of the past.

17. Other critical positions regarding the sharp distinction between memory and history can be found in Peter Novick, *The Holocaust in American Life* (Boston: Houghton Mifflin Company, 1999); and Tzvetan Todorov, *Memoria del mal, tentación del bien. Indagación sobre el siglo XX* (Barcelona: Península, 2002). Todorov's work was originally published as *Mémoire du mal, tentation du bien* (Paris: Robert Laffont, 2000).

18. "I have always been interested in how figurative language can be used to create images of objects no longer perceivable and endow them with an aura of a kind of 'reality' and in such a way as to render them susceptible to the techniques of explanation and interpretation chosen by a given historian for their explication." White, "Hecho y figuración en el discurso histórico" ("Fact and Figuration in Historical Discourse"), preface to *El texto histórico como artefacto literario*, trans. Verónica Tozzi and Nicolás Lavagnino (Paidós: Barcelona, 2003), 51.

19. My reconstruction of White's exposition of "figural realism" from his "Auerbach's Literary Theory" is further developed, together with some answers to possible objections, in Verónica Tozzi, "La historia como promesa incumplida. Hayden White, heurística y realismo figural." *Diánoia*, México, UNAM, 51, no. 57 (November 2006), 103–31.

20. "I do not argue that certain kinds of events, persons, processes, groups, institutions, and so on, roughly corresponding to the terms used by historians to refer to and describe them, did not exist in the past. . . . And I argued that *historiographical debates are often resolved by the elimination or revision of a certain way of naming historical phenomena and the substitution of a new way.*" White, preface to *El texto*), 51, in Spanish translation. Emphasis added.

21. Erich Auerbach, *Mimesis: The Representation of Reality in Western Literature* (Princeton, NJ: Princeton UP, 1968). The analysis goes from Homer up to Proust's and Woolf's literary modernism.

22. "The notion of figural causation might provide a key to an understanding of what is distinctively historicist *and* modernist in Auerbach's concept of literary history, if not of history in general." White, "Auerbach's Literary Theory," 87.

23. The idea that sustains and reveals itself in the history recounted in *Mimesis* is that of "figure" or "figural representation," which "establishes a connection between two events or persons in such a way that the first signifies not only itself but also the second, while the second involves or fulfills the first." Auerbach, *Mimesis*, 73. Along the same lines, Frank Ankersmit points out in "Why Realism? Auerbach on the Representation of Reality," in Ankersmit, *Historical Representation* (Stanford: Stanford UP, 2001), that Auerbach's work implies that "*realism* can only be defined by means of a *history* of realism" (197). "Realism only exists for him in the many variants in which it has shown itself in the course of the long history investigated in this book" (198).

24. The schema of figure fulfillment is not a causal or genetic relationship, nor is it teleological (the goal is never ultimately realizable); rather, it is a genealogical one. See White, "Auerbach's Literary Theory," 90, 91.

25. Ibid., 96.

26. For Auerbach, "the representative literary text may be at once (1) a fulfillment of a previous text and (2) a potential prefiguration of some later text, but also (3) a figuration of its author's experience of a piece of historical milieu, and therefore (4) a fulfillment of a piece of historical reality." Ibid., 93.

27. The notion of "heuristic appraisal" differs from that of "epistemic appraisal"—which is a frequent focus of philosophers' analysis—in that it judges a theory's merit not by its past record of predictive success or failure, but by its ability to initiate new research areas for scientific community members interested in it. See Nickles, "Heuristic Appraisal," 176. I have applied this notion to historiography in Tozzi, "Evaluación heurística en la historiografía. El debate

Browning-Goldhagen," in *Los enigmas del descubrimiento científico*, ed. Gregorio Klimovsky (Alianza: Buenos Aires, 2005), 185–206.

28. See Auerbach, *Mimesis*, 75.

29. Consonantly with promise fulfillment, "The making of a promise can be deduced retrospectively from a fulfillment, but a fulfillment cannot be inferred prospectively from the making of a promise." White, "Auerbach's Literary Theory," 89.

30. Ibid., 88, 89.

31. Hayden White, *Metahistory: The Historical Imagination in Nineteenth-Century Europe* (Baltimore: Johns Hopkins UP, 1973), 22.

32. Dirk Moses, "Hayden White, Traumatic Nationalism, and the Public Role of History," *History and Theory* 44, no. 3 (2005): 314.

33. "The Modernist Event," in White, *Figural Realism*.

34. As moviemaker Claude Lanzmann proposes.

35. See Todorov, *Memoria del bien*, 174.

36. Ibid., 175.

37. White, *Metahistory*, 11.

38. Jan Kott, *Shakespeare Our Contemporary*, trans. Boleslaw Taborski, 2nd ed. (London: Routledge, 1967), particularly part 1, "Tragedies," 2 and 30.

39. See White, *Metahistory*, 200. In this respect, adds White, Tocqueville is closer to his contemporary Michelet and further from Ranke, who in combining comic genre, an organicist model, and conservative ideology, tends to blandness and to a certain unfounded assurance. See 191.

40. "Whereas the drama of America showed itself to be . . . a struggle of men against nature solely for the establishment of the principle of equality . . . the European drama was essentially a sociopolitical one, involving conflicting ideas of society, a state power which transcended and opposed these ideas and used them to its own advantage, and the revolutionary tradition which in turn opposed the principle of state power and periodically dissolved it in the service of the ideal of liberty. . . . The European, as against the American, drama had all the ingredients of a real Tragedy." Ibid., 210.

41. See Guber, *De chicos*, 21.

42. Ibid., 24.

43. The film was introduced as a progressive voice on the armed conflict. Scriptwriter Miguel Bonasso is a renowned activist from left-wing Peronism of the seventies, a writer exiled during the regime and a human rights advocate. *Iluminados por el fuego* drew public attention, was screened at various film festivals, and received Argentinean Film Critics Association Awards as well as Goya Awards in several categories.

44. Edgardo Esteban, *Malvinas, diario del regreso*, 4th ed. (Buenos Aires: Sudamericana, 2005).

45. Federico Penelas drew my attention to this scene and its "parodical" mes-

sage. The point is important because cinema in Argentina has played a crucial role in the forming of public representations of our last dictatorship's events and experiences. In the eighties, three films crystallized three recurring images: *La noche de los lápices* (Night of the Pencils), directed by Héctor Olivera, 1986, with an image of illegal repression's violence; *La historia oficial* (The Official Story), directed by Luis Puenzo, 1985, with that of a society "unaware" of what was happening; and *Los chicos de la guerra* (The Boys of the War), directed by Bebe Kamin, 1984 (inspired by Daniel Kon's much more sophisticated and complex book *Los chicos de la guerra*, 1982), with that of ex-soldiers as "chicos." Curiously enough, the last image is repeated in *Iluminados por el fuego*, unchanged despite there being over twenty years between one film and the other.

46. In this case, "veterans" refers to some unspecified Malvinas ex-combatant association.

47. Graciela Speranza and Fernando Cittadini, *Partes de guerra, Malvinas 1982* (Buenos Aires: Edhasa, 2005). I believe the title itself, *War Reports*—as opposed to "recollections" or "memoirs"—aims at emphasizing the active dimension of the story they wish to relate. Issuing a report implies making a decision in relation to a subsequent action, rather than just being carried by images of the past.

48. Ibid., 11.

49. "First-person narrative, although crucial for the study and writing of recent history, can make us lose view of historical processes, while rendering stories much more colorful and emotional. This text aims precisely at going back and forth from one space to the other: a defence of individual experience as a way of returning complexity to historical explanations, yet without losing sight of their circumstances." Lorenz, *Las guerras por Malvinas* (Buenos Aires: Edhasa, 2006), 97.

50. "*War* is not regarded *as war* solely by analyzing it as another aspect of the régime's politics. Even if this is a valid perspective, it is inevitably incomplete, since it overlooks the fact that a war, just like any social phenomenon, has its particular characteristics." Ibid., 308. The reduction of war analysis to politics is, according to Lorenz, another instance of "the logics guiding politics during the second half of the twentieth century . . . that of extrapolating war categories to political discussion." Ibid.

51. "No wonder, then, that patriotic discourse—retained by the Armed Forces due to the acts or omissions of other social actors during the eighties—is still operative, even after having been crushed by 1982 events. It so happens that for survivors, for the families of the deceased—and for many Argentines—it is the only one still referring to a turning point in their histories: the war." Ibid., 309.

13

Primo Levi for the Present

Judith Butler

> Even the most rigorously objective and determinedly 'clear' and literal language
> cannot do justice to the Holocaust without recourse to myth, poetry, and 'liter-
> ary' writing.
> —Hayden White

What follows is a set of reflections on Primo Levi, whose task was
to render the reality of the Nazi concentration camps through a fiction
that was faithful to that historical reality. I take as my point of departure
Hayden White's essay, "Figural Realism in Witness Literature."[1] Levi's reflections on this issue are vexed and interesting, but what becomes clear,
especially in his later works, is that there is some tension in his work between memory, which he calls a fallacious instrument, and the demands
of a story or a narrative. He was well aware that the history of that period
would be told time and again and that the stories might well take the
place of memories and, eventually, would take their place, once there were
no more living survivors. In his last years, he gave a set of interviews that
included some which asked him about his relationship to Jewishness, to
Israel, and to the abiding ethical and political implications of the Shoah
for thinking through politics in the early 1980s. But toward the end of his
life, he asked not to speak about this topic in interviews anymore. How
do we understand Levi's relationship to what can and cannot be spoken
about, and how does that which seems unspeakable or irretrievable become conveyed through the language he uses?

Let's assume that not only in the cases of historical trauma that be-set an author like Primo Levi, but in the course of life more generally, there are gaps or fissures in the accounts that we give, and that we have no account to give of why that part of life cannot be recalled or given in narrative form. This becomes especially acute when we ask others, or ourselves, to give an account of themselves in order precisely to hold them accountable for their actions, in an effort to locate or assign responsibil-ity to a set of actions that led to injurious consequences. In such cases, we depend upon the capacity of another to give an account in order to determine responsibility, and when and where that capacity breaks down, we may turn to other kinds of evidence to determine the agency of the action at issue. This surely happens in legal contexts and in courts of law, where a juridical notion of responsibility is operative, and clearly must be. But are we right to import such a model of responsibility into nonjuridi-cal domains of human relationality? After all, in giving an account, one addresses one's speech to someone, to another, and this mode of address has an ethical significance that is distinct from the sequence of events that are relayed through the narrative. We might then ask: might other ethical values be lost when the juridical notion of accountability becomes equated with our understanding of responsibility more generally?

I ask this question because it would seem that if traumatic events make giving an account difficult or impossible, that some compassion toward this inability to narrate the issue of agency is important to main-tain. Moreover, when we refer to someone giving a narrative account of a life, we generally think about narrative in terms of the content of what is said. But a narrative proceeds by way of figures, and those might in-clude irony and ellipsis. The moment of ellipsis is precisely one in which something is not told, a moment of withdrawal or lapse within the narra-tive, but also part of narrative, a formal feature of its possible trajectory. Hence, if traumatic events make giving an account difficult or impos-sible, or if they produce elision or ellipsis within a narrative, then it would seem that precisely what is not spoken is nevertheless conveyed through that figure. What is unspoken is nevertheless relayed or conveyed in some way, suggesting that the narrative also has to be understood as a mode of address, one that makes a bid for our understanding. According to auto-genetic schemes of narrative self-accounting, the "I" makes itself into the inaugural moment of a sequence of acts and so places itself at the center of the action in question. But what is the status of such a narrative when a series of circumstances and actors are acting upon the scene at once, all of which are acted on by other circumstances and actors, the history of which cannot be fully known or narrated at the time, if ever? The "I" is neither the first and foremost "cause" in a sequence of events nor the fully passive "effect" of such a sequence, which has led Hayden White, for instance, to wonder whether it might be possible to reanimate the middle voice to enunciate the fully equivocal status of a subject at once acted upon and acting.

I would add that there might be some humility to be valued in recognizing that one's actions do not always completely and utterly originate with the "I," and that, correspondingly, there is some forgiveness, if you will, which correlates with this acknowledgement that giving a full account of oneself in that sense is impossible. The impossibility follows not only from an inability to secure the subject as the first cause of a historical sequence of events, but also because language falters when it is charged with the task of elaborating that sequence in terms of its content alone. Giving an account is thus not so much a matter of disclosing or concealing the truth of what has happened (elaborating a content in and by language); the ideal of full disclosure leads to certain failure, and not necessarily or only because the narrator is deceitful. The impossibility of the ideal of full disclosure exposes a fallibility at the heart of narrative itself, and this fallibility is elaborated through those figures that do something other than convey a positive content, understood as the delineation of "what happened."

I want to suggest provisionally a link between such figures and fallibility more generally and remark further that we need such an understanding in order to separate the question of the "what" that is conveyed, from the mode of address that may seek an audience, even when, or precisely when, it may not be possible to give a seamless narrative account. Something is still said, and it is said to someone (even if that someone is only figured anonymously through apostrophe). That there is faltering in narrative reconstruction is a sign that there is such a mode of address; indeed, there can be no reach without that fallibility and faltering. Although the emphasis on the scene of address implied by this account of narrative suggests that testimony has to be something other than securing a verifiable sequence of events, it is bound up with the communication of a reality. Indeed, the task of communicating such a reality, as Hayden White points out, involves making use of the rhetorical features of language to convey *the emotional reality* running counter to the positivist demand that language act only and always transparently with regard to the facts.

There are at least two points to be made from the outset. The first is that the suturing of a sequence of events is only one way to communicate a reality. The second is that the reality communicated consists not only in "what happened," but also *that* it happened, and the *that* requires language to assert its reality and its force. There is a task at work in testimony that is different from the transmission and preservation of a sequence of events. For the account to communicate a reality, it needs to relay the meaning of the events in question, even when, precisely when, the events produce a crisis for meaning-making activity. Communication does not take place if the mode of relaying events seeks to separate the happening of those events from their affective and psychic dimensions. Theoretically, this means both that the demands of evidence require figuration and that we cannot usefully separate content from form. White argues that such accounts rely on figures precisely to relay an affective reality: "The most vivid scenes of the horrors of life in the camps produced by Levi consist less in the delineation of 'facts' as conventionally conceived than of the sequences of figures he creates by which to endow the facts with passion, his own feelings about and the value he therefore attaches to them" (White, 119). If White is right, then a sequence of figures may sometimes be more important than a sequence of facts. Indeed, it may well be that no communication of the facts can take place without a linguistic assertion that relies to some extent on figuration. As will be seen, sometimes the figures are required to convey an emotional reality, and other times Levi invokes them precisely to mark a certain distance between the story of what happened and the memory of the emotional reality.

One figure that recurs in Primo Levi's work is "crystallization." It marks a certain problem that emerges when the linguistic effort to convey what happened becomes reiterated over time. It comes up for him most prominently when, in trying to refute the revisionists by offering a definitive account of what happened, he finds that he must *re*count the events, and that this recounting actively affects his memory. As White points out, Levi tries to void his account of figures only to produce an account for which no such evacuation is possible. On the one hand, Levi seeks a clear and transparent language, one that might rise to the level of scientific rigor in order to refute those revisionists who are ready to claim that the reports on the Shoah are "just stories." On the other hand, he is aware of how the stories of memory congeal and "crystallize" over time, which suggests that they are anchored in something other than memory. How does he broker this crystallization effect? Does the Shoah assume a linguistic life that unanchors it from memory and historical reality? Can such an effect be countered? And what consequences does it have for us, in the present, as we consider the discursive life that the Shoah has assumed?

The linguistic form in which Levi preserves and conveys the historical experience of the camps produces at least two different kinds of difficulties, and these, in turn, constitute two different political problems. On the one hand, there are the revisionists who must be refused through a reconstitution of the historical and experiential record; on the other hand, there are those who "use" the Shoah to justify excessive Israeli militarism, an exploitation that Levi also openly opposed. What is it in language that gives rise to both the denial and the exploitation of the Shoah in such instances? How can these forms of effacement and deployment be averted, and is there something in language that can resist these two political trajectories, both of which Levi finds unacceptable? At stake is not only a political position, but also a way to position himself morally in relation to the experience he has undergone. He needs to tell the story to preserve its historical status against those who would deny it, but he also needs to tell the story in order to come to terms with his own accountability. The first task seems to require that language be transparent, but the second demands that a sequence be secured for the events in question, in order to negotiate the status of his own agency and complicity.

In at least two of his books, *Survival in Auschwitz*,[2] and *The Drowned and the Saved*,[3] Levi focuses on the need to preserve and convey the lives and deaths of those in the camps with him, but also to determine his moral position in that context. Although there are times when he simply maintains that there were victims and executioners, at other times he points to the "grey zone," where lines of accountability are more difficult to ascertain. In that zone, he addresses the actions that prisoners took under constraint, indeed, under the threat of death, and seeks to show that though they participated in activities that could be said to maintain the death and labor camps, their actions were in large part coerced. He portrays yet other prisoners, though, who became the notorious "kapos" and identifies in them an overreaching, a zealous, if not sadistic, entry into the lower ranks of the SS, and so to a collaborationist practice that he finds morally repugnant. Levi vacillates between holding himself accountable for surviving, seeing his survival as evidence of a certain guilt, and insisting that the responsibility for the destruction of human lives in the camps resides with the SS and the explicit collaborators.

At one point, Levi claims that inmates made the assumption that if they were arrested and imprisoned, they must be guilty of something, and so lived their days in an effort to expiate a guilt that was nameless and without any basis in reality. It was only after the camps were liberated that suicide rates increased for former prisoners. He elaborates the tragic form of psychic reasoning that leads to this conclusion:

Suicide is born from a feeling of guilt that no punishment has attenuated; now, the harshness of imprisonment was perceived as punishment, and the feeling of guilt (if there is punishment, there must have been guilt) was relegated to the background, only to re-emerge after the Liberation. In other words, there was no need to punish oneself because of a (true or presumed) guilt: one was already expiating it by one's daily suffering. (Levi 1989, 76)

Levi clearly sees that the guilt is induced unjustly, that it follows from a need to find a reason for the internment, a reason that tragically establishes the self as the "cause." And though Levi can outline this faulty line of reasoning, he sometimes succumbs to its terms. Levi clearly understands that it is by accident that he himself survived. For instance, he relays how he came down with an illness that landed him in an infirmary just when the rest of his barracks was taken out for a death march in the late Spring of 1944, leading to his inadvertent survival and rescue. He writes with clarity: "I do know that I was a guiltless victim and that I was not a murderer" (Levi 1989, 48). At other times, though, it would appear that Levi thought that he survived at the expense of someone else, that his own action or inaction was accountable for the deaths of others, and that it was unbearable that he should survive when another could not, understanding that, it would seem, he survived in the place of another, and so experienced his survival as an illegitimate usurpation of another person's place in life. Thus, he writes,

It is no more than a supposition, indeed the shadow of a suspicion: that each man is his brother's Cain, that each one of us (but this time I say "us" in a much vaster, indeed, universal sense) has usurped his neighbor's place and lived in his stead. It is a supposition, but it gnaws at us; it has nestled deeply like a woodworm; although unseen from the outside, it gnaws and rasps. (Levi 1989, 82)

   Usurp is clearly an active verb, and fortifies the conviction that one's survival is the cause of another's death (if, according to this economy, one takes life at the expense of another, then to give up one's life is to let the other live). One might well come, then, to wish for one's own death as a way of reanimating the other's life. If Levi's portraits of various characters in the camp were efforts to "bring back to life" those who were killed, we might consider that this "reanimating" function of literary portraiture prefigures suicide. In suicide, the insupportable logic of usurpation is reversed: one does not live at the expense of the other, but one gives one's life so that the other may live. Such a logic of guilt inflates the power of the subject to decide matters of life and death, installing the cause of the other's death in the surviving subject. This can only be read as a painful displacement of the machinery of mass death onto and into the causal agency of the self, effectively refiguring the self, an incarcerated victim, as the machinery of mass death itself. My fear, in reading Levi's biographies and writings, is that he did suffer from that sense of baseless but acute guilt over survival as such, but that is merely speculation on my part. And though many still argue about whether his final fall was a suicidal effort or not, the question of course remains whether he could ever reconcile himself to surviving and whether he experienced that survival as a kind of guilt.

   In the time that he did survive, however, Levi tried to tell the stories of Auschwitz again and again, not only to keep the historical record straight and perhaps come to terms with his own position in the camps, but also to make sure that such a phenomenon could not recur in history. His reflections on politics are profoundly informed by this extraordinary experience of suffering and his enormous commitment to witnessing, even as he understood himself as someone who could not give a full or adequate testimony to what happened there. As he took stands on political issues, he was alert to the threat and excesses of fascism, to the persistence of anti-Semitism, but also to the way in which the Shoah itself could be used to justify a set of politics that he thought no survivor could or should condone.

Levi understood it as his public responsibility as a Jew and as a survivor to make clear his opposition to the bombing of Beirut and the massacres at Sabra and Shatila in 1982. Although he clearly valued the founding of Israel as a refuge for Jews from the Nazi destruction, and even as a place where Jews might maintain a right of return, he sought to distinguish between an argument that valued Israel's existence as permanent refuge for the Jews from then contemporary Israeli state policies. As a result, he became critical of both Begin and Sharon in the early 1980s and called for their resignations after Sabra and Shatila (*La Stampa*, June 24, 1982). Later, he received letters from Israel criticizing him for taking a public stand against Israel (though in actuality he was taking a public stand against some Israeli military actions, not Israel as such). Levi opposed the bombings of Beirut, which devastated much of southern Lebanon and killed thousands of Arabs living there, and he opposed the building of settlements in the occupied territories. Such actions, Levi maintained, caused him "shame and anguish," and yet he held out for the possibility that conditions could change. In an interview titled "Judaism and Israel," he writes, "I am not such a pessimist as to think that Israel will always be like this." And when asked by his interlocutor how he responds to the letters from Israel, from those who ask him whether or not he can see "all the Jewish blood spilled in all these years," he replies:

I reply that the blood spilled pains me just as much as the blood spilled by all other human beings. But there are still harrowing letters. And I am tormented by them, because I know that Israel was founded by people like me, only less fortunate than me. Men with a number from Auschwitz tattooed on their arms, with no home nor homeland, escaping from the horrors of the Second World War who found in Israel a home and a homeland. I know all this. But I also know that this is Begin's favourite defense. And I deny any validity to this defense."[4]

In denying any validity to this defense, Levi is clearly maintaining that it will not do to call upon the Shoah as a way of legitimating arbitrary and lethal Israeli violence against civilian populations. It is a moment in which Levi clearly, though tormented by the letters he received from Israelis rebuking him for his public criticism, does not fall prey to a sense of guilt that would lead him to retract his public views. Instead, he asserts the authority of the "I" to deny validity to this defense. And he surely knows that this "I" is not any "I" but the first-person declaration of the most articulate and influential of European survivors of the Shoah. It would seem that the torment might have silenced him, but in the place of that silence, he reasserts the "I" that would rationalize the use of excessive violence in the name of Shoah. At the same time, it is important to note that Levi refused the identification of Israel with Nazi Germany, and he decried the upsurge of anti-Semitism that became public in Italy after 1982. He worried that Israel itself might be responsible for fostering anti-Semitism, but he also was very clear that neither Israeli state violence of the time nor anti-Semitism would ever be acceptable to him.

I mean to point out at least two dimensions of the Shoah that seem to be at work not only for Levi, but more broadly in the available discourses we have on this topic, even now. On the one hand, the Shoah is what traumatizes and what disrupts or deforms the possibility of giving an account of himself. It is a set of memories that cannot always be maintained or sustained, and it makes very difficult any full or comprehensible accounting, even at times, for Levi, any exhaustive understanding of accountability in light of the "grey zone" in which the agency of the prisoner is at afflicted by coercion and the threat of death. On the other hand, the "Shoah" has been used to rationalize state violence, and to this Levi delivers an unequivocal moral and political objection. Can we then think about the relationship between a discourse interrupted and confounded by trauma, on the one hand, and available to political instrumentalization, on the other?[5] As traumatic, the Shoah makes use of Levi's language, of the language of those who survive and those who continue to live in the aftermath of that most horrific destruction of human life. As instrumentalized, the Shoah becomes a way of silencing critique, rationalizing state violence and lending legitimacy to Israeli practices that ought properly to be objected to and refused, as Levi clearly did.

Levi has two predominant problems that follow from a certain seizure of memory by discourse. He has to solve these problems somehow in order to refuse both revisionism and the political exploitation of memory. Let us then recount how these problems emerge for him in order to understand how these discursive formations produce both the possibility and liability of communication. If what I am calling here "discursive seizure" and what White specifies as a "sequence of figurations" are not to be understood as mere "constructions" that abandon the reality they are meant to communicate, then it seems we have to understand in what sense these discursive seizures are modes of referentiality. White makes clear, for instance, that a series of portraits Levi provides of camp interns constitutes a "sequence of figurations [that] is fully and explicitly referential." The fact that Levi's description "expresses the moral charge which inspires its form" is not a reason to debunk the referentiality of the form. Rather, it is a reason to understand the moral charge as part of the objective reality being transmitted. How precisely that is done, and with what effect, are questions that remain for us to explore in the latter part of this essay.

Primo Levi starts *The Drowned and the Saved* by letting his readers know that the Nazis sought not only to destroy lives, but also to eradicate the evidence of their destruction. The Third Reich, he writes, "waged a war against memory" (Levi 1989, 31). Thus, the narrative voice in Levi's text not only relays this fact, but, in its very existence, constitutes a kind of evidence. Insofar as Levi writes this text, he provides a narrative voice that, in its telling, proves that this one was not fully destroyed and so, in this way, foils the plot that the Nazis devised to eradicate any evidentiary trace of their exterminations. That there is still a speaking subject is itself refutation of that attempted effacement. If the Nazi thought was, as Elie Wiesel surmised, that no one would believe such a thing (that is, they themselves understood themselves as enacting the unbelievable) or that no one would survive to testify, then Levi, in testifying, disrupts their plan and sabotages their ongoing machinery, since they sought not only to act during the war years, but to continue to act upon any future in which a history might be told about what they did. Levi's telling, his story, proves that their machinery broke down. He will be a surviving witness, provide evidence, and so confirm what they would deny.

As soon as Levi begins this task of establishing evidence, however, he is beset by problems; he is writing forty years later, and he must inquire about the veracity of his memory, an inquiry that raises for him the relation of memory to trauma or, at least, to what resists remembering, and also, the relationship between memory and story. Can he still tell the story? And does his story confirm his memory? Did the Nazis perchance succeed in making the event untellable, unnarratable? If the narration proves to be not fully tellable, would that be a Nazi success story? Or can we safeguard the fallibility in and of narrative for another purpose? Is there a way to consider the fallibility of narrative, its very breakdown, as the evidentiary trace of trauma itself?

Although the book starts with a strong claim about the Nazis seeking to destroy memory, to render the future witness impossible, it turns within a few pages to the problems that obstruct a simple reconstruction of memory. Calling memory a "suspect source" (Levi 1989, 34), especially the memory of suffering, he notes first that the memory of suffering has a way of "crystallizing" as story. This crystallized story then takes on a life of its own; in turn, the memory, in being told and crystallized, in this way in turn begins to restructure memory itself. Indeed, the telling of the story performs a crystallization of that memory of suffering that transforms memory such that some of the original memory is lost. In this way, then, the story takes on a life that comes at the expense of the memory. Paradoxically and painfully, the story can actually become the means by which the original suffering becomes lost to memory. Here is his language: "a memory invoked too often, and expressed in the form of a story, tends to become fixed in stereotype, in a form tested by experience crystallized, perfected, adorned, installing itself in the place of the raw memory and growing at its expense" (Levi 1989, 24).

The idea is, of course, frightening: that the more such a story is told, the more it crystallizes, the more we lose the memory of suffering that prompts the story. And though Levi resists the consequences of this insight, he is truthful enough to articulate it anyway. We might consider that what Levi fears, and also what he knows to be partially true, is that there can be a loss of the loss itself, and that this can be the result of the story we tell. Of course, Levi's story is told in order to make sure that the Nazi project does not achieve the goal of destroying evidence, and it is told precisely against the revisionists who would question the very facts of the extermination camps. The story is there to establish evidence, to acknowledge that there was an enormous, if not unfathomable, loss of life, and to provide the explicit recognition of loss that mourning requires. But if the story makes more remote the memory of suffering and the memory of loss, then the story might be said to institute a kind of melancholia in which the suffering and loss are denied. The story threatens to substitute for the events it relays, and crystallization is the means of that substitution. The substitution comes at the cost of the event, and so it would seem that a certain strict accountability applies: the story is purchased at the expense of the event itself, just as the life of the survivor is understood to come at the expense of the dead.

That crystallization, however, is not strictly responsible for the loss of the referent. The unbearability of loss and guilt gnaws at the referential capacity of language. But it would also have to be said, with White, that the "moral charge that inspires the form" is part of the objective reality to be relayed. If referentiality is still troubled, this has to do with the difficulty of remembering or recalling that suffering, a difficulty that afflicts the very capacity to retain a form for memory. Levi points out that "many survivors of wars or other complex and traumatic experiences tend unconsciously to filter their memory . . . they dwell on moments of respite . . . the most painful episodes . . . lose their contours" (Levi 1989, 32). He refers earlier to this loss of contour in the context of those who recite their memories, substituting descriptions for memories, and moving from bad faith to good faith. Of those who seek to substitute a description for a memory, he writes that "the distinction between true and false progressively loses its contours, and man ends up fully believing the story he has told so many times and continues to tell." This starts as a moral failure, although it becomes a form of self-deception sustained by no explicit intention to falsify. But then, in the next paragraph, he suggests that this capacity of the story to substitute for memory may well happen as "events fade into the past." Under such conditions, "the construction of convenient truth grows and is perfected" (Levi 1989, 27). It is only pages later that he returns to this problem to suggest that it may well be the painfulness of the memory itself that prompts the story that ends up taking its place. At this point, the story emerges briefly, no longer as a sign of moral failure, but of trauma.

The trauma works to undo the painful memory as a bounded event, and the story, in crystallizing the memory, offers relief from precisely this traumatic encounter. It seems worth considering that the story works in tandem with a certain forgetfulness, a forgetfulness that is actually needed for survival. The story that seeks to establish evidence of suffering on the basis of memory crystallizes that suffering, inducing a forgetfulness that helps the teller survive. It would seem that the requirements of survival sometimes work against the requirements to provide evidence. The story does not return to the original memory, but helps to vanquish it, and though Levi believes that the original memory, preserved, will lend veracity to his telling, his telling is also in the service of his surviving, and so must act upon that memory, alleviate its traumatic effect, and even take its place. What is communicated as a result is the effect that trauma has on storytelling, and Levi's written reflection worrying whether the story will be rooted in reality communicates precisely this reality of a trauma that unsettles the conventional function of the story. Although Levi's writing contains stories and portraits, vignettes, historical forays, and speculations, they do not settle on a single form. Something is to be communicated here that makes form into a problem, and that registers in the forms that Levi provides. It is in this sense that we can continue to maintain the referentiality of his writing, despite his own doubts, for the reasons that White supplies: the moral charge inspires the form and so, too, we might add, does the fear of moral failure. Further, one writes not only in relation to the event, but also in relation to the audience, and Levi had to struggle to make the story believable. That struggle also registers at the level of form.

Levi's struggle with truth and narrative is not uniquely his own. Charlotte Delbo, for example, writes in the foreword to *Auschwitz and After*, "When I talk to you about Auschwitz, it is not from deep memory (sense memory) my words issue. They come from external memory (*mémoire externe*), the memory connected with the thinking process."[6] This last is a memory that precisely does not relive the event in order to tell it. If she were reliving it, she would not be able to tell it. Indeed, in her own work that narrative capacity occasionally breaks down as sense memory interrupts what she calls "external memory." This suggests that "telling" is always at some remove from reliving, and must be. At one point, she relates a story about standing in the roll call at Auschwitz in the early hours of the morning in freezing weather, and she claims that, while standing there, that thought how one day she might tell the story of standing there at roll call. Yet in the next sentence, she writes, "That is actually not true at all. I was thinking nothing. I could not think at all." She asks further whether it is reasonable to think that anyone who underwent this experience would be able to give an account of it. They are not (Delbo, 64). This does not mean, though, that therefore no account should be given. On the contrary: to paraphrase Derrida, precisely because one *cannot* give an account, one *must* give an account. The capacity for narration to be suspended or debilitated by the trauma is precisely what emerges as the sign and evidence of a capacity to live on and survive. And Delbo, when she reflects upon the veracity of her own account, concludes that she does not know whether it is true, but that she does know that it is *truthful.*[7]

So, given the complex relations among memory, story, and trauma at work here, it makes sense to ground an evidentiary refutation of revisionists on something other than the claim of memory to veracity. Of course the archives of survivor stories are based on memory, but let us be clear that the story can only aspire to truthfulness and perhaps not to truth. Testimony acts in ways that memories cannot, and memories depend on stories to be transmitted and to endure.

Language not only records, preserves, and transmits, though on occasion it does all those things. Language also invariably works upon the material it records, preserves, and transmits. Hayden White, for instance, argues that, for Levi, testimony "produces the referent," and we have to be careful here to understand what he means. This production of the referent has to be distinguished from the view that says there is no referent, only language, that is, the point of view that language nullifies referentiality as such. White contends that if the traumatic events are to be transmitted to an audience, they must be relayed in rhetorical terms that produce or orchestrate that referent for us, that bring the referent into legibility and endow it with sense. At one point, White argues, figures are needed in order to "grasp . . . a real situation" (White, 116). In this same essay, he remarks as well that Levi's turn away from realist representation, when it happens, "has the effect of actually producing the referent rather than merely pointing to it—and much more vividly than any kind of impersonal registration of the 'facts' could ever have done" (White, 119).

If, against the revisionists, one wants language to preserve the referentiality of events and so to act archivally, then perhaps the means by which they are both preserved and transmitted is also the means by which language acts upon the referent. There seems to be no way around this, and we might even speculate that the psychoanalytic notion of "working through" depends precisely on this possibility of language to act upon past events. But there are at least two even stronger points. First, to preserve the referent, one *must* act upon it, and to act upon it is to transform it in some way; without acting on the referent, the archive cannot be preserved. Second, for the reality to be communicated—which means that conditions of incredulity must be overcome—language must act on the facts to produce them as a graspable reality. This last is no easy task, since it means coming up with forms that will communicate this reality, a task at once rhetorical and referential.

Stories, of course, are not the only discursive means by which memories are acted upon and displaced. It may be that when we refer to trauma, we are indexing that which is not quite on the order of a memory, although it constitutes a past; it is distinguished as a past that does not stop happening. The trauma continues, but not seamlessly; it must repeat, and its repetition invariably takes a certain syntactical form. Moreover, to be known or communicated, the retelling must be, to some extent, a reliving; otherwise, to read or, indeed, to listen to what is said will not lead to a full "emotional reality" (White's term) of the narrative sequence of events. To say that certain narrative retellings are traumatic is to maintain that the means, the syntax, of that retelling is not precisely decided, but rather, compelled. But then we are in a complex situation, one in which a crystallization of events that is meant to preserve and transmit the reality of those events not only acts upon those events to achieve those purposes, but takes on new discursive effects that exceed the purposes for which the narrative crystallization was devised. Something makes use of the story that is not the choice of the narrator, and we can see this not only in the quasi-independence of the crystallization effect: is that my story, another's story, the story I have told so often that I no longer know precisely what is the narrative account, and what is the referent? Crystallization names a certain operation of discursive seizure, one that is necessary and unavoidable.

To say that there is a repetition of storytelling that belongs to a traumatic compulsion to repeat is already to say that we cannot fully control the discursive uses of the story. If there is no retelling and reliving of the narrative without also acting upon it, then this acting upon is crucial to the relaying of the story and forms one of its necessary rhetorical dimensions. But those who receive the story also retell it, and though the traumatic effect is transmitted—along with the crisis of volition that comes with that trauma—it can become unmoored from its original aims. This seems to me to be the invariable risk of crystallization.

Crystallization thus seems to be both the condition and risk of the archive and, hence, the precondition for refuting revisionism. But as we have seen, the very process of crystallization is linked up with an acute sense of accountability. It is this latter, I would suggest, that is at work in the political exploitation of the Shoah. The primary aim of that exploitation is to heighten a certain sense of accountability and to mobilize this accusation as a way of rendering an opposing political viewpoint morally reprehensible. The rhetorical invocation reanimates the trauma in the service of an accusation that works to render the contemporary enemy into an "effective Nazi" and, so, to legitimate any and every violence against them.

In these political contexts, the reanimation of the trauma does not serve to preserve a referential history—even when its slogan is "never again!"—but, rather, to intervene with a discursive weapon in the field of contemporary politics. Can we understand this as another permutation of crystallization? In this case, however, the substitution of discourse for memory does not simply establish a distance from unbearable suffering and guilt for the subject; it also levels an accusation in which guilt is fully (and infinitely) externalized and the other is constituted as fully accountable for one's continued suffering. The accusation reanimates the suffering to support the accusation, and the accusation, in turn, alleviates a baseless guilt through identifying its "cause" as the contemporary other, thus continuing that traumatic temporality in which the past does not cease being past, eclipsing the historical distance between then and now. The transferability of the affect, the transmissibility of the trauma, is essential to this historical transposition from one political reality to another. I am not sure how to locate agency in this process, since, as I have suggested above, the traumatic aspect confounds any usual recourse to volition. And yet, we can see on both sides of the political debates on the Middle East a certain strategic use or exploitation of this nexus of trauma and language to wage an accusation of paralyzing proportions. The discursive means by which the Holocaust is reinvoked is precisely a way of calling upon the pain of its repetition, and mobilizing that repetition and pain for other means. The question is whether it is mobilized for political purposes with the consequence of displacing the pain (and closing the historical gap between present and past) and losing the referent itself.

If Levi is right that the story of the Holocaust can grow at the expense of the memory of suffering, the story of the Holocaust can also grow at the expense of apprehending human suffering. And this can happen in at least two ways: first, by denying the Shoah and its continuing traumatic significance; second, by exploiting its traumatic significance in order to justify all military aggression as a necessary self-defense. Both tactics fail to consider what kind of ethical and political framework might usefully be derived from the Holocaust for the present. To ask this question is to consider, first, that it may not be the most useful paradigm for thinking about the present. But it is also to consider that some historical translations have to be made that allow the Holocaust to become history, rather than the kind of trauma that knows no historical distinction between then and now.[8]

Levi comes to form his own view on the founding aims of the Israeli state:

The State of Israel was supposed to change the history of the Jewish people, but in a very precise sense: it was supposed to be a life raft, the sanctuary to which Jews threatened in other countries would be able to run. That was the idea of the founding fathers, and it preceded the Nazi tragedy; the Nazi tragedy multiplied it a thousandfold. Jews could no longer do without that country of salvation. Nobody stopped to think that there were Arabs in that country.[9]

In 1976, though, he tells an interviewer: "I must admit that after 1950 this image of the Jewish homeland gradually faded in me."[10] Indeed, there were more than 700,000 Palestinians who were forcibly dispossessed of their lands and their homes through the establishment of Israel in 1948, and surely the Israeli Defense Forces did have those Arab populations in mind when it seized those lands.

As we know, trauma takes on the character of repetition. It breaks into the present and reabsorbs the very possibility of the present into the past, maintaining those who are traumatized in an uncertain historical time in which the agents who inflict traumatic suffering repopulate one's world and foreclose upon the possibility of opening to a different future. There was a symptomatic moment in 1982 when Begin announced that he had with his military forces successfully encircled Berlin, when he meant to say Beirut. Can we read in that slip something like the work of trauma to reabsorb every present circumstance into the recurrent and ravenous pain of the past? What would it mean to awake to a present that would learn from the Holocaust the necessity of opposing fascism, racism, state

violence, and forcible detention? It would mean that we have to understand that those kinds of actions can recur, and do recur, in different
historical circumstances, that they are not always the same, but that they
are to be opposed, vocally and insistently, wherever and whenever they
do recur. It would also mean that no one is exempt, by historical fiat, of
occupying the position of the oppressor or the perpetrator, and this Levi
already knew when he considered the actions of the Jewish collaborators.
There is no innocence that pertains to Jews or Palestinians as such. There
is only a historical demand to produce a political practice and mode of
engagement that respects and institutionalizes protection for the precari-
ousness of life itself.

There is, of course, a difference between a politics that is animated
by trauma and that seeks, tactically, to reanimate trauma for its own uses,
and a politics that reflects on what political conditions would be necessary to foreclose crimes against humanity such as these. This latter is
surely an ethical and political framework derived from the Holocaust, but
it is one that is forced to derive principles from a past for the purposes of
living in and negotiating a present. That transposition or translation can
only work if there is an apprehension of the difference between "then"
and "now," but cannot work if the "then" replaces and absorbs the "now,"
because that can only produce a blindness towards and in the present.
Indeed, paradoxically, only by allowing the Shoah to become past can we
begin to derive those principles of justice and equality and respect for life
and property on the basis of that experience. It would be a different way
never to forget, because it would not install the past as the present, but
rather consult the past in order to conduct the comparative and reflective work that would allow us to derive principles of human conduct that
would make good on the promise not to reiterate in any way the crimes of
that historical time.

Trauma does not in itself legitimate a political claim, except, perhaps, the claim that it is imperative to ameliorate trauma for every con-
ceivable person, regardless of ethnicity, religion, or race. Trauma is not
itself entitlement, though it can lead us to reflect upon how best to insti-
tutionalize entitlements so that trauma is ameliorated and foreclosed for
every possible human. In a reactive relation to trauma, the trauma determines us unilaterally, even as we operate within its horizon and by way
of its internal logic. The refusal of the present and of what we might call

the *concrete other* is the consequence of this kind of hermeticism; waking from trauma is the only way to forestall its endless reiteration. Indeed, in this way we might say that trauma presents us with a specific responsibility precisely because it threatens to render us as pure victims who, by definition, cannot take responsibility for the present or the conditions we impose upon others. Although trauma cannot be willed away, it can be worked through to the extent that we can become mindful of the way in which it threatens to absorb the present into the past or, rather, reenact the past as the present, bypassing the experience of historical distance, the interval needed to reflect upon and consider how best to make a history now in light of such a past.

Levi's own reflections led him over time to consider that a "diasporic" condition for the Jewish people was the better alternative to Israel. In 1984, three years before his death, Levi spoke again about Israel after a self-imposed period of censorship: "I have thought about this a great deal: the centre is in the Diaspora, it is coming back to the Diaspora. . . . I would prefer the centre of gravity of Judaism to stay outside Israel." And then again, "I would say that the best of Jewish culture is bound to the fact of being dispersed, polycentric. . . . The history of the Diaspora has been a history of persecution but also of interethnic exchange and relations, in other words, a school for tolerance."[11]

Levi understood the Holocaust to provide a moral framework for his own criticisms of Israel, and he would not listen to those who said that, in his position, he ought to remain silent. On the eve of his departure to revisit Auschwitz in 1982, he signed the open letter in *La Repubblica* calling for the withdrawal of Israeli troops from Lebanon. He refused to understand the Israeli army as representing a persecuted minority. The discourse of persecution could not be used for such a purpose; and, over and against those who would revive the images of the camps to authorize Israeli aggression, he wrote provocatively in *Il Manifesto*: "Everybody is somebody's Jew. And today the Palestinians are the Jews of the Israelis" (*Il Manifesto*, 1982).

Of course, this is a controversial claim, and we are surely right to reject it as unwise. After all, if Levi says that the Palestinians are the Jews of the Israelis, he is transposing the victimized position of the "Jews" under the Nazis to the victimized position of the Palestinians under the Israelis. We might think that this, too, is a crude and cynical use of a Holocaustal resonance. But consider that he is also saying that just as the Jew was persecuted under the Nazis, so others can be in the position of being persecuted, and if we equate the Jew with the persecuted, then today others can be Jews, including Palestinians. Further, Israelis—understood as the Israeli government—are not the same as Jews. When asked later about his controversial formulation, Levi made clear that he did not think that Begin and Sharon were Nazis.[12] And in response to an interviewer from *La Repubblica* who asked, "Are the Palestinians in the same position as the Jews under the Nazis?" he replied that he does not accept such simplistic analogies and that "there is no policy to exterminate the Palestinians." After he joined with other Italian and Jewish intellectuals to publicly ask both Begin and Sharon to resign, he was also horrified by the anti-Semitic slogans that appeared on the walls of his town, equating Jews with Nazis.

This was a radically untenable situation that produced a conflict: could he continue to elaborate those principles derived from his experience of Auschwitz to condemn state violence without contributing to an anti-Semitic seizure of the event? This was the issue he had to negotiate. Within a few months, Levi fell silent on this issue, and even descended into a serious depression, one that doubtless had several causes but could not have been helped by the impasse before him. His political predicament was not far from our own, since to speak at all against Israeli policies can excite those who would condemn not only Israel, but Jews more generally, in the spirit of anti-Semitism. Is this a reason not to speak, or does it mean that when and if we speak, we must speak against that anti-Semitism at the same time that we articulate moral and political objections to wanton state violence? Similarly, if we say that the Holocaust is deployed for the purposes of justifying state and military actions, we must also say that the Holocaust is not reducible to this deployment, and that it devalues and effaces the specific suffering and political challenge of the Holocaust to make such a reduction.

It is crucial, as White has shown, to show that the rhetorical means through which the Holocaust is relayed can be a way of trying to "grasp" the reality, to register its moral force in the form by which it is conveyed. It is equally crucial to understand that the "moral charge" of the story can be transposed and displaced, and that this happens in ways that are open to debate. The problem is not rhetoric versus reference, but rather, *which* rhetoric, and for what purposes, and with what obligation to tell the story in a way that attempts to do it justice. If Levi considered one quandary when he wrote *The Drowned and the Saved*, he found himself in the midst of another toward the end of his life. His effort to refute the revisionists continued in his work both to counter the anti-Semites as well as those who would mobilize that history for the purposes of legitimating state power. The discursive seizure of the Holocaust was inevitable, even necessary, to rebut those who would deny it. But it brought along new risks, ones that seemed to spell a nearly full muteness for Levi in relation to contemporary politics.

Levi spoke out in 1982, and then softened his remarks, often then saying he would only give interviews on the condition that they not bring up Israel. Something traumatic had to be set aside, and neither Levi nor any other individual could remake the political lexicon within which he was compelled to live and speak. But we know that muteness is no answer, and that in this way, his situation bids us not to follow him there. And a few political principles did emerge from the impasse he faced. When asked whether he hated Germans, Levi said that he did not believe one should or could categorize an entire people on the basis of their national character. When asked about his alleged insensitivity to the loss of Jewish blood, he responded that Jewish blood ought not to be privileged over any other. His final word on the topic: we must not allow the sufferings of the Holocaust to justify everything. And if this simple sentence cannot be uttered, then we are doubtless learning the wrong lesson from the atrocities of World War II, namely, the lesson that we must not speak, that muteness is the only alternative. To separate that historical suffering from contemporary political exploitations of any kind is part of what must be done if we are to follow Levi's lead to do justice to history, and to struggle for justice in the present.

Notes

1. Hayden White, "Figural Realism in Witness Literature," *Parallax* 10, no. 1 (2004): 113–24.
2. Primo Levi, *Survival in Auschwitz: The Nazi Assault on Humanity*, trans. Stuart Woolf (New York: Macmillan, 1961).
3. Primo Levi, *The Drowned and the Saved*, trans. Raymond Rosenthal (New York: Random House, 1989).

4. Primo Levi, *The Voice of Memory: Interviews 1961–1987*, ed. Marco Belpoliti and Robert Gordon, trans. Robert Gordon (New York: New Press, 2001), 285–86.

5. For an excellent and singularly capacious discussion of this vexed position, see Idith Zertal's *Israel's Holocaust and the Politics of Nationhood* (Cambridge: Cambridge University Press, 2005), 52–71.

6. Charlotte Delbo, *Auschwitz and After*, trans. Rosette Lamonte (New Haven: Yale University Press, 1995), xiii–xiv.

7. Ibid. The original French uses "veridique" for truthful, suggesting a continuing link with verifiability.

8. This phenomenon is not exactly new. The discursive circulation of the Holocaust for politically strategic reasons has been there from the start. If I understand her correctly, Jacqueline Rose argues that for messianic Zionism, the Holocaust becomes the modern exemplar of the catastrophe that is bound to recur, and without which the messianic strain in Judaism cannot renew itself. In other words, the Holocaust must be renewed within contemporary politics in order to reinvigorate the messianic goal of collecting and authorizing the Jewish people as a nation. In effect, for her there can be no renewal of the messianic aims of Zionism without a catastrophe. Jacqueline Rose, *The Question of Zion* (Princeton: Princeton University Press, 2005).

9. Ferdinando Camon, *Conversations with Primo Levi* (Evanston: IL: Marlboro Press, 1989), 54.

10. Levi, *The Voice of Memory*, 263.

11. Ibid., 292–93.

12. Carole Angier, *The Double Bond: Primo Levi, A Biography* (New York: Farrar, Straus and Giroux, 2003), 629.

14

Hayden White, Historian

Richard T. Vann

In 1999 Hayden White characterized his approach to "structuralism, modernism, and postmodernism" as from the perspective of "a historian, critic, and social theorist."[1] His work as a critic and social theorist has become well-known, not to say notorious; as a historian, rather less so. Indeed, treating Hayden White as a historian reads against the grain—or more precisely, reads the back parts of his books. Some believe he has never been a "proper" historian (that is, presumably, a delver into archives and obscure texts). To these, having an informed opinion of any kind on structuralism, much less postmodernism, may already compromise his disciplinary credentials. Others think that he began as a historian, but in the mid-1970s stopped being one; and some believe that his work, if attended to by historians, would make *them* stop being proper historians. This might happen—in the unlikely event that masses of historians started reading him—if White credibly argued that there is no difference between works of history and works of pure fiction such as novels. But, as any careful reader of his work should know, he believes no such thing. His historical writings extend—unevenly—over forty years and, besides being valuable in themselves, shed light on his better-known theory and criticism.

I

White's original training was as a historian of the medieval church; his dissertation was on Bernard of Clairvaux and the papal schism of 1130. In 1958 and 1960 he published articles in this field—solid professional work, exhaustively footnoted, in eminently respectable journals.[2] These are worth the attention of those who believe that White has no experience of archival work.

Even earlier, though—in fact it was his first publication—he began writing on philosophy of history, with an article on R. G. Collingwood and Arnold Toynbee.[3] Drawing on Collingwood's *Autobiography* and his *Religion and Philosophy* as well as on *The Idea of History*, White emphasizes the importance of Collingwood's idea that purposive thought is what differentiates history from nature; but he objects that Collingwood has "avoided empiricism and positivism only to identify historical knowledge with philosophy" and failed to create a scientific basis for the study of human affairs by establishing a criterion for truth which is "purely relativistic, existing only in the mind of the individual historian." He concludes that possibly Collingwood's concept of history would become "one of those which historians will have to consider as the demand for answers from history becomes more violent."[4]

In the last few pages White turns to Toynbee, whom he calls the St. Augustine of the fall of the British Empire, sympathizing with Toynbee's "theosophy of history." Next he took up another off-beat historian, Christopher Dawson, whom he found in "a twilight zone between science on the one hand and art on the other."[5] White praises Dawson's work "at its best" for "doing justice to the true multiplicity of historical forms of thought and action."[6]

These essays in intellectual history, now almost forgotten, established White's interest in intellectual history, and especially the kind which summarizes some work of a thinker and presents a critique of it. They already signal White's interest in the history of historiography and his sympathy, unusual then as now, for speculative systems like those of Dawson and Toynbee, as well as detecting an "increasingly violent" demand for "answers from history" while English historiography—and others—were "in a twilight zone between art and science." White was interested in philosophy as an undergraduate at Wayne State University, but found what was on offer from logical positivism or analytical philosophy "tame" and unresponsive to social and moral issues.[7] This led him to "drift" into the "existentialist version of Marxism," which was "an ethical socialism" to which the existentialist emphasis on choice and commitment could appeal.[8]

In the late 1950s White turned his attention from English to Continental European thinking about history. His earliest views on historical knowledge criticize "objective" historiography, which "merely 'entertained' the data and consciously tried to avoid interpreting it."[9] While emphasizing the constructive or creative powers of the historian, he also cautions against making historiography purely aesthetic by overemphasizing the "original, imaginative creation of the individual historian." That would "release history from any obligation to truth in any form" and plunge historiography into "radical relativism, a nihilism, which held that since history was unknowable by any canons of scientific, religious, or philosophical knowledge, its proper mode of investigation must lie in art." White gives Michelet, Burckhardt, and Carlyle as examples of this "radical relativism," whose "high priest" was Friedrich Nietzsche.[10] After distinguishing four types of nineteenth-century historicism, all trying to resolve history into some other form of thought (art, philosophy, positive science, or empirical science), White concludes that Benedetto Croce succeeded in synthesizing the forms of historicism.[11]

II

White was eventually "productive" in almost every genre of historiography: general surveys, book reviews, edited volumes, translations, essays collected and uncollected, forewords, afterwords, introductions, notes correcting the errors of other scholars, and, in 1973, two books. What he didn't do was produce a book-length historical monograph, as almost all prestigious universities require for tenure. However, he was at the University of Rochester, where Norman O. Brown was teaching, and the history department there decided it could accept another unorthodox colleague.

In 1966 White published his well-known call in "The Burden of History" for a radical reformation, or perhaps dissolution, of the fuddy-duddy American historical profession.[12] Its concerns recur throughout his subsequent career. Having advised historians what to do, he turned for several years to historical writing, producing some essays and a two-volume survey of European intellectual history from the Renaissance to the present, written in collaboration with Willson Coates, and organized around the congenial theme of liberal humanism.[13]

The first volume, *The Emergence of Liberal Humanism*, is particularly skillful in illuminating climates of opinion and juxtaposing thinkers who don't form part of the canonical parade with those who do. The organization of the book shows what Coates and White were up to: it divides intellectual history into its religious, political, social, and economic aspects. While the Reformation, philosophy, and natural science (especially celestial mechanics) necessarily loom large, there are perceptive discussions of the psychology, historiography, and aesthetic thought of the times, and a number of quite unexpected insights.[14] What other treatment of the Scientific Revolution associates it with the Germanic barbarians? (Both, they say, had a basically hostile attitude towards the natural world.) Beyond the usual facts about John Locke there is an extensive discussion of his correspondence with William Molyneux about the "Molyneux problem," the question about the interrelationship of the senses that goes to the heart of the eighteenth-century cult of empiricism.

The Ordeal of Liberal Humanism gives it a somewhat less prominent role (befitting its "ordeal"). The authors organized it—with the exception of the admirable treatment of modern science—by what they call "total postures," such as romanticism, German idealism, social radicalism, and existentialism, thus grouping some thinkers seldom associated. These get three- to five-page mini-essays, some (on Johann Gottlieb Fichte and Herbert Spencer, for example) brilliant. The chapter "Science as a Substitute for Metaphysics," after a section on Auguste Comte and the Anglo-Saxon attitudes of Henry Thomas Buckle, Herbert Spencer, and T. H. Huxley, treats the materialist Young Hegelians, Otto Strauss and Ludwig Feuerbach, then Leopold von Ranke and Hippolyte Taine, and finally—surprisingly—Walter Bagehot. Similarly, the next chapter, "Supercommunity and Superman: The Foundations of the Radical Right and the Origins of Totalitarianism," features Joseph de Maistre, Jules Michelet, Heinrich von Treitschke, and Arthur de Gobineau as advocates for the "supercommunity," whether it be the Roman Catholic Church, France, the state (especially Germany), or a dominant race. Their antitypes are Max Stirner,

Carlyle, Kierkegaard, and of course Nietzsche. Surprised as some of these would have found it to be in one another's company, their juxtaposition makes sense in light of the thematics of the book.

It is hard to know what to make of these two volumes on the history of humanism. I would be tempted to call them "good of their kind," if I could be sure what kind they are. Their publisher or editor may have exerted some influence on the way they were written, and the books provide no information about who wrote what. They have some of the characteristics of textbooks—a trade publisher, wide scope, footnote references to other surveys, and occasional invocation of stock phrases like the "rising middle class"; familiar thinkers are sometimes represented by their most familiar passages. Yet the chapters in the first volume average almost thirty pages of fairly small print, and there are no breaks or subheads within these chapters. The prose is clear and occasionally epigrammatic, but makes no concessions to novice readers; ideas are clarified, but not simplified. The books could thus challenge even the brightest undergraduate, and few historians would fail to learn something from them.[15] They display qualities that historians admire—broad erudition, novel insights, lucid style, and narrative skill; but they are not exactly samples of the program for historiography adumbrated in "The Burden of History."

III

The best predominantly historical writing that White has done can be found in essays that he wrote in the early 1970s, especially the dialectical pair of "Wild Man" and "Noble Savage."[16] The essay on the Wild Man begins by disavowing "the flowing narrative of the historian." White characterizes his work as "little more than the historian's equivalent of a field archaeologist's notes, reflections on a search for archetypal forms rather than an account of their variations, combinations, and permutations during the late medieval and early modern ages" (*TD*, 150–51). This is excessively modest. Though he makes abundant use of his inveterate tendency to classify, he does not present the reader with discrete thematic lumps in the style of Foucault's *The Order of Things*. He does remark on, if not fully account for, the "variations, combinations, and permutations" of the archetypal forms, and he carries the analysis into the twentieth century, redefining his theme as a transition of the Wild Man "from myth to fiction to myth again, with the modern form of the myth assuming a pseudoscientific aspect in the various theories of the psyche currently clamoring for our attention" (*TD*, 154).

Both Hebrew and Greek myths recognized two sorts of humans and one species of humanoid creature: the Wild Man. The Jews had inherited the Promise made originally to Abraham; gentiles were humans in their natural state. Hebrew thought about the origins of the Wild Man emphasized that God had cursed Cain and Ham, a curse later construed as a sort of species corruption, afflicting those who committed such sins as mixing of kinds through inter-species matings or even sowing different kinds of seeds in the same field, and resulting in gigantism, blackness, and "wildness" (*TD*, 160–61).

For the Greeks and Romans, humans differed primarily physically and culturally. The Greeks importantly distinguished between civilized men—and I do mean men—who were inhabitants of a polis, and barbarians, who at least lived under *some* law (they had established families, for example). Relationships thus established human status, whereas Wild Men had no social institutions and lived alone, or at most with a mate—who, if she gave birth, abandoned the infant. In this solitary state they offered little threat to civilized society, but they did threaten individuals—lurking near their settlements, stealing domestic animals and sometimes women and children.

Greek mythology—and Roman insofar as they adopted it—was lavishly furnished with the results of inter-species mating (if one can thus describe god-on-human sex). Such creatures as fauns, satyrs, and sileni lived in unconstrained instinctual gratification; White calls them "little more than ambulatory genitalia." Others indulged their aggressive impulses with equal enthusiasm (*TD*, 170). Thus, although Wild Men were a source of anxiety in the Jewish and Christian traditions, in the pagan societies of Greece and Rome this anxiety was tinged with suppressed desire.

Christianity introduced the possibility of redemption of even the wildest humans, maintained though medieval schoolmen debated whether God could create humans devoid of a soul, so bestial as to be beyond the reach of divine grace and therefore appropriately used by humans like animals. The debate suggests some anxiety that a human could so degenerate, and indeed Wild Men (and Women) were "generally believed to be an instance of human regression to an animal state," but though Wild Persons incessantly offended against human and divine laws, they did so in madness, thus incurring no real guilt (*TD*, 164–67). In practice, however, White finds Christian universalism "not notably less egocentric, in a confessional sense, than its ancient Hebrew prototype" (*TD*, 162–63).

The Graeco-Roman and the Hebraic and Christian traditions met and "took root" in the Middle Ages (*TD*, 156) when the Wild Man united "the specific anxieties underlying the three securities supposedly provided by the specifically Christian institutions of civilized life": sex (through the family), sustenance (provided through political, social, and economic institutions), and salvation (via the church). He—or she—enjoyed none of the benefits of these institutions, but did not have to pay the price in repression that membership in them demanded (*TD*, 166–67). It doesn't take Freud to suspect that some envy accompanied the disgust, loathing, and fear surrounding wild humanity.

Now White notes, and tries to account for, the transformation of the Wild Man "from an object of loathing and fear (and only secret envy) into an object of open envy and even admiration." This emerges in the fourteenth and fifteenth centuries, the same time—though he does not argue for a causal relationship—when "the social bonds of medieval culture began to disintegrate." In "an age of general cultural revolution" the Wild Man was reinterpreted as a model of a lost—and free—humanity. The "idealized image" of the Wild Man could be used even to justify revolution against civilization itself. This "redemption" looks like a by-product of the Renaissance, associated with the recovery of classical culture, the revival of humanistic values, and the "improvisation of a new conception of nature more classical than Christian in inspiration" (*TD*, 168). But, apparently complicating this chronology, White suggests this process began in the twelfth century, when "Wild Men began to appear in folklore as protectors of animals and forests and as teachers of a wisdom more useful to the peasants than the 'magic' of the Christian priest."[17] He speculates that this may have had something to do with "a more bucolic view of nature" associated with new agricultural tools and techniques which brought "vast areas" of Europe under cultivation, entailing cutting down forests and turning "the back country" into sheep runs. Or it "may reflect a kind of peasant resistance to Christian missionaries, who were once more taking up the task of Christianizing Europe, started in earlier times but interrupted by the Viking invasions, Muslim assaults, and feudal warfare." But "whatever the reason,"

the beneficent Wild Man, the protector and teacher of peasants, is attended by his identification with the satyrs, fauns, nymphs, and sileni of ancient times. And this identification complements, on the popular level, the vindication of nature by intellectuals through the revival of classical thought, and especially of Aristotelianism, that was occurring at the same time. (*TD*, 168)

To elucidate this development, White proposes a distinction between archaism and primitivism: "Primitivism seeks to idealize *any group* as yet unbroken to civilizational discipline; archaism, by contrast, tends toward the idealization of real or legendary *remote ancestors*, either wild or civilized." Archaism can justify conventional values as well as departure from conventional behavior, whereas "primitivism is quintessentially a radical doctrine," because it is based on "the conviction that men are really the same throughout all time and space but have been made evil in certain times and places by the imposition of social restraints upon them." It "simply invites men to be themselves. . . . Like archaism, then, primitivism holds up a vision of a lost world, but unlike archaism, it insists that this lost world is still latently present in modern, corrupt, and civilized man—and is there for the taking" (*TD*, 170–71).

Whereas archaists often imagine nature as "red in tooth and claw," primitivists conceive it as pastoral, populated by shepherds and shepherdesses who innocently lie down together—in other words, "the world of the picnic." This conception of nature is required for the transformation of the Wild Man into the Noble Savage signaled by the poetry of Edmund Spenser and Hans Sachs in the sixteenth century (*TD*, 172). Thus, by the end of the Middle Ages, there were two images of the Wild Man. One, thinking of animal nature, saw the "Wild Man as the antitype of the *desirable humanity*, as a warning of what men would fall into if they definitively rejected society and its norms." The other, thinking of nature as cultivated, "saw society, with all its struggle, as a fall away from natural perfection" and so tended to populate nature with "Wild Men as antitypes of *social* existence." This changed the myth, with its "essence" of wildness, into a "fiction" which could be "turned to limited use as an instrument of intracultural criticism." Locke and Spenser, Montesquieu and Rousseau, and more recently, Camus and Lévi-Strauss draw upon this version of the Wild Man, while Machiavelli, Hobbes, Vico, Freud, and Sartre are in the other tradition (*TD*, 173).

Tacitus in his *Germania*, Montaigne in the essay on cannibals, and Lévi-Strauss in *La Pensée sauvage* use this "fictive" notion of wildness ironically—that is, set up an antithesis between a "natural" and an "artificial" humanity, which draws us, "by the dialectic of thought itself," to "torture" each of these extreme conceptions with the other, so that we can "gradually approximate a truth about a world that is as complex and changing as our possible ways of comprehending that world." Such a comprehension is thwarted by the "mythical" tendency "to take signs and symbols for the things they represent, to take metaphors literally, and to let the fluid world indicated by the use of analogy and simile slip its grasp" (*TD*, 177).

The final pages of the essay take the story—and it is that, by now—of primitivism into the nineteenth and twentieth centuries, from mainly an anthropological to mainly (in popular thinking, at least) a psychological category. We now recognize the Victorian concept of "backwards" people they dominated as ethnocentric, if not racist, while we see "wildness" as a pathology reflecting "a personality malfunction in the individual's relation with society, rather than as a species variation or ontological differentiation" (*TD*, 179).

Finally, White notes that "the three most revolutionary thinkers of the nineteenth century" (Freud, Marx, and Nietzsche) took "as their special subject matter" the three securities in social life (sex, sustenance, and salvation) that the Wild Man seemed to threaten. As radical atheists, they redefined the problem of salvation in purely human terms and saw its solution in the "reexamination of the *creative* forms of *human* vitality," which required them to imagine "what primal man, precivilized man, the *Wild Man* who existed before history—i.e. outside the social state—might have been like." They did not idealize the freedom of precivilized humans, because the "fall" into society arose from a crucial scarcity (in goods, women, and/or power). The "primitive food-gatherers, primal horde, and barbarians" imagined by Marx, Freud, and Nietzsche solved the problem of scarcity "in essentially the same way: through the alienation and oppression of other men." This in turn gave rise to "the creation of a false consciousness, or self-alienation, necessary to the myth that a fragment of mankind might incarnate the *essence* of all humanity." This is why the archetype of the Wild Man kept reappearing in the Western imagination, as "Wild Man, monster, or devil," sometimes as a threat, at other times as a goal, sometimes "as an abyss into which mankind might fall, and again as a summit to be scaled; but always as a criticism of whatever security and peace of mind one group of men in society had purchased at the cost of the suffering of others" (*TD*, 179–80). So the story has a characteristic moral: human life is built on oppression, and it is good to disturb the peace of mind of the oppressors.

This essay is fertile in suggestions why images of the Wild Man developed as they did. It gestures toward the sorts of explanation a social historian might offer (feudal bonds loosening, new agricultural techniques, for example) and mentions other more or less concurrent intellectual changes which might have been influential, though White doesn't tell us how. (Such ideas as that adoption of Aristotelian logic in scholastic philosophy "complemented" the association of Wild Men with fauns, sileni, or satyrs do seem to require some further substantiation.) However, White seems more at home with purely dialectical or "internalist" explanations, such as that the mutual "torturing" of the ideas of natural and artificial humanity is driven just by the dialectic of thought itself to produce a more complex and adequate conception of the world.

Three years later White turned to the other half of the dialectical pair with "The Noble Savage Theme as Fetish." He uses "fetish" in three senses: natural objects believed to have magical powers; extravagant, irrational devotion (as to a body part in psychoanalytic parlance); and "pathological displacement of libidinal interest and satisfaction to a fetish." Insofar as the Noble Savage was "a putative description of a part of humanity" it was magical; it was "extravagant and irrational in the kind of devotion it was meant to inspire"; and as a "pathological displacement of libidinal interest," led to a form of racism dependent on the idea of "wild humanity" to justify it (*TD*, 184).

His argument focuses on the European imagination of the indigenous populations of the Americas. It does not map easily onto his earlier account of how the more benign version of the Wild Man began to emerge among the European peasantry in the twelfth century. Here he claims the Noble Savage theme is implicit in the Europeans' original metaphorical characterizations of the peoples of the New World: both men and women naked, without personal property, a king, or government, mating randomly with no proper form of marriage, cannibalistic, and (if they avoided being eaten) living healthily for 150 years.

This makes a heady brew of "gold, land, incest, sexual promiscuity, cannibalism, longevity, health, violence, passivity, disease, all mixed in with a compulsive concern for the souls of the natives." The natives contravened five taboos of the Europeans: against (public) nakedness, community of property, lawlessness, sexual promiscuity, and cannibalism; yet they enjoyed the "robust health and longevity" formerly available only to the Patriarchs of the Old Testament—in short, "moral depravity and a kind of physical superhumanity." These anomalies had to be resolved either by conceiving of the "savages" as super animals (which would account for both their remarkable health and their violations of European norms) or as a "breed of degenerate men (descendants of the lost tribes of Israel or a race of men rendered destitute of reason and moral sense by the effects of a harsh climate)." This established an opposition between normal (European) and abnormal (native) people, which led, no matter how the choice was made, to the reduction of native Americans to mere objects, commodified, as Bartolomé de las Casas said in 1619, like pieces of wood or flocks of sheep. But, echoing Hegel's well-known master-slave dialectic, White argues that using them meant they were desirable, increasing the suspicion that they did in fact share a common humanity (*TD*, 186–88).

The relationship between "normal" and "abnormal" humans could be conceived in two ways. The tradition of the great chain of being saw it in terms of continuity.[18] The fact that humans formed part of such a chain meant that they had at least some things in common, and complicated drawing a line between the normal and abnormal. Those who argued, on the basis of the deleterious environment of the New World, that all its species, including humans, were degenerate and congenitally inferior to their European counterparts were thinking in a mode of contiguity, simply setting the two types alongside one another. (Although White does not use the terms found in *Metahistory*, these are synecdochic and metonymic modes, respectively.) The mode of continuity is naturally "more productive of tolerance and mediation by degree"—and of attempted proselytization and conversion—than that of contiguity, which could be used to justify war, extermination, or the slave trade (*TD*, 190, 193–94).

Having shown, by what he calls "a purely linguistic operation," how the indigenous population of the Americas (and elsewhere) could come to be thought of as Noble Savages, White explains why this happened after the "pacification" (that is, subjugation) of these peoples in the second half of the eighteenth century. He ties together the threads of his argument by asserting that in this moment when the theme was most potent, it was being conceived on two levels of meaning simultaneously—that is, ironically. He points out that the concept of the Noble Savage was being used not to elevate the position of the "savages," but to degrade that of "nobles." It appeared everywhere the nobility were otherwise under attack, and it had no effect on the actual treatment of natives nor on the way their oppressors viewed them. Although "on the literal level, the concept asserts the nobility of the savage," better ethnographic information from such explorers as Captain Cook was showing how different native cultures were. If proponents of the idea had a real interest in the welfare of the "savages," they should have insisted "on the natives' rights to 'life, liberty, and property,' which they claimed for the European middle classes of the time." So, he concludes, the idea that savages are noble (in spite of the evidence they were backward) had "the effect . . . of demeaning the idea of nobility itself. The hidden or suppressed referent of the Noble Savage idea is, in short, that of nobility itself" (*TD*, 192).

This reflects the middle-class ambivalence towards the nobility, since they desired privileges like the ones which they felt the nobility unjustly enjoyed and monopolized. So "the concept of the Noble Savage served their ideological needs perfectly, for it at once undermined the nobility's claim to a special human status and extended that status to the whole of humanity." Its insincerity is shown by the fact that once attaining some power, the bourgeoisie set about dehumanizing the "dangerous" peasants and workers of Europe with a "fetishism of class" which White considers even "more virulent" (*TD*, 194–95).

These two historical articles illustrate White's contention that no absolute distinction can be made between historiography and the philosophy of history. Stripped of the various theories and tropes implicit in them, they would simply be an unintelligible heap of facts. His receptivity to these and his versatility in deploying them allows him to bring together superficially disparate themes—or, as he might say, "constitute the facts."

Any really good social or political historian could have come up with some of these, and undoubtedly would have mustered more evidence to explain them. The value White adds comes from the linguistic theory he applies, rather unobtrusively in "The Wild Man" and overtly in "The Noble Savage." Their persistent dualisms show the influence of structuralism, which White has never foresworn,[19] while the tropology found in the essay on the noble savage is a rare example of how it works in White's own historical writing.

White has published only two substantial historical articles since 1980. One undertakes to explain why rhetoric, after its long neglect, was revived in the late twentieth century. He argues that rhetoric was "suppressed" in the early nineteenth century so that literature could be "mystified." "It is no accident," he contends, that 'literacy' and 'literature' were coined and entered into general usage at about the same time, in the early nineteenth century." This is because creation of these categories was part of "the same process of a general reorganization of culture," which saw the establishment and integration of the nation-state, the transition from an "estate" to a "class" organization of society, the advent of corporate capitalism, and the transformation of the masses from subjects into citizens capable of taking their place as functionaries in a system of production and exchange for profit rather than use.

The ideological formation supporting these changes combined "aestheticism" with utilitarianism. Ordinary citizens required only literacy, since literature was "useless" to them as "functionaries," and so was "literature," because they were deprived of "cognitive authority." Rhetoric as the Greeks conceived it, unlike poetics, grammar, and logic, addressed the politics of language use; so its suppression effectively deprived students "of the practical knowledge without which they can never develop their political capacities fully."[20]

In contrast to the *marxisant* tenor of this article is one about how "facts" are manufactured from events. The "event" was an avalanche of mud which descended on Salerno and several other towns in southern Italy. He questions how "the custodians of rationalizing knowledge . . . produced mythic accounts of the nature of the disaster." Once the "extremity of the event had been registered," they unleashed "a virtual shower of discourses"—moral and political, blaming victims and hinting of Mafia involvement. The event was thus "overdetermined" by "being subjected to so many varying accounts of its real importance" that it was "sublimated . . . into a spectacle which could be forgotten once its drama had been played out." White notes the same process would have happened to earlier events if there had been the abundance of sources which we now have.[21]

IV

Just as some of his historical pieces betray their theoretical underpinnings, White's more theoretical ones are never too remote from the practice of historiography, even when most critical of it. He doesn't think much of appeals to the historian's "craft." A historian's specialized training, he writes,

consists for the most part of study in a few languages, journeyman work in the archives, and the performance of a few set exercises to acquaint him with standard reference works and journals in his field. For the rest, a general experience of human affairs, reading in peripheral fields, self-discipline, and *Sitzfleisch* are all that are necessary. Anyone can master the requirements fairly easily. (*TD*, 40)

Instead of the disciplinary paradigm which he took to be endemic in American historical work, White advocated a style of historical explanation organized by the "governing metaphor" of the historical work, conceived as *"a heuristic rule which self-consciously eliminates certain kinds of data from consideration as evidence."* He takes a resolutely constructivist view of both art and natural science. Most scientists, he claims, recognize that facts are "not so much found as constructed by the kinds of questions which the investigator asks of the phenomena before him. The artist and the historian face the common problem of *"what constitutes the facts themselves"* and try to solve it in the choice of the metaphor which "orders his world, past, present, and future" (*TD*, 43, 46–47). Because there are many possible choices of governing metaphor, this approach precludes the possibility that a work of history can be definitive.

What, if anything, keeps this position from falling into the utter relativism that White had earlier tried to avoid? Nothing, if by "constitutes the facts themselves" he meant "makes them up"; and not much, if he advocates that inconvenient facts simply be left out if they don't fit the governing metaphor. But "constitute" can also mean "bring together," and so it surely does here. Furthermore, and none too soon, "data" now come into view, and somehow these can call into question the constitution of facts by the governing metaphor. We readers should "ask only that the historian show some tact" in the use of governing metaphors. This means she should exploit the metaphor to the limit, but not "overburden it with data" and be ready to abandon it for a richer one when it can't accommodate certain kinds of data. White compares this to "the same way that a scientist abandons a hypothesis when its use is exhausted" (*TD*, 47).

Thus White's early challenge to professional historians goes beyond claiming that not much is required to be one. They should use contemporary scientific and artistic insights without lapsing into radical relativism and making history into propaganda, or into "that fatal monism which has always heretofore resulted from attempts to wed history and science." They could then consider using various modes of representation "for dramatizing the significance of data which they have uncovered but which, all too frequently, they are prohibited from seriously contemplating as evidence" (*TD*, 47–48). (It is unclear why it seems to be data that call for adequate metaphors; also unclear is why governing metaphors, instead of self-consciously excluding some data from consideration, allow more to be included. If it is really only the governing metaphor that solves the problem of what constitutes the facts, it would seem impossible for "data" to force the creation of a new metaphor.)

This onslaught on conventional historiography raises this question: if it is to lose its autonomy and muddle along with modest requirements for its practitioners, why bother doing history at all? White's answer invokes historiography's "golden age," from 1800 to 1850, whose best representatives (Hegel, Balzac, and Tocqueville) agreed that "the task of the historian was less to remind men of their obligation to the past than to force upon them an awareness of how the past could be used to effect an ethically responsible transition from present to future." Their "tragic sense" came from an apprehension of "the absurdity of individual human aspiration" combined with the sense that such aspirations were required to save humans from the "potentially destructive awareness of the movement of time" (*TD*, 48–49). So these proto-existentialists (as White sees them) provide the inspiration historians today require, since "*the burden of the historian* in our time is to . . . transform historical studies in such a way as to allow the historian to participate positively in the liberation of the present from *the burden of history*" (*TD*, 40–41).

V

Metahistory: The Historical Imagination in the Nineteenth Century has been called many things, but seldom—except by White—"just a study of nineteenth-century historical writing."[22] Nine-tenths of the text is indeed devoted to nineteenth-century European historical thought, not just historiography as practiced by most historians. Its remaining tenth, the introduction, has almost eclipsed the rest of the book, however.[23]

The manuscript White first submitted had a methodological section, but "a very modest one."[24] Its great expansion in the final text caused Fredric Jameson to complain that "access to White's methodological thesis is encumbered by the presence of his substantive application of it to his texts."[25] I hope to show that the historiographical nine-tenths is not an encumbrance.

There are several ways to organize a study of nineteenth-century European historiography. White does not present a conventional "internalist" account (stressing the influence of previous historians on the four on whom it concentrates, or that which they might have had on one another). He does not evaluate the previous state of historical writing on the Renaissance, the French Revolution, or the European state system, nor show what the four "master historians" did with their sources. Most importantly, he gives us a history of thought and writing rather than of erudition, and so takes as givens all the nineteenth-century accomplishments of philological refinement and the mining of archives. He has not even written a history of historians' "styles" in the manner of G. M. Trevelyan or Peter Gay.[26]

He does present, intermittently, some of the things that an "externalist" or contextualist would look for. He explains that he chose to focus on Michelet as the "presiding genius of the Romantic school"; Ranke as "founder of the historical school" and a paradigm for academic historiography; Tocqueville as the virtual founder of social history; and Burckhardt as the "archetypal cultural historian" (*M*, 141). However, he gives no institutional history of these schools or scholarly traditions, nor discusses their national peculiarities. There is not much more on professionaliza-tion of historiography (establishment of academic appointments chairs in history, publication of historical documents, founding of national jour-nals, and the like). White mentions these only to note their ideological implications. The appeal to methodological rigor and nonpartisanship which attended the professionalization of history, he says, actually aimed "to remove historical study from the uses to which it was being put by Radicals and Reactionaries on the political scene, and to serve—by the disciplinization of historical studies—the interests and values of the new social orders and classes which had come to power after the Revolution-ary Age" (*M*, 137–38).

One difficulty a historian confronts when writing a comprehensive history of historiography is that historians wrote about so many differ-ent things. Since there are such diverse subjects of historical works, com-parison (or any persuasive treatment of possible progress in historiogra-phy) based on substantive analyses of their works becomes quite difficult. White evades some problems of well-known approaches to the history of historiography by choosing a method which, he says, treats the histori-cal work "as what it most manifestly is: a verbal structure in the form of a narrative prose discourse" (*M*, ix). The words "structure" and "form" indicate that White's approach—never previously applied to the history of historiography—will be structuralist and formalist. Those requiring an introduction to it will find the best one in "Interpretation in History."[27]

Formalist treatment of historical texts yields intriguing readings of them. White's categories can be applied to any text, the more complex the better; and "satire" is sufficiently flexible to accommodate plots not easily assigned to the other three. However, White, rather than settle for insightful "readings" of the master historians and philosophers, as a New Critic might have done,[28] does—in a way—write a history of nineteenth-century European historical thinking. To do this he resorts to his well-known tropology, based on the four "master tropes" of Renaissance rhetorical theory: Metaphor, Metonymy, Synecdoche, and Irony, thus extending his treatment of "metaphor" in "The Burden of History."

Metaphor characterizes phenomena in terms of their similarity to (and difference from) one another—like "My love, a rose." Metonymy substitutes the name of the part of a thing for the whole ("fifty sail" for "fifty ships"). Synecdoche uses the part to symbolize some quality presumed to inhere in the whole. White's example is "He is all heart." Both metonymy and synecdoche are ways of talking about part-whole relationships, but the relationship between part and whole is "extrinsic" in metonymy, as between causes and effects, whereas synecdoche implies "an *intrinsic* relationship of shared *qualities*," seeing a whole which is "*qualitatively* different from the sum of the parts." These three tropes are "naïve," in that they depend on "the belief in language's capacity to grasp the nature of things in figurative terms." By contrast, irony is a "metatrope," a "way of negating on the figurative level what is positively affirmed on the literal level" that casts doubt on this capacity. By using, for example, absurd metaphors (catachresis) or self-contradictory ones (oxymorons), it directs attention to the fallibility of all figurative speech (*M*, 36–37).

Irony and metaphor are pretty clear. I may be able to make the relevance of these tropes to historical writing more evident if I translate—with the treasons attending translations—metonymy and synecdoche into ordinary English. Jack Hexter once contrasted his approach to seventeenth-century English history with that of the Marxist historian Christopher Hill. Hill, to Hexter, was an inveterate "lumper"—that is, he tended to interpret facts as parts of greater social or religious groups and movements. Hexter, on the other hand, generally sought to dissolve these groups to create what White calls "a set of *dispersed* entities" which are "subsumable under no general rule, either of causation or of classificatory entailment" (*TD*, 63). "Lumping" (Hill's technique) is synecdochic, "splitting" (Hexter's method) metonymic. (This is the tropological version of the familiar issue of "methodological individualism" as against "methodological holism," which arises in the philosophy of history and social sciences.)[29]

Hexter the liberal and Hill the Marxist cannot reconcile their differences in interpreting the English Civil War by proving that all historians should split or lump—or split the difference. They simply irreducibly see the world differently.

As he often does, White "points both ways" in discussing the ontological status of the tropes. He avoids terming them "laws of thought," stressing instead their conventional character in Western discourse; but there are also passages which lead Hans Kellner to say they "look very much like a mental structure, a natural part of human cognition."[30]

Fortunately I need not try to make up White's mind. The tropes give him the organizing principles for the really short history—but it is a history—of "the deep structure of its historical imagination of the nineteenth century" which concludes the introduction. He conceives this as a "closed-cycle development" which evolved from Metaphorical through Metonymical and Synecdochic comprehensions of the historical world into an "Ironic apprehension of the irreducible relativism of all knowledge" (*M*, 38). This "closed cycle" started after the ironic views reached by such eighteenth-century writers on history as Voltaire, Gibbon, Hume, Kant, and Robertson were coming under attack. However, it did not begin, chronologically at least, with widespread acceptance of a metaphorical view of history. In the first third of the nineteenth century, irony was discredited, but all three of the other tropes were in play. In its first decade, White says, Hegel refused to see history either ironically or metaphorically, arguing for a synecdochic conception of its course. Meanwhile the French positivists, especially Comte, combined mechanistic theories of explanation typical of the Enlightenment with an organicist conception of the historical process whose belief in inevitable progress made their emplotments comic. All these approaches were live options in the period from 1830 to 1870, when "the four great 'masters' of nineteenth-century historiography . . . produced their principal works" (*M*, 39).

But they all led to irony. Both Right and Left Hegelians in the mid-nineteenth century tried to go beyond Hegel's position, but only Marx succeeded, by combining "the Metonymical strategies of the political economy of his time" with the "Synecdochic strategies of Hegel." His view of history was far from ironical, but he was "sensitive to the ideological implications of any conception of history which claimed the status of a 'realistic' vision of the world." This could ironically undercut such conceptions (including his own) and lead to a "descent into Irony" which characterized the "crisis of historicism" in the last third of the nineteenth century (*M*, 40). But White says that even had Marx never written, "the consistent elaboration of a number of equally comprehensive and plausible, yet apparently mutually exclusive, conceptions of the same set of events was enough to undermine confidence in history's claim to 'objectivity,' 'scientificity,' and 'realism.'" Burckhardt responded with an "aestheticist, skeptical, cynical, and pessimistic" attitude "towards any effort to know the 'real' truth of things." Burckhardt's friend Nietzsche took these presuppositions as philosophical problems, and attempted to "dissolve" irony and return to a romantic or metaphorical conception of history, but he could not, and did not try to, revive the romanticism of Herder or Burke. Instead he embraced a self-conscious romanticism which was "Metaphorically Ironic in its intention." Nietzsche's analysis of the psychology of historical consciousness, revealing its "specifically poetic apprehension of reality," accentuated the "crisis of historicism" (*M*, 41).

Finally, Croce, like Nietzsche, diagnosed the ironical character of the crisis of historicism, and like him "hoped to purge it of this irony by assimilating it to art." However, White's early enthusiasm for Croce had now cooled; he concluded that Croce's efforts to escape skepticism by assimilating history to philosophy resulted in historicizing philosophy, thereby making it as aware of its ironic condition as historiography had become (*M*, 41).

White concludes that the evolution of philosophy of history in the nineteenth century from Hegel through Marx and Nietzsche to Croce paralleled that of historiography from Michelet through Ranke and Tocqueville to Burckhardt—except that the sequence of tropes was different. No matter: what is important is that both ended in the same Ironic condition, although with greater sophistication and erudition than was available in the eighteenth century (*M*, 42).

Historians, aside from Burckhardt, do not figure much in this introductory sketch. White talks more about their choices of emplotment and modes of explanation than about the tropes in their work. White credits them with a high degree of theoretical self-consciousness, but no consciousness of the poetics of historiography. Like M. Jourdain, they were employing metaphoric, metonymic, synecdochic, or ironic tropes without knowing it. What they thought they were doing was striving to establish criteria for a genuine "realistic" historiography—yet they "succeeded only in producing as many different species of 'realism' as there were modalities for construing the world in figurative discourse" (*M*, 40).

VI

Metahistory is an unprecedented history of historiography. Its focus on "historical thinking" allows the inclusion of philosophers as well as historians. While four historians receive intensive treatment, others (Numa Denis Fustel de Coulanges, Augustin Thierry, and Thomas Babington Macaulay, for example) are not mentioned at all, and few dates appear. He does make the case, though, that "philosophy of history" is not a contaminant of "proper" history; the distinction between the two, he says, is now "little more than a preaccepted cliché."[31]

The book can certainly be read as a series of formalistic "readings," but there is considerable history of historiography in the chapters on the transition from Enlightenment to early nineteenth-century historiography and on the revival of philosophy of history in the later nineteenth century. The clue to understanding nineteenth-century historical thought, White says, is what it objected to in its eighteenth-century predecessors—not its optimism and belief in progress, but its *essential irony*, just as what it objected to most in its cultural reflection was its *skepticism*." This kept it from providing "adequate cognitive justification" for its optimistic belief in progress" (*M*, 47). This requires him to analyze "the eighteenth century's failure in historical thinking." He does not attribute this to a lack of scholarly achievement, an "inadequate theory of historical reflection," or failure to anticipate the insights of historicism. The failure lay instead in the inability of the Enlightenment's outstanding historical thinkers to transcend the "Ironic mode in which both scholarly inquiry and theoretical syntheses were cast" (*M*, 48).

The first generation of *philosophes* saw the past in dualistic terms: reason vs. various forms of unreason. (White calls this "an epic prefiguration of the historical field.")[32] They of course anticipated that reason would win because they saw it winning in their own generation. They also had a vision of the essential unity of the human race, although they "could not take it as a *presupposition* of their historical writing," because the data did not bear it out, but also because "it did not accord with their own experience of their own social worlds." Their sense of satisfaction with their own times eventually eroded, helping to lead subsequent generations of Enlightenment historians to adopt an ironic view of history (*M*, 62–66).

White is saying here things we don't expect. Historians are constrained by data and by the "experience of their own social worlds." Furthermore, their choices amount to a "failure in historical thinking"—so much for White's allegedly invariable relativism. However, he has no intention of leaving it at that. He next analyzes the manifest level of what

Enlightenment historians thought about historiography. They carried on the classical tradition in emphasizing that the historian above all must tell only the truth, avoiding figurative language and any elements of invention. Like Voltaire, they conventionally distinguished between true, fabulous (which made up facts), and satirical historiography. They found it difficult to classify any particular sample of historical writing. This required them to presuppose a fourth type of historical consciousness: a "metahistorical consciousness that stands above, and adjudicates between, the claims which the three kinds of historiography . . . might make upon the reader" (*M*, 49–51).

White praises this as a real advance in thinking about history. Nevertheless, although Enlightenment rationalists realized the need for the "*meta*historical principles by which the general truths derived from contemplation of past facts in their individuality and concreteness could be substantiated *on rational grounds*," they failed to find one, because they lacked an adequate psychological theory. Opposing reason, the source of truth, to imagination or fantasy, the source of error, blinded them to "the *continuity* between reason and fantasy" (*M*, 51).

Enlightenment historical thinkers also did not go far enough into the problem of historical representation. They did not get beyond questioning whether comedy, tragedy, or epic was the right emplotment. They generally agreed that neither epic nor tragedy was likely to be an appropriate plot; Voltaire thought Charles XII was the only subject fit for a tragic history, but finally came up only with a mock epic, and White points out that there was also no great tragic theater in the Enlightenment (*M*, 54, 66). Such failures contributed to the skepticism of Gibbon, Hume, and Kant, who by the end of the Enlightenment had "effectively dissolved the distinction between history and fiction on which earlier thinkers such as Bayle and Voltaire had based their historiographical enterprises" (*M*, 48).

So here is another layer of explanation, focusing on emplotment and formal thought; but White's are like Russian dolls. Beneath ones like these working on the manifest levels is the tropological one. White says that *the* [my italics] reason that Enlightenment historiography ended in "essential irony" was the incompatibility of the two tropes and two modes of explanation which it attempted to employ. It originally tried to apply to the data of history metonymical strategies of reduction (that is, seeking causal relationships) so as to "justify belief in the possibility of a human community conceived in the Synecdochic mode." However, the worm of irony was already at the heart of Metonymy, because historians who begin apprehending history as dominated by cause-effect relations will ultimately "regard anything in this field . . . as nothing but an 'effect' of some causal nexus"—a "contingent (hence determined) reality, and thus . . . *irrational* in its essence" (*M*, 66).

White depicts the tensions among the tropes in the Enlightenment as even more complex, because its historians and theorists tended to characterize the objects of historical knowledge metaphorically—that is, sought to make an iconic representation of them—while treating individuals "in terms of species and genera," a synecdochic procedure.

Yet White also "puts it another way," invoking emplotments, ideology, and modes of explanation to account for the way Enlightenment historiography fell into irony. He says the original "creative tension" between "Comic and Tragic conceptions of the plot of history, Mechanistic and Organicist conceptions of its processes, and the Conservative and Radical implications that might be drawn from these" eventually stopped being creative, gradually throwing "all the principal problems of both historiographical representation and general social goals" into doubt. By 1775, "historical epistemology . . . was Skeptical in the extreme," and thus led to a "manifestly relativistic ethical attitude" (*M*, 48).

Not only can White apparently characterize this development without invoking tropes; it seems that plots (epic, at least) can "prefigure the historical field." Epic also comes first in the sequence; after historians abandoned it, they "finally recognized that a Comic representation of historical occurrences can be sustained only on dogmatic grounds . . . and never on empirical ones, as Bayle and Voltaire had hoped to do." Their commitment to causal explanations made a truly tragic emplotment impossible because, since human nature was causally determined, "every potential Tragic flaw in a protagonist became a genuine corruption rather than a virtue which has been transformed by excess into a vice." Finding neither satisfactory, historical thought, like the philosophical and literary sensibility of the age, was carried into the mode of Satire, which is the 'fictional' form that Irony takes" (*M*, 66–67).

VI

White's roles as historian and literary critic inflect, though do not determine, one another. Naturally, the interrelationships between them are not free of tensions. White the radical relativist and voluntarist still calls himself a Marxist and is—or certainly was—a believer in "purely linguistic or logical necessity," as when an initially metonymic or causal approach inevitably ends in an ironical one. Furthermore, if we take his hints that the tropes follow one another in the—almost!—invariable sequence of metaphor, metonymy, synecdoche, and irony, then metaphor and synecdoche will also wind up at the same address. One closed cycle of tropological development has occurred, and White cites Vico's historical *corso* beginning with the metaphoric mode typifying the age of gods and proceeding through metonymy and synecdoche to the irony characteristic of an age of prose and science.

This makes White, notwithstanding his consistent preferences for relativism, sound like a determinist, on two grounds: that he sees figurative language, and especially tropes, as constraining what historians write, and that historiography, like other cultural phenomena, can be explained by social changes. He holds that all historians are "equally limited by the language chosen in which to delimit what it is possible to say about the subject under study"; but if limits prevent our saying *x*, we need not therefore say *y*. And such soft determinism, because it is "linguistic," would allow translating from one mode of discourse to another, thus making it possible "to imagine how our representations of the historical world aggregate into a comprehensive total vision of that world, and how progress in our understanding of it is possible" (*TD*, 117–18).

Sometimes in his writings it appears impossible to escape the ironic perspective from which *Metahistory*, like "most of modern academic historiography," is written, but White suggests "recognition of this Ironic perspective provides the grounds for a transcendence of it" since there are a number of "possible perspectives on history, each of which has its own good reasons for existence" (*M*, xii, 434).

White carefully leaves space in his historical writings for other "possible perspectives." He handles the tropological grid (which could easily become Procrustean) flexibly, offering alternatives involving emplotment, modes of explanation, and ideological implication rather than tropes. His historical essays show no obsession with hunting down tropes and figures and he is as chary of recommending methodological procedures to other historians as he is of gathering disciples or creating a "school."[33]

Vico held that "the order of ideas must follow the order of institutions,"[34] and so it seems to do in White's essays on the Wild Man, the Noble Savage, and the suppression of rhetoric—if indeed ideas are not laggards. These describe social changes which (in Vichian language) are "followed" by changes in ideas. White characterizes the epochal changes in our own times as full implications of industrialization (massive population expansion, urbanization, and international economics) and its effects (mass famine, boom-and-bust economic cycles, pollution of the ecosphere, world wars, and mass death by techno-weapons) whose "scale, intensity, and reach . . . render them impervious to the traditional categories of historical representation and explanation."[35] They call not only for novel representations, drawing on the many fictive possibilities created by modern media, but also for new types of historical writing—"antinarrative nonstories produced by literary modernism," which "offer the only prospect for adequate representation of the kind of 'unnatural' events—including the Holocaust—that mark our era and distinguish it absolutely from all of the history that has come before it" (FR, 81). This language recalls that of "The Burden of History," urging historians to unleash their imaginations on a chaotic past and expand their stylistic repertoires. If such a "call" were to be answered, historiography would "follow" (though not necessarily be determined by) these social changes. White in Figural Realism and in other places leaves details of the relationships between world and word unspecified.

So far this call has pretty much reposed silently on the English and American historical professions' answering machine, though "historical thinking" in contemporary Europe (represented in a string of figures from André Malraux and W. B. Yeats to Michel Foucault and Georg Lukács, none of them professional historians) may have, as White believes, sought to overcome the profession's ironic perspective (M, 433–34). As a theorist, White makes it imaginable that "the historical imagination" need not be confined to nineteenth-century Europe. As a historian, he consistently tries to bring together wide arrays of apparently unrelated facts, which marks his dominant mode as synecdoche rather than irony; but he doesn't offer his historical work as a model or even as an example of how his theoretical apparatus might be applied or extended.

Expectations that he do so miss the point. White's contribution to contemporary historiography lies not in stipulation but in suggestion and provocation. He has resisted emulation; if historians are to be free artists, they must be free of him. But he remains convinced that an historiography adequate to our times cannot be bound by the "mind-forged manacles" of the contemporary "craft" or "discipline" of history. He has at the very least done his best to strike these off.

Notes

1. Hayden White, afterword to *Beyond the Cultural Turn: New Directions in the Study of Society and Culture*, ed. Victoria E. Bonnell and Lynn Hunt (Berkeley: University of California Press, 1999), 315.

2. "Pontius of Cluny, the Curia Romana and the End of Gregorianism in Rome," *Church History* 27 (1958): 195–219; "The Gregorian Ideal and Saint Bernard of Clairvaux," *Journal of the History of Ideas* 21 (1960): 321–48.

3. "Collingwood and Toynbee: Transitions in English Historical Thought," *English Miscellany* 8 (1957): 147–78.

4. Ibid., 166–68. In a later review essay on Alan Donagan's *Later Philosophy of R. G. Collingwood*, in *History and Theory* 4 (1965): 250, White acknowledges that Collingwood was not a relativist.

5. "Religion, Culture and Western Civilization in Christopher Dawson's Idea of History," *English Miscellany* 9 (1958): 244–87.

6. Ibid., 252.

7. As a graduate student White took seminars in philosophy of history with Maurice Mandelbaum, but never shared Mandelbaum's interest in pursuing the analogies between history and biology. He told Keith Jenkins he was always interested in "the relationship between history and poesis." See Jenkins, "A Conversation with Hayden White," *Teaching History* 7 (1998): 72–74.

8. He emphasizes the "protoexistentialism" of "original Marxism" in *The Ordeal of Liberal Humanism: An Intellectual History of Western Europe*, vol. 2, *Since the French Revolution* (New York: McGraw-Hill, 1970), 232.

9. White's translator's introduction to Carlo Antoni, *From History to Sociology: The Transition in German Historical Thought* (Detroit: Wayne State University Press, 1959), xxi. White takes quite a different view of Croce in *Metahistory*.

10. Ibid., xxiii.

11. White has identified Collingwood and Croce, both historians and philosophers, as the two main influences on his early thought; see Ewa Domańska, *Encounters: Philosophy of History After Postmodernism* (Charlottesville: University Press of Virginia, 1998), 18.

12. Reprinted in *Tropics of Discourse* (1978). Henceforth this will be cited as

TD. Other books by White are cited as follows: *M = Metahistory (1973)*; *CF = The Content of the Form: Narrative Discourse and Historial Representation* (1987); and *FR = Figural Realism: Studies in the Mimesis Effect* (1999).

13. Coates is the first-named author (although this may have been merely by alphabetical order) of *The Emergence of Liberal Humanism* (1966) and *The Ordeal of Liberal Humanism* (1970).

14. See, for example, *Emergence*, 18–20, 61, 148, 169–70, 186–87, 194–96, 209–20, 301–7.

15. White also wrote a survey clearly intended for undergraduates, *The Greco-Roman Tradition* (1973).

16. These are "The Forms of Wildness: Archaeology of an Idea" in *The Wild Man Within: An Image in Western Thought from the Renaissance to Romanticism*, ed. Edward Dudley and Maximilian E. Novak (Pittsburgh: University of Pittsburgh Press, 1972); and "The Noble Savage Theme as Fetish" in *First Images of America: The Impact of the New World and the Old*, ed. Fredi Chiappelli (Berkeley: University of California Press, 1976), both reprinted in *TD*.

17. *TD*, 168; Richard Bernheimer, *Wild Men in the Middle Ages* (Cambridge, MA: Harvard University Press, 1952), 24–25. White acknowledges the degree to which his article draws on Bernheimer's book.

18. Arthur O. Lovejoy, *The Great Chain of Being: A Study of the History of an Idea* (Cambridge, MA: Harvard University Press, 1936), 52–58.

19. Domańska, *Encounters*, 19, 27.

20. "The Suppression of Rhetoric in the Nineteenth Century," in *The Rhetoric Canon*, ed. Brenda Deen Schildgen (Detroit: Wayne State University Press, 1997), 22–28. Generalizing about all of Europe is questionable; the *Shorter Oxford English Dictionary* gives earlier dates for both literacy and literature.

21. "Catastrophe, Communal Memory and Mythic Discourse: The Use of Myth in the Reconstruction of Society," in *Myth and Memory in the Construction of Community*, ed. Bo Stråth (Brussels: P.I.E.-P. Lang, 2000), 73.

22. Ibid., 18.

23. In this respect *Metahistory* is like Hegel's *Lectures on the Philosophy of History*, which also has a theoretical introduction that everybody reads and then a much longer substantive—and brilliant—survey of universal history.

24. Ibid., 15.

25. "Figural Relativism, or the Poetics of Historiography," *Diacritics* 6, no. 1 (Spring 1976): 4.

26. George Macaulay Trevelyan, *Clio, a Muse and Other Essays Literary and Pedestrian* (London: Longmans, 1913); Peter Gay, *Style in History* (New York: McGraw-Hill, 1974).

27. Published in 1973 and reprinted in *TD*.

28. In a brilliant article, Nancy Partner wonders whether White's works "insidiously open the gates to deconstruction, replace representation with semi-

otics, and contaminate factual evidence with fictional anxiety." Her answer is "yes"—but not intentionally. "This is not from the route of Saussure to Barthes to Derrida, but rather from New Criticism, replacing authorial with textual intentions." "Hayden White: The Form of the Content," *History and Theory* 37 (1998): 170–71.

29. Arthur Danto, "Methodological Individualism and Methodological Holism," in *Philosophical Analysis and History*, ed. William H. Dray (New York: Harper & Row, 1966); and Brian Fay, *Contemporary Philosophy of Social Science: A Multicultural Approach* (Oxford: Blackwell, 1996), 50–54.

30. Kellner, "Hayden White and the Kantian Discourse: Tropology, Narrative, and Freedom," *Philosophy of Discourse*, ed. Chip Sills and George H. Jensen (Portsmouth, NH: Boynton/Cook Publishers, 1992), 2.253.

31. *M*, 427. See also Haskell Fain, *Between Philosophy and History: The Resurrection of Speculative Philosophy of History within the Analytic Tradition* (Princeton, NJ: Princeton University Press, 1970).

32. Note that prefiguration is normally the province of the tropes; also "epic" now appears as a fifth emplotment.

33. He told Domańska in 1993: "Young people . . . write me letters and say: 'You say so and so. What do you mean?' I reply: I do not know. I was writing in a different milieu at that time and . . . for different purposes, than I would write for today and for a different audience" (*Encounters*, 25, 30).

34. Giambattista Vico, *The New Science*, 3rd ed., trans. Thomas Goddard Bergin and Max Harold Fisch (Ithaca, NY: Cornell University Press, 1948), 64.

35. "Postmodernism and Textual Anxieties," in *The Postmodern Challenge: Perspectives East and West*, ed. Bo Stråth and Nina Witoszek (London: Sage Publications, 1999), 30. See also "The Modernist Event" in *FR*, 66–86.

15

Hayden White

AN ACADEMIC TEACHER

Ewa Domańska
Translated by Magdalena Zapedowska

According to Jean-François Lyotard, we live in a postmodern era characterized by the collapse of "grand narratives," associated not only with a crisis of belief in truth and a crisis of metaphysics, but also with a crisis of the university. In his *Postmodern Condition*, Lyotard makes much of the commercialization of knowledge, pointing out that in the postmodern era the main factors which legitimate knowledge are its efficiency and usefulness. The goal of research is "not to find truth, but to augment power." The cognitive function of science is thus inseparable from its socio-political function. Under the control of those who manage its financial resources, the role of the university changes: it is expected to produce competent researchers, not to generate ideals.[1]

Many historians claim that the declared crisis of history is of an institutional or technical rather than epistemological character. The arguments they use to support this claim are similar to Lyotard's: changes in the ways of financing institutions of higher education; the reduced autonomy of universities, controlled by authorities that promote particular kinds of research and provide funds for it; the commercialization of historical science (the heritage industry; the past as an object of trade which can be purchased and sold); the reduced number of history classes in elementary and high schools (the supposed uselessness of the humanities; the tendency toward specialized education); fewer funds allocated for education; the mass character of higher education (producing job seekers with university degrees; college studies as a means of preventing unemployment among young people); the deteriorating quality of education; the lessened status of historians, who used to be widely respected intellectuals and have become experts invited to television quiz shows and talk shows; the decreasing number of young people employed in historical institutions, which leads to gerontocracy, etc. While this approach to the crisis of history treats epistemological crisis as an effect of institutional crisis, the fact is that the two should be considered together.[2]

This essay does not discuss Hayden White's work in the context of the epistemological crisis of history, with which he is often associated. Instead, it draws attention to the crisis of the university and White's reactions to situations in which this crisis has manifested itself. It will focus on an issue rarely addressed in scholarly essays on White: the ways in which his style and engagement as a teacher and mentor embody a desirable model of intellectual work.

The Stanford Incident

On April 6, 2006, Stanford University organized a discussion of Hans Ulrich Gumbrecht's book *The Production of Presence*.[3] Hayden White, Gumbrecht's longtime friend and department colleague, was among the participants (as was the author of this essay). Instead of a debate, however, the meeting proceeded in a series of lavish compliments on Gumbrecht's book. Having listened for almost two hours, White spoke up angrily, harshly criticizing not so much the book itself as the uncritical and congratulatory tone of the whole event. Over the next few days White and Gumbrecht exchanged many e-mails. In a message of April 7, 2007, White wrote:

My tone? Yes, irritated. But not so much with you as with the atmosphere of these kinds of events—advertised as discussions—which are so genteel and so self-congratulatory and so self-satisfied that there is no room or time for self-reflection and serious thinking. . . . If these kinds of occasions were intended to be serious intellectual events, they would not be regulated so rigorously, would be more open-ended, and would go on for as long as anyone wanted to speak.[4]

This incident can serve as a starting point for reflection on Hayden White's integrity as an academic teacher. His intervention was a response to the violation of the idea of serious academic debate. His sense of responsibility for the education of undergraduate and graduate students, who attended the event in large numbers, prompted him to rebuke a scholar as distinguished as Gumbrecht, whom he had often treated with a fatherly sort of care. It was a disappointed mentor's reaction to the behavior of a disciple who betrayed his teachings.

Everyone who has attended White's seminars and lectures knows that White loves teaching and thinks of himself first and foremost as a teacher whose principal aim is to provide a model of a certain kind of intellectual work, not produce disciples who promote his own views. White has not created his own school and has never aspired to do so; however, he played a major role in creating the History of Consciousness program at the University of California, Santa Cruz (UCSC), which was a place for interdisciplinary, critical, and "rebellious" work.

The History of Consciousness program was founded in the mid-1960s at UCSC by Page Smith, Maurice Natanson, and Albert Hofstadter. Hayden White was the first full-time appointee in the program, in 1978, charged with the task of reorganizing and sustaining it. He was supposed to do this alone, but appointed James Clifford, then an instructor in history at Harvard. With the aid of the new dean of humanities, Helene Moglen, White expanded the department, adding two people in women's studies—Donna Haraway and Teresa de Lauretis—and two scholars from other departments—Barbara Epstein and Gary Lease. Before White left the program (1995), two more were added to the faculty: Victor Burgin in cinema and Angela Davis in critical studies. They expanded the student base and embarked on a program of recruiting ethnic minorities. By the late 1980s, HistCon had produced more ethnic minority PhDs in the humanities than all the other campuses of the UC system combined. Thus, as I observed above, there is no "school of Hayden White" because the knowledge he disseminates is supposed to liberate his students as co-workers rather than restrain them. White does not want his students to absorb and apply his theories but to develop their own approaches and modes of expression. HistCon is a proof of this attitude. White did not hire his followers or former students, but rather a set of strong people who shared a fierce commitment to interdisciplinary work and to a socially and politically engaged academy, but who had various visions and priorities and were definitely not afraid to defend their differences.

Hayden White has many independent disciples who continue and extend his mode of studying history and also, more importantly, his way of thinking about people and the world, as well as his way of teaching. Above all, White teaches his students how to rebel, so that in the future they can create a world in which human beings can be themselves. White approaches education as the practice of freedom.[5]

For White, "to be a historian is not a choice of career; it is an existential choice."[6] In his own case, this choice has determined his ethical approach as well as his attitude toward teaching. White does not only want to study the past. He wants to shape the future by educating new generations of scholars. His preferred audience is not made up of other professors, but of students, since, as White often says, students are still open to teaching and their views are not completely shaped, while mature scholars are mainly preoccupied with getting others to accept their views. Teaching students to be responsible for their existential choices and to respect other people, to act professionally and engage in critical but friendly debates, are White's main goals in his pedagogical work. Thanks to his teaching philosophy, those of us who pride ourselves on being his disciples see White not only as a professor but also as mentor, friend, and advisor. White's pedagogical talent may be an aspect of his personality, but it is also a product of his own education. He was fortunate to have an excellent teacher.

William J. Bossenbrook as a Model Mentor

Hayden White went to college at Wayne State University in Detroit, Michigan. It was there in the late 1940s that he met the person who exerted an immense influence on his way of thinking: William J. Bossenbrook, professor of history. In a way, Bossenbrook created Hayden White.

Arthur C. Danto, who attended Wayne University at the same time as White, admits that his own interest in history was inspired by Bossenbrook, "a powerful and visionary teacher." Danto mainly remembers Bossenbrook's courses in medieval history and the Renaissance, which he found "tremendously exciting":

Bossenbrook read very widely in philosophy, and brought his reading to bear on the subject at hand. The immediate post-war years brought Existentialism to America, and I found that philosophy very compelling, especially in the way

Bossenbrook used it to illuminate the past. His classes are impossible to describe, but one felt that nothing was irrelevant, and that everything he saw somehow connected with everything else. . . . He was really like some sort of shaman.[7]

In his preface to the Festschrift for Bossenbrook, White expressed gratitude and admiration for his mentor. "We saw him as Olympian," White wrote. "He bewitched us."[8] The charismatic power of Bossenbrook's intellect allowed him to liberate students from conventional approaches to history as well as shape their thinking. He taught "wisdom" rather than "information." Indeed, Hayden White's research interests show the fundamental influence of his mentor. White's understanding of history and his interest in particular thinkers are largely Bossenbrook's heritage.

White came to share Bossenbrook's interest in the philosophy of history and high regard for Kant, Hegel, Toynbee, Spengler, Collingwood, and Croce. He also came to share Bossenbrook's appreciation for the great "reflective" historians like Huizinga and Burckhardt. Moreover, as Giorgio Tagliacozzo observes, White was "Vichianized" by Bossenbrook, himself a devotee of Vico. White's indebtedness to his charismatic teacher is evident in his early writings, which address such issues as the rationale for the study of history, history's social function, its status as a discipline and its relation to other disciplines, aspects of intellectual history and different theories of the historical process, the changing concept of history, and intellectual rebellions against positivistic notions of history, as well as specific historical problems such as the crisis of Western culture and its secularization, the anthropocentric or humanistic understanding of the world. Finally, there are the ethical issues, such as choice and freedom. Those interests demonstrate how much of White's entire intellectual formation is owed to Bossenbrook. But Bossenbrook also influenced White's teaching style.

Bossenbrook was sans pareil as a teacher. I never met anyone else like him. But his was a style that was openly and even aggressively "masculinist," even "macho." As Danto said, he was like a wizard who had the capacity to conjure up ideas as if they were living presences. He strode the lecture room, moving amongst the students, sometimes laying a hand on a shoulder to emphasize a point, using the blackboard as a vast canvas on which a whole dialectic unfolded before our very eyes. One was exhausted after the two-hour sessions he typically held. How could one—especially a young male—not wish to emulate him?[9]

"[Bossenbrook] always insisted that the principal aim of the college teacher of history was to help prepare young people to come to grips with the world of affairs, not to populate the globe with scholars," White wrote.[10] Each of White's students, including myself, can certainly say the same about White's own idea and practice of teaching.

But there was another influence on White that was equally strong: that of certain feminists whom he encountered on the West Coast teaching at the University of California, Los Angeles, and the University of California, Santa Cruz, from 1978 to 1996. As White recollects:

My first classes at UCSC were attended by three remarkable women who have subsequently become well known in historiography and critical history: Susan Foster, Sharon Traweek, and Chela Sandoval. I am honored that all three of these remarkably talented women have publicly cited me as one of their mentors. But they taught me much more than I taught them about tone, style, mood, and tact in the classroom situation. Perhaps they were unaware of the changes wrought in my sense of my own pedagogical technique by their gentle coaching of my masculinist impulses into something more responsible to difference than they had formerly been. And of course my wife, Margaret Brose, herself a great teacher of Dante, has constantly over our thirty-some years of marriage been indefatigable, patient, and loving in her efforts to curb my congenital narcissism and tendency to go for effect rather than substance in public performance. Speaking of performance, I believe that teaching in the humanities has to be something more akin to acting a role than to "communication" of a content. It goes without saying, that the acting has to be "authentic" rather than "fake" and the teacher subordinated to the "role" rather than to his or her own ego-needs or *amour propre*. After all, a teacher is, in the final analysis, a medium rather than a message incarnated.[11]

Just as Bossenbrook "bewitched" White, White has "bewitched" many of his students. When I attended his seminars as a Fulbright fellow at the University of California, Berkeley, in 1995–1996, I was seeking, more or less consciously, an alternative to the Communist model of school as factory, where the teacher is a technician producing submissive citizens. I was looking for a professor who would continue the work of my previous teachers, who in the 1970s and 1980s were involved in the Solidarity movement and taught me to rebel against the repressive system. In Hayden White, who teaches and supports rebellion and who attempts to liberate the minds of his students rather than subjugating them, I saw an embodiment of the familiar model of rebel teacher, faithful to himself and the idea of education, and not to the school encapsulating the Althusserian "ideological state apparatus."

Back in the mid-1990s, just as today, I believed that the creation of a new society—which is the task of the young democracies in Central and Eastern Europe—must be founded upon the education of free, responsible, and open-minded individuals whose sense of identity involves a critical approach to reality rather than passive submission to the mind-controlling state apparatus. I thus joined those intellectuals who criticized the idea of the university as an institution producing graduates eager to acquiesce to the demands of authority. I think that today's crisis of the university reveals the need for "new teachers." Thus, it is the academic education of students, some of whom will become teachers, and of academic teachers themselves that should be debated. If a field is to be revolutionized, those who want to revolutionize it should first rethink and revise their own values. "Novelty" should not refer to the object that is expected to produce (the effect of) novelty, such as a change of political system, a change of government, or any other change of context. Rather, "novelty" should apply to the subject who is talking about it. In other words, for the university to be renewed and reinvigorated, we need a new kind of academic teacher, teachers who can become models for those who will later create the new university. In his work as a professor, Hayden White presents an example for those who care about the future of the university as an institution that both conducts research and educates the younger generation.

The Pedagogical Body as "Docile Body"

In his *Discipline and Punish*, Michel Foucault argues that power and knowledge are inseparably connected: "Power produces knowledge."[12] Foucault emphasizes the fundamental importance of the power/knowledge dyad to the development of individual subjectivity and the definition of the limits and conditions of cognition. The power/knowledge relation also affects bodies, both biological and institutional. As Foucault argues,

The body is directly involved in a political field; power relations have an immediate hold upon it; they invest it, mark it, train it, torture it, force it to carry out tasks, to perform ceremonies, to emit signs. . . . [T]he body is invested with relations of power and domination; . . . the body becomes a useful force only if it is both a productive body and a subjected body.[13]

The history of the last few decades has demonstrated that the pedagogical body at different levels of education is a "docile body," a body that can easily be trained to adopt certain behaviors. In the course of the current debate about educational reform, it would be worthwhile to examine the weak points of this "body," in which power and knowledge intersect. Perhaps the very mode of the debate about reform demonstrates its control by the structures of power. Education is a field controlled by the state, and unless we become aware of those relations, we will not be able to formulate the goals of the "renewed university."

Poland is now undergoing the process of corporatization and the difficult social accommodation to capitalism. Drawing upon Foucault, Stephen J. Ball observes that in education, corporatization manifests itself in the "industrialization" of schools and universities. Governed by managers who follow the "efficiency imperative," schools and universities induce their technician teachers to produce "submissive and well-trained" bodies of professionals. Industrial models are adopted in education (management, training, and evaluation of personnel). Management itself is a mode of power. "Management," Ball writes, "is also an imperialistic discourse. . . . The language of management deploys rationality and efficiency to promote control."[14]

Of course, it is impossible for Poland to bypass capitalism, but Polish people are fortunate to be able to learn about its dangers from the experience of those countries that have a long history of capitalism. In the debate about "new schooling," it would be worthwhile to seek less limiting alternatives. In the following part of this essay I propose one such alternative as I suggest a different way of thinking and talking about the renewed university, the academic teacher, the student, and learning. Such an alternative discourse would use "live metaphors" and would have a different goal and point of reference than the modern conception of the world and the human being, governed as it is by the technological metaphors of mechanism, machine, objectification, and management, whose values are violence, control, and manipulation.

The Liminal Phase, or the Pedagogical Body as a Close-Knit/Open Body: *Communitas*

The phase of social life which Poland has been undergoing for almost two decades can be described as liminal: it is a transformation, the passage from one system to another. The concept of liminality, which the U.S. anthropologist Victor Turner borrowed from Arnold van Gennep's theory of rites of passage (*rites de passage*), refers to the middle stage of those rites. It occurs between the preliminal and postliminal phases, which are marked, respectively, by a rite of exclusion (for example, a symbolic death) and a rite of inclusion (a symbolic rebirth). Turner emphasizes the importance of the liminal state to individual development, arguing that it is a state of the individual's ontological transformation related to a change in his/her gender or social role: maturity entails a higher social status. Liminality, which Turner also describes as a "betwixt and between," is a positive phase, a phase when the old structure is revaluated and its elements form a new pattern. Turner then applied those observations to social life at large.

The liminal phase of social life is marked by the appearance of *communitates*. They are opposed to structures, defined by Turner as a system of hierarchical positions in which individuals are important to the system insofar as they play the role assigned to them by those in power, in other words, insofar as they become personae in the narrative of power. Structure thus corresponds to the culture of the mask, and in the context of this essay can be related to the model of the university as a factory or company. In contrast, *communitas* is a certain utopia, a renewed university which individuals and communities should strive to bring into being. Turner writes:

[Communitas represents] the desire for a total, unmediated relationship between person and person, a relationship which nevertheless does not submerge one in the other but safeguards their uniqueness in the very act of realizing their commonness. Communitas does not merge identities; it liberates them from conformity to general norms, though this is necessarily a transient condition if society is to continue to operate in an orderly fashion.[15]

In relation to structure, communitas, which arises in the liminal phase, is an antistructure, a body whose freshness, vigor, and spontaneity threaten the existing order. But communitas is actually a positive force, an opportunity for the old, stagnant structure to be reinvigorated. The phase of communitas is a transitional, liminal phase that exists between one structure and another. It is a time of chaos, opening, and transgression, a time of new ideas, new birth, entering a new world and creating it. Communitas and liminality provide favorable conditions for the emergence of new conceptual archetypes, new root metaphors, and new paradigms.

People involved in the life of a structure are absorbed in playing their roles, while the repressive truth of the authority they have to obey forestalls speculation and free intellectual play, enforcing movement within binary oppositions. By contrast, the liminal state encourages creativity and uses masks only for the purpose of dialogue with an archetype (Turner speaks of "the liberating masks of liminal masquerade"). Communitas is related to spontaneity and freedom, whereas structure involves duty and law. In contrast to the culture of the mask, communitas is a culture of the face, a culture which promotes self-creation and authenticity, rejecting games, labeling, and structural segregation, and which expresses itself through simplicity, sincerity, and friendliness. Relationships within a communitas are not structural or institutional, but existential.

Liminality and the emergence of communitas (anti-structure) would be a desirable state for the old educational system (structure), a state that would prepare the ground for the appearance of new teachers (anti-teachers). However, the utopian hope for a *communitas* of teachers following an idealist vocation is only a first step toward "novelty."

In a neophyte's experience, the liminal state involves a duality: something is neither this nor that, it is both this and that; someone is no longer a boy and not yet a man. The liminal state describes an individual at a transitional stage, which Turner terms "a transitional being" or "a liminal persona." The rites of passage related to the liminal phase are important for the present argument as rites of identity, which emerges through dialogue with an archetype. The liminal phase involves a peculiar symbolism since a person in the process of metamorphosis is difficult to classify. Neither alive nor dead (zombie), neither male nor female (androgyne), this person has a dual nature. The archetypes defining a neophyte are therefore hybrid beings. Liminality is the realm of monsters. Monsters, as Turner argues, are invented in order to teach neophytes how to recognize different elements of their culture and understand them in ways adopted by this culture.[16] Monsters help develop critical thinking and distance toward one's own culture because they inspire reflection about those elements of a culture that were previously regarded as natural. As Turner argues, "One classical prototype of this revealed duality is the centaur Chiron, half wise old man, half stallion, who in his mountain cavern—epitomizing outsiderhood and liminality—instructed, even initiated, the adolescent sons of Achaean kings and princes, who would later occupy leading positions in the social and political structure of Hellas. Human wisdom and animal force meet in this liminal figure, who is both horse and man."[17]

I believe that the mythical figure of Chiron can serve as an alternative to the owl, a traditional symbol for education. The owl as symbol of wisdom has become a dead metaphor of education for two reasons: firstly, the modern school-as-factory has little relation to wisdom, and secondly, the owl represents solitude, passivity, boredom, secular teaching, rational knowledge, homeliness, sorrow, and melancholia, as well as darkness and the demon. In addition, the owl is believed to presage death. It is thus an appropriate symbol for the old kind of school, which stifles creativity and imposes the norm, but is inappropriate for the new kind. Chiron can become the new archetype that shapes the student's individual subjectivity through dialogue, as well as an archetype of the desired attitude of the academic teacher. The self can be defined through a set of symbols in the course of the neophyte disciple's dialogue with the archetype represented by the teacher. In the final stage of initiation (the doctoral defense as a sign of intellectual maturity), as the student puts on the mask of a monster, s/he acquires the monster's features and becomes the monster.

Chiron as an Archetype of Mentor/Sage

Chiron (Gk. Χείρων, Lat. *Cheiron*) was the divine centaur: half man, half horse, the son of Philyra (daughter of Okeanos) and Kronos, who, surprised by Rhea, changed into a stallion and fled, leaving his semen in the nymph's womb. He was the only centaur to have the status of a god and hence immortality, and the only one to have a family. Unlike the other centaurs, who were represented as wild, violent, cruel, and intemperate, Chiron was kind and restrained, and, most importantly, wise, knowledgeable, and just. He was a prophet as well as an accomplished healer, warrior, hunter (specializing in archery), practical moralist, and musician. Greek gods and heroes left their children in his care, asking him to raise and teach them. Chiron helped the children discover their destiny and develop their potential, which became their future strength. His disciples included Achilles (Chiron's foster son), Asclepius, Jason, Heracles, Aeneas, and Odysseus. It was Heracles, Chiron's beloved disciple and friend, who accidentally shot him in the knee with a poisoned arrow. Chiron prepared a medicine to heal the wound, but it could not serve as an antidote for the poison of the Hydra's blood. Because he was immortal, he suffered in his cave, doomed to eternal agony.[18] However, Heracles learned about Prometheus's curse, which was to be lifted when an immortal gave Prometheus his eternal life. Using Heracles as messenger, Chiron transferred his immortality to Prometheus and died. Zeus placed him in the sky as the constellation of Sagittarius. He can be seen there as a centaur archer preparing to shoot.[19]

As an archetype, Chiron combines animality (intuition, the unconscious) with humanity (reason, consciousness). He manifests the desired fusion of the human and animal worlds. He also symbolizes the dichotomies of barbarism/civilization, body/spirit, physical strength/intellectual power, passion/rationality, natural law/human law, violence/kindness, all of which refer to the fundamental opposition of nature and culture. Like any other hybrid, the centaur tests the liminality of the oppositions, demonstrating the liminality of opposites and intimating ways of transcending them. As neither man nor horse, he is the "liminal persona" Turner describes. Chiron transcends the limitations of his species and is thus a symbol of transgression: the process that is necessary for the development of a culture at the liminal stage. At the same time, Chiron symbolizes problems with self-realization because his difference alienates him from the other centaurs.

Chiron is also a monster. In the context of this argument, a monster, especially in hybrid form, is a positive phenomenon, a dialectical "other." The symbolic "return of monsters" resembles the Freudian "return of the repressed," revealing our fears, hopes, and desires, and shows the neurotic condition of contemporary culture, which addresses questions of its identity, tolerance, and openness to visitors from its margins. Monstrosity thus becomes a kind of cultural discourse where the hybrid refers us to the archetypal past, and points toward the future it heralds.[20]

Combining human wisdom with animal strength, the centaur is an ideal figure to inspire abstract thinking about the standards of normalcy and the boundaries between the opposite qualities he embodies. Chiron taught heroes how to attain a multilevel (hybrid) personality and how to transcend and exploit the limits of duality effectively. His way of teaching emphasized the integrated physical, spiritual, ethical, and intellectual development of his students, this integration being the only way for the hero to recognize his true nature, his destiny, and the meaning of his life. Chiron was a teacher, healer, sage, and prophet. He can be considered an archetype of the mentor, guru, and leader.[21]

Conclusion

Referring to the liminal phase in which the Polish society has found itself, I seek "new" archetypes and fresh metaphors which could help us change our way of thinking, create a new discourse, and speak differently when talking about the rebirth of the university and the desired model of academic teacher. I assume that there are academics interested in finding an alternative to the university-as-factory paradigm, that we are aware of how education is entangled in politics (power), and hence, that many of us sympathize with "rebellion": we do not want to be the kind of teachers the state tries to make us, as it applies a variety of instruments of control (low education subsidies, low teacher salaries, low social status of teachers, high enrollment limits imposed on many schools and colleges, very large classes, etc.). We do not want to become office workers in the service of the state: we want to be faithful to ourselves and our institutions. We want our subjectivities and those of our students to be constituted through active choice rather than passive acceptance, however convenient the latter would be. We are unwilling to think about the pedagogical body as a docile, controlled, objectified body. We prefer to think of it as a "close-knit/open body," a self-constituting, subjective body, a communitas. We realize that by shaping the views of the younger generation, the teacher is shaping the future.

Of course, I am aware of my idealism and the utopian character of this project. However, I believe that the debate about college education needs a different language, a different discourse, and different symbols. Perhaps it is worth thinking again about education not as the production of specialists but as an initiation rite which should bring about the metamorphosis of the individual. An examination could be imagined not as a test of knowledge and exercise of power but as a step toward finding one's own self. It depends on us whether the teacher will be a technician or a mentor and whether the student will be a small wheel in a machine or a neophyte. Every teacher has a choice, as implied by the very word *education*. The Latin *educare* means to feed and cultivate, but also to take care, to bring up. It is a choice between the university as factory and the university as "Chiron's cave." However, the anagram of the word *monster* is *mentors*, the synonym of pedagogues, caregivers, and wise advisors.

Many of us who were fortunate to work with Hayden White find ourselves in a "Chiron's cave" having long face-to-face discussions that begin with intellectual matters and end with existential problems. White does not fit the model of an ideal mentor such as Socrates, who always wins in his arguments with others, whom he purports or pretends to treat as equals but whom he always "reduces" to something less than fully mature and free. Never too tired to listen, never impatient with our questions, sensitive to various forms of oppression, White taught us how to say "no." However, Hayden White himself is critical of his pedagogical skills. He said: "I have had many failures as a teacher. I have not always succeeded in conforming to my own ideal of what a great teacher should be and do. I have alienated students and, inadvertently, to be sure, hurt some of them. It turns out that teaching is no more of a science than medicine, and even less of an art."[22] Thus, if we follow in Hayden White's footsteps, adopting his way of teaching and attitude toward students, we must realize that the possibility of becoming a mentor like him involves the danger of becoming a monster.

Notes

1. Jean-François Lyotard, *The Postmodern Condition: A Report on Knowledge*, trans. Geoff Bennington and Brian Massumi (Minneapolis: University of Minnesota Press, 1984), 46–53.

2. Cf. James Vernon, "Thoughts on the Present 'Crisis of History' in Britain," *Reviews in History*, November 1999, http://www.ihrinfo.ac.uk/ihr/Focus/Whatishistory/vernon.html. Similar questions are addressed by Gérard Noiriel in his *Sur la "crise" de l'histoire* (Paris: Belin, 1996).

3. Hans Ulrich Gumbrecht, *The Production of Presence: What Meaning Cannot Convey* (Stanford: Stanford University Press, 2004).

4. E-mail message from Hayden White to Hans Ulrich Gumbrecht, April 7, 2006. The incident of April 6 echoed far and wide, not only among Stanford intellectuals. One thread of the White-Gumbrecht debate, concerning Gumbrecht's book *In Praise of Athletic Beauty*, which White criticized, was published in the *Chronicle of Higher Education*. Gumbrecht's book describes sports as an aesthetic experience, while White objects to the commercialization of college sports. See "The Place and Value of College Sports: 2 Views": Hayden White, "They Have Betrayed Their Educational Purpose," and Hans Ulrich Gumbrecht, "They Have a Powerful Aesthetic Appeal," *Chronicle of Higher Education* 52, no. 42 (2006): B10.

5. Cf. bell hooks, *Teaching to Transgress: Education as the Practice of Freedom* (New York: Routledge, 1994).

6. Ewa Domańska's notes from Hayden White's course Rhetoric/Culture/Society, University of California at Berkeley, September 19, 1995.

7. Ewa Domańska, "An Interview with Arthur C. Danto," in *Encounters: Philosophy of History After Postmodernism*, ed. Ewa Domańska (Charlottesville: University Press of Virginia, 1998), 166.

8. Hayden White, preface to *The Uses of History: Essays in Intellectual and Social History*, ed. Hayden V. White, with a foreword by Alfred H. Kelly (Detroit: Wayne State University Press, 1968), 10.

9. Hayden White, interview by Eva Domańska, April 5, 2007. Authorized by Hayden White.

10. White, *The Uses of History*, 9.

11. White, interview.

12. Michel Foucault, *Discipline and Punish: The Birth of the Prison*, trans. Alan Sheridan (New York: Vintage Books, 1995), 27.

13. Ibid., 25–26.

14. Stephen J. Ball, "Management as Moral Technology: A Luddite Analysis," in *Foucault and Education: Disciplines and Knowledge*, ed. Stephen J. Ball (London: Routledge, 1990), 157. On the "corporatization" and "managerialism" of universities, see also: Ian Curry and Janice Newson, eds., *Universities and Globalization. Critical Perspectives* (Thousand Oaks, CA: Sage, 1998); and Nicholas C. Burbules and Carlos Alberto Torres, eds., *Globalization and Education. Critical Perspectives* (New York: Routledge, 2000).

15. Victor Turner, *Dramas, Fields, and Metaphors. Symbolic Action in Human Society* (Ithaca, NY: Cornell University Press, 1974), 274.

16. Victor Turner, "Betwixt and Between: The Liminal Period in *Rites de Passage*," in *The Forest of Symbols. Aspects of Ndembu Ritual* (Ithaca, NY: Cornell University Press, 1967), 105.

17. Ibid., 253.

18. This is why Chiron is an archetype of the wounded healer who wants to heal his wounds and finds a remedy that cannot help him but will help others.

19. On centaurs and Chiron, see Hesiod's *Theogony* and Homer's *The Iliad* (6.219; 11.832; 26.143; 19.391). See also Page duBois, *Centaurs and Amazons* (Ann Arbor: University of Michigan Press, 1987); Robert Graves, *The Greek Myths: Complete Edition* (London: Penguin, 1993); Judith J. Kolleman, "The Centaur," in *Mythical and Fabulous Creatures*, ed. Malcolm South (New York: Greenwood, 1987); Elizabeth Atwood Lawrence, "The Centaur: Its History and Meaning in Human Culture," *Journal of Popular Culture* 27, no. 4 (1994).

20. I refer to Derrida's observation that the future can only herald and present itself as monstrosity. In an interview, Derrida said that the monster (hybrid) is a figure of the future. To be open to the future is to be open to the arrival of monsters, to show hospitality to everyone and everything that is different, strange, and unfamiliar. It is an attempt to domesticate this otherness and make it part of the household, an acceptance of different customs which will mingle with our own and create a new quality. See Jacques Derrida, *Of Grammatology*, trans. Gayatri Chakravorty Spivak (Baltimore: Johns Hopkins University Press, 1976), 5; and Jacques Derrida and Elisabeth Weber, "Passages—From Traumatism to Promise," in *Points-Interviews 1974–1994*, ed. Elisabeth Weber, trans. Peggy Kamuf et al. (Stanford: Stanford University Press, 1995), 386–87.

21. John Updike's novel *The Centaur* (1963), winner of the National Book Award, describes the relationship between a father, a high school teacher of natural science, and a son, who also becomes a teacher. For his son, the father becomes a Chiron, the symbol of caregiver, teacher, and mentor. The son, Professor George W. Caldwell, becomes such a symbol for the narrator. The book begins with Caldwell being shot in the leg during class by one of his students, just as the mythical centaur was.

22. White, interview.

REFERENCE MATTER

Bibliography of Hayden White

WORKS IN ENGLISH

Compiled by Ewa Domańska

Books

From History to Sociology: The Transition in German Historical Thinking by Carlo Antoni, with a foreword by Benedetto Croce, translated from the Italian by Hayden White. Detroit: Wayne State University Press, 1959. Includes translator's preface (pp. ix–xii) and introduction (pp. xv–xxviii).

Reviewed in
Mazlish, Bruce. *History and Theory* 1, no. 2 (1961): pp. 219–27.

The Emergence of Liberal Humanism: An Intellectual History of Western Europe, vol. 1, *From the Italian Renaissance to the French Revolution*, by Willson Coates, Hayden V. White, and J. Salwyn Schapiro. New York: McGraw-Hill, 1966.

The Uses of History: Essays in Intellectual and Social History, edited by Hayden V. White. Detroit: Wayne State University Press, 1968. Includes preface (pp. 9–13) and "Romanticism, Historicism, and Realism: Toward a Period Concept for Early 19th Century Intellectual History" (pp. 45–58).

Reviewed in
Barnes, Sherman B. *The Historian: A Journal of History* 31, no. 1 (November 1968): p. 90.
Saunders, Richard M. *The American Historical Review* 74, no. 3 (February 1969): p. 939.
Wilkins, Burleigh T. *The Journal of Southern History* 35, no. 3 (August 1969): pp. 397–98.
Burnet, J. F. *English Historical Review* 85, no. 1 (January 1970): pp. 222–23.
HK. "Historicism Again and Again." *Clio* 1, no. 1 (October 1971): pp. 73–74.

Giambattista Vico: An International Symposium, edited by Giorgio Tagliacozzo and Hayden V. White. Baltimore: Johns Hopkins University Press, 1969. Includes "What Is Living and What Is Dead in Croce's Criticism of Vico" (pp. 379–89).

The Ordeal of Liberal Humanism: An Intellectual History of Western Europe, vol. 2,

Since the French Revolution, by Willson Coates and Hayden V. White. New York: McGraw-Hill, 1970.

The Greco-Roman Tradition, by Hayden V. White. New York: Harper & Row, 1973.

Metahistory: The Historical Imagination in Nineteenth-Century Europe, by Hayden V. White. Baltimore: Johns Hopkins University Press, 1973.

Reviewed in

Deininger, Whitaker I. *History: Reviews of New Books* 2, no. 5 (March 1974).

Clive, John. *Journal of Modern History* 47, no. 3 (September 1975): pp. 542–43.

Ermarth, Michael. *American Historical Review* 80, no. 4 (October 1975): pp. 962–63.

Nelson, John S. *History and Theory* 14, no. 1 (1975): pp. 74–91.

Carroll, Robert C. *Nineteenth-Century French Studies* 4, no. 4 (Summer 1976): pp. 548–50.

Kuzminski, Adrian. "A New Science?" *Comparative Studies in Society and History* 18, no. 1 (January 1976): pp. 129–43.

Jameson, Fredric. "Figural Relativism, or the Poetics of Historiography." *Diacritics* 6, no. 1 (Spring 1976): pp. 2–9.

Iggers, Georg G. "Style in History: History as an Art and as Science." *Reviews in European History* 2, no. 2 (June 1976): pp. 171–81.

Carroll, David. "On Tropology: The Forms of History." *Diacritics* 6, no. 3 (Fall 1976): pp. 58–64.

Rubino, Carl A. *Modern Language Notes* 91, no. 5 (October 1976): pp. 1131–35.

Ezergailis, Andrew. *Clio* 5, no. 2 (Winter 1976): pp. 235–45.

Bérard, Robert N. "Approaches to Nineteenth-Century Historiography." *New Scholar* 5, no. 2 (1978): pp. 369–75.

Pierson, Stanley. *Comparative Literature* 30, no. 2 (Spring 1978): pp. 178–81.

Oexle, Otto Gerhard. "Sehnsucht nach Klio. Hayden Whites *Metahistory*— und wie man der darüber hinwegkommt." *Rechtshistorisches Journal* 11 (1992): pp. 1–18.

Walther, Gerrit. "Fernes Kampfgetümmel. Zur angeblichen Aktualität von Hayden White's *Metahistory*." *Rechtshistorisches Journal* 11 (1992): pp. 19–40.

Tropics of Discourse: Essays in Cultural Criticism, by Hayden V. White. Baltimore: Johns Hopkins University Press, 1978.

Reviewed in

Gates, Barbara. *Clio* 6, no. 3 (Spring 1977): pp. 351–54.

LaCapra, Dominick. *Modern Language Notes* 93, no. 5 (December 1978): pp. 1037–43.

King, Richard. *Virginia Quarterly Review* 55, no. 3 (Summer 1979): pp. 568–72.

Carroll, Robert C. *Nineteenth-Century French Studies* 8, no. 1/2 (Fall/Winter 1979/1980): pp. 162–64.

Gunn, Giles. *American Literature* 52, no. 4 (January 1981): pp. 649–53.

Johnston, William M. *New Vico Studies* 1 (1983): pp. 86–90.

Durant, Alan. *Prose Studies* 9, no. 3 (December 1986): pp. 112–13.

Representing Kenneth Burke, edited by Margaret Brose and Hayden V. White. Baltimore: Johns Hopkins University Press, 1982. Includes preface by White (pp. vii–ix).

The Content of the Form: Narrative Discourse and Historical Representation, by Hayden V. White. Baltimore: Johns Hopkins University Press, 1987.

Reviewed in

McCullagh, Behan. *Poetics Today* 8, no. 2 (1987): pp. 469–70.

Burke, Peter. "Rethinking the Historian's Craft." *Times Literary Supplement*, 6–12 (November 1987): p. 1231.

Raval, Suresh. "Recent Books on Narrative Theory: An Essay-Review." *Modern Fiction Studies* 33, no. 3 (Autumn 1987): pp. 559–70.

Flores, Ralph. *Modern Language Notes* 102 (December 1987): pp. 1191–96.

Scott, Robert Lee. *Quarterly Journal of Speech* 74, no. 1 (February 1988): pp. 114–16.

Wellek, René. *Partisan Review* 55, no. 2 (Spring 1988): pp. 334–37.

Tambling, Jeremy. *Modern Language Quarterly* 49, no. 2 (June 1988): pp. 192–94.

Gross, David S. *World Literature Today* 62, no. 3 (Summer 1988): p. 516.

Pagden, Anthony. "Rethinking the Linguistic Turn: Current Anxieties in Intellectual History." *Journal of the History of Ideas* 49, no. 3 (July/September 1988): pp. 519–29.

LaCapra, Dominick. *American Historical Review* 93, no. 4 (October 1988): pp. 1007–8.

Dray, William. *History and Theory* 27, no. 3 (1988): pp. 282–87.

Carrier, David. *British Journal of Aesthetics*, vol. 28, no. 1 (1988): pp. 84–85.

Mellard, James M. *Style* 22 (Winter 1988): pp. 657–61.

Gunn, Giles. "The Kingdoms of Theory and the New Historicism in America." *Yale Review* 77, no. 2 (1988): pp. 207–36.

Woolf, Daniel R. *Queen's Quarterly* 95, no. 4 (Winter 1988): pp. 908–10.

McCallum, Pamela. *University of Toronto Quarterly* 58 (Summer 1989): pp. 538–39.

Engebretsen, Terry. *Southern Humanities Review* 23, no. 4 (Fall 1989): pp. 377–80.

Brook, Thomas. *Novel: A Forum on Fiction* 22, no. 2 (Winter 1989): pp. 247–49.

Toews, John E. *History of the Human Sciences* 4, no. 1 (February 1991): pp. 154–59.

Rigney, Ann. "Narrativity and Historical Representation." *Poetics Today* 12, no. 3 (Fall 1991): pp. 591–605.

Figural Realism. Studies in the Mimesis Effect. Baltimore: Johns Hopkins University Press, 1999.

Reviewed in

Tempelhoff, Johann W. N. "Exploring the Semblance of Realism in Historical Thought." *H-Net Reviews in the Humanities and Social Sciences*, August 1999. http://www.h-net.org/reviews/showrev.php?id=3325.

Carrol, Noel. "Tropology and Narration." *History and Theory* 39, no. 3 (2000): 396–404.

Golden, Cameron. *Symploke* 8, no. 1–2 (2000): 227–28.

Carrard, Philippe. *Clio* 29, no. 2 (Winter 2000): 229–32.

Jenkins, Keith. *Literature & History* 9, no. 1 (Spring 2000): 114–15.

Megill, Allan. *Journal of Modern History* 72, no. 3 (Sept. 2000): 777–78.

Folks, Jeffrey J. *College Literature* 27, no. 3 (Fall 2000): 171–73.

Plass, Ulrich. *Comparative Literature Studies* 38, no. 2 (2001): 173–79.

Tambling, J. *Modern Language Review* 96, no. 2 (April 2001): 452–54.

Kisantal, Tamás. *Helikon* 3 (2002): 369–70.

Barbour, Charles. "White's Mythology." *Canadian Literature* 173 (Summer 2002): 187–89.

Erickson, Jon. *Modern Language Quarterly* 63, no. 3 (September 2002): 405–9.

ARTICLES

"Collingwood and Toynbee: Transitions in English Historical Thought." *English Miscellany* 8 (1957): pp. 147–78.

"Religion, Culture, and Western Civilization in Christopher Dawson's Idea of History." *English Miscellany* 9 (1958): pp. 247–87.

"Pontius of Cluny, the *Curia Romana* and the End of Gregorianism in Rome." *Church History* 27, no. 3 (September 1958): pp. 195–219.

"The Gregorian Ideal and Saint Bernard of Clairvaux." *Journal of the History of Ideas* 21, no. 3 (July–September 1960): pp. 321–48.

"The Abiding Relevance of Croce's Idea of History." *Journal of Modern History* 35, no. 2 (June 1963): pp. 109–24.

"The Burden of History." *History and Theory* 5, no. 2 (1966): pp. 111–34.

"Hegel: Historicism as Tragic Realism." *Colloquium* 5, no. 2 (1966): pp. 10–19.

"The Task of Intellectual History." *The Monist* 53, no. 4 (October 1969): pp. 606–30.

"Literary History: The Point of It All." *New Literary History* 2, no. 1 (Autumn 1970): pp. 173–85.

"Croce and Becker: A Note on the Evidence of Influence." *History and Theory* 10, no. 2 (1971): pp. 222–27.

"The Culture of Criticism." In *Liberations. New Essays on the Humanities Revolution*, edited by Ihab Hassan. Middletown, CT: Wesleyan University Press, 1971, pp. 55–69.

Hayden White, Allen W. Wood, Theodore M. Brown, David I. Grossvogel, and Robert Matthews. "Interview with Ernst Gombrich." *Diacritics* 1, no. 2 (Winter 1971): pp. 47–51.

"The Structure of Historical Narrative." *Clio* 1, no. 3 (1972): pp. 5–20.

"The Irrational and the Problem of Historical Knowledge." In *Studies in Eighteenth-Century Culture*, vol. 2, *Irrationalism in the Eighteenth Century*, edited by Harold E. Pagliaro. Cleveland: Press of Case Western Reserve University, 1972, pp. 303–21.

"The Forms of Wildness: Archeology of an Idea." In *The Wild Man Within: An Image in Western Thought from the Renaissance to Romanticism*, edited by Edward Dudley and Maximilian E. Novak. Pittsburgh: University of Pittsburgh Press, 1972, pp. 3–38.

"What Is a Historical System?" In *Biology, History and Natural Philosophy*, edited by Allen D. Breck and Wolfgang Yourgrau. New York: Plenum Press, 1972, pp. 233–42.

"Interpretation in History." *New Literary History* 4, no. 2 (Winter 1972): pp. 281–314.

"The Structure of Historical Narrative." *Clio* 1, no. 3 (June 1972): pp. 5–20.

"Foucault Decoded: Notes from Underground." *History and Theory* 12, no. 1 (1973): pp. 23–54.

"The Politics of Contemporary Philosophy of History." *Clio* 3, no. 1 (October 1973): pp. 35–54.

"The Historical Text as Literary Artifact." *Clio* 3, no. 3 (June 1974): pp. 277–303.

"Structuralism and Popular Culture." *Journal of Popular Culture* 7, no. 4 (Spring 1974): pp. 759–75.

"The Problem of Change in Literary History." *New Literary History* 7, no. 1 (Autumn 1975): pp. 97–111.

"Historicism, History, and the Figurative Imagination." In "Essays on Historicism," special issue, *History and Theory* 14, no. 4 (1975): pp. 48–67.

"The Noble Savage Theme as Fetish." In *First Images of America: The Impact of the New World and the Old*, edited by Fredi Chiappelli. Berkeley: University of California Press, 1976, pp. 121–35.

"The Tropics of History: The Deep Structure of the New Science." In *Giambat-*

tista Vico's Science of Humanity, edited by Giorgio Tagliacozzo and Donald Philip Verene. Baltimore: Johns Hopkins University Press, 1976, pp. 65–85.

Introduction to *Augustin Thierry and Liberal Historiography*, by Lionel Gossman. Middletown, CT: Wesleyan University Press, 1976.

"The Absurdist Moment in Contemporary Literary Theory." *Contemporary Literature* 17, no. 3 (Summer 1976): pp. 378–403. Also published in *Directions for Criticism: Structuralism and Its Alternatives*, edited by Murray Krieger and L. S. Dembo. Madison: University of Wisconsin Press, 1977.

"The Fictions of Factual Representation." In *The Literature of Fact*, edited by Angus Fletcher. New York: Columbia University Press, 1976, pp. 21–44.

"Rhetoric and History." In *Theories of History*. Papers read at the Clark Library Seminar, March 6, 1976, by Hayden White and Frank E. Manuel. Los Angeles: William Andrews Clark Memorial Library, 1978, pp. 7–25.

"Michel Foucault." In *Structuralism and Since: From Lévi-Strauss to Derrida*, edited by John Sturrock. Oxford: Oxford University Press, 1979, pp. 81–115.

"The Problem of Style in Realistic Representation: Marx and Flaubert." In *The Concept of Style*, edited by Berel Lang. Philadelphia: University of Pennsylvania Press, 1979, pp. 213–29.

"The Discourse of History." *Humanities in Society* 2, no. 1 (Winter 1979): pp. 1–15. Discussion in the same volume: John Carlos Rowe, "Structuralism or Post-Structuralism: The Problem of 'The Discourse of History,'" pp. 17–23; Jan D. Dekema, "Hermeneutics and the Discourse of History: A Response to Hayden White," pp. 25–30.

"Literature and Social Action: Reflections on the Reflection Theory of Literary Art." *New Literary History* 11, no. 2 (Winter 1980): pp. 363–80.

"The Value of Narrativity in the Representation of Reality." *Critical Inquiry* 7, no. 1 (1980): pp. 5–27. Discussion: Louis O. Mink, "Everyman His or Her Own Annalist"; Marilyn Robinson Waldman, "'The Otherwise Unnoteworthy Year 711': A Reply to Hayden White"; Hayden White's reply: "The Narrativization of Real Events." In *Critical Inquiry* 7, no. 4 (Summer 1981). Cf. also: Peter de Bolla, "Disfiguring History." *Diacritics* 16, no. 4 (Winter 1986): pp. 49–58.

"Conventional Conflicts." *New Literary History* 13, no. 1 (Autumn 1981): pp. 145–60.

"The Politics of Historical Interpretation: Discipline and De-Sublimation." *Critical Inquiry* 9, no. 1 (September 1982): pp. 113–38.

"Getting Out of History." *Diacritics* 12, no. 3 (Fall 1982): pp. 2–13.

"Method and Ideology in Intellectual History: The Case of Henry Adams." In *Modern European Intellectual History. Reappraisals and New Perspectives*, edited by Dominick LaCapra and Steven L. Kaplan. Ithaca, NY: Cornell University Press, 1982, pp. 280–310.

"The Limits of Relativism in the Arts." In *Relativism in the Arts*, edited by Betty Jean Craige. Athens: University of Georgia Press, 1983, pp. 45–74.

"Vico and the Radical Wing of Structuralist/Poststructuralism Thought Today." *New Vico Studies* 1 (1983): pp. 63–68.

"The Question of Narrative in Contemporary Historical Theory." *History and Theory* 23, no. 1 (1984): pp. 1–33.

"The Italian Difference and the Politics of Culture." *Graduate Faculty Philosophical Journal* 10, no. 1 (Spring 1984): pp. 117–22.

"The Interpretation of Texts." *Berkshire Review* 19 (1984): pp. 7–23.

"The Rule of Narrativity: Symbolic Discourse and the Experience of Time in Ricoeur's Thought." *University of Ottawa Quarterly* 55, no. 4 (1985): pp. 287–99.

"Historical Pluralism." *Critical Inquiry* 12, no. 3 (Spring 1986): pp. 480–93.

"The XIXth Century as Chronotype." *Nineteenth-Century Context* 11, no. 2 (1987): pp. 119–30.

"Historiography and Historiophoty." *American Historical Review* 95, no. 5 (December 1988): pp. 1193–99.

"The Rhetoric of Interpretation." *Poetics Today* 9, no. 2 (1988): pp. 253–74.

"New Historicism: A Comment." In *The New Historicism*, edited by H. Aram Vesser. New York: Routledge, 1989, pp. 293–302.

"Romantic Historiography." In *A New History of French Literature*, edited by Denis Hollier. Cambridge, MA: Harvard University Press, 1989, pp. 1823–27.

"Introduction" to "History and Memory in European Romanticism," special issue, *Stanford Literature Review* 6, no. 1 (Spring 1989): pp. 5–14.

"'Figuring the Nature of the Times Deceased': Literary Theory and Historical Writing." In *The Future of Literary Theory*, edited by Ralph Cohen. New York: Routledge, 1989, pp. 19–43.

Introduction to *Lotte in Weimar: The Beloved Returns*, by Thomas Mann, translated by H. T. Lowe-Porter. Berkeley: University of California Press, 1990, pp. v–xi.

"Ideology and Counterideology in the Anatomy." In *Visionary Poetics: Essays on Northrop Frye's Criticism*, edited by Robert D. Denham and Thomas Willard. New York: Peter Lang, 1991, 101–11.

"Form, Reference, and Ideology in Musical Discourse." In *Music and Text: Critical Inquiries*, edited by Steven Paul Scher. Cambridge: Cambridge University Press, 1991, pp. 288–319.

"Historical Emplotment and the Problem of Truth." In *Probing the Limits of Representation: Nazism and the "Final Solution,"* edited by Saul Friedlander. Cambridge, MA: Harvard University Press, 1992, pp. 37–53. Discussion in the same volume: Carlo Ginzburg, "Just One Witness," and Amos Funkenstein, "History, Counterhistory, Narrative."

"Writing in the Middle Voice." *Stanford Literature Review* 9, no. 2 (Fall 1992): pp. 179–87.

"Historiography as Narration." In *Telling Facts: History and Narration in Psycho-analysis*, edited by Joseph H. Smith and Humphrey Morris. Baltimore: Johns Hopkins University Press, 1992, pp. 284–99. Also published in *Psychiatry and the Humanities* 13 (1992): 284–300.

"Frye's Place in Contemporary Cultural Studies." In *The Legacy of Northrop Frye*, edited by Alvin Lee and Robert Denham. Toronto: University of Toronto Press, 1994, pp. 28–39.

"Foreword: Rancière's Revisionism." In *The Names of History: On the Poetics of Knowledge*, by Jacques Rancière. Minneapolis, London: University of Minnesota Press, 1994, pp. vii–xix.

"Age-Old Problem." *Times Higher Education Supplement*, no. 1151, November 25, 1995, p. 17.

"A Rejoinder. A Response to Professor Chartier's Four Questions." *Storia della storiografia* 27 (1995): pp. 63–70. Cf. Roger Chartier, "Quatre Questions à Hayden White." *Storia della storiografia* 24 (1993): pp. 133–42.

"Response to Arthur Marwick." *Journal of Contemporary History* 30, no. 2 (April 1995): pp. 233–46. Cf.: Arthur Marwick, "Two Approaches to Historical Study: The Metaphysical (Including 'Postmodernism') and the Historical." *Journal of Contemporary History* 30, no. 1 (January 1995): pp. 5–35; further discussion: Christopher Lloyd, "For Realism and Against the Inadequacies of Common Sense: A Response to Arthur Marwick"; Beverley Southgate, "History and Metahistory: Marwick Versus White"; Wulf Kansteiner, "Searching for an Audience: The Historical Profession in the Media Age—A Comment on Arthur Marwick and Hayden White"; Geoffrey Roberts, "Narrative History as a Way of Life." *Journal of Contemporary History* 31, no. 1 (January 1996).

"Bodies and Their Plots." In *Choreographing History*, edited by Susan Leigh Foster. Bloomington: Indiana University Press, 1995, pp. 229–34.

"The Modernist Event." In *The Persistence of History: Cinema, Television, and the Modern Event*, edited by Vivian Sobchack. New York: Routledge, 1996, pp. 17–38.

"Commentary" to the thematic issue of *History of the Human Sciences* ("Identity, Memory and History") 9, no. 4 (November 1996): pp. 123–38.

"Auerbach's Literary History: Figural Causation and Modernist Historicism." In *Literary History and the Challenge of Philology*, edited by Seth Lerer. Stanford: Stanford University Press, 1996, pp. 123–43.

"Storytelling: Historical and Ideological." In *Centuries' Ends, Narrative Means*, edited by Robert Newman. Stanford: Stanford University Press, 1996, pp. 58–78.

"Literature Against Fiction." *La Torre* (Universidad de Puerto Rico) 2, no. 4–5 (1997): pp. 194–207.

"The Suppression of Rhetoric in the Nineteenth Century." In *The Rhetoric Canon*, edited by Brenda Deen Schildgen. Detroit: Wayne State University Press, 1997, pp. 21–32.

"The Problem with Modern Patriotism." *2B (Two Be)*, no. 13 (1998): pp. 119–30.

"The End of Narrative Historiography." In *Swiat historii [The World of History]. Essays Presented to Jerzy Topolski on his 70th birthday*, edited by Wojciech Wrzosek. Poznan, Poland: IH UAM, 1998, pp. 393–409.

Afterword to *Beyond the Cultural Turn: New Directions in the Study of Society and Culture*, edited by Victoria E. Bonnell and Lynn Hunt. Berkeley: University of California Press, 1999, pp. 315–24.

"Postmodernism, Textualism, and History." In *Literaturforschung Heute*, edited by Eckart Goebel and Wolfgang Klein. Berlin: Akademie Verlag, 1999, pp. 173–84.

"Postmodernism and Textual Anxieties." In *The Postmodern Challenge: Perspectives East and West*, edited by Nina Witoszek and Bo Stråth. London: Sage Publications, 1999, pp. 27–45.

"The Discourse of Europe and the Search for European Identity." In *Europe and the Other, Europe as the Other*, edited by Bo Stråth. Brussels: P.I.E./Peter Lang, 2000, pp. 67–86.

"Catastrophe, Communal Memory, and Mythic Discourse: The Uses of Myth in the Reconstruction of Society." In *Myth and Memory in the Construction of Community: Historical Patterns in Europe and Beyond*, edited by Bo Stråth. Brussels: P.I.E./Peter Lang, 2000, pp. 49–74.

"An Old Question Raised Again: Is Historiography Art or Science? (Response to Iggers)." *Rethinking History* 4, no. 3 (December 2000): pp. 391–406. See also Georg G. Iggers, "Historiography Between Scholarship and Poetry: Reflections on Hayden White's Approach to Historiography." *Rethinking History* 4, no. 3 (December 2000): pp. 373–90.

"Posthumanism and the Liberation of Humankind." *Design Book Review* 41/42 (Winter/Spring 2000): pp. 10–13.

"Figura and Historical Subalternation." In *Kontaktzone Amerika. Literarische Verkehrsformen kultureller Übersetzung*, edited by Utz Riese and Doris Dziwas. Heidelberg: Universitatsverlag, 2000.

Foreword to *The Practice of Conceptual History*, by Reinhart Koselleck, translated by Todd Presner and Kerstin Behnke. Stanford: Stanford University Press, 2002, pp. ix–xiv.

"Reply to Professor Ankersmit." *Groniek*, no. 161 (2003): pp. 465–66.

"Commentary: Good of Their Kind." *New Literary History* 34, no. 2 (2003): pp. 367–376.

"Anomalies of Genre: The Utility of Theory and History for the Study of Literary Genres." *New Literary History* 34, no. 3 (2004): pp. 597–615.

"The Metaphysics of Western Historiography." *Taiwan Journal of East Asian Studies* 1, no. 1 (2004): pp. 1–16. See also: Hayden White, "The Metaphysics of (Western) Historiography," *Call*, no. 2 (2004): pp. 148–55.

"Figural Realism in Witness Literature." *Parallax* 10, no. 1 (January–March 2004): pp. 113–24.

"Historical Fiction, Fictional History, and Historical Reality." *Rethinking History* 9, no. 2–3 (2005): pp. 147–57.

"The Public Relevance of Historical Studies: A Reply to Dirk Moses." *History and Theory* 44 (October 2005): pp. 333–38. In the same volume, compare A. Dirk Moses, "Hayden White, Traumatic Nationalism, and the Public Role of History," pp. 311–32, as well as Moses's "The Public Relevance of Historical Studies: A Rejoinder to Hayden White," pp. 339–47.

"Historical Discourse and Literary Writing." In *Tropes for the Past: Hayden White and the History/Literature Debate*, edited by Kuisma Korhonen. 96 Internationale Forschungen zur Allgemeinen und Vergleichenden Literaturwissenschaft. Amsterdam: Rodopi, 2006, pp. 25–33.

"They Have Betrayed Their Educational Purpose." *Chronicle of Higher Education* 52, no. 42 (June 23, 2006): p. B10.

Foreword to *Criticism in the Wilderness: The Study of Literature Today*, by Geoffrey Hartman, 2nd edition. New Haven: Yale University Press, 2007, pp. xi–xviii.

"Against Historical Realism. A Reading of *War and Peace*." *New Left Review*, no. 46 (July–August 2007): 89–110.

"Response: The Dark Side of Art History." *Art Bulletin* 89, no. 1 (March 2007): 21–26.

Afterword to *Manifestos for History*, edited by Keith Jenkins, Sue Morgan, and Alun Munslow. New York: Routledge, 2007, pp. 220–31.

"The Future of Utopia in History." *Historein. A Review of the Past and Other Stories* 7 (2007): 5–19.

ENCYCLOPEDIC ENTRIES

"Gabineau, Comte Joseph Arthur de," "Feuerbach, Ludwig Andreas," "Klages, Ludwig," "Strauss, David Friedrich," and "Windelband, Wilhelm." In *The Encyclopedia of Philosophy*, edited by Paul Edwards. New York: Macmillan, 1967, pp. 25–26, 190–92, 320–22, 342–43, 343–44.

"Vico, Giovanni Battista." In *International Encyclopedia of the Social Sciences*, edited by David L. Sills, vol. 16. New York: The Macmillan Company and The Free Press, 1968, pp. 313–16.

REVIEWS BY HAYDEN WHITE

"Ibn Khaldun World Philosophy of History." Review of *The Muquaddimah*, by Ibn Khaldun, translated by Franz Rosenthal. *Comparative Studies Society and History* 2, no. 1 (October 1959): pp. 110–25.

Review of *The Later Philosophy of R. G. Collingwood*, by Alan Donagan. *History and Theory* 4, no. 2 (1965): pp. 244–52.

Review of *Idealism, Politics, and History: Sources of Hegelian Thought*, by George Armstrong Kelly. *History and Theory* 9, no. 3 (1970): pp. 343–63.

"The Historians at the Bridge of Sighs." Review of *The Historian Between the Ethnologist and the Futurologist*, edited by Jerome Dumoulin and Dominique Moisi. *Reviews in European History* 1, no. 4 (March 1975): pp. 437–45.

Review of *Vico: A Study of the "New Science,"* by Leon Pompa. *History and Theory* 15, no. 2 (1976): pp. 186–202.

"Criticism as Cultural Politics." Review of *Beginnings: Intention and Method*, by Edward Said. *Diacritics* (Fall 1976): pp. 8–13.

"The Archeology of Sex." Review of *Histoire de la sexualité*, by Michel Foucault. *Times Literary Supplement*, May 6, 1977, p. 565.

Review of *Surveiller et punir*, by Michel Foucault. *American Historical Review* 82, no. 3 (June 1977): pp. 605–6.

"Ethnological 'Lie' and Mythical 'Truth.'" Review of *Violence and the Sacred*, by René Girard. *Diacritics* (March 1978): pp. 2–9.

"Power and the Word." Review of *Discipline and Punish* and *Language, Counter-memory, Practice*, by Michel Foucault. *Canto* 2, no. 1 (Spring 1978): pp. 164–72.

Review of *Historik*, by Johann Gustav Droysen. *History and Theory* 19, no. 1 (1980): 73–94.

Review of *The Origin of Table Manners*, by Claude Lévi-Strauss. *Annales of Science* 37, no. 2 (March 1980): pp. 249–51.

"Fiery Numbers and Strange Productions: A Cento of Thoughts on Ihab Hassan." Review of *The Right Promethean Fire*, by Ihab Hassan. *Diacritics* 10, no. 4 (Winter 1980): pp. 50–59.

"A Critical Garden." Review of *Criticism in the Wilderness: The Study of Literature Today*, by Geoffrey Hartman. *Partisan Review* 48, no. 4 (1981): 646–49.

Review of *The Origin of Formalism in Social Science*, by Jeffrey T. Bergner. *American Historical Review* 87, no. 3 (June 1982): pp. 746–47.

"Painting and Beholder." Review of *Absorption and Theatricality: Painting and Beholders in the Age of Diderot*, by Michael Fried. *The Eighteenth Century* 24, no. 2 (Spring 1983): pp. 173–77.

"The Worm in the Apple." Review of *From Locke to Saussure*, by Hans Aarsleff. *Partisan Review* 50, no. 4 (1983): pp. 618–22.

Review of *Narrative Logic*, by F. R. Ankersmit. *American Historical Review* 89 (October 1984): pp. 1037–38.

"He Merged Myth and History." Review of *Victor Hugo and the Visionary Novel*, by Victor H. Brombert. *New York Times Book Review*, December 23, 1984, s. 7.

Review of *The Paradox of History*, by Nicola Chiaromonte. *New York Times Book Review*, September 22, 1985, s. 7.

"Between Science and Symbol." Review of *Writing History*, by Paul Veyne; *Justifying Historical Description*, by Behan McCullagh; *Historical Reason*, by José Ortega y Gasset; and *History and Criticism* by Dominick LaCapra. *Times Literary Supplement*, January 31, 1986, pp. 109–10.

Review of *Future Past*, by Reinhart Koselleck. *American Historical Review* 92 (December 1987): pp. 1175–76.

Review of *The Growth of Minds and Cultures*, by Willem H. Vanderburg. *Isis* 79 (September 1988): pp. 493–94.

Review of *After Philosophy: End or Transformation?* edited by Kenneth Baynes, James Bohman, and Thomas McCarthy. *New Vico Studies* 6 (1988): pp. 167–68.

Review of *Anthropology Through the Looking-Glass*, by Michael Herzfeld. *New Vico Studies* 7 (1989): pp. 126–29.

Review of *Vico in the Tradition of Rhetoric*, by Michael Mooney. *Eighteenth-Century Studies* 22 (Winter 1988/89): pp. 219–22.

"Vattimo's 'Weak' Thought and Vico's 'New' Science." Review of *The End of Modernity: Nihilism and Hermeneutics in Postmodern Culture*, by Gianni Vattimo. *New Vico Studies* 9 (1991): pp. 61–68.

Review of *The Production of Space*, by Henri Lefebvre. *Design Book Review* 29/30 (Summer/Fall 1993): pp. 90–93.

Review of *G. B. Vico: The Making of an Anti-Modern*, by Mark Lilla. *Political Theory* 22 (August 1994): pp. 509–11.

Review of *The Arbor Scientiae Reconceived and the History of Vico's Resurrection*, by Giorgio Tagliacozzo. *New Vico Studies* 12 (1994): pp. 114–21.

Review of *The New History*, by Alun Munslow. *Rethinking History* 9, no. 1 (March 2005): pp. 129–37.

"Guilty of History? The *Longue Durée* of Paul Ricoeur." Review of *History, Memory, Forgetting*, by Paul Ricoeur. *History and Theory* 46, no. 2 (May 2007): pp. 233–51.

ON HAYDEN WHITE

LaCapra, Dominick. "A Poetics of Historiography: Hayden White's *Tropics of Discourse*." In *Rethinking Intellectual History*. Ithaca, NY: Cornell University Press, 1983, pp. 72–83. Originally published in *Modern Language Notes* 93, no. 5 (December 1978).

"Metahistory: Six Critiques." *History and Theory* 19, no. 4 (1980).

Momigliano, Arnaldo. "The Rhetoric of History and the History of Rhetoric: On Hayden White's Tropes." *Comparative Criticism* 3 (1981): pp. 259–68.

Goodman, David. ". . . and Then the Academics." *Melbourne Historical Journal* 13 (1981): pp. 29–35.

Konstan, David. "The Function of Narrative in Hayden White's Metahistory." *Clio* 11, no. 1 (1981): pp. 65–78.

Grossman, Marshall. "Hayden White and Literary Criticism: The Tropology of Discourse." *Papers on Language and Literature* 17, no. 4 (Fall 1981): pp. 424–45.

Leitch, Vincent B. "The (Inter)Textualization of Context." Chapter 6 in *Deconstructive Criticism: An Advanced Introduction*. New York: Columbia University Press, 1983.

Gearhart, Suzanne. "(Voltaire) The Question of Genre: White, Genette, and the Limits of Formalism." In *The Open Boundary of History and Fiction: A Critical Approach to the French Enlightenment*. Princeton, NJ: Princeton University Press, 1984, pp. 57–94.

Ankersmit, F. R. "Hayden White's Appeal to the Historians." *History and Theory* 37, no. 2 (1988): pp. 182–93.

Roth, Michael S. "Cultural Criticism and Political Theory: Hayden White's Rhetorics of History." *Political Theory* 16, no. 4 (Nov. 1988): pp. 636–46.

Kramer, Lloyd. "Literature, Criticism, and Historical Imagination: The Literary Challenge of Hayden White and Dominick LaCapra." In *The New Cultural History*, edited by Lynn Hunt. Berkeley: University of California Press, 1989, pp. 97–128.

Ostrowski, Donald. "A Metahistorical Analysis: Hayden White and Four Narratives of 'Russian' History." *Clio* 19, no. 3 (1990): pp. 215–36.

Bahners, Patrick. "Die Ordnung der Geschichte. Über Hayden White." *Merkur* (1992): pp. 506–21.

Kellner, Hans. "Hayden White and the Kantian Discourse. Tropology, Narrative, and Freedom." In *The Philosophy of Discourse. The Rhetorical Turn in Twentieth-Century Thought*, vol. 1, edited by Chip Sills and George H. Jansen. Portsmouth, NH: Boynton/Cook Publishers, 1992, pp. 246–67.

Roth, Paul A. "Hayden White and the Aesthetics of Historiography." *History of the Human Sciences* 5, no. 1 (1992): pp. 17–35.

Himmelfarb, Gertrude. "Telling It As You Like It. Post-Modernist History and the Flight from Fact." *Times Literary Supplement*, October 16, 1992, pp. 12–15.

Kansteiner, Wulf. "Hayden White's Critique of the Writing of History." *History and Theory* 32, no. 3 (1993): pp. 273–95.

"Hayden White's *Metahistory* Twenty Years After." Pt. 1, "Interpreting Tropology." *Storia della storiografia* 24 (1993). Pt. 2, "*Metahistory* and the Practice of History." *Storia della storiografia* 25 (1994).

Dami, Roberto. *I tropi della Storia. La narrazione nella teoria della storiografia de Hayden White.* Milano: Franco Angeli, 1994.

Kellner, Hans. "Hayden White." In *The Johns Hopkins Guide to Literary Theory and Criticism*, edited by Michael Groden and Martin Krieiswirth. Baltimore: Johns Hopkins University Press, 1994.

Jenkins, Keith. "Beyond the Old Dichotomies: Some Reflections on Hayden White." *Teaching History* 74 (January 1994): pp. 10–16.

Jenkins, Keith. *On "What Is History?" From Carr and Elton to Rorty and White.* London: Routledge, 1995.

Duncan, James. S. "Me(trope)olis: Or Hayden White Among the Urbanists." In *Re-presenting the City: Ethnicity, Capital and Culture in the Twenty-First Century Metropolis*, edited by Anthony D. King. New York: New York University Press, 1996, pp. 253–68.

Harlan, David. "The Return of the Moral Imagination." In *The Degradation of American History.* Chicago: University of Chicago Press, 1997, pp. 105–26.

Munslow, Alun. "Hayden White and Deconstructionist History." In *Deconstructing History.* London: Routledge, 1997, pp. 140–62.

Stückrath, Jörn, and Jürg Zbinden. *Metageschichte. Hayden White und Paul Ricoeur. Dargestellte Wirklichkeit in der europäischen Kultur im Kontext von Husserl, Weber, Auerbach, Gombrich.* Baden-Baden: Nomos, 1997.

Murphy, Richard J. "Metahistory and Metafiction: Historiography and the Fictive in the Work of Hayden White." *Sources: Revue d'Etudes anglophones* 2 (Spring 1997): pp. 3–12.

Partner, Nancy. "Hayden White (and the Content and the Form and Everyone Else) at the AHA." *History and Theory* 36, no. 4 (December 1997): pp. 102–10.

"Hayden White: Twenty-five Years On." *History and Theory* 37, no. 2 (May 1998). Issue includes Frank Ankersmit, "Hayden White's Appeal to the Historians"; Ewa Domańska, "Hayden White: Beyond Irony"; Nancy Partner, "Hayden White: The Form of the Content"; and Richard Vann, "The Reception of Hayden White."

Jenkins, Keith. "On Hayden White." In *Why History? Ethics and Postmodernity.* London: Routledge, 1999, pp. 89–158.

Carignan, Michael I. "Fiction as History or History as Fiction? George Eliot, Hayden White, and Nineteenth-Century Historicism." *Clio* 29, no. 4 (2000): pp. 395–415.

Hughes-Warrington, Marnie. "Hayden White." In *Fifty Key Thinkers on History.* London: Routledge, 2000, pp. 350–57.

Day, Frank. "Hayden White." In *Twentieth-Century American Cultural Theorists*, edited by Paul Hansom. Detroit: Gale Group, 2001, pp. 380–94.

Domańska, Ewa. "Hayden White." In *Postmodernism: Key Figures*, edited by Hans Bertens and Joseph Natoli. Cambridge, MA: Blackwell, 2001, pp. 321–26.

Kisantal, Tamás, and Gábor Szeberényi. "On Hayden White's 'Advantages and Disadvantages': Narratological Challenges in Historiography." *Aetas* 1 (2001): 116–33.

Kisantal, Tamás, and Gábor Szeberényi. "White's Mythology. Rhetorics, Tropology, and Narrativity in Hayden White's Theory of History." In *Crossings: Deconstruction, Rhetoric, and Understanding in the Recent Criticism*, edited by Antal Bókay and Edina Sándorfi. Budapest: Osiris, 2003, pp. 250–75.

Söder, Hans-Peter. "The Return of Cultural History? 'Literary' Historiography from Nietzsche to Hayden White." *History of European Ideas* 29 (2003): pp. 73–84.

Leeson, David. "Cutting Through History: Hayden White, William S. Burroughs, and Surrealistic Battle Narratives." *Left History* 10, no. 1 (Fall/Winter 2004): pp. 13–43. Discussion in the same volume: Nancy Partner, "Reading, Writing, Getting It Right: A Response to David Leeson's 'Cutting Through History'"; Robert M. Stein, "Fictional Plots and Historical Explanation: A Response to David Leeson's 'Cutting Through History'"; David Leeson, "Who Shall Decide, When Doctors Disagree? David Leeson Responds in Turn," pp. 44–53.

Paul, Herman. "Metahistorical Prefigurations: Toward a Re-Interpretation of Tropology in Hayden White." *Journal of Interdisciplinary Studies in History and Archaeology* 1, no. 2 (Winter 2004): pp. 1–19.

Moses, A. Dirk. "Hayden White, Traumatic Nationalism, and the Public Role of History." *History and Theory* 44 (October 2005): pp. 311–32.

Kellner, Hans. "Hayden White." In *Le dictionnaire des sciences humaines*, edited by P. Savidan and S. Mesure. Paris: Presses Universitaires Français, 2006, pp. 1230–31.

Korhonen, Kuisma, ed. *Tropes for the Past: Hayden White and the History/Literature Debate*. 96 Internationale Forschungen zur Allgemeinen und Vergleichenden Literaturwissenschaft. Amsterdam: Rodopi, 2006.

Finney, Patrick. "Hayden White, International History and Questions Too Seldom Posed." *Rethinking History* 12, no. 1 (2008): pp. 103–23.

Paul, Herman. "A Weberian Medievalist: Hayden White in the 1950s." *Rethinking History* 12, no. 1 (2008): pp. 75–102.

Pihlainen, Kalle. "History in the World: Hayden White and the Consumer of History." *Rethinking History* 12, no. 1 (2008): pp. 23–39.

Daddow, Oliver. "Exploding History: Hayden White on Disciplinization." *Rethinking History* 12, no. 1 (March 2008): pp. 41–58.

SELECTED INTERVIEWS WITH HAYDEN WHITE

Domańska, Ewa. "The Human Face of a Scientific Mind: An Interview with Hayden V. White." *Storia della storiografia* 24, no. 2 (1993): pp. 5–21. Republished in *Encounters: Philosophy of History After Postmodernism.* Charlottesville: University Press of Virginia, 1998. See also "The Image of Self-Presentation." *Diacritics* (Spring 1994): pp. 91–100.

Soldán, Paz, and José Edmundo. "Interview with Hayden White." *Lucero. A Journal of Iberian and Latin American Studies*, no. 6 (1995): pp. 3–7.

Murphy, Richard J. "Hayden White on 'Facts, Fictions, and Metahistory.'" *Sources: Revue d'Etudes anglophones*, no. 2 (Spring 1997): pp. 13–30.

Jenkins, Keith. "A Conversation with Hayden White." *Literature and History* 7, no. 1 (1998): pp. 68–82.

Koufou, Angelica, and Margarita Miliori. "The Ironic Poetics of Late Modernity. An Interview with Hayden White." *Historein, A Review of the Past and Other Stories* (Athens) 2 (2000).

Aldama, Frederick. "Hayden White Talks Trash." *Bad Subjects* 55 (May 2001). http://bad.eserver.org/issues/2001/55/white.html.

Domańska, Ewa. "A Conversation with Hayden White." *Rethinking History* 12, no. 1 (March 2008): 3–21.

Contributors

FRANK ANKERSMIT is professor of intellectual history and historical theory at Groningen University. He has published fifteen books (*Aesthetic Politics: Political Philosophy Beyond Fact and Value*, 1996; *Historical Representation*, 2001; *Political Representation*, 2002; *Sublime Historical Experience*, 2005—among others), coedited twelve others, and written some two hundred essays on philosophy of history and political philosophy. He founded a new journal, the *Journal of Philosophy of History*, in 2007, and is its chief editor.

ANDREW BAIRD has a PhD from the Board of Studies in History of Consciousness at University of California, Santa Cruz. He studies the intersections of history, philosophy, and psychoanalytic theory. He is currently working on a book titled *Historicality and Narcissistic Closure*.

STEPHEN BANN is professor of history of art at the University of Bristol (United Kingdom) and a fellow of the British Academy. He has published work on historiography and historical representation since the 1970s, including *The Clothing of Clio* (1984) and *Romanticism and the Rise of History* (1995). Among his recent books are *Parallel Lines: Printmakers, Painters and Photographers in Nineteenth-Century France* (2001) and *Ways Around Modernism* (2007).

JUDITH BUTLER is Maxine Elliot Professor in the Departments of Rhetoric and Comparative Literature at the University of California, Berkeley. Her recent books include *Antigone's Claim: Kinship Between Life and Death* (2000); *Hegemony, Contingency, Universality*, with Ernesto Laclau and Slavoj Žižek (2000); *Precarious Life: Powers of Violence and Mourning* (2004); *Undoing Gender* (2004); and *Giving an Account of Oneself* (2005).

DAVID CARR is Charles Howard Candler Professor of Philosophy at Emory University. His main interests are phenomenology and the philosophy of history. His books include *The Paradox of Subjectivity* (1999), *Interpreting Husserl* (1987), and *Time, Narrative and History* (1986).

EWA DOMAŃSKA is associate professor of theory and history of historiography in the Department of History, Adam Mickiewicz University, Poznan

(Poland), and since 2002, visiting associate professor in the Department of Anthropology, Stanford University. She is the author of *Microhistories: Encounters in-between-worlds* (1999; 2005 in Polish) and *Unconventional Histories: Reflections on the Past in the New Humanities* (2006, in Polish) and editor of several books including *Encounters: Philosophy of History After Postmodernism* (1998) and collections of the works of Hayden White and Frank Ankersmit in Polish (2002; 2004).

DAVID HARLAN is an associate professor in the History Department, California State University at San Luis Obispo. He is the author of *The Degradation of American History* (1997) and has served as North American editor of the journal *Rethinking History*. He is working on a book about the challenges academic history faces from the rise of popular history.

KEITH JENKINS is professor of historical theory at the University of Chichester (United Kingdom). He is the author of six books on historical theory including *On "What Is History?": From Carr and Elton to Rorty and White* (1995); *Why History? Ethics and Postmodernity* (1999); and *Refiguring History: New Thoughts on an Old Discipline* (2003). He coedited *The Nature of History Reader* (2004) with Alun Munslow, and *Manifestos for History* (2007) with Alun Munslow and Sue Morgan.

HANS KELLNER teaches at North Carolina State University. He is the author of *Language and Historical Representation: Getting the Story Crooked* (1989) and essays in historical and rhetorical theory. With Frank Ankersmit, he coedited *A New Philosophy of History*.

DOMINICK LACAPRA teaches at Cornell University, where he is professor of history and comparative literature, the Bryce and Edith M. Bowmar Professor of Humanistic Studies, and director of the School of Criticism and Theory. His interests include modern European intellectual and cultural history, critical theory, and Holocaust studies. He is the author of twelve books, the most recent of which are *History and Reading: Tocqueville, Foucault, French Studies* (2000); *Writing History, Writing Trauma* (2001); and *History in Transit: Experience, Identity, Critical Theory* (2004). He has also edited or coedited two other books.

ALLAN MEGILL is professor of history at the University of Virginia. He teaches modern European intellectual history and historical theory. His books include *Karl Marx: The Burden of Reason* (2001) and *Historical Knowledge, Historical Error: A Contemporary Guide to Practice* (2007), and he also edited the collection *Rethinking Objectivity* (1994).

NANCY PARTNER is professor of history at McGill University. Her interests in historical theory focus on narrative theory, concepts of fictionality, epistemology, and psychoanalytic theory, as well as medieval historical writing. She edited *Writing Medieval History* (2005), and is currently working (with coeditor Sarah Foot) on *The Handbook of Historical Theory* for Sage Publications.

HERMAN PAUL is a lecturer in philosophy of history at Leiden University and a research fellow in modern intellectual history at the University of Groningen, the Netherlands. His primary research areas are philosophy of history, historiography, and religious memory cultures. A book version of his 2006 PhD dissertation on Hayden White is in preparation. He is currently working on the crisis of historicism in early-twentieth-century Europe.

VERÓNICA TOZZI is professor of philosophy of history at the University of Buenos Aires, Argentina. She is interested in epistemology of history of the recent past and the philosophy of social sciences. One of the editors of *El giro pragmatico en la filosofía* (2003), she also translated Hayden White's work for the Spanish-language compendium *El texto historico como artefacto literario* (2003), which she also edited.

RICHARD T. VANN is senior editor of *History and Theory* and professor of history and letters, emeritus, at Wesleyan University. He has written a number of articles on the rhetoric and logic of historiography (to appear in a collection of his essays) and of two books about the social and population history of the British Quakers. He also edited a number of volumes including *Historical Understanding: Essays of Louis Mink* (1987), with Brian Fay and Eugene O. Golob; *History and Theory: Contemporary Readings* (1998), with Brian Fay and Philip Pomper; and *World History: Ideologies, Structures, and Identities* (1998), with Philip Pomper and Richard H. Elphick.

Index

academic history. *See* professional (academic) history

actor: human as, 60; the "I" as, 284; state as, 48–49; World Spirit as, 22–23. *See also* agent

Adler, Mortimer J., 189n58

Aeneid (Virgil), 228

agent: in Israeli-Palestinian narrative, 98–99; role of, in narrative, 24–26. *See also* actor

Albanian narrative, 92–93

Alltagsgeschichte (Practice of Everyday Life), 139–40, 239–42

"America Made Easy" (Wilentz), 179

American Historical Review (journal), suspension of film reviews, 178, 182

anabasis, 124–25, 137–42

Anabasis (Xenophon), 124, 138, 140–42

analogy, 217–18, 220, 223

Analytical Philosophy of History (Danto), 198

analytic tools, 148, 157, 240

ancestors, choosing one's, 3–6, 73n36, 133, 174–75, 230n23

animals. *See* human species

Annales school, 157, 159–60

anthropocentrism, 242, 246–47, 249n7, 336

Antoni, Carlo, 59

aporia, 109, 244

Arab/Palestinian narrative, 96–99, 269–70

Argentina, 262–65, 273–76

Aristotle, 98, 116, 174

Auerbach, Erich, 6–7, 38, 191–93, 266

Auschwitz and After (Delbo), 294–95

authenticity. *See* truth, attaining

Badiou, Alain, 79, 124–29, 137–41, 248n3

Ball, Stephen J., 339

Barthes, Roland, 89, 145–47, 152, 155–58

Baudrillard, Jean, 220

Bauer, Tristán, 274–75

beginnings, 53n17, 98–99, 192–95

Beirut, bombing of, 289

Berlin, Isaiah, 46–47

biological systems, cultures compared with, 3, 5–6, 338–39

Bitterlemons.org (Israeli-Palestinian website), 97

Bosnian narrative, 93–96

Bossenbrook, William J., 197–202, 205, 335–37

Burckhardt, Jacob, 64, 319, 322–23

Burke, Kenneth, 147

Burke, Peter, 177

Butterfield, Herbert, 185n17

Campbell, David, 95

Carr, Edward Hallett, 171–73

catachresis, 108–9, 111, 321

"Catastrophe, Memory and Identity" (Sa'di), 97

causality, 36–37, 52n3, 219

Centaur, The (Updike), 347n21

Nagasaki bombings, 252n21; historical, 217–25, 228; Kant and the, 216–18, 225; pricing out of the market, 218; in radical constructivism, 236
superstition. *See* myth
Survival in Auschwitz (Levi), 286
survivor's guilt, 286–88
syllogism, historical discourse and, 116, 151–52
synecdoche: defined, 320–21; as dominant trope, 158, 328; in Enlightenment historiography, 68, 326; Herder's integration of history and myth, 63; HW's own use of, 64. *See also* tropes

testimonies of witnesses: demand for representation and, 269–70; epistemic privilege of, 264–65, 273–76; as essential voice, 238–39; fallibility of, 284–85, 291–92; Malvinas ex-soldiers providing, 263–64, 268–69, 275; narrative analysis of, 95. *See also* Levi, Primo
textualism, 237–38
textuality, 83–84
Time and Narrative (Ricoeur), 96
Tocqueville, Alexis de, 66, 227–28, 272–73, 319
Todorov, Tzvetan, 271–73
Toews, John E., 194, 240
tools, analytic, 148, 157, 240
Toynbee, Arnold J., 18, 194–95, 305
tradition, lure of, 159
tragedy, past as, 271–73
transcendentalist narrative: in HW's philosophy, 35–40; Kant on, 36–37; politics of, 46–50
transcendental realism, 106–7
transference, 245
transhistorical, the, 232–37
trauma: compulsive repetition in, 231, 296; difficulty in recounting, 283–86, 292–97; foundational, 243, 248n4; middle voice and, 167; overcom-

ing, 167, 231; temporal ambiguity and, 263–64; transhistorical, 232–35; witnesses to, 238–39, 270; working-through, 243–47. *See also* testimonies of witnesses
Troeltsch, Ernst, 56–58, 65
tropes: as analytical tools, 148; closed cycle of, 322, 327; HW on, 158, 320–27; HW's own use of, 23–24, 62, 133, 153, 316; and Kant's analytics of the beautiful, 42–44; and Kant's categories of understanding, 36–37; optionalism of, 36–38, 40. *See also* *individual tropes*
tropology grid, 35–36, 327–28
truth, attaining: evidence and, 20, 83–84, 114, 208–9, 316–18; historical facts and, 155, 171–73, 179, 192–96, 317–18; historical referent and, 78–79, 106–8, 113–16, 291, 293–97; search for universals and, 23–29, 48, 56–57, 60, 66–67, 109. *See also* reality and representation; testimonies of witnesses
Turner, Victor, 340–42
twenty-first century, 124–25

Unfashionable Observation (Nietzsche), 125–26
unfulfilled figures, 223–28
Ungleichzeitigkeit (nonsimultaneity), 57
"unified organic force," 60, 63
Updike, John, 347n21

values. *See* morality
"verum ipsum factum," 153
Vezzetti, Hugo, 264–65
Vico, Giambattista, 147–48, 152–57, 327–28, 336
victimization narratives, 97–98, 252, 271, 300
victims. *See* testimonies of witnesses
violence: first-level, 108–9; second-level, 109–10; third-level, 110–11
Virgil, 226, 228
vision. *See* myth

Cultural Memory | in the Present

Jennifer A. Jordan, *Structures of Memory: Understanding German Change in Berlin and Beyond*

Christoph Menke, *Reflections of Equality*

Marlène Zarader, *The Unthought Debt: Heidegger and the Hebraic Heritage*

Jan Assmann, *Religion and Cultural Memory: Ten Studies*

David Scott and Charles Hirschkind, *Powers of the Secular Modern: Talal Asad and His Interlocutors*

Gyanendra Pandey, *Routine Violence: Nations, Fragments, Histories*

James Siegel, *Naming the Witch*

J. M. Bernstein, *Against Voluptuous Bodies: Late Modernism and the Meaning of Painting*

Theodore W. Jennings, Jr., *Reading Derrida / Thinking Paul: On Justice*

Richard Rorty and Eduardo Mendieta, *Take Care of Freedom and Truth Will Take Care of Itself: Interviews with Richard Rorty*

Jacques Derrida, *Paper Machine*

Renaud Barbaras, *Desire and Distance: Introduction to a Phenomenology of Perception*

Jill Bennett, *Empathic Vision: Affect, Trauma, and Contemporary Art*

Ban Wang, *Illuminations from the Past: Trauma, Memory, and History in Modern China*

James Phillips, *Heidegger's* Volk: *Between National Socialism and Poetry*

Frank Ankersmit, *Sublime Historical Experience*

István Rév, *Retroactive Justice: Prehistory of Post-Communism*

Paola Marrati, *Genesis and Trace: Derrida Reading Husserl and Heidegger*

Krzysztof Ziarek, *The Force of Art*

Marie-José Mondzain, *Image, Icon, Economy: The Byzantine Origins of the Contemporary Imaginary*

Cecilia Sjöholm, *The Antigone Complex: Ethics and the Invention of Feminine Desire*

Jacques Derrida and Elisabeth Roudinesco, *For What Tomorrow . . . : A Dialogue*

Elisabeth Weber, *Questioning Judaism: Interviews by Elisabeth Weber*

Jacques Derrida and Catherine Malabou, *Counterpath: Traveling with Jacques Derrida*

Martin Seel, *Aesthetics of Appearing*

Nanette Salomon, *Shifting Priorities: Gender and Genre in Seventeenth-Century Dutch Painting*

Jacob Taubes, *The Political Theology of Paul*

Jean-Luc Marion, *The Crossing of the Visible*

Eric Michaud, *The Cult of Art in Nazi Germany*

Anne Freadman, *The Machinery of Talk: Charles Peirce and the Sign Hypothesis*

Stanley Cavell, *Emerson's Transcendental Etudes*

Stuart McLean, *The Event and Its Terrors: Ireland, Famine, Modernity*

Beate Rössler, ed., *Privacies: Philosophical Evaluations*

Bernard Faure, *Double Exposure: Cutting Across Buddhist and Western Discourses*

Alessia Ricciardi, *The Ends of Mourning: Psychoanalysis, Literature, Film*

Alain Badiou, *Saint Paul: The Foundation of Universalism*

Gil Anidjar, *The Jew, the Arab: A History of the Enemy*

Jonathan Culler and Kevin Lamb, eds., *Just Being Difficult? Academic Writing in the Public Arena*

Jean-Luc Nancy, *A Finite Thinking*, edited by Simon Sparks

Theodor W. Adorno, *Can One Live After Auschwitz? A Philosophical Reader*, edited by Rolf Tiedemann

Patricia Pisters, *The Matrix of Visual Culture: Working with Deleuze in Film Theory*

Andreas Huyssen, *Present Pasts: Urban Palimpsests and the Politics of Memory*

Talal Asad, *Formations of the Secular: Christianity, Islam, Modernity*

Dorothea von Mücke, *The Rise of the Fantastic Tale*

Marc Redfield, *The Politics of Aesthetics: Nationalism, Gender, Romanticism*

Emmanuel Levinas, *On Escape*

Dan Zahavi, *Husserl's Phenomenology*

Rodolphe Gasché, *The Idea of Form: Rethinking Kant's Aesthetics*

Michael Naas, *Taking on the Tradition: Jacques Derrida and the Legacies of Deconstruction*

Herlinde Pauer-Studer, ed., *Constructions of Practical Reason: Interviews on Moral and Political Philosophy*

Jean-Luc Marion, *Being Given That: Toward a Phenomenology of Givenness*

Theodor W. Adorno and Max Horkheimer, *Dialectic of Enlightenment*

Ian Balfour, *The Rhetoric of Romantic Prophecy*

Martin Stokhof, *World and Life as One: Ethics and Ontology in Wittgenstein's Early Thought*

Gianni Vattimo, *Nietzsche: An Introduction*

Jacques Derrida, *Negotiations: Interventions and Interviews, 1971–1998*, ed. Elizabeth Rottenberg

Brett Levinson, *The Ends of Literature: The Latin American "Boom" in the Neoliberal Marketplace*

Timothy J. Reiss, *Against Autonomy: Cultural Instruments, Mutualities, and the Fictive Imagination*

Hent de Vries and Samuel Weber, eds., *Religion and Media*

Niklas Luhmann, *Theories of Distinction: Re-Describing the Descriptions of Modernity*, ed. and introd. William Rasch

Johannes Fabian, *Anthropology with an Attitude: Critical Essays*

Michel Henry, *I Am the Truth: Toward a Philosophy of Christianity*

Gil Anidjar, *"Our Place in Al-Andalus": Kabbalah, Philosophy, Literature in Arab-Jewish Letters*

Hélène Cixous and Jacques Derrida, *Veils*

F. R. Ankersmit, *Historical Representation*

F. R. Ankersmit, *Political Representation*

Elissa Marder, *Dead Time: Temporal Disorders in the Wake of Modernity (Baudelaire and Flaubert)*

Reinhart Koselleck, *The Practice of Conceptual History: Timing History, Spacing Concepts*

Niklas Luhmann, *The Reality of the Mass Media*

Hubert Damisch, *A Theory of /Cloud/: Toward a History of Painting*

Jean-Luc Nancy, *The Speculative Remark: (One of Hegel's bon mots)*

Jean-François Lyotard, *Soundproof Room: Malraux's Anti-Aesthetics*

Jan Patočka, *Plato and Europe*

Hubert Damisch, *Skyline: The Narcissistic City*

Isabel Hoving, *In Praise of New Travelers: Reading Caribbean Migrant Women Writers*

Richard Rand, ed., *Futures: Of Jacques Derrida*

William Rasch, *Niklas Luhmann's Modernity: The Paradoxes of Differentiation*

Jacques Derrida and Anne Dufourmantelle, *Of Hospitality*

Jean-François Lyotard, *The Confession of Augustine*

Kaja Silverman, *World Spectators*

Samuel Weber, *Institution and Interpretation: Expanded Edition*

Jeffrey S. Librett, *The Rhetoric of Cultural Dialogue: Jews and Germans in the Epoch of Emancipation*

Ulrich Baer, *Remnants of Song: Trauma and the Experience of Modernity in Charles Baudelaire and Paul Celan*

Samuel C. Wheeler III, *Deconstruction as Analytic Philosophy*

David S. Ferris, *Silent Urns: Romanticism, Hellenism, Modernity*

Rodolphe Gasché, *Of Minimal Things: Studies on the Notion of Relation*

Sarah Winter, *Freud and the Institution of Psychoanalytic Knowledge*

Samuel Weber, *The Legend of Freud: Expanded Edition*

Aris Fioretos, ed., *The Solid Letter: Readings of Friedrich Hölderlin*

J. Hillis Miller / Manuel Asensi, *Black Holes / J. Hillis Miller; or, Boustrophedonic Reading*

Miryam Sas, *Fault Lines: Cultural Memory and Japanese Surrealism*

Peter Schwenger, *Fantasm and Fiction: On Textual Envisioning*

Didier Maleuvre, *Museum Memories: History, Technology, Art*

Jacques Derrida, *Monolingualism of the Other; or, The Prosthesis of Origin*

Andrew Baruch Wachtel, *Making a Nation, Breaking a Nation: Literature and Cultural Politics in Yugoslavia*

Niklas Luhmann, *Love as Passion: The Codification of Intimacy*

Mieke Bal, ed., *The Practice of Cultural Analysis: Exposing Interdisciplinary Interpretation*

Jacques Derrida and Gianni Vattimo, eds., *Religion*